P9-DGI-554

Frommer's 96

London

by Darwin Porter
& Danforth Prince

Macmillan • USA

ABOUT THE AUTHORS

A native of North Carolina, **Darwin Porter** was a bureau chief of *The Miami Herald* when he was 21, and later worked in television advertising. A veteran travel writer, he is the author of numerous bestselling Frommer Guides, notably to England, France, the Caribbean, Italy, and Spain. When not traveling (which is rare) he lives in New York City. His coauthor is **Danforth Prince,** formerly of the Paris bureau of *The New York Times.*

MACMILLAN TRAVEL

A Simon & Schuster Macmillan Company
1633 Broadway
New York, NY 10019

Copyright © 1977, 1979, 1981, 1983, 1985, 1987, 1989, 1991, 1992, 1993, 1994, 1995 by Simon & Schuster, Inc.

All rights reserved. No part of this book may be reproduced or transmitted in any form or by any means, electronic or mechanical, including photo-copying, recording, or by any information storage and retrieval system, without permission in writing from the Publisher.

Macmillan is a registered trademark of Macmillan, Inc.

ISBN 0-02-860638-8
ISSN 0899-2886

Editor: Peter Katucki
Production Editor: Liz Powell
Map Editor: Douglas Stallings
Design by Michele Laseau
Digital Cartography by Jim Moore

SPECIAL SALES

Bulk purchases (10+ copies) of Frommer's Travel Guides are available to corporations at special discounts. The Special Sales Department can produce custom editions to be used as premiums and/or for sales promotion to suit individual needs. Existing editions can be produced with custom cover imprints such as corporate logos. For more information write to: Special Sales, Simon & Schuster, 1230 Avenue of the Americas, New York, NY 10020.

Manufactured in the United States of America

Contents

List of Maps

AN INVITATION TO THE READER

In researching this book, we discovered many wonderful places—hotels, restaurants, shops, and more. We're sure you'll find others. Please tell us about them, so we can share the information with your fellow travelers in upcoming editions. If you were disappointed with a recommendation, we'd love to know that, too. Please write to:

Darwin Porter
Frommer's London '96
Macmillan Travel
1633 Broadway
New York, NY 10019

AN ADDITIONAL NOTE

Please be advised that travel information is subject to change at any time—and this is especially true of prices. We therefore suggest that you write or call ahead for confirmation when making your travel plans. The authors, editors, and publisher cannot be held responsible for the experiences of readers while traveling. Your safety is important to us, however, so we encourage you to stay alert and be aware of your surroundings. Keep a close eye on cameras, purses, and wallets, all favorite targets of thieves and pickpockets.

WHAT THE SYMBOLS MEAN

✪ Frommer's Favorites

Hotels, restaurants, attractions, and entertainment you should not miss.

⑤ Super-Special Values

Hotels and restaurants that offer great value for your money.

The following abbreviations are used for credit cards:

AE	American Express	EU	Eurocard
CB	Carte Blanche	JCB	Japan Credit Bank
DC	Diners Club	MC	MasterCard
DISC	Discover	V	Visa

Introducing London

When Henry James moved to London in 1881, he recorded his impression of the city. "It is not a pleasant place; it is not agreeable, or cheerful, or easy, or exempt from reproach. It is only magnificent." He concluded that in spite of what he cited as the dirt, the darkness, the wet, the ugliness, and the brutal size of the place, "London is on the whole the most possible form of life." The author's reservations and endorsement still ring true today as London approaches the millennium.

Of course, since James wrote those words, London has been through the end of the Victorian era, the Edwardian era, the "Great War," the turbulent '20s, the depressive '30s with the dim-witted Duke of Windsor and his snobbish duchess, and a blitz ordered by Hitler to destroy the city and demoralize its people. London survived all that and went on to outwear the Swinging '60s with Mary Quant and Carnaby Street. Londoners even outlived the nouvelle cuisine craze of the '80s. By the '90s, London is still there, perhaps a little battered from all the wear and tear.

The House of Windsor, certainly, isn't as discreet as it used to be, with all that toe-sucking and nudie pictures of royal princes splashed across racy tabloids all around the world. Except for the queen, that is. She remains as serene as ever, in spite of her opening her home, Buckingham Palace, to the masses, or suggesting to drillers they might have carte blanche to dig for oil on the grounds of Windsor Castle. Even Her Majesty has bills to pay—a lot of them—now that she's agreed to pay taxes, and fire-ravaged Windsor Castle, her favorite residence, needs restoration.

It strikes some visitors with sheer amazement that there's so much fun to be had in staid old London. Perhaps they'd planned on an obligatory duty call to see the monuments, including the Tower of London and the British Museum, before rushing off to Paris for some real fun. Even the very name, LON–DON, sounds heavy, ponderous, like the ringing of Big Ben in one of those old black and white English mystery films that the Rank group used to churn out on low budgets. Big Ben somberly strikes the hour as if setting the dull, gray tone of life in London, but some seven million Londoners rarely march to the sound of that clock. They're too busy getting on with the job of living.

Sure, London is dull and staid in parts, and you're supposed to act proper and not spill your tea if the duchess of Bedford invites you to the Ritz or Brown's for a "cuppa." But when you're not with Her Ladyship, you can get out and explore, discover, and have a good time—from the depths of a Soho dive to an elegant Mayfair gaming club, from having a pint in an East End drag pub (a favorite English custom) to getting packed into the already packed Ronnie Scott's for some cool jazz.

More and more, London is becoming less English and more international in flavor, at least continental. The trend was noticed when food critics in the early '80s noted that every waiter they encountered was born on some shore far removed from "merrie olde England." They wrote at the time, "A knowledge of foreign languages is absolutely essential for dining out in London today." That's even truer now than then. It seems that foreigners have virtually taken over the catering business. As one cynic not too keen on British food observed, "And not a minute too soon."

The gent with the bowler hat has long gone out of fashion. If you are to meet a Londoner for the first time in person, even a "Londoner born and bred," don't expect a Peter Sellers–like English character to show up. For all you know, this Londoner might arrive in a turban or whatever.

Increasingly, London is home to many of the world's immigrants and refugees—arriving both rich and poor, from all reaches of the world. Racial tension among these widely diverse cultures is all too evident in London today. So is overcrowding. What's amazing is that the city works as well as it does. Violent crime is still relatively rare—most often it's domestic-related.

Discovering London and making it your own is a bit of a challenge, especially if you have little time. Even in the 18th century, Daniel Defoe found London, "Stretched out in buildings, straggling, confused, out of all shape, uncompact and unequal; neither long nor broad, round nor square." Defoe could have been describing the London of the 1990s.

London is a city that has never quite made up its mind about its own size. For "The City of London" proper is merely one square mile of very expensive real estate around the Bank of England, inhabited at night by only a few hundred nightwatchpeople and caretakers, several score police officers, and innumerable cats.

All the gargantuan rest is made up of separate cities, boroughs, and corporations called Westminster, Chelsea, Hampstead, Kensington,

Impressions

Londoners like to talk of their city as a great magnet, but the image of Dracula is equally accurate. It drains the rest of the country in the same ways as the oil rigs are draining the North Sea. One goes there at last as Americans go to New York: to experience the shock of vitality from so many millions living together and to see the country in a melting pot.
—W. J. Wetherby, *Guardian* (August 22, 1979)

Camden Town, etc., each with its own mayor and administration and ready to fight for its independent status at the drop of an ordinance. Together, however, they add up to a mammoth metropolis, once the largest on the globe.

The millions of people loosely governed by the Greater London Council live on a parcel of land that's more than 609 square miles. Luckily, only a minute fraction of this territory need concern us: The rest is simply boring, monotonous suburbs, stretching endlessly into the horizon, red-roofed and bristling with TV antennas.

But the heart, the brick and mortar core of this giant is one of the most fascinating areas on earth. For about a century, one-quarter of the world was ruled from there. With almost every step you take, you'll come across some sign of the tremendous influence this city has exerted over our past thoughts and actions . . . and still wields today.

London is a very old city, even by European standards. The Roman conquerors of Britain founded Londinium in A.D. 43 by settling and fortifying two small hills on the north bank of the River Thames and linking them with the rest of the island by a military network of roads.

More than a thousand years later, another conqueror turned the city into his capital. This was William of Normandy, who defeated the last Saxon ruler of England, Harold, in 1066. Not much remains of the Roman period, but William the Conqueror left his imprint on London for all time to come. For a start, he had himself crowned in Westminster Abbey on Christmas Day in 1066. Almost all British monarchs have been crowned there since, right up to the present queen. He also built the White Tower, which today forms part of the Tower of London.

London is a mass of contradictions. On the one hand, it's a decidedly royal city, studded with palaces, court gardens, coats-of-arms, and other regal paraphernalia. Yet London is also the home of the world's second-oldest parliamentary assembly (Iceland has the oldest). It should be noted that way back in 1649 when handsome and rash King Charles I tried to defy the members of Parliament, he found himself swept off his throne and onto a scaffold.

1 Frommer's Favorite London Experiences

- **Watching the Sunset at Waterloo Bridge.** Waterloo Bridge is the ideal place in London to watch the sun set over Westminster in the west. From here, the last rays of sunlight can be seen bouncing off the City spires in East End, too.
- **Enjoying a Pub Lunch.** In the bustling, overcrowded atmosphere of a London pub, place your order at the bar for a roast-beef sandwich and a mug of lager.
- **Enjoying a Traditional English Tea.** Nothing is more typically British. To avoid making advance reservations, try the Hotel Goring, dating from 1910. From the lounge, you'll have a view of a small garden as you enjoy "finger" sandwiches (often watercress or cucumber), the hotel's special Ceylon blend tea, scones, and the chef's famous "light fruit cake," offered from a trolley.

- **Brass Rubbing.** Re-create all those costumed ladies and knights in armor from England's age of chivalry. One good place for brass rubbings is the crypt of St. Martin-in-the-Fields in Trafalgar Square.

- **A Night at the West End Theater.** London is the theatrical capital of the world. The live stage offers a unique combination of variety, accessibility, and economy—and perhaps a look at next year's Broadway hit.

- **Cruising London's Waterways.** In addition to the Thames, London is riddled with an antique canal system, complete with towpath walks, bridges, and wharves. Replaced by the railroad, the canal system remained forgotten until it was rediscovered by a new generation. Now, the old system has been restored, bridges painted and repaired, and towpaths cleaned up—it's been called "industrial archeology." The major water link is a 28-mile canal near the north bank of the Thames. To take a ride, call Bridgewater Boats (☎ **11442/863615**), the firm names its boats after T. S. Eliot's famous cats.

- **Studying the Turners at the Tate.** Upon his death in 1851, J. M. W. Turner bequeathed his personal collection of 19,000 watercolors and some 300 paintings to the people of Britain. He wanted his finished works, some 100 paintings, displayed under one roof. For 125 years, Turner's wish was unfulfilled. The expansion of the Clore Gallery changed this. Today, you get not only Turner, but glimpses of the Thames through the museum's windows, which is appropriate. The artist lived and died on its banks in Chelsea, and painted the river in its many changing moods.

- **Sunday in London.** Some find it dull, but it needn't be. Begin by looking for some smart fashion at Camden Market, a Sunday affair in the northern reaches of Camden High Street. There, stallholders hawk designer jewelry and clothing. Next, walk up to Hampstead Heath off Well Walk, take the right fork, which will lead you to an open field with a panoramic view of London. If you walk long and hard enough, you'll be ready for a traditional roast beef lunch at Jack Straw's Castle at North End Way. Cap your meal with a visit to the Freud Museum at 20 Maresfield Gardens, which remains open on Sunday till 5pm.

- **Treasure Hunt for an Antique.** It's estimated that some 2,000 antiquarians live within the city limits of London. Check with the tourist office to see if a major antiques fair is occurring at the time of your visit; the Dorchester Fair and Grosvenor House Fair take place in June. If not, head for one of the following antiques centers selling everything from plain old junk (mugs with Prince Philip's face on them) to rare bric-a-brac. The best ones are Gray's and Gray's in the Mews, 58 Davies St. (tube: Bond Street); Chelsea Antiques Market, 245A–53 King's Rd. (tube: Sloane Square), and Alfie's Antique Market, 13–25 Church St. (tube: Edgware Road).

- **A Shopping Trip to Harrods.** Regardless of how many times you visit London, few can resist a visit to this vast emporium at

Knightsbridge. It is the "supplier of provisions and household goods to HM the Queen." Spread across 15 acres, Harrods proclaims as its motto *Omnia Omnibus Ubique* or "everything for everyone, everywhere." They mean it, too. Want an elephant? Go to Harrods. Someone didn't believe the claim, and in 1975 called Harrods at midnight and ordered that a baby elephant be delivered to the home of the governor of California and his First Lady, Mr. and Mrs. Ronald Reagan in Sacramento. The animal arrived safely, albeit a bit bewildered. (Nancy even sent a "thank you" note.) The food hall is my favorite venue, with some 500 different cheeses and some 163 brands of whisky, among zillions of other goodies. It is estimated that at Christmas, Harrods sells 100 tons of Christmas puddings. You can even arrange your funeral at the store.

- **Rowing on the Serpentine.** When the weather's right, we always like to head to this 41-acre artificial lake dating from 1730. A stream, which no longer exists, was dammed to create the artificial lake whose name derives from its winding, snakelike shape. At the Boathouse, you can rent (they call it "hire") a boat by the hour. With the right companion, it's one of the most idyllic ways to spend an afternoon in sunny London. Renoir must have agreed. He depicted the custom on canvas.

- **Dinner at Rules.** At 35 Maiden Lane (WC2), Rules dates from 1798, when it was first established as an oyster bar. It may, in fact be the oldest restaurant in London. Long a venue for the theatrical elite and literary *beau monde,* it still serves the same dishes that delighted Edward VII and his mistress, Lillie Langtry. They always began with champagne and oysters behind a closed door upstairs. Charles Dickens liked the place so much he had a regular table. Over the years, it has fed its pheasant and grouse to everyone from William Thackeray to Clark Gable. If it's feathered or furred, it's likely to be served here—Highland red deer, wild duck, and where else can you get a good purée of parsnips these days, anyway? As for the puddings (the English call all desserts puddings), its treacle sponge for those who want unreconstructed British cuisine. As for the apple suet pudding, how English can you get?

- **Strolling Through Covent Garden.** George Bernard Shaw got his inspiration for *Pygmalion* here, and the character of Eliza Doolittle, who sold violets to wealthy operagoers, became a household name around the world. The old fruit and vegetable market, with its cockney cauliflower peddlers and butchers in blood-soaked aprons, is long gone. What's left is just as interesting. Covent Garden today is London's best example of urban renewal. In the footsteps of Chippendale and Dickens, you can wander about, discovering colorful street stalls, an array of boutiques, shops selling one-of-a-kind merchandise, and all the while enjoying the best sidewalk entertainment in London. There's an antique market within the piazza on Monday, and a crafts market Tuesday through Saturday. When you're thirsty, plenty of pubs in the area will quench your thirst. The most noteworthy of these is the Nag's Head, an Edwardian pub that will serve you a draft Guinness and a plate of pork cooked in cider.

- **Sunday Morning at Speakers' Corner.** At the northeastern corner of Hyde Park, near Marble Arch, a British tradition from the 19th century carries on. Speakers sound off on any subject they want, and "In Your Face" hecklers are part of the show and fun. You might hear everything from denunciations of the monarchy to antigay rhetoric. Anyone can get up and speak. The only rules: One cannot blaspheme, one cannot be obscene, and one cannot incite a riot. The tradition began in 1855 when a mob of 150,000 gathered to attack a proposed Sunday Trading Bill, this occurred before there was a legal right of assembly. That wasn't guaranteed until 1872, and orators from all over Britain have been taking advantage of it since.

- **A Pub Crawl.** Americans bar hop, Londoners do a pub crawl. With some 5,000 pubs within the city limits, you would be crawling indeed if you tried to have a drink in each of them. Many pubs today are only for "lager louts," these places have given way to Formica, loud jukeboxes, and a sometimes obsessive concern with football (soccer) or rugby scores. But enough traditional ones remain, especially in central London, with their long mahogany bars, dark wood paneling, and Victorian curlicued mirrors to make it worthwhile to go on a crawl. While making the rounds, you can partake of that peculiarly British fare known as "pub grub," which might include everything from a ploughman's lunch (a hunk of bread, cheese, and a pickle) to a ground-meat concoction called cottage pie that is likely to contain anything the cook had left over.

  Here's our favorite crawl, which gives you a chance to see several of London's districts: Begin at Dickens Inn by the tower on St. Katharine's Way (E1), then go on to The Cheshire Cheese, Wine Office Court, 145 Fleet St. (EC4) before making your way to Cittie of Yorke at 22–23 High Holborn (WC1). Then it's off to Old Coffee House at 49 Beak St. (W1) in Soho, before descending on Red Lion, 2 Duke of York St. (SW1). If you're still standing, rush to Shepherd's Tavern, 50 Hertford St. (W1) in Mayfair before the publican rings the bell for "final call."

2 A Look at the Past

Dateline

- 55 B.C. Julius Caesar invades England; he lands just a short distance from present-day London.

continues

THE CELTS, ROMANS & EARLY MIDDLE AGES The oldest artifacts ever discovered in London and the first historical reference to the city, date from its occupation by the ancient Romans, who adapted a local Celtic name into the latinized form, Londinium.

Julius Caesar raided England in 55 and 54 B.C., fording the Thames with his armies somewhere downstream from today's London. The bulk of written history dates from about a century later, during the era of Claudius's military campaigns of A.D. 43. Londinium became a thriving port by A.D. 61. That same year a union of Celtic tribes, led by Boadicea, attacked the unprotected rear flank of the Roman armies during one of their northern campaigns; the Celts burned the fortified camp of Londinium to the ground, too. The Romans erected a much larger camp (excavations reveal that it covered about 11 square acres); its grid-work street plan was later altered into a convoluted tangle by medieval Londoners. Before they left, the Romans developed the city, but not to the status of a capital. (The heyday of London's excavations of the Roman occupation coincided with the clearing of World War II's rubble, when a Roman temple and statues dedicated to Mithras, Serapis, and Ptolemaic Greek deities were revealed.)

The Romans advanced into northern England, as far as the site of Hadrian's Wall, but they faced continuous insurrections. In the year 410, by which time the seeds of Christianity had been sown in England, the emperor Honorius ordered the Roman legions back to the Continent, leaving England isolated from the European mainland for centuries.

In the 600s, London's first bishop, Mellitus, built a church in honor of St. Paul, but for the most part, London slumbered and stagnated. A hodgepodge of medieval houses arose, some reportedly in the middle of thoroughfares. The irregularity of medieval construction and property lines was reinforced by later generations of Londoners, who were usually required to respect the legal claims of earlier owners and builders. As a result independent neighborhoods and private enclaves developed.

THE SAXONS, DANES & VIKINGS After the Romans, the next major invaders of London were the Teutonic Saxons and Danes, who arrived on the southeastern (Kentish) coast of England about 449. Depending on who was in power, they either embraced or rejected Christianity. Mellitus, the reigning bishop, was banished and London remained rigidly and lustily pagan.

One ruler who emerged from England's early Middle Ages was Alfred, King of the Saxons, who spent much of his career battling the Norse Vikings. In 886, Alfred strengthened London's

- **A.D. 43** Roman armies defeat Celts, establishing a fortified camp called Londinium.
- **61** Celts from East Anglia burn and sack Londinium, but the settlement is repossessed by Romans.
- **410** Romans retreat from London and return to Europe.
- **449** Arrival of Saxons on the Kentish coast.
- **886** King Alfred, a Saxon, conquers London but rules from his capital at Winchester.
- **900–1050** Saxons ward off Viking invasions.
- **1066** Norman invasion of England. William the Conqueror defeats Harold at the Battle of Hastings and is crowned in Westminster Abbey.
- **1100s** London asserts its right for some measure of self-government, establishing the office of lord mayor.
- **1400s** Trade flourishes in London.
- **1509–47** Reign of Henry VIII. His feud with Rome over his

continues

divorce leads
to the English
Reformation;
church property
is confiscated,
and the English
monarch is
declared head
of Church of
England.

- **1558** Elizabeth I
ascends throne.

- **1586** William
Shakespeare
moves to London
and buys part of
the Globe
Theatre.

- **1640s** Much
fighting between
Cromwellians
and Royalists.
King Charles I
is beheaded
at London's
Whitehall (1649).

- **1660** Charles II
ascends throne.

- **1665** A plague
decimates the
population.

- **1666** Great Fire
demolishes much
of the city.

- **1710** St. Paul's
Cathedral
completed.

- **1710–1820** The
arts thrive and
London's popul-
ation increases.
Industrial Revol-
ution begins.

- **1837–1901**
Reign of Victoria.

- **1901** Edward VII
ascends throne.

- **1939–45** World
War II. Much of
London is

continues

fortifications: He appointed his son-in-law as
governor, while he continued to rule his growing
kingdom from his capital at Winchester. For a
century after Alfred's death (around 900), his
heirs were occupied almost exclusively with securing and protecting their holdings against the
Viking invaders.

THE NORMANS   Though London was still
not defined as the country's capital, more and
more treaties, rites of succession, and military
conferences were hosted within its walls. The last
Saxon king was Harold, who chose London as
the site of his election. He ruled for only nine
months before the fateful Battle of Hastings in
1066. There, the politics, bloodlines, language,
and destiny of London were to change forever after the victory of the Norman armies, led
by William the Conqueror, over the Saxon
kingdom.

William the Conqueror might have been the
first ruler to recognize fully the political importance of London. His coronation took place in
Westminster Abbey, establishing a precedent that
has been observed by almost all British monarchs
since. He recognized the capital status of London
and the power and rights of London's medieval
church. Strengthening his political hold in the
process, he acquiesced to the Saxon ecclesiastics
by granting them many well-defined rights and
privileges. He also constructed the White Tower,
a fortification incorporated into the Tower of
London by later monarchs.

During the 1100s, London asserted its right to
some independence from the rest of England,
reinforcing the role of its lord mayor. English
monarchs, eager for the support of the country's wealthiest and most influential populace,
bid for the fealty and allegiance of Londoners
in the hopes that holding London was the key
to controlling England.

By the 1400s, the banks of the Thames were
lined with buildings as depicted in the engravings produced prior to the Great Fire of 1666.
London-based merchants built massive residences
atop or beside their riverfront warehouses. Ferryboats plied the Thames, and life burgeoned on
both banks of the river. The city was dotted with
ecclesiastical buildings that were later confiscated
by Henry VIII during the Reformation but
whose neighborhoods and Catholic images

(Blackfriars, Greyfriars, and Whitefriars) still remain as part of modern London.

TUDOR & ELIZABETHAN LONDON   The modern history of London begins with the Tudors. Sadly, Henry VIII's Reformation (1530s) led to the physical destruction of many medieval buildings, and London—as the centerpiece of the country's political and religious conflicts—was sometimes a willing participant in many of the changes. Tower Hill saw the execution of two of Henry's wives, and two of England's most prominent ecclesiastics (Sir Thomas More and Bishop John Fisher).

The wealth of the medieval churches was confiscated and redistributed to a newly appointed aristocracy willing to comply with Henry's wishes. The medieval gardens, convents, and priories of the Catholic church were knocked apart and subdivided into narrow streets and courtyards (whose overcrowding led to the increased danger of fire). The cripples and beggars who had been dependent on the church were unleashed, without resources, on the population of London. Many recalcitrant nuns and monks, refusing to acknowledge the ecclesiastical leadership of the English monarch, were dragged through the streets to the scaffold, hanged by the neck, and disemboweled.

damaged by bombs dropped by the Nazis.
- **1953** Elizabeth II ascends throne.
- **1987** Conservatives under Margaret Thatcher win third term.
- **1990** John Major becomes prime minister.
- **1992** Royal couple jolted by fire at Windsor Castle and marital troubles of their two sons.
- **1994** For the first time since the Ice Age, England is linked to the Continent— this time by the Chunnel under the English Channel.

From the dissent, bloodshed, and strife of Reformation London sprang the creative juices of Elizabethan England, named after the great queen who reigned from 1558 to 1603. William Shakespeare, arriving in London in 1586, bought part ownership of the Globe Theatre, which was strategically located a short distance outside the puritanical jurisdiction of the corporation of London. Along with the flowering of the arts, England (and especially London) simultaneously entered a period of mercantile and colonial expansion in the Americas, Asia, and Africa.

PLAGUE, FIRE & THE JACOBEAN ERA   By the mid-1600s, during the Jacobean era, London was crowded, with half-timbered

Impressions

By October of 1969 Funky Chic was flying through London like an infected bat, which is to say, silently, blindly, insanely, and at night, fangs afoam . . . but with an infallible aim for the main vein . . . much like the Sideburns Fairy, who had been cruising about the city since 1966, visiting young groovies in their sleep and causing them to awake with sideburns running down their jaw-bones.—Tom Wolfe, "Funky Chic," in *Mauve Gloves and Madmen, Clutter and Vine* (1976) gabled houses topped by tile roofs. Streets were hopelessly narrow, especially those near the river, a result of reliance on the Thames for transport and commerce.

In the 1640s, London saw much fighting between the Puritan troops of Oliver Cromwell and the Royalist followers of Charles I, which culminated with Charles's execution in 1649 on the scaffold at Whitehall. Not until 1660, the year of Charles II's accession to the throne, was the House of Stuart restored to power.

In 1665, a plague swept through the city's overcrowded slums, claiming an estimated 75,000 lives. A year later, the Great Fire, which began in a bakery on Pudding Lane near London Bridge, destroyed much of the town, including 89 churches and 13,200 homes.

THE 18TH CENTURY   Despite the tragedy of fire, urban planners, spearheaded by Sir Christopher Wren, used the disaster to redesign and rebuild London. The beauty of Wren's churches remains unmatched in all Britain. They include St. Mary-le-Bow, one of the most famous, as well as the new St. Paul's Cathedral, both finished by 1710.

By this time the aristocracy had begun migrating westward toward Covent Garden and Whitehall. The most convenient method of transportation was still via the Thames, while the sedan chair allowed aristocrats to be carried over the filthy streets, where dung, sewage, and refuse littered the undrained cobblestones.

Despite the hardships, the arts and sciences flourished in London. In the second half of the century, Joshua Reynolds painted his portraits; James Boswell wrote his reminiscences of lexicographer/critic/poet Samuel Johnson; David Garrick performed his famous Shakespearean roles; and some of the best landscape painting in the history of Europe was about to flower.

The spatial proportions of Georgian and (later) Regency architecture changed the facades of thousands of houses throughout London. For a limited number of citizens, the good life was bountiful, and London was the seat of all that was powerful, beautiful, desirable, intelligent, and witty.

THE VICTORIAN ERA   The most visible progress, as well as the greatest expansion of London, occurred during the Victorian era, when railroad lines and steam engines, sewage systems, cabs, underground trains, and new building techniques transformed London into a modern metropolis and hugely expanded its borders. Massive slums in the city's interior were cleared, but their occupants ended up in newer, more remote slums that remain legendary as examples of the Industrial Revolution's most horrible urban blight. Traffic arteries were rammed through the city's center from west to east. And an unlikely meadow known as Porridge Island was transformed into Trafalgar Square.

Victorian London was the center of the largest empire the world had ever seen. Londoners left their homes to fill military and administrative posts in such faraway dependencies as Calcutta, Kenya, Singapore, and Hong Kong. The art treasures of the world filled London's museums and private houses. In poorer neighborhoods, dyed-in-the-wool Londoners evolved a series of dialects and attitudes later identified as cockney; its accents and humor filled the city's music halls and vaudeville houses and subsequently influenced the entertainment industry from Sydney to San Francisco. London thrived, burgeoning into one of the most complicated and diverse capitals of Europe.

THE EDWARDIAN ERA   During the early 1900s, Victoria's successor, Edward VII, brought elaborate pageantry back to affairs of state (and a welcome laissez-faire attitude to affairs of the heart). Buckingham Palace was enlarged and newly sheathed in a honey-colored layer of stone, and a massive statue to Victoria was erected in front of its newly opened processional avenue leading to the Admiralty Arch. The neo-Gothic grandeur of the Albert Memorial, although not escaping criticism, helped define the era's architectural style, which permeated vast neighborhoods of London with its eclecticism, ornateness, and high individualism.

THE WORLD WARS   World War I sent shock waves through Britain, although George V, who ascended the throne in 1910, ruled steadfastly from his London seat. Even if the damage was relatively minor compared to that later inflicted by World War II, 922 incendiary and explosive bombs fell on the financial district (the City), causing great damage and killing or injuring almost 2,500 people. The enraged Londoners poured their national effort into a conflict that was to be idealistically defined as "the War to End All Wars."

During World War II, however, at least 30,000 people died and vast tracts of London were destroyed by aerial bombing. Westminster Abbey (parts of which had stood unmolested since the 11th century) and the magnificent bulk of the Houses of Parliament were seriously damaged over two nights in May 1941. During a period remembered for the indomitable spirit of the people, thousands of Londoners systematically moved their mattresses and bedclothes every night to the city's subway tunnels, considered safe from Nazi bombing.

Although the neighborhood that surrounded it was almost completely destroyed, St. Paul's Cathedral amazingly escaped with only minor damage, rising majestically above the rubble like a beacon of hope for the sorely tested people of London.

Following World War II, vast rebuilding projects replaced London's bombed-out rubble. The transportation system was improved. Then, in 1953, the coronation of Elizabeth II sparked a period of beautification with myriad houses painted and millions of flower beds planted.

TODAY'S LONDON   In the 1970s and 1980s, a revitalized economy led to the revival of some run-down districts (Notting Hill, parts of Chelsea, the Docklands) into chic and desirable neighborhoods. English wits estimate that at one time or another since the end of World War II, virtually every corner of London has been covered with scaffolding, as builders, homeowners, and real estate moguls add structural support, modernized comforts, and new life to virtually every building.

Prime Minister Margaret Thatcher's reforms of the 1980s created new and modernized financial institutions, including a computerized London Stock Exchange, whose presence has reinforced London's traditional role as a financial, shipping, and insurance center. In 1990,

Thatcher was replaced as prime minister by another member of the Conservative party, the less flamboyant but also controversial John Major. In 1992, it wasn't the prime minister but the House of Windsor that got the boldest headlines. In a year that Elizabeth II labeled *annus horribilis,* a fire swept Windsor Castle; the queen agreed to pay income taxes for the first time; and the marriages of two sons seemed to crumble as Princes Charles and Andrew separated from their wives, Diana and Sarah. Princess Anne, however, remarried.

Although England's (and London's) problems such as unemployment and terrorist bombings continued to dominate the headlines in 1993, the problems of the royal family captured the most print and TV time. That year was launched by what the press dubbed "Camillagate," the release of alleged and sexually explicit phone conversations between Prince Charles and his longtime companion, the then-married Camilla Parker-Bowles. British author Anthony Holden wrote that the Crown was dragged "as deep into the mud as at any time in the 500 years since Henry VII found it there at Bosworth Field."

The future of the monarchy—specifically the House of Windsor—continues to attract world attention. In 1994, talk and speculation continued to focus on the House of Windsor, but it was an engineering feat that captured London's attention even more. Queen Elizabeth II and François Mitterrand of France officially opened the Chunnel under the English Channel, the first link between Britain and France since the Ice Age. Although some pessimists predicted the "end of London as we know it before the foreign hordes descend," that hasn't happened yet. Now, there's a fast, efficient way to reach Paris in near-record time without getting seasick while tossed by the turbulent waves of the English Channel with its notorious bad weather.

Chastened, sadder, and probably wiser after the ruin of the 1940s and the loss of the empire, not to mention today's racial and economic tensions, London remains one of the most vital, interesting, and influential cities in the world. Its allure to foreigners, be they English-speaking or not, is potent, providing one of the most intriguing, varied, and appealing tourist destinations in the world. More true than ever is Samuel Johnson's dictum, uttered some 200 years ago: "When a man is tired of London, he is tired of life." Surely the same could be said for a woman as well.

4   Art & Architecture

ART

You can read about English art, but it's better to experience it firsthand in some of London's great galleries. Most noted are London's National Gallery and the Tate Gallery, but there are dozens of others.

During the Anglo-Saxon and medieval periods, intricately wrought crosses, religious statuary, and illuminated manuscripts were the major art objects. Ornate tombs with sculpted effigies of the dead marked the resting places of the nobility and the princes of the church, and the cathedrals became art galleries of awesome beauty. By the 13th century, as the Gothic period gathered momentum, embroidered tapestries, metalwork, frescoes, panel painting, and stained glass also served as mediums of religious artistic expression. Inevitably, such ornamentation overflowed into secular life as well.

During the Renaissance, portraiture assumed primacy in secular painting, especially as executed by the great Hans Holbein the Younger, a Swiss-born artist who became painter to Henry VIII.

Henry's massive frame and little "piggy eyes" were famously depicted in the Holbein portrait. It was so unflattering that it's amazing that the king, known for his six wives didn't have the portrait painter beheaded. The great miniaturist Nicholas Hilliard and his pupil Isaac Oliver rendered similar service to Elizabeth I, Henry's daughter.

Among the outstanding painters of the Stuart period, neither Sir Anthony Van Dyck nor Sir Peter Lely was English-born. Van Dyck (1599–1641), the Flemish painter, studied under Rubens and assisted that great artist on some of his most important canvases. Van Dyck came first to England in 1620 and was there again from 1632 when he was knighted by Charles I of England who appointed him court painter. Van Dyck was known for his use of color and for portraying delicate emotion in his portraits, producing more than 500 of them. Sir Peter Lely (1618–80), from Westphalia (Germany), came to England in 1641 and painted both historical subjects and landscapes, although he is mainly known for his portraits of the royal family, including the 1660s series, *Windsor Beauties* (even if the subjects weren't).

William Hogarth (1697–1764), the English painter and engraver who once owned his own engraver's shop, is today remembered chiefly for his satirical narrative pictures. He is known for such works as *The Beggar's Opera* (1728) and *Marriage à la Mode* (1745). Many Londoners of the time were scandalized by his two series of engravings, *A Harlot's Progress* and *A Rake's Progress*.

By the 18th century, English painting had come into its own and didn't have to be imported from abroad. Some critics claim that the main contribution of England to Western art derived from its long tradition of landscape painting. Even though much of the scenery these artists captured on canvas is gone forever, much remains to give fresh inspiration to today's landscape painter.

The harbinger of this genre was Richard Wilson, born in Wales in 1714. As a young man, he was heavily influenced by the French artist, Claude Lorrain. Although poverty-stricken throughout much of his life, he painted native Welsh mountains set across from limpid lakes and tried to get the world to buy them. In time they would, but perhaps too late to help the struggling artist's finances.

The landscape painting giants that followed Wilson did get the world to take an intense interest in their work. These included Suffolk-born artist Thomas Gainsborough (1727–88), who was one of the original members of the Royal Academy of Fine Arts, which although established in 1768, is still flourishing in Piccadilly today. In the salons of Bath and London, Gainsborough gained fame as a portrait painter of the rich. "His touch was as light as the sweep of a cloud and swift as the flash of a sunbeam," wrote John Ruskin, the Victorian critic. In his final years, he turned to seascapes and often painted rather idealized pictures of country rustics and children. Even people who know nothing of art have seen reproductions of his 1770 *The Blue Boy*.

From the same landscapes of East Anglia emerged John Constable (1776–1837), some half a century after Gainsborough. Hayfields, river scenes, church spires, horses and wagons, all of these captured his fantasy and imagination. He wrote of "Light, dews, breezes, bloom, and freshness." At first, the English didn't appreciate him, but he eventually won recognition in France beginning in 1824. Some of his most memorable paintings, all landscapes, included *Salisbury Cathedral, Dedham Vale,* and *Hay Wain.*

Painting at the same time as Constable was an even greater name in English art, Joseph Mallord William (J. M. W.) Turner (1775–1851). John Ruskin had words for him, too: "He saw that there were more clouds in every sky than had ever been painted, more trees in every forest, more crags on every hillside, and set himself with all his strength to proclaim the great quantity of the universe." Living in Chelsea, and fascinated by the River Thames, Turner painted romantic landscapes, great cathedrals, country houses, river scenes, the landscapes of the Lake District, the Yorkshire Dales. He became increasingly fascinated by light, as evoked by his 1807 painting, *Sun Rising Through Vapour.* Turner in the final phase of his life became more poetic and dreamlike in his paintings. He also produced engravings and thousands of watercolors, 19,000 of which he left to the Tate Gallery in London upon his death.

The multitalented William Blake (1757–1827), English mystic, artist, and poet, made illustrations for the Bible, Milton's *Paradise Lost,* and Blair's *The Grave,* among other works. His fantastical paintings and illustrations earned him fame in his day. He printed from etched copper plates a series of his own illustrations for his own lyrical poems, including the 1789 *Songs of Innocence.* At the time of his death, he was preparing engravings for Dante's *Divine Comedy.*

In time came the Pre-Raphaelites, including Sir Edward Burne-Jones (1833–1898), the English painter and designer who first became known for his large oils such as *Le Chant d'Armour* from 1877. A contemporary of Burne-Jones, Dante Gabriel Rossetti (1828–82), the English painter and poet, founded, along with others, the pre- Raphaelite school of painting in 1848.

One of the most important portrait painters of the 20th century was Augustus John (1878–1961), whose works included portraits of George Bernard Shaw, Tallulah Bankhead, Dylan Thomas, and Lloyd George.

England gave the world many great names in art during the 20th century, including Francis Bacon, Ben Nicholson, and Graham Sutherland. Sutherland painted in Pembrokeshire before and after the war, winning world acclaim. Bacon's "bloody meat" portraits disturbed many, and won him both praise and condemnation. Nicholson became known for semiabstract still lifes and landscapes, sometimes rendered in relief.

Most early British sculpture was commissioned by the church. The religious conflicts of the 16th and 17th centuries temporarily ended the lavish ornamentation of churches, but in the late 17th and early 18th centuries, sculpture came back into vogue, producing such artists as Grinling Gibbons (1648–1721), who was employed by Sir Christopher Wren to carve the stalls in St. Paul's. He also worked for the Royal family at Windsor, Whitehall, and Kensington.

Henry Moore (1898–1986) and Dame Barbara Hepworth (1903–75) became towering figures in 20th-century British sculpture. Moore created abstract—often mammoth—sculptures inspired by organic forms, especially in stone and bronze. He is best remembered for his undulating reclining nudes. Many critics consider him the greatest sculptor of the 20th century; other critics have denounced his work as pointless.

His sometimes companion, the above-mentioned Dame Barbara Hepworth, also pursued the abstract in sculpture. Her works are hailed for their mastery of texture. She created an interplay of mass and interior space by the use of painted hollows, voids, and perforations. Much of her work was commissioned, including the 1962 *Single Form* for the United Nations. Her *Reclining Figure* from 1932 brought her early acclaim.

ARCHITECTURE

Originally, London was a collection of scattered villages and towns that were unified under the pressure of the Industrial Revolution in the 18th and 19th centuries. A little of the city's original flavor and feeling remains in such places as Whitechapel, Chelsea, Hammersmith, and Hampstead. During the 18th century, when the principles of "picturesque planning" were being evolved for a rapidly expanding London, planners consciously incorporated the best of the greens, riverbank terraces, and small-scale layouts of the original villages. These rural features (rigorously preserved by neighborhood residents today) are now completely enclosed by the bulk and congestion of urban London.

Other than an ancient Roman temple of Mithras, excavated in the 1950s on Queen Victoria Street, and the ruins of a fortified wall discovered near Trinity Place, few architectural remnants of the city's Roman colonization exist.

London's first major architectural style was imported from northern France. Defined as Norman Gothic, it was solid, majestic, and ideal for such defensive structures as gatehouses and castles. Decoration was blunt and geometric, arches were rounded. The style thrived in Britain until about 1190. It can best be admired today in the Tower of London, St. Bartholomew's, and the Temple Church.

EARLY ENGLISH GOTHIC   As medieval England grew more sophisticated, both structural arches and the frames that surrounded windows were designed with pointed ("broken") tops, and exterior buttresses took on more solidity as the windows became larger. Cathedrals grew taller, with roofs and spires angled more steeply. The cathedrals of Ely, York, and Salisbury are the best examples of this Early English Gothic style; in London it was manifested in Westminster Abbey's Chapter House.

During the 1300s, the solid rectilinear lines of English cathedrals gave way to increasing ornateness as vaultings grew more complex and windows became ever larger. Eventually, cathedrals were highlighted with huge expanses of glass and fan-shaped vaulting that resembled the trunks and branches of trees gracefully frozen into stone ribbing. The style became known as Gothic Perpendicular. Its best examples can be seen in the cathedrals of Bath and Gloucester and in St. George's Chapel at Windsor. Its best London manifestation is in Henry VII's chapel in Westminster Abbey.

TUDOR TO JACOBEAN ERAS   The true surge in London's building didn't begin until the population explosion and outward urban expansion of the Renaissance. Until the early 1500s, London was contained by the original Roman walls, having only 50,000 inhabitants (about 20% more than it had when occupied by the Romans). By 1600, however, the population had passed the quarter-million mark, with about 75,000 living within the walls.

The main inspirations for Tudor architecture were the Gothic lines and masses that had characterized ecclesiastical building since the 11th century, but this style was now applied to private residences. London's best examples of this style are St. James's Palace and Hampton Court, the home originally built by Henry VIII's Cardinal Wolsey.

By 1660, the population of London had reached half a million, many of whom lived in overcrowded and filthy conditions. London Bridge, until 1739 the only bridge crossing the Thames, today is described as Elizabethan. Picturesque, but highly flammable, houses had a framework of oak beams whose open spaces were filled with mud, plaster, and chopped straw, and were sometimes whitewashed. More elaborate houses were constructed of brick and tile or slate in a style eventually identified as Jacobean. Low-ceilinged, with dark paneling and leaded-glass windows, they gave off a richly gorgeous feeling of comfort and carried Elizabethan motifs to a grander and larger scale.

INIGO JONES TO CHRISTOPHER WREN   Inigo Jones (1573–1652), considered the first great modern British architect, introduced the airily and mathematically precise designs promoted by Italian Renaissance architect Andrea Palladio. This style opted for strict spatial ratios of windows to doors, plus a balanced symmetry that often combined the three classic Greek orders (Doric, Ionic, and Corinthian) in gracefully symmetrical neoclassical grandeur. In London, two of Jones's most famous buildings are the Banqueting House at Whitehall and the Queen's House at Greenwich.

The Great Fire of 1666, which devastated huge neighborhoods of London, resulted in a revolutionary code of building. Borrowing heavily from construction techniques used in Holland, Sir Christopher Wren did much to replace a city previously built of wood with brick, stone, and (later) stucco. He rebuilt more than 50 churches, dozens of public buildings, and many private homes, making him the most prolific architect in Britain's history. His dignified yet graceful designs have been relentlessly copied throughout the world. The greater part of his work was erected in London, the most famous building being St. Paul's

Cathedral. Other examples of his work include Kensington Palace, the Royal Hospital in Chelsea, and portions of Hampton Court Palace.

Wren had submitted a plan to rebuild London on a French baroque–inspired plan of plazas, traffic circles, and panoramic avenues. Fearing the number of land disputes this would have involved, Charles II rejected the plan and the city was rebuilt on a less grand and less coherent scale—one that respected the property lines and medieval layouts that had existed prior to the fire.

London, however, was about to embark on one of its greatest expansions. Where the municipal government failed in imposing a logical order on the city's architectural layout, private speculators created developments that usually included a series of almost identical facades opening onto a plaza, square, or garden.

Covent Garden (designed by Inigo Jones himself in 1631) was the first of the monumental squares. Laden with neoclassical details and grand in its proportions, Covent Garden was followed by dozens of imitations, including such famous ones as Portman Square, Soho Square, Grosvenor Square, and Berkeley Square. Later, in the early 19th century, these were copied by private entrepreneurs who created the regular and rhythmic, less monumental neighborhoods of Belgravia, Bloomsbury, Finsbury, and Paddington. The architectural taste of the era (Palladian classical) was endlessly reproduced. This last development partly explains the comparative lack of gargantuan structures in many London neighborhoods, where a sense of privacy and shelter behind walled gardens stems from the British yearning for privacy.

VICTORIAN ERA   During the 19th century, the population of London exploded once again, so that by 1902 it had reached almost 4.5 million inhabitants. (The opening of the Underground in 1863 was in part the City Council's attempt to cope with this expansion.) The architecture of this period was eclectic and whimsical, with the Gothic tradition as the main inspiration but adapted in idiosyncratic and clever ways. Today, Victorian architecture seems to dominate the city, but the quintessential example is the memorial erected by Queen Victoria to her departed husband, Albert. Ringed with bronzes of allegorical female figures representing the world's continents, it stands surrounded by greenery in South Kensington.

The English love of gardens, the expansion of London from a series of villages in Europe's biggest metropolis, and the encroachment of urban sprawl on rural areas—all helped to form the concept of the city of gardens, of the "corner of the country within the city." In 1898,

Impressions

More than any other city in Europe, London is a show, living by bluff and display. People have always remarked upon its theatrical nature. . . . It is, surprisingly, a very volatile capital: the U.S. ambassador recently diagnosed it as manic-depressive, on top of the world one day, all despondency the next.   —Jan Morris, *Destinations* (1980) industrial planner Ebeneser Howard conceived of a low-income garden city: an autonomous urban center that contained within its borders outlets both for earning a livelihood and for living within sight of greenery. The first of these developments was Letchworth, a few miles north of London, built in 1903.

EDWARDIAN ERA TO POST 1945 During the early 20th century, Edwardian architects (the most deservedly celebrated of whom was Sir Edwin Lutyens) created what some critics consider the finest examples of domestic architecture in the world. They corrected many of the mistakes of, and improved the designs of, their Victorian predecessors. Often building with earth-colored brick and incorporating elements of Arthurian legend, art nouveau, and the arts-and-crafts movement, they added whimsy and great comfort to thousands of buildings, usually siting and landscaping them gracefully. Inside were oversized bathrooms, extra pantries, and reading nooks. Excellent examples of the Edwardian style include most of the grand hotels of London's Park Lane (most notably the Park Lane, the Ritz, and the somewhat newer art deco Dorchester), as well as the Admiralty Arch.

The blitz that Hitler launched on London during World War II destroyed not only much of the city's great architecture but also the slums of Whitechapel in the East End. This neighborhood—made equally famous by Charles Dickens and Jack the Ripper—had been London's festering sore, having among the worst housing conditions in the Western world. The London City Council rebuilt most of the area into rather drab but infinitely preferable rows of apartment blocks.

This postwar building boom may have made London a little less "quaint," but it also made it a more healthful place in which to live. A consciousness of good modern architecture was much promoted in the 1980s by the articulate efforts of Prince Charles.

2

Planning a Trip to London

After people decide where to travel, most have two fundamental questions: What will it cost? and How do I get there? This chapter tackles the hows of your trip to London—all those issues required to get your trip together and take it on the road, whether you're a regular traveler or are disabled, a senior citizen, a single traveler, a student, or a family traveling together. In addition to helping you decide when to take your vacation (climate, events), this chapter discusses what to take, where to gather information, and what documents you need to obtain.

1 Visitor Information & Entry Requirements

VISITOR INFORMATION

In the United States and Canada, you can obtain information about Great Britain from the following British Tourist Authority offices: 551 Fifth Ave., Suite 701, **New York,** NY 10176-0799 (☎ 212/986-2200); and 111 Avenue Rd., Suite 450, **Toronto,** ON M5R 3J8, Canada (☎ 416/925-6326).

In London, London Tourist Board's **Tourist Information Centre,** Victoria Station Forecourt, SW1 (tube: Victoria Station), can help you with almost anything that might be of touristic interest to a visitor. The center deals chiefly with accommodations in all size and price categories, and can handle the whole spectrum of travelers. It also arranges for travel, tour-ticket sales, and theater reservations, and operates a shop offering a wide selection of books and souvenirs. The center is open for personal callers between Easter and October, daily from 8am to 7pm and from November to Easter, Monday to Saturday from 8am to 6pm and Sunday from 9am to 4pm.

The tourist board also maintains an office in the basement of one of London's largest department stores, **Selfridges,** Oxford Street, W1 (tube: Bond Street), Duke Street Entrance, open during store hours. Other offices are at **Heathrow** Terminals 1, 2, and 3, and on the Underground Concourse at **Liverpool Street Railway Station.**

For a full information pack on London, write to London Tourist Board, P.O. Box 151, London E15 2HF. You can also telephone the recorded-message service, Visitorcall, which is available 24 hours a day. Various topics are listed on this number, which is 01839/123456. Calls cost 39p (60¢) per minute cheap rate (Monday to Friday from 6pm to

8am and all day Saturday and Sunday) and 49p (75¢) per minute at all other times.

For accommodation booking by credit card (MasterCard or VISA), telephone 0171/824-8844.

ENTRY REQUIREMENTS

DOCUMENTS U.S. citizens, Canadians, Australians, New Zealanders, and South Africans all require a passport to enter the United Kingdom, but no visa. Some Customs officials will request proof that you have the means to eventually leave the country (usually a round-trip ticket) and visible means of support while you're in Britain. If you're planning to fly to another country from the United Kingdom, it's wise to secure the visa before your arrival in Britain.

CUSTOMS For visitors to England, goods fall into two basic categories—the first category includes goods purchased in a non-European Community (EC) country or bought tax-free within the EC; the second category is goods purchased tax-paid in the EC. In the first category, limits on imports by individuals (17 and older) include 200 cigarettes (or 50 cigars or 250 grams of loose tobacco), 2 liters of still table wine, 1 liter of liquor (over 22% alcohol content) or 2 liters of liquor (under 22%), and 2 fluid ounces of perfume. In the second category, limits are much higher. An individual may import 800 cigarettes bought tax-paid in the EC, 200 cigars, and 1 kilogram of loose tobacco, 90 liters of wine, 10 liters of alcohol (over 22%), and 110 liters of beer, plus unlimited amounts of perfume.

Foreign vacationers in England may not bring along pets. An illegally imported animal is liable to be destroyed.

If you make purchases in Britain, keep receipts. On gifts, the duty-free limit for U.S. citizens is $50. For more information, see "Taxes" under "Fast Facts: London" in Chapter 3 (which covers England's value-added tax, or VAT) and Section 1 of Chapter 8 (which discusses sending gifts home).

2 Money

CURRENCY

POUNDS & PENCE Britain's decimal monetary system is based on the pound sterling (£), which is made up of 100 pence (written as "p"). There are now £1 coins (called "quid" by Britons), plus coins of 50p, 20p, 10p, 5p, 2p, and 1p. The 0.5p coin has been officially discontinued, although it will be around for a while. Banknotes come in denominations of £5, £10, £20, and £50.

As a general guideline, the price conversions in this book have been computed at the rate of £1 equaling U.S. $1.58. Bear in mind, however, that exchange rates fluctuate daily.

In general, banks in London proper offer the best exchange rates, and you're likely to obtain a better rate for traveler's checks than for cash. There are also branches of the main banks at London's airports, but they charge a small fee. There are in addition bureaus de change

The British Pound & the U.S. Dollar

£	U.S.$	£	U.S.$
0.05	0.08	15	23.85
0.10	0.16	20	31.60
0.25	0.40	25	39.50
0.50	0.79	30	47.40
0.75	1.19	35	55.30
1	1.58	40	63.20
2	3.16	45	71.11
3	4.74	50	79.00
4	6.36	55	87.45
5	7.90	60	95.40
6	9.48	65	102.70
7	11.06	70	110.60
8	12.64	75	118.50
9	14.22	100	158.00
10	15.90	125	197.50

Note: The rate of exchange at press time was approximately $1.58 U.S. to £1, and that was the rate used to compile the chart listed above. Because rates change almost daily, however, check the current value of the pound in a newspaper or at a bank.

at the airports and around London that charge a fee for cashing traveler's checks and for changing foreign currency into pounds sterling. Some travel agencies, such as American Express and Thomas Cook, also provide currency-exchange services. It's wise to check around to find the best exchange rate—you usually won't find it in hotels and shops.

TRAVELER'S CHECKS   Before leaving home, purchase traveler's checks and arrange to carry some ready cash (usually about $250, depending on your habits and needs). In the event of theft, if the checks are properly documented, the value of your checks will be refunded. Most large banks sell traveler's checks, charging fees that average between 1% and 2% of the value of the checks you buy, although some out-of-the-way banks, in rare instances, have charged as much as 7%. If your bank wants more than a 2% commission, it sometimes pays to call the traveler's check issuers directly for the address of outlets where this commission will cost less.

For more information, contact the following companies: **American Express** (☎ 800/221-7282 in the U.S. and Canada); **Citicorp** (☎ 800/645-6556 in the U.S. and Canada, or 813/623-1709 collect from other parts of the world); or **Thomas Cook** (☎ 800/223-7373 in the U.S. or Canada or 609/987-7300 collect from other parts of the world).

What Things Cost in London	U.S. $
Taxi from Victoria Station to Paddington hotel	12.50
Underground from Heathrow Airport to central London	5.25
Local telephone call	0.20
Very expensive double room (at The Dorchester)	355.50
Moderate double room (at Bryanston Court Hotel)	142.20
Inexpensive double room (at Regent Palace Hotel)	121.70
Moderate lunch for one (at Sheekeys)	28.90
Inexpensive lunch for one (at Cheshire Cheese)	15.00
Very expensive dinner for one, without wine (at Le Gavroche)	90.00
Moderate dinner for one, without wine (at Bracewells)	37.00
Inexpensive dinner for one, without wine (at Porter's English Restaurant)	23.60
Pint of beer	2.90
Coca-Cola in a café	1.60
Cup of coffee	1.30
Roll of ASA 100 color film, 36 exposures	8.00
Admission to the British Museum	Free
Movie ticket	7.50
Theater ticket	15.00–52.50

PERSONAL CHECKS   Some British hotels require an advance deposit in pounds to make reservations. An easy way to obtain a check for this is through **Ruesch International,** 825 14th St. NW, Washington, DC 20005 (☎ 202/408-1200, or toll free 800/ 424-2923). To place an order, call and tell them the amount of the sterling-denominated check you need. Ruesch will quote a U.S. dollar equivalent, adding a $2 service fee per check. After receiving your dollar-denominated personal check, Ruesch will mail you a sterling-denominated bank draft, drawn at a British bank and payable to the party you specify. Ruesch will also convert checks in a foreign currency to U.S. dollars, change currency for more than 120 countries, and sell traveler's checks payable in dollars or six foreign currencies, including pounds. In addition to the Washington office, Ruesch maintains offices in Zurich, London, New York, Los Angeles, Chicago, Atlanta, and Boston. Any of these offices can supply draft and traveler's check by mail or phone.

CREDIT CARDS   Credit cards are widely used in London. American Express, VISA, and Diners Club are the most commonly recognized. A Eurocard or Access sign displayed at an establishment means that it accepts MasterCard.

3   When to Go

THE CLIMATE

Charles Dudley Warner (in a remark most often attributed to Mark Twain) once said that the trouble with the weather is that everybody talks about it but nobody does anything about it. Well, Londoners talk about weather more than anyone, but they have also done something about it—air-pollution control, which has resulted in the virtual disappearance of the pea-soup fogs that once blanketed the city.

A typical London-area weather forecast for a summer day predicts "scattered clouds with sunny periods and showers, possibly heavy at times." Summer temperatures seldom rise above 78° Fahrenheit, nor do they drop below 35° Fahrenheit in winter.

The British consider chilliness wholesome and usually try to keep room temperatures about 10° below the American comfort level.

London's Average Daytime Temperature & Rainfall

	Jan	Feb	Mar	Apr	May	June	July	Aug	Sept	Oct	Nov	Dec
Temp (°F)	40	40	44	49	55	61	64	64	59	52	46	42
Rainfall (")	2.1	1.6	1.5	1.5	1.8	1.8	2.2	2.3	1.9	2.2	2.5	1.9

CURRENT WEATHER CONDITIONS   In the United States, you can dial 1/900-WEATHER, then press the first four letters of the desired foreign city—in this case, LOND for London—for the time of day in that city, plus current temperatures, weather conditions, and forecasts. The cost is 95¢ per minute.

HOLIDAYS

In England, public holidays include New Year's Day, Good Friday, Easter Monday, May Day (first Monday in May), spring and summer bank holidays (last Monday in May and August, respectively), Christmas Day, and Boxing Day (December 26).

LONDON CALENDAR OF EVENTS

January

- **London International Boat Show,** Earl's Court Exhibition Centre, Warwick Road. The largest boat show in Europe. First two weeks in January.
- **Charles I Commemoration.** Anniversary of the execution of King Charles I "in the name of freedom and democracy." Hundreds of cavaliers march through central London in 17th-century dress, and prayers are said at the Banqueting House in Whitehall. Free. Last Sunday in January.

February

- **Chinese New Year.** The famous Lion Dancers in Soho. Free. February 13.

April

- **Easter Parade,** around Battersea Park. Brightly colored floats and marching bands; a full day of Easter Sunday activities. Free. April 3.

May

- **Outdoor Shakespeare Performances.** If you want to see *Macbeth, Hamlet,* or *Romeo and Juliet* (or any other Shakespeare play), the advice is always to "bring a blanket and a bottle of wine" to watch the Bard's works performed at the Open Air Theatre, Inner Circle, Regent's Park, NW1. Take the tube to Regent's Park or Baker Street. Previews begin in late May and last throughout the summer. Times are Monday, Tuesday, and Friday at 8pm; Wednesday, Thursday, and Saturday at 2:30 and 8pm. Call 0171/486-2431 for more information.

- **Chelsea Flower Show,** Chelsea Royal Hospital. The best of British gardening, with displays of plants and flowers of all seasons. Tickets are available abroad from overseas reservations agents; contact your local British Tourist Authority office to find out which agency is handling ticket sales this year, or write to the Chelsea Show Ticket Office, P.O. Box 1426, London W6 OLQ. Late May. Call 0171/630-7422 for more information.

June

- **Epsom Derby Stakes.** Famous horse-racing event at Epsom Racecourse, Epsom, Surrey. It's the best-known event on the British horse-racing calendar and a chance for men to wear top hats and women, including the queen, to put on silly millinery creations. The "darby" (as it's called here) is run in early June. Grandstand tickets range from £9 to £20 ($14.20 to $31.60). Call 01372/726311 for more information.

- **Grosvenor House Antique Fair,** Grosvenor House. A very prestigious antiques fair. Second week of June.

- **Kenwood Lakeside Concerts,** annual concerts on the north side of Hampstead Heath, a British tradition of outdoor performances for nearly 50 years. Firework displays and laser shows help to enliven the premier musical performances staged here. Music drifts to the fans from a performance shell across the lake every Saturday in summer from mid-June to early September.

- **Royal Academy's Summer Exhibition.** This institution, founded in 1768 with Sir Joshua Reynolds as president, and with Gainsborough as a member, for some two centuries has sponsored Summer Exhibitions of living painters. Visitors can both browse and make art purchases, many of them quite reasonable in price. Exhibitions are presented daily at Burlington House, Piccadilly Circus, W1. Call 0171/439-7438 for more information. Gala opening of exhibition draws London's artistic elite. June 4 to August 13.

- **Royal Ascot Week.** Ascot Racecourse is open all year round for guided tours, events, exhibitions, and conferences. There are 23 race days throughout the year with the feature race meetings being the Royal Meeting in June, Diamond Day in July, and the Festival at Ascot in September. For further information please contact Ascot Racecourse, Ascot, Berkshire SL5 7JN (☎ 01344/22211).

✪ **Trooping the Colour**   The official birthday of the queen. Seated in a carriage (no longer on horseback), the royal monarch inspects her regiments and takes their salute as they parade their colors before her. A quintessential British event religiously watched by the populace on TV. The pageantry and pomp are exquisite. Depending on the weather, the young men under the bearskins have been known to pass out from the heat.

Where: Horse Guards Parade, Whitehall. **When:** A day designated in June (not necessarily the queen's actual birthday). **How:** Tickets for the actual parade and two reviews, held on preceding Saturdays, are allocated by ballot. Those interested in attending must write to apply for tickets between January 1 and the end of February, enclosing a stamped, self-addressed envelope or International Reply Coupon—exact dates and ticket prices will be supplied later. The ballot is held in mid-March, and successful applicants *only* are informed in April. For full details write to HQ Household Division, Horse Guards, Whitehall, London SW1X 6AA, enclosing a self-addressed envelope with an International Reply Coupon.

✪ **Lawn Tennis Championships**   Ever since the players in flannels and bonnets took to the grass courts at Wimbledon in 1877, this tournament has drawn a socially prominent crowd. Although the courts are now crowded with all kinds of tennis fans, there's still an excited hush at the Centre Court and a certain thrill in being there. Savor the strawberries and cream that are part of the experience.

Where: Wimbledon, Southwest London. **When:** Late June to early July. **How:** Tickets for Centre and Number One courts obtainable through a lottery. Write in October to Lawn Tennis Association, P.O. Box 98, Church Road, Wimbledon, London SW19 5AE (☎0181/946-2244). Outside court tickets available daily, but prepared to wait in line.

July

- **City of London Festival,** annual arts festival throughout the city. Call 0181/377-0540 for information about the various programs and venues. Early to mid-July.

- **Royal Tournament,** Earl's Court Exhibition Centre, Warwick Road. British armed forces put on dazzling displays of athletic and military skills, which have been called "military pomp, show biz, and outright jingoism." For information and details about performance times and tickets, call 0171/373-8141. Late July.

- **The Proms.** A night at "The Proms"—the annual Henry Wood Promenade Concerts at Royal Albert Hall—attracts music aficionados from around the world. Staged almost daily (except for a few

Sundays) these traditional concerts were launched in 1895 and are the principal summer venue for the BBC Symphony Orchestra. Cheering, clapping, Union Jacks on parade, banners and balloons create summer fun. Mid-July through mid-September.

August

- **African-Caribbean Street Fair,** Notting Hill. One of the largest street festivals in Europe, attracting over half a million people annually. Live reggae and soul music combine with great Caribbean food. Free. Two days in late August.

October

✪ **Opening of Parliament**   Ever since the 17th century, when the English cut off the head of Charles I, the British monarch has had no right to enter the House of Commons. Instead, the monarch opens Parliament in the House of Lords, reading an official speech that is written by the government of the day. The monarch rides from Buckingham Palace to Westminster in a royal coach accompanied by the Yeoman of the Guard and the Household Cavalry.

   Where: House of Lords, Westminster. **When:** First Monday in October. **How:** Strangers' Gallery is open on a first-come, first-served basis.

- **Horse of the Year Show.** At Wembley Arena, Wembley, outside London, this event is the premier equestrian highlight on the English calendar. Riders fly in from all continents to join in this festive display of horseflesh (much appreciated by the queen herself). The British press call it "an equine extravaganza." For more information, call 0181/902-8833. October 3–8.

November

- **Fireworks Night.** Commemorating the anniversary of the Gunpowder Plot, an attempt to blow up James I and his Parliament. Huge organized bonfires are lit throughout the city, and Guy Fawkes, the plot's most famous conspirator, is burned in effigy. Free. Early November.

✪ **Lord Mayor's Procession and Show**   This impressive annual event marks the inauguration of the new lord mayor of the City of London. The queen must ask permission to enter the City's square mile—a right that has been jealously guarded by London merchants from the 17th century to this very day.

   Where: From the Guildhall to the Royal Courts of Justice, in the City. **When:** Second week in November. **How:** You can watch the procession from the street; the banquet is by invitation only.

4 Tips for Special Travelers

FOR TRAVELERS WITH DISABILITIES

Before you go, there are many agencies to check with about information for the disabled.

One is the **Travel Information Service,** MossRehab Hospital, 1200 W. Tabor Rd., Philadelphia, PA 19141, which provides information to telephone callers only: Call 215/456-9603 for assistance with your travel needs.

You can also obtain a copy of **"Air Transportation of Handi- capped Persons,"** published by the U.S. Department of Transporta- tion. A copy is sent free by writing for Free Advisory Circular No. AC12032, Distribution Unit, U.S. Department of Transportation, Publications Division, M-4332, Washington, DC 20590.

You may also want to consider joining a tour specifically for disabled visitors. Names and addresses of such tour operators can be obtained by contacting the **Society for the Advancement of Travel for the Handicapped,** 347 Fifth Ave., New York, NY 10016 (☎ 212/ 447-7284). Yearly membership dues are $45, $25 for senior citizens and students. Send a stamped self-addressed envelope.

You might also consider the **Federation of the Handicapped (FEDCAP),** 154 W. 14th St., New York, NY 10011 (☎ 212/ 727-4200), which offers summer tours for its members, who pay a yearly membership fee of $4.

The **Information Center for Individuals with Disabilities,** Fort Point Place, 27–43 Wormwood St., Boston, MA 02210 (☎ 617/ 727-5540), is another good source. It has lists of travel agents who spe- cialize in tours for the disabled.

For the blind or visually impaired, the best source is the **American Foundation for the Blind,** 15 W. 16th St., New York, NY 10011 (☎ 212/620-2147 or toll free 800/232-5463 for ordering of informa- tion kits and supplies). It offers information on travel and various requirements for the transport and border formalities for Seeing Eye dogs. It also issues identification cards to those who are legally blind.

One of the best organizations serving the needs of the dis- abled (wheelchairs and walkers) is **Flying Wheels Travel,** 143 West Bridge, P.O. Box 382, Owatoona, MN 55060 (☎ 507/451-5005, or toll free 800/535-6790), offering various escorted tours and cruises internationally.

For a $20 annual fee, consider joining **Mobility International USA,** P.O. Box 10767, Eugene, OR 97440 (☎ 503/343-1284). It answers questions on various destinations and also offers discounts on videos, publications, and programs it sponsors.

Finally, a bimonthly publication, **Handicapped Travel Newsletter,** keeps you current on accessible sights worldwide for the disabled. To order an annual subscription for $15, call 903/677-1260.

Many London hotels, museums, restaurants, and sightseeing attrac- tions have wheelchair ramps. Disabled people are often granted special discounts at attractions and, in some cases, nightclubs. These are called "concessions" in Britain. It always pays to ask. Free information and advice is available from **Holiday Care Service,** 2 Old Bank Chambers, Station Road, Horley, Surrey RH6 9HW (☎ 01293/774535). The British Tourist Authority sells *London Made Easy* (£2.50 [$3.80]), a booklet offering advice and describing facilities for the handicapped. Bookstores often carry *Access in London* (£4 [$6]), an even more helpful publication listing facilities for the handicapped, among other things.

London's most visible organization for information about access to theaters, cinemas, galleries, museums, and restaurants is **Artsline,** 54 Chalton St., London NW1 1HS (☎ 0171/388-2227). Funded by the London Arts Board and staffed for the most part by disabled people, it offers free information about wheelchair access, theaters with hearing aids, tourist attractions, and restaurants. Artsline will mail information to North America, but it's even more helpful to contact Artsline after your arrival in London. Call from 9:30am to 5:30pm on Monday through Friday.

An organization that cooperates closely with Artsline is **Tripscope,** The Courtyard, 4 Evelyn Rd., London W4 5JL (☎ 0181/994-9294), which offers advice on travel for disabled persons in Britain and elsewhere.

FOR GAY & LESBIAN TRAVELERS

The **Lesbian and Gay Switchboard** (☎ 0171/837-7324) is open 24 hours a day, providing information about gay-related London activities or advice in general.

The **Bisexual Helpline** (☎ 0181/569-7500) offers useful information but only on Tuesday and Wednesday from 7:30 to 9:30pm. Harassment, gay bashing, and other such matters are handled by **Gay and Lesbian Legal Advice** (☎ 0171/253-2043) on Monday through Friday from 7 to 10pm.

FOR SENIORS

Many discounts are available for seniors. Be advised, however, that in England you often have to be a member of an association to obtain discounts. Public transportation reductions, for example, are available only to holders of British Pension books. However, many attractions do offer discounts for senior citizens (women 60 or over and men 65 or over). Even if discounts aren't posted, you might ask if they are available. Of course, showing your passport as proof of your age is also necessary.

You can write for a helpful publication, **"101 Tips for the Mature Traveler,"** available from Grand Circle Travel, 347 Congress St., Boston, MA 02210 (☎ 617/350-7500, or toll free 800/221-2610); this travel agency also offers escorted tours and cruises for seniors.

SAGA International Holidays is well known for its affordable all-inclusive tours for seniors, preferably those 50 years old or older. Both medical and trip cancellation insurance are included in the net price of any of their tours, except cruises. Contact SAGA International Holidays, 222 Berkeley St., Boston, MA 02116 (☎ toll free 800/ 343-0273).

The **American Association of Retired Persons (AARP),** 601 E. St. NW, Washington, DC 20049 (☎ 202/434-AARP), is the best U.S. organization for seniors. Members are offered discounts on car rentals and hotels.

Information on travel for seniors is also available from the **National Council of Senior Citizens,** 1331 F St. NW, Washington, DC 20004 (☎ 202/347-8800). A nonprofit organization, the council charges a membership fee of $12 per couple for which you receive a monthly newsletter and membership benefits, including travel services. Benefits of membership include discounts on hotels, motels, and auto rentals, and also include supplemental medical insurance for members.

Mature Outlook, 6001 N. Clark St., Chicago, IL 60660 (☎ toll free 800/336-6330), is a travel organization for people over 50 years of age. Members are offered discounts at ITC-member hotels and will receive a bimonthly magazine. Annual membership is $9.95, which entitles its members to discounts and in some cases free coupons for discounted merchandise from Sears Roebuck Co.

FOR FAMILIES

If you have a very small child, you will probably want to take along such standard items as children's aspirin, a thermometer, Band-Aids, and similar supplies.

On airlines, you must request a special menu for children at least 24 hours in advance. If baby food is required, however, bring your own and ask a flight attendant to warm it to the right temperature.

Take along a "security blanket" for your child. This might be a pacifier, a favorite toy or book, or, for older children, a baseball cap or favorite T-shirt.

Arrange ahead of time for such necessities as a crib, bottle warmer, and car seat. (In England small children aren't allowed to ride in the front seat.) Find out if the place at which you're staying stocks baby food. If it doesn't, take some with you and plan to buy more abroad in supermarkets.

Babysitters can be found for you at most hotels.

"Family Travel Times" is published 10 times a year by TWYCH (Travel With Your Children) and includes a weekly call-in service for subscribers. Subscriptions ($55 a year) can be ordered from TWYCH, 45 W. 18th St., 7th floor, New York, NY 10011 (☎ 212/206-0688). TWYCH also publishes two nitty-gritty information guides, *Skiing with Children* and *Cruising with Children,* which sell for $29 and $22, respectively, but are discounted to newsletter subscribers. An information packet, including a sample newsletter, is available for $2.

Families Welcome!, 21 W. Colony Place, Suite 140, Durham, NC 27705 (☎ 919/489-2555, or toll free 800/326-0724), a travel company specializing in worry-free vacations for families, offers "City Kids" packages to London, featuring accommodations in family-friendly hotels or apartments. Some hotels include a second room for children free or at a reduced rate (either/or depending on house count, availability, etc.) during certain time periods. Individually designed family packages can include car rentals, train and ferry passes, and special air prices. A welcome kit is distributed, containing "insider's information" for families traveling in London—such as reliable babysitters, where to buy Pampers, and a list of family friendly restaurants.

FOR STUDENTS

Council Travel (a subsidiary of the Council on International Educational Exchange) is America's largest student, youth, and budget travel group, with more than 60 offices worldwide. The main office is at 205 E. 42nd St., New York, NY 10017 (☎ 212/661-1450). Council Travel's London Centre is conveniently located at 28A Poland St., W1V 3DB, just off Oxford Circus (☎ 071/287-3337 for European destinations, 0171/437-7767 for other destinations). International Student Identity Cards, issuable to all bona fide students for $16, entitle holders to generous travel and other discounts. Discounted international and domestic air tickets are available.

Eurotrain rail passes, YHA passes, weekend packages, overland safaris, and hostel/hotel accommodations are also bookable. Council Travel sells a number of publications for young people, including *Work, Study, Travel Abroad: The Whole World Handbook; Volunteer: The Comprehensive Guide to Voluntary Service in the U.S. and Abroad;* and *Going Places: The High School Student's Guide to Study, Travel, and Adventure Abroad.*

For real budget travelers it's worth joining **Hostelling/International/IYHF** (International Youth Hostel Federation). For information, write Hostelling Information/American Youth Hostels (HI-AYH), 733 15th St. NW, No. 840, Washington, DC 20005 (☎ 202/783-6161). Membership costs $25 annually, but those under age 18 pay $10 and those over 54 pay $15.

STA Travel is the only worldwide company specializing in student- and youth-discounted airfares. Located at 86 Old Brompton Rd., SW7 3LQ, it is open 9:30am to 7pm Monday to Thursday, 10am to 6pm on Friday, 10am to 4pm on Saturday. Telephone 0171/937-9921 for more information. Tube: South Kensington.

The International Student House, 229 Great Portland St., W1 (☎ 0171/631-3223), lies at the foot of Regent's Park across from the tube stop for Great Portland Street. It's a beehive of student activity such as discos and film showings. It rents blandly furnished, very institutional rooms, charging £23.40 ($36.95) in a double, £19.75 ($31.20) per person in a double, and £16.60 ($26.25) per person in a triple. An English breakfast is included. Laundry facilities are available, and a £10 ($15.80) key deposit is charged. Reserve way in advance.

The **University of London Student Union,** 1 Malet St., WC1E 7HY (v 0171/580-9551; tube: Goodge Street), the largest of its kind in the world, is the best place to go to learn about student activities in the Greater London area. The Union contains a swimming pool, a fitness center, a gymnasium, a general store, a sports shop, a ticket agency, banks, bars, discos, inexpensive restaurants, venues for live events, an office of STA Travel, and many other facilities. It is open Monday through Friday from 8:30am to 11pm, Saturday from 9am to 11pm, and Sunday from 9:30am to 10:30pm. Bulletin boards at the union provide a rundown on sponsored events, some of which you might be able to attend; others might be "closed door."

5 Getting There

BY PLANE

The deregulation of the airline industry made world headlines in 1979, and since then, any vestige of uniformity in price structures for trans-atlantic flights has disappeared.

The best strategy for securing the least expensive airfare is to shop around and, above all, to remain as flexible as possible. Keep calling the airlines. If a flight is not fully booked, an airline might discount tickets in an attempt to achieve a full load, allowing you to buy a lower-priced ticket at the last minute.

Most airlines charge different fares according to season. For flights to Europe, the fares are most expensive during midsummer—the peak travel time. The basic season, which falls (with a few exceptions) in the winter months, offers the least expensive fares. Travel during Christmas and Easter weeks is usually more expensive than in the weeks just before or after those holidays. The periods between basic and peak seasons are called shoulder seasons. Also note that prices tend to be higher on the weekend, which is usually defined as Friday, Saturday, and Sunday.

Even within the various seasons, most airlines also offer heavily discounted promotional fares available according to last-minute market plans. But be warned: The less expensive your ticket is, the more stringent the restrictions will be. The most common and frequently used such fare is the APEX, or advance-purchase excursion (see below).

THE MAJOR AIRLINES

Following is a list of several of the airlines that fly the enormously popular routes from North America to Great Britain.

For travelers departing from Canada, **Air Canada** (☎ toll free 800/776-3000) flies daily to London Heathrow nonstop from Vancouver, Montréal, and Toronto. There are also frequent direct services from Edmonton, Calgary, Winnipeg, Ottawa, Halifax, and St. John's. All flights provide a smoke-free environment.

American Airlines (☎ toll free 800/624-6262) offers daily routes to London Heathrow Airport from half a dozen U.S. gateways—New York's JFK (five times daily), Chicago's O'Hare (twice daily), Miami International (usually once daily), and Los Angeles International, Philadelphia International, and Boston's Logan (each once daily).

British Airways (☎ toll free 800/AIRWAYS) offers flights from some 18 U.S. cities to Heathrow and Gatwick airports, as well as many others to Manchester, Birmingham, and Glasgow. Just about all flights are nonstop. With more add-on options than any other airline, BA can make a visit to Britain cheaper than you might have expected. The 1993 union of some of BA's functions and routings with USAir has opened additional North American gateways to BA, improved services, and reduced some of its fares—making BA more competitive as a transglobal carrier. Of particular interest are the "Value Plus,"

"London on the Town," and "Europe Escorted" packages that include both airfare and hotel accommodations throughout Britain at heavily discounted prices.

Depending on day and season, **Delta** (☎ toll free 800/241-4141) runs either one or two daily nonstops between Atlanta and Gatwick, near London. Delta also offers nonstop daily service from Cincinnati and Miami to Gatwick.

Northwest Airlines (☎ toll free 800/447-4747) flies nonstop from both Minneapolis and Boston to Gatwick.

TWA (☎ toll free 800/221-2000) flies nonstop to Gatwick every day from its hub in St. Louis. Connections are possible through St. Louis from most of North America.

United Airlines (☎ toll free 800/241-6522) flies nonstop from New York's JFK to Heathrow two to three times a day, depending on the season. United also offers nonstop service twice a day from Dulles International, near Washington, D.C., plus once-a-day service from Newark, N.J.; Los Angeles; San Francisco; and Seattle.

Virgin Atlantic Airways (☎ toll free 800/862-8621) flies daily to either Gatwick or Heathrow from Boston; Newark, N.J.; New York's JFK; Los Angeles; and San Francisco. The airline also flies to Gatwick four times a week from Miami, and five times a week from Orlando.

Virgin Atlantic also offers flights to London from Chicago through interconnecting, jointly marketed service on **Kiwi Airlines.** Passengers depart from Chicago's Midway airport on Kiwi, then transfer in either Boston or one of the New York area airports for connections on to London. Booking both sections of the itinerary simultaneously is less expensive than if both legs had been purchased as separate entities. For information, call Virgin Atlantic or Kiwi (☎ toll free 800/JET-KIWI).

LONDON AIRPORTS

London Heathrow Airport, located west of London in Hounslow (☎ 0181/759-4321 for flight information), is one of the world's busiest airports, with flights arriving from around the world and throughout Great Britain. It is divided into four terminals, each relatively self-contained. Terminal 4, the most modern, handles the long-haul and transatlantic operations of British Airways. Most transatlantic flights of U.S.-based airlines arrive at Terminal 3. Terminals 1 and 2 receive intra-European flights of several European airlines.

It takes 50 minutes by Underground and costs £3.10 ($4.90) to make the 15-mile trip from Heathrow to center city. You can also take the Airbus, which gets you into central London in about an hour and costs £6 ($9.50) for adults and £4 ($6.30) for children. A taxi is likely to cost at least £30 ($47.40).

Many charter and some scheduled flights land at relatively remote **Gatwick Airport** (☎ 01293/535-353 for flight information), located some 25 miles south of London in West Sussex.

From Gatwick, express trains leave for Victoria Station in London every 15 minutes during the day and every hour at night. The charge is £8.50 ($13.45) for adults and £4.25 ($6.70) for children under 15.

There is also an express bus from Gatwick to Victoria every half hour from 6:30am to 8pm and every hour from 8 to 11pm; this Flightline Bus 777 costs £7.50 ($11.85) per person. A taxi from Gatwick to central London usually costs £50 to £60 ($79 to $94.80). However, you must negotiate a fare with the driver before you enter the cab; the meter does not apply because Gatwick lies outside the Metropolitan Police District.

London Stansted Airport (☎ 0171/474-5555), located some 30 miles northeast of central London, mostly handles flights to and from the European continent. Actually, Stansted is not in London but in Stansted, Essex, part of East Anglia.

If your arrival is in Stansted (and many international flights land here), your best bet to reach central London is the Stansted Express to Liverpool Street Station, costing £10 ($15.80) for adults and £5 ($7.90) for children under 15. Service is every 40 minutes Monday through Friday from 5:30am to 11pm, every 30 minutes on Saturday from 6:30am to 11pm, and every 30 minutes on Sunday from 7am to 11pm. Trip time: 45 minutes.

London City Airport (☎ 0171/474-5555) receives mainly short-haul flights from Britain and northern Europe, making it popular with the business and financial communities.

From London City Airport, there are three ways to reach the center of London. First, blue-and-white bus charges £3 ($4.75) each way to and from the Liverpool Street Station, where passengers can get rail and Underground transport to almost anywhere in England. The bus runs every 20 minutes Monday through Friday, and every 30 minutes on Saturday and Sunday during open hours of the airport—roughly from 7am to 8:30pm. Second, there's a shuttle bus to Canary Wharf, where trains from the Dockland Line Railway make frequent 10-minute runs to the heart of London's financial district, the City. There, passengers can catch an Underground from the Bank tube stop. Third, London Transport bus no. 473 goes from the City Airport to East London. There, passengers can board any Underground line at the Plaistow tube stop.

BY TRAIN

Most arrivals of trains originating in Paris are at **Victoria Station** in the center of London. Visitors from Amsterdam arrive at **Liverpool Street Station,** and those journeying south by rail from Edinburgh arrive at **King's Cross Station.** Each station is connected to London's vast bus and Underground (subway) network, and each has phones, restaurants, pubs, luggage-storage areas, and London Regional Transport Information Centres.

If you're traveling to London from elsewhere in the United Kingdom, consider buying a **BritRail Pass,** which allows unlimited rail travel during a set time period (8 days, 15 days, or one month). A Eurailpass is not accepted in Britain, although it is accepted in Ireland if you're going on there. A BritRail Pass costs $219 for 8 days, $339 for 15 days, $425 for 22 days, or $495 for an entire month. Senior citizens pay $199, $305, $379, and $425, respectively. Those between 16 and 25 years of age are charged $179, $269, $339, and $395, respectively. Children 5 to 15 pay half the adult fare, and there's no charge for children 4 and under.

Americans can secure a BritRail pass at **BritRail Travel International,** 1500 Broadway, New York, NY 10036 (☎ 212/575-2667). Canadians can write to 2161 Yonge St., Suite 812, Toronto, ON M4F 386 (☎ 416/484-0571).

UNDER THE CHANNEL

Queen Elizabeth and President François Mitterrand officially opened the Channel Tunnel, and the Eurostar Express in 1994 began twice-daily passenger service between London and both Paris and Brussels. The $15 billion tunnel, one of the great engineering feats of all time, is the first link between Britain and the continent since the Ice Age. The 31-mile journey between France and Great Britain takes 35 minutes, although actual chunnel time is only 19 minutes.

Rail Europe (☎ toll free 800/94-CHUNNEL for information) sells tickets on the Eurostar direct train service between Paris and Brussels and London. A round-trip first-class fare between Paris and London, for example, costs $312, $248 in second class. But you can cut costs to $152 with a second-class, 14-day advance purchase (nonrefundable) round-trip fare. In London make reservations for Eurostar at 01345/300003; in Paris at 44-51-06-02, and in the United States toll free at 800/387-6782.

Chunnel train traffic is roughly competitive with air travel, if you calculate door-to-door travel time. Trains leave Paris from the Gare du Nord and arrive at London's Waterloo Station.

BY BUS

If you're traveling to London from elsewhere in the United Kingdom, consider purchasing a **Britexpress Card,** which entitles you to a 30% discount on National Express (England and Wales) and Caledonian Express (Scotland) buses. Contact a travel agent.

Bus connections to Britain from the Continent are generally not very comfortable, though some lines are more convenient than others. One line with a relatively good reputation is **Euroways Eurolines, Ltd.,** 52 Grosvenor Gardens, London SW1W OUA (☎ 0171/730-8235). Their service will book passage on buses traveling once a day between London and Paris (9 hours); Amsterdam (10 hours); Munich (24 hours); and Stockholm (44 hours). On the longer routes, which employ two alternating drivers, the bus proceeds almost without interruption, taking occasional breaks for meals.

BY CAR

If you plan to take a rented car across or under the Channel, check carefully with the rental company before you leave about license and insurance requirements.

There are many "drive-on, drive-off" car-ferry services across the Channel. The most popular ports in France for Channel crossings are

Boulogne and Calais, where you can board Sealink ferries taking you to the English ports of Dover and Folkestone. At Calais you can take Le Shuttle under the English Channel.

The tunnel not only accommodates trains but passenger cars, charter buses, taxis, and motorcycles, all taken under the English Channel from Calais, France, to Folkestone, England, or vice versa. It operates 24 hours a day, 365 days a year, running every 15 minutes during peak travel times and at least once an hour at night. Tickets may be purchased at the toll booth. With "Le Shuttle," gone are weather-related delays, seasickness, and a need for reservations.

Motorists drive onto a half-mile-long train and travel though an underground tunnel built beneath the seabed through a layer of impermeable chalk marl and sealed with a reinforced-concrete lining.

Before boarding Le Shuttle, motorists stop at a toll booth and then pass through Immigration for both countries at one time. During the ride, motorists stay in bright, air-conditioned carriages, remaining inside their cars or stepping outside to stretch their legs. When the trip is completed, motorists simply drive off toward their destinations—in our case, heading on to London. Total travel time between the French and English highway system is about one hour.

Stores selling duty-free goods, restaurants, and service stations are available to travelers on both sides of the Channel. A bilingual staff is on hand to assist travelers at both the British and French terminals.

Remember to drive on the left if you're coming from the Continent. London is circled by two roadways—the A406 and A205 combination close in and the M25 farther out. Determine which part of the city you wish to enter and follow signposts. I suggest you confine driving in London to the bare minimum, which means arriving and parking.

Parking is scarce and expensive. Before arrival in London, call your hotel and inquire if it has a garage (and what the charges are) or ask the staff to give you the name and address of a garage nearby.

BY SHIP
OCEAN LINER

Cunard Line, 555 Fifth Ave., New York, NY 10017 (☎ 212/880-7500, or toll free 800/221-4770), boasts that its flagship, *Queen Elizabeth 2,* is the only five-star-plus luxury ocean liner providing regular transatlantic service—some 27 sailings a year between April and December. Many passengers appreciate its graceful introduction to British mores, as well as the absolute lack of jet lag that an ocean crossing can provide.

Fares are extremely complicated, based on cabin standard and location and the season of sailing. During the thrift/superthrift season—roughly defined as late autumn or early spring—sailings usually cost a minimum of $2,230 in transatlantic class and around $4,660 in first class. These prices are per person, double occupancy. All passengers also pay a $175 port tax. Many packages are offered, which include inexpensive airfare from your home city to the part of departure plus a return flight to your home city from London on British Airways.

FERRY & HOVERCRAFT

For centuries, sailing ships and ferryboats have traversed the English Channel bearing supplies, merchandise, and passengers. Today, the major carriers are P&O Channel Lines, Hoverspeed, and Sealink.

P&O Channel Lines (☎ 01233/203388) operates car and passenger ferries between Portsmouth and Cherbourg, France (three sailings a day; $4^3/_4$ hours each way); between Portsmouth and Le Havre, France (three sailings a day; $5^3/_4$ hours each way); between Dover and Calais, France (sailings every 90 minutes; 75 minutes each way); and between Felixstowe and Zeebrugge, Belgium (two sailings a day; $5^3/_4$ hours each way).

P&O's major competitor is **Stena Sealink** (☎ 01233/647047), which carries both passengers and vehicles on its routes. This company is represented in North America by BritRail (☎ 212/575-2667 New York, or toll free 800/677-8585 in the U.S. for more information).

By far the most popular route across the Channel is between Calais and Dover. Hoverspeed operates at least 12 daily 35-minute Hovercraft crossings, as well as slightly longer crossings via Seacat (a catamaran propelled by jet engines) between Boulogne and Folkestone. Seacats cross about four times a day and require 55 minutes.

Stena Sealink operates conventional ferryboat service between Cherbourg and Southampton (one or two sailings a day taking six to eight hours) and between Dieppe and Newhaven (four sailings a day taking four hours). Very popular are Sealink's conventional car-ferries between Calais and Dover, which depart 20 times a day in either direction and take 90 minutes for the crossing. Typical fares between France and England are as follows: £25 ($39.50) for adults one-way, £15 ($23.70) for children. One-way Stena fares are £26 ($41.10) for adults, £22 ($34.75) for seniors and students, and £14 ($22.10) for children.

Traveling by Hovercraft or SeaCat cuts your journey time from the Continent to the U.K. A Hovercraft trip is definitely a fun adventure, as the vessel is technically "flying" over the water. A SeaCat crossing from Folkestone to Bologne is longer in miles but more time-saving to passengers than the Calais-Dover route used by conventional ferryboats. SeaCats also travel from the mainland of Britain to the Isle of Wight, Belfast, and the Isle of Man. For reservations and information call HoverSpeed (☎ 01304/240-241). Typical one-way fares are £26 ($41.10) per person.

3

Getting to Know London

Europe's largest city is like a great wheel, with Piccadilly Circus at the hub and dozens of communities branching out from it. Since London is such a conglomeration of sections—each having its own life (hotels, restaurants, pubs)—first-time visitors may be intimidated until they get the hang of it. Most visitors spend all their time in the West End, where most of the attractions are located, except for the historic part of London known as the City, where the Tower of London stands.

This chapter will help you get your bearings. It provides a brief orientation and a preview of the city's most important neighborhoods and answers questions you need to know about getting around London by transportation or on foot. It also presents a "Fast Facts" section covering everything from babysitters to shoe repairs.

1 Orientation

VISITOR INFORMATION

The **British Travel Centre,** Rex House, 4–12 Lower Regent St., London SW1 4PQ (tube: Piccadilly Circus), caters to walk-in visitors who need information about all parts of Britain. Telephone information has been suspended—you must show up in person and wait in line—often long. On the modern premises you'll find a British Rail ticket office, travel and theater-ticket agencies, a hotel-booking service, a bookshop, and a souvenir shop. Hours are 9am to 6:30pm on Monday through Friday and 10am to 4pm on Saturday and Sunday, with extended hours on Saturday during June through September.

CITY LAYOUT

MAIN DISTRICTS, SQUARES & STREETS

There is—fortunately—an immense difference between the sprawling vastness of Greater London and the pocket-size chunk north of the River Thames that might be called "Prime Tourist Territory." This tourist's London begins at **Chelsea,** on the north bank of the river, and stretches for roughly five miles north to **Hampstead.** Its western boundary runs through **Kensington,** while the eastern boundary lies five miles away at Tower Bridge. Within this five-by-five-mile square, you'll find all the hotels and restaurants and nearly all the sights that are usually of interest to visitors.

Make no mistake: This is still a hefty portion of land to cover, and a really thorough exploration of it would take a couple of years. But it has the advantage of being flat and eminently walkable, besides boasting one of the best public transportation systems ever devised.

The logical (although not geographical) center of this area is **Trafalgar Square,** which we'll therefore take as our orientation point. If you stand facing the steps of the imposing National Gallery, you're looking northwest. That is the direction of **Piccadilly Circus**—the real core of tourist London—and the maze of streets that make up **Soho.** Farther north is **Oxford Street,** London's gift to moderate shopping, and still farther northwest lies Regent's Park with London Zoo.

At your back—that is, south—is **Whitehall,** which houses or skirts nearly every British government building, from the Ministry of Defence to the official residence of the prime minister at no. 10 Downing Street. In the same direction, a bit farther south, stand the Houses of Parliament and Westminster Abbey.

Flowing southwest from Trafalgar Square is the table-smooth **Mall,** flanked by magnificent parks and mansions and leading to Buckingham Palace, residence of the queen. Farther in the same direction lie **Belgravia** and **Knightsbridge,** the city's plushest residential areas, and south of them lies the aforementioned **Chelsea,** with its chic flavor, plus **King's Road,** principally a boulevard for shopping.

Due west of Trafalgar Square stretches the superb and distinctly high-priced shopping area bordered by **Regent Street** and **Piccadilly Street** (as distinct from the Circus). Farther west lie the equally elegant shops and even more elegant homes of **Mayfair.** Then comes **Park Lane.** On the other side of Park Lane is Hyde Park, the biggest park in London and one of the largest in the world.

Charing Cross Road runs north from Trafalgar Square, past **Leicester Square,** and intersects with **Shaftesbury Avenue.** This is London's theaterland. A bit farther along, Charing Cross Road turns into a browser's paradise, lined with shops selling new and secondhand books.

Finally, it funnels into **St. Giles Circus.** This is where you enter **Bloomsbury,** site of the University of London, the British Museum, and some of the best budget hotels, as well as the erstwhile stamping ground of the famed Bloomsbury Group, led by Virginia Woolf.

Northeast of your position lies **Covent Garden,** known for its Royal Opera House and today a major shopping, restaurant, and café district.

Following the **Strand** eastward from Trafalgar Square, you'll come into **Fleet Street.** Beginning in the 19th century, this corner of London became the most concentrated newspaper district in the world. Where the Strand becomes Fleet Street stands Temple Bar, and only here do you enter the actual City of London, or the City. Its focal point and shrine is the Bank of England on **Threadneedle Street,** with the Stock Exchange next door and the Royal Exchange across the street. In the midst of all the hustle and bustle rises St. Paul's Cathedral, a monument to beauty and tranquillity.

At the far eastern fringe of the City looms the Tower of London, shrouded in legend, blood, and history, and permanently besieged by battalions of visitors.

And this, as far as we will be concerned, concludes the London circle.

FINDING AN ADDRESS

London's street layout follows no real pattern, and both street names and house numbers seem to have been perpetrated by xenophobes with equal grudges against postal carriers and foreigners. Don't think, for instance, that Southampton Row is anywhere near Southampton Street or that either of these places has any connection with Southampton Road.

London is checkered with innumerable squares, mews, closes, and terraces, which jut into or cross or overlap or interrupt whatever street you're trying to follow, usually without the slightest warning. You may be walking along ruler-straight Albany Street and suddenly find yourself flanked by Colosseum Terrace (with a different numbering system). Just keep on walking and after a couple of blocks you're right back on Albany Street (and the original house numbers) without having encountered the faintest reason for the sudden change in labels.

House numbers run in odds and evens, clockwise and counter-clockwise, as the wind blows. *That is, when numbers exist at all, and frequently they don't.* Many establishments in London, such as the Four Seasons Hotel or Langan's Brasserie, *do not use house numbers,* although a building right next door might be numbered. Happily, Londoners are generally glad to assist a bewildered foreigner.

Every so often you'll come upon a square that is called a *square* on the south side, a *road* on the north, a *park* on the east, and possibly a something or other *close* on the west. Your only chance is to consult a map or ask your way as you go along.

STREET MAPS

If you're going to explore London in any depth, you'll need a detailed street map with an index—not one of those superficial overviews given away at many hotels or tourist offices. The best ones are published by Falk, and they're available at most newsstands and nearly all bookstores, including **W. & G. Foyle Ltd.,** 113–119 Charing Cross Rd., WC2 (☎ 0171/439-8501), which carries a wide range of maps and guides.

NEIGHBORHOODS IN BRIEF

Belgravia South of Knightsbridge, this has long been the aristocratic quarter of London, rivaling Mayfair in grandness and richness. Although it reached the pinnacle of its prestige during the reign of Queen Victoria, it is still a chic address—the duke and duchess of Westminster, one of England's richest families, still live at Eaton Square. No, not in a palace but in an upper-story apartment, and they own more real estate in London than the queen. Once an area for "duels at dawn" and sheep grazing, Belgravia eventually marked the westward expansion of London. Its centerpiece is Belgrave Square (1825–35). When the town houses were built, the aristocrats followed—the duke of Connaught, the earl of Essex, even Queen Victoria's mother, the duchess of Kent. Chopin on a holiday in 1837 was impressed: "And the English! And the houses! And the palaces! And

London at a Glance

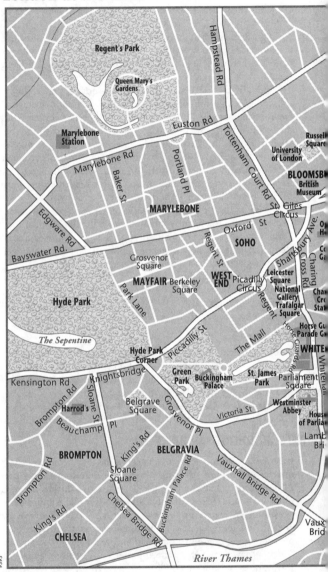

9595

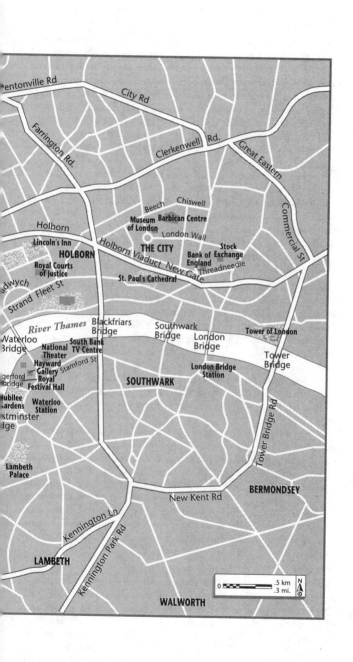

the pomp, and the carriages! Everything from soap to the razors is extraordinary."

Bloomsbury   This district, a world within itself, lies northeast of Piccadilly Circus, beyond Soho. It is, among other things, the academic heart of London; here you'll find the University of London, several other colleges, and many bookstores. Despite its student overtones, the section is fairly staid. Its reputation has been fanned by such writers as Virginia Woolf, who lived within its bounds (it figured in her novel *Jacob's Room*). The novelist and her husband, Leonard, were once the unofficial leaders of a group of artists and writers known as "the Bloomsbury Group"—nicknamed "Bloomsberries"—which at times included Bertrand Russell.

The heart of Bloomsbury is **Russell Square,** and the streets jutting off from the square are lined with hotels and B&Bs. Russell Square was laid out between 1800 and 1814, and Thackeray in his novel *Vanity Fair* made it the stamping ground of the Osbornes and the Sedleys. Most visitors, even though not living in a hotel in Bloomsbury, enter the district to see the British Museum, one of the world's greatest repositories of treasures—everything from the Rosetta Stone to the Elgin Marbles.

Chelsea   A stylish district stretching along the Thames, Chelsea lies south of Belgravia. It begins at Sloane Square, with Gilbert Ledward's Venus fountain playing watery music if the noise of the traffic doesn't drown it out. Flower sellers hustle their flamboyant blooms here year-round. The area has always been a favorite of writers and artists, including such names as Oscar Wilde (who was arrested here), George Eliot, James Whistler, J. M. W. Turner, Henry James, Augustus John, and Thomas Carlyle (whose former home can be visited). Mick Jagger and Margaret Thatcher (not together) have been more recent residents, and Princess Diana and her Sloane Rangers of the '80s gave it even more fame.

Its major boulevard is King's Road where Mary Quant launched the miniskirt in the 1960s and the Rolling Stones once lived. It was where the English punk look began. King's Road runs the entire length of Chelsea, and the best time to visit is on a Saturday when it's at its liveliest. Originally the route was the royal carriage route Charles II took to Hampton Court. The hip-hop of King's Road is not typical of upmarket Chelsea, which is filled with town houses and little mews dwellings that only the rich or very successful London professionals such as stockbrokers and solicitors can afford. Real estate prices are astronomical.

The City   When the English speak of "the City," (EC2, EC3,) they don't mean London. The City is the British version of Wall Street, and buildings in this district are known all over the world: the Bank of England on Threadneedle Street, the London Stock Exchange, and the financially troubled Lloyd's of London. This was the origin of Londinium in A.D. 43, so called by the Roman conquerors. Landmarks include St. Paul's Cathedral, the masterpiece of Sir Christopher Wren, which withstood the London Blitz. Some 2,000 years of history unfold at the Museum of London and the Barbican Centre, opened by Queen Elizabeth in 1982, and hailed by her as a "wonder" of the cultural world. At the Guildhall, the first lord mayor of London was installed in 1192. Lady Jane Grey, wife of Henry VIII, was tried here for "treason."

Covent Garden   The flower, fruit, and "veg" market is long gone (since 1970), but memories of Professor Higgins and his "squashed cabbage leaf," Eliza Doolittle, linger on. Even without the market, Covent Garden is still associated with food, as it contains the liveliest group of restaurants, pubs, and cafés in London, outside Soho. The tradition of food dates from the time when monks of Westminster Abbey dumped their surplus homegrown vegetables here. Charles II in 1670 granted the Earl of Bedford the right to "sell roots and herbs, whatsoever" in the district. The king's mistress, Nell Gwynne, once peddled oranges on Drury Lane. The restored marketplace with its glass and iron roofs has been called a "magnificent example of urban recycling." It's not all about food. Inigo Jones built St. Paul's Covent Garden between 1631 and 1633. Jones's "handsomest barn in Europe" was rebuilt after a fire in 1795 and is still attended by actors and artists, attracting over the years everybody from Ellen Terry to Vivien Leigh. The Theatre Royal Drury Lane was where Nell Gwynne made her debut in 1665, and the Irish actress, Dorothea Jordan, first caught the eye of the duke of Clarence, later William IV. She not only became his mistress, but the mother of 10 of his children.

The East End   Traditionally this was one of London's poorest districts, and was nearly bombed out of existence by the Nazis. Hitler, in the words of one commentator at the time, created "instant urban renewal." It is the home of the cockney, surely one of London's most colorful characters. To be a true cockney, it is said you must have been born "within the sound of Bow Bells," a reference to a church, St. Mary-le-Bow, rebuilt by Sir Christopher Wren in 1670. Many immigrants to London have found a home here.

The East End extends from the City Walls east encompassing Stepney, Bow, Poplar, West Ham, Canning Town, and other districts. The East End has always been filled with legend and lore. The area beyond the East End, the docklands, has been called "an emerging third city of London," filled with offices, Thames-side "flats," museums, entertainment complexes, and sports centers, certainly shopping malls, and an ever-growing list of restaurants.

Holborn   The old borough of Holborn takes in the heart of legal London—home of the city's barristers, solicitors, and law clerks. Still Dickensian in spirit, the area lets you follow in the Victorian author's footsteps, passing the two Inns of Court and arriving at Bleeding Heart Yard of *Little Dorritt* fame. A 14-year-old Dickens was once employed as a solicitor's clerk at Lincoln's Inn Fields. Old Bailey has stood for English justice down through the years (Fagin went to the gallows from this site in *Oliver Twist*). Everything here seems steeped in history. Even as you're quenching your thirst with a half pint of bitter at the Viaduct Tavern, 126 Newgate St. (tube: St. Paul's), you learn the pub was built over the notorious Newgate Prison (which specialized in death by pressing) and was named after the Holborn Viaduct, the world's first overpass.

Kensington   The Royal Borough (W8) lies west of Kensington Gardens and Hyde Park and is traversed by two of London's major shopping streets, Kensington High Street and Kensington Church Street. Since 1689 when asthmatic William III fled Whitehall Palace for Nottingham House (where the air was fresher), the district has enjoyed royal associations. Nottingham House in time became Kensington Palace, and the royals grabbed a chunk of Hyde Park to plant their roses. Queen Victoria was born here. "KP," as the royals say, is still home to Princess Margaret (20 rooms with a view), Prince and Princess Michael of Kent, and the duke and duchess of Gloucester. In residence at Kensington Palace at the moment is the Princess of Wales and her two little princes. The queen permits all these royals to live there free, but insists they pay their own phone, heat, and electricity.

Kensington Gardens is now open to the public ever since George II decreed that "respectably dressed" people would be permitted in only on Saturday—providing that no servants, soldiers, or sailors came. In the footsteps of William III, Kensington Square developed, attracting artists and writers. In time, a maid decided to use Thomas Caryle's manuscript of *The French Revolution* to light a fire, and he had to write it again. Thackeray lived here from 1846 to 1853 and during that time wrote *Vanity Fair.* Over the years Kensington High Street became a mecca for rich shoppers.

Knightsbridge   One of London's most fashionable neighborhoods, Knightsbridge is a top residential and shopping district, just south of Hyde Park. Harrods on Brompton Road is its chief attraction. Founded in 1901, it's been called "the Notre Dame of department stores"—it sells everything from Rayne pumps worn by the queen to a Baccarat crystal table valued at one million pounds. There's a department that will even arrange your burial. Right nearby Beauchamp Place (pronounced *Beech*-am) is one of London's most fashionable shopping streets, a Regency-era boutique-lined little street with a scattering of restaurants such as San Lorenzo, frequented often by Princess Diana and those who'd like to get a look at her. Shops include Bruce Oldfield at 27 Beauchamp Place, where Princess Diana and even Joan Collins show up to purchase his evening dresses. And, at the end of a shopping day, if Harrods's five restaurants and five bars haven't tempted you, retreat to Bill Bentley's at 31 Beauchamp Place for a dozen oysters washed down with a few glasses of muscadet.

Mayfair   Bounded by Piccadilly, Hyde Park, and Oxford and Regent streets, this section of London is considered the most elegant, fashionable section of London. Luxury hotels exist side by side with Georgian town houses and swank shops. Grosvenor Square (pronounced *Grov*-nor) is nicknamed "Little America," because it contains the American embassy and a statue of Franklin D. Roosevelt. Berkeley (pronounced *Bark*-ley) is the home of the English Speaking Union. At least once you'll want to dip into this exclusive section, or perhaps visit

Carnaby Street, a block from Regent Street, if you want to remember London from the Swinging '60s. One of the curiosities of Mayfair is Shepherd Market, a tiny village of pubs, two-story inns, book and food stalls, and restaurants—all sandwiched between Mayfair's greatness.

Paddington/Bayswater The Paddington section centers around Paddington Station, north of Kensington Gardens and Hyde Park. It's one of the major centers in London attracting budget travelers who fill up the B&Bs at such places as Sussex Gardens and Norfolk Square. After the first railway was introduced in London in 1836, it was followed by a circle of sprawling railway termini, including Paddington Station in 1838. That marked the growth of this somewhat middle class and prosperous area, now blighted in parts. Just south of Paddington is Bayswater, a sort of unofficial area also filled with a large number of B&Bs, attracting budget travelers. As London moved west, the area north of Hyde Park known as Tyburnia eventually developed into Bayswater. Inspired by St. Marylebone and elegant Mayfair, terrace houses and spacious squares became home to a relatively prosperous set of Victorians from the mercantile class.

Piccadilly This is the very heart and soul of London, with Piccadilly Circus and its statue of Eros being the virtual gaudy "living room" of London. The circus isn't New York's Times Square yet, but its traffic, neon, and jostling crowds don't do anything to make it fashionable. Circus might be an apt word. The thoroughfare Piccadilly was always known as "the magic mile." Traditionally the western road out of town, it was named for the "picadil," a ruffled collar created by Robert Baker, a tailor in the 1600s. He built a mansion called Piccadilly Hall, and the name is still used today. If you want a little more grandeur, retreat to the Regency promenade of exclusive shops, the Burlington Arcade, designed in 1819. The English gentry—tired of being mud-splashed by horses and carriages along Piccadilly—came here to do their shopping. Some 35 shops, a treasure trove of goodies, await you. Or make your way to Fortnum & Mason, 181 Piccadilly, the world's most luxurious grocery store, which was launched in 1788. The store sent hams to the Duke of Wellington's army, baskets of "tinned" goodies to Florence Nightingale in the Crimea, and the store packed a "picnic basket" for Stanley when he went looking for Livingstone.

St. James's Often called "Royal London," St. James's basks in its associations with everybody from the "merrie monarch" Charles II, to today's Elizabeth II who lives at its most fabled address, Buckingham Palace. Beginning at Piccadilly Circus and moving southwest, it's "frightfully convenient," as the English say, enclosing such addresses as American Express on Haymarket and many of London's leading department stores. In this bastion of aristocracy and royalty, a certain pomp is still carried out—gentlemen still go to private clubs, and English tradition never dies. The district evokes memories of such figures as Oscar Wilde, George Meredith, and Edward VII.

Marylebone An area enjoying famous associations with the likes of Turner or Elizabeth Barrett (waiting for the return of Robert Browning), St. Marylebone lies south of Regent's Park and north of

Oxford Street. All first-time visitors head here, exploring Madame Tussaud's waxworks or walking along Baker Street in the make-believe footsteps of Sherlock Holmes. Right north of the district at Regent's Park you can visit Queen Mary's Gardens or in summer see Shakespeare performed in an Open-Air Theatre. Robert Adam laid out Portland Place, one of the most characteristic squares from 1776 to 1780, and it was at Cavendish Square that Mrs. Horatio Nelson waited—often in vain—for the return of the admiral. Marylebone Lane and High Street still retain some of their former village atmosphere. Dickens (who seems to have lived everywhere) wrote nearly a dozen books when he resided in St. Marylebone.

Soho   This district in a sense is a Jekyll and Hyde quarter. In the daytime, it's a paradise for the searcher of spices, continental foods, fruits, fish, and sausages, and has at least two street markets offering fruits and vegetables. But at night, it's a dazzle of strip joints, gay clubs, porno movies, and sex emporiums, all intermingled with international restaurants that offer good values. In fact, this section of crisscrossed narrow lanes and crooked streets is the site of many of the city's best foreign restaurants, and Gerrard Street has succeeded in becoming London's first Chinatown.

Soho starts at Piccadilly Circus and spreads out, ending at Oxford Street. One side borders the theater center on Shaftesbury Avenue. From Piccadilly Circus, walk northeast and you'll come to Soho, to the left of Shaftesbury. This jumbled section can also be approached from the Tottenham Court Road tube station: Walk south along Charing Cross Road and Soho will be to your right.

South Kensington   Lying southeast of Kensington Gardens and Earl's Court, South Kensington is primarily residential and is often called "museumland" because of the many museums located there. These include the Natural History Museum, once part of the British Museum, containing everything from specimens of Charles Darwin's historic voyage on the HMS *Beagle* to dinosaurs. One of the district's chief curiosities is the extravagant Albert Memorial completed in 1872 by Sir George Gilbert Scott. For sheer excess, the Victorian monument is unequaled in the world.

The Strand and Fleet Street   Beginning at Trafalgar Square, the Strand runs east into Fleet Street and is flanked with theaters, shops, hotels, and restaurants. Ye Olde Cheshire Cheese with "ye olde" roast beef, Dr. Johnson's House, Twinings English tea (which the queen herself prefers for her "cuppa")—all these evoke memories of the rich heyday of this district. The Strand runs parallel to the River Thames, and to walk it would be to follow in the footsteps of Charles Lamb, Mark Twain, Henry Fielding, James Boswell, William Thackeray, and most definitely Sir Walter Raleigh. The Savoy Theatre helped make Gilbert & Sullivan a household word. Henry James called the Strand "a tremendous chapter of accidents." Fleet Street has long been London's journalistic hub, and well it should be. William Caxton printed the first book in English here. *The Daily Consort*, first daily newspaper printed in England, was launched at Ludgate Circus in 1702.

Westminster/Whitehall Dominated by the Houses of Parliament and Westminster Abbey, this has been the seat of the British government since the days of Edward the Confessor. Even if that power isn't what it used to be, the House of Commons and the House of Lords go about running what's left of the empire. Trafalgar Square, one of the major landmarks, remains a testament to England's victory over Napoléon in 1805, and the paintings in its landmark National Gallery will restore your soul.

Originally the home of Cardinal Thomas Wolsey, Whitehall was a royal residence for some 160 years—everybody from Henry VIII to James II called it home. Today it's more of a street, linking Trafalgar Square with Parliament Square. In the district you can visit Churchill's Cabinet War Rooms and walk down Downing Street to see No. 10, considered the world's most famous street address. One of its longest tenants: Margaret Thatcher, Britain's first woman prime minister. No visit is complete without a call at Westminster Abbey, one of the greatest English/French Gothic churches in the world. It's witnessed a parade of English history beginning when William the Conqueror was crowned here on Christmas Day 1066.

The City of Westminster also encompasses Victoria, an area that takes its unofficial name from bustling Victoria Station, known as "the gateway to the Continent."

2 Getting Around

BY PUBLIC TRANSPORTATION

If you know the ropes, transportation in London can be easy and inexpensive. Both the Underground (subway or tube) and bus systems are operated by London Transport.

Travel Information Centres are located in the Underground stations at Hammersmith, King's Cross, Oxford Circus, St. James's Park, Liverpool Street Station, and Piccadilly Circus, as well as in the British Rail stations at Euston and Victoria and in each of the terminals at Heathrow Airport. They take reservations for London Transport's guided tours and offer free Underground and bus maps and other information leaflets. A 24-hour telephone information service is available (☎ 0171/222-1234). Information is also obtainable by writing London Transport, Travel Information Service, 55 Broadway, London SW1H 0BD.

London Transport offers **Travelcards** for use on bus, Underground, and British Rail services in Greater London. Available in combinations of adjacent zones, Travelcards can be purchased for a minimum of seven days or for any period (including odd days) from a month to a year. A Travelcard allowing travel in two zones for one week costs adults £13.80 ($21.80) and children £4.50 ($7.10).

Travelcards must be used in conjunction with a Photocard (a photo ID used for identification by London Transport as well as by several other entities in London). A free Photocard is issued simultaneously with your Travelcard—bring along a passport photo of yourself—when you buy your Travelcard at main post offices in the London area, the ticket window of any tube station, or at the Travel Information Service of London Transport (see address above).

For shorter stays in London, you may want to consider the **One-Day Off-Peak Travelcard.** This Travelcard can be used on most bus, Underground, and British Rail services throughout Greater London after 9:30am on Monday through Friday and at any time on weekends and bank holidays. The Travelcard is available from Underground ticket offices, bus garages, Travel Information Centres, and some newsstands. For two zones, the cost is £2.80 ($4.40) for adults and £1.50 ($2.35) for children 5 to 15. Children 4 and under go free.

The **Visitor Travelcard,** allowing unlimited travel on almost the entire London Underground and bus system for up to seven days, can be purchased in North America (but not in London). Contact a British Tourist Authority office.

UNDERGROUND

Known as the tube, the Underground is the fastest and easiest (although not the most interesting) way to get from place to place.

All Underground stations are clearly marked with a red circle and blue crossbar. You descend by stairways, escalators, or huge elevators, depending on the depth. Some Underground stations have complete subterranean shopping arcades and several boast high-tech gadgets, such as push-button information machines.

You pick the station for which you're heading on the large diagram displayed on the wall, which includes an alphabetical index. You note the color of the line (Bakerloo is brown, Central is red, and so on). Then, by merely following the colored band, you can see at a glance whether and where you'll have to change and how many stops there are to your destination.

If you have British coins, you can purchase your ticket at one of the vending machines. Otherwise, you must buy it at the ticket office. You can transfer as many times as you like so long as you stay in the Underground. The flat fee for one trip within the Central zone is £1 ($1.60). Trips from the Central zone to destinations in the suburbs range from £1 to £4 ($1.60 to $6.30) in most cases.

Note: Be sure to keep your ticket; it must be presented when you get off. If you are caught without a valid ticket, you will be fined £10 ($15.80) on the spot. If you owe extra, you'll be asked to pay the difference by the attendant. And if you're out on the town and dependent on the Underground, watch your time carefully; many trains stop running at midnight (11:30pm on Sunday).

BUSES

The first thing you learn about London buses is that nobody just boards them. You "queue up"—that is, form a single-file line at the bus stop.

The comparably priced bus system is almost as good as the Underground, and you have a better view. To find out about current routes, pick up a free bus map at one of London Transport's Travel Information

Centres, listed above. The map is available to personal callers only, not by mail.

London still has old-style Routemaster buses, with both driver and conductor. Once on a bus, a conductor will come to your seat. You pay a fare based on your destination, and receive a ticket in return. This type of bus is being phased out and replaced with buses that have only a driver. You pay the driver as you enter, and exit via a rear door. As with the Underground, the fares vary according to distance traveled. Generally, bus fares are 50p to £1.70 (80¢ to $2.70) cheaper than tube fares. If you travel for two or three stops, the cost is 60p (95¢); longer runs within zone 1 cost 80p ($1.25). If you want your stop called out, simply ask the conductor. (See map, "Central London Bus Routes.") Call a 24-hour hot line, 222-1234, for schedules and fares.

BY TAXI

London cabs are among the most comfortable and best-designed in the world. You can pick one up either by heading for a cab rank or by hailing one in the street. (The taxi is free if the yellow TAXI sign on the roof is lighted.) For a **radio cab,** you can telephone 0171/272-0272 or 0171/253-5000.

The minimum taxi fare is £1 ($1.60) for the first 564 yards or 1 minute and 54 seconds, with increments of 20p (30¢) thereafter—based on distance or time. Each additional passenger is charged 30p (50¢). Passengers pay 10p (15¢) for each piece of luggage in the driver's compartment and any other item more than two feet long. Surcharges are imposed after 8pm and on weekends and public holidays. All these tariffs include VAT. Fares usually increase annually. It's recommended that you tip 10% to 15% of the fare.

Warning: If you telephone for a cab, the meter starts running when the taxi receives instructions from the dispatcher. So you could find £1 ($1.60) or more already on the meter when you enter the taxi. Minicabs are also available, and they are often useful when the regular taxis become scarce or when the tube stops running. These cabs are meterless, so the fare must be negotiated in advance. Unlike regular cabs, minicabs are forbidden by law to cruise for fares. They operate from sidewalk kiosks, such as those around Leicester Square. Many minicab companies are listed in the yellow pages.

If you have a complaint about taxi service, or if you leave something in a cab, contact the Public Carriage Office, 15 Penton St., N1 9PU (☎ 0171/833-0996; tube: Angel Station). If it's a complaint, you must have the cab number, which is displayed in the passenger compartment.

Cab sharing is permitted in London, as British law allows cabbies to offer rides for two to five persons. The taxis accepting such riders display a notice on yellow plastic, with the words SHARED TAXI. Each of two riders sharing is charged 65% of the fare a lone passenger would be charged. Three persons pay 55%, four pay 45%, and five (the seating capacity of all new London cabs) pay 40% of the single-passenger fare.

Central London Bus Routes

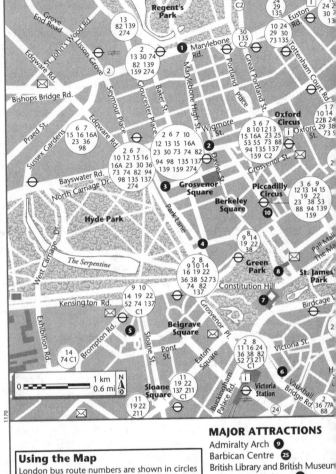

Using the Map

London bus route numbers are shown in circles at places where routes cross. Locate where you are going and then follow the route circles back toward your starting point. This will show if and where you need to change buses and the bus route number or numbers for your trip.

MAJOR ATTRACTIONS

Admiralty Arch **9**
Barbican Centre **25**
British Library and British Museum
Buckingham Palace **7**
Downing Street **16**
Harrods **5**
Horse Guards **15**
Houses of Parliament **18**
Imperial War Museum **20**

BY CAR

RENTALS

Car rentals are relatively expensive, and London offers a large array of companies to choose from. Most will accept your U.S. or Canadian driver's license, provided you've held it for more than a year. There is also an age requirement: 23 for cars rented through Avis, or 25 for cars arranged through Budget Rent-a-Car, British Airways, and Hertz. Don't forget that the steering wheel will be on the "wrong" side.

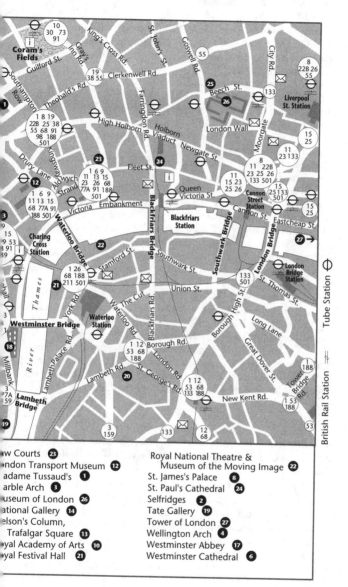

	Royal National Theatre &
w Courts **23**	Museum of the Moving Image **22**
ndon Transport Museum **12**	St. James's Palace **8**
adame Tussaud's **1**	St. Paul's Cathedral **24**
arble Arch **3**	Selfridges **2**
useum of London **26**	Tate Gallery **19**
ational Gallery **14**	Tower of London **27**
elson's Column,	Wellington Arch **4**
Trafalgar Square **13**	Westminster Abbey **17**
yal Academy of Arts **10**	Westminster Cathedral **6**
yal Festival Hall **21**	

Many companies grant discounts to clients who reserve their cars in advance (usually 48 weekday hours) through the toll-free reservations offices in a renter's home country and rent for periods longer than a week. When renting, be sure to ask if the price quoted includes the $17\frac{1}{2}$ % value-added tax (VAT), personal accident insurance (PAI), collision damage waiver (CDW), and other insurance options. If not, ask what these will cost because they can make a big difference in your bottom line.

As in the United States, the CDW and some added insurance are offered free by certain credit cards if you use them to rent a car. Check to see if you are covered by the credit card you use, thus avoiding the added expense.

The following are major rental firms.

Avis (☎ toll free 800/331-2112 in the U.S. and Canada) offers a one-day rental of the small but peppy Ford Fiesta with CDW and unlimited mileage for £64 ($101.10) plus taxes. At presstime, however, a full week's rental of a similar car, if reserved 14 days in advance, was a much better bargain at £173 ($273.35). The main Avis office is in Mayfair at 8 Balderton St., London W1 (☎ 071/917-6700; tube: Bond Street).

British Airways (☎ toll free 800/AIRWAYS in the U.S. and Canada) offers a relatively inexpensive way to rent a car in Britain through its reservations service. As the U.K.'s largest car renter, BA can offer discounted rates. Depending on size, horsepower, and amenities, as well as season, cars range in price from $20 to $92 per day, plus VAT and insurance. Child seats are available free. Understandably, these arrangements are offered only to passengers flying into Britain on BA.

Budget Rent-a-Car (☎ toll free 800/472-3325 in the U.S. and Canada) maintains 10 offices in London, including at the major airports, and about 100 others throughout the United Kingdom. The busiest London office is near Marble Arch at 89 Wigmore St., W1 (☎ 0171/723-8038; tube: Marble Arch). If you reserve from North America at least eight business hours prior to pickup, cars will cost from £34 ($53.70) per day for short rentals and from £95 ($150.10) per week (less during promotions)—with unlimited mileage, VAT, and CDW included in the net fee.

Hertz (☎ toll free 800/654-3001 in the U.S. and Canada) offers an unlimited-mileage Fiat Uno for as low as £155 ($244.90) per week, including CDW, theft insurance, and VAT. The main Hertz office is at 35 Edgware Rd., Marble Arch, London W1 (☎ 0171/402-4242; tube: Marble Arch).

PARKING   Driving around London is a tricky business. The city is a warren of one-way streets, and parking spots are at a premium.

In addition to strategically placed, expensive garages, central London offers metered parking. But be aware that traffic wardens are famous for issuing substantial fines when the meter runs out. The time limit and the cost of metered parking are posted on the meter. Zones marked "Permit Holders Only" are for local residents. If you violate these sacrosanct places, your vehicle is likely to be towed away. A yellow line along the curb indicates "No Parking"; a double yellow line signifies "No Waiting." However, at night (meters indicate exact times) and on Sunday, you're allowed to park along a curb with a single yellow line.

DRIVING RULES & REQUIREMENTS   In England, as you probably know, you drive on the left and pass on the right. Road signs are clear and the international symbols unmistakable.

Your passport and driver's license must be presented when you rent a car. No special British license is needed. The prudent driver will secure a copy of the *British Highway Code,* available from almost any stationer or newsstand. Wearing of seat belts by both front- and rear-seat occupants is mandatory in the British Isles.

Warning: Pedestrian crossings are marked by striped lines (zebra striping) on the road; flashing lights near the curb indicate that drivers must stop and yield the right of way if a pedestrian has stepped into the zebra zone to cross the street.

ROAD MAPS   The best road map of the country, especially if you're trying to locate an obscure village, is *Ordinance Survey Motor Atlas of Great Britain,* revised annually and published by Temple Press. It's available at most bookstores, including W. & G. Foyle Ltd., 113–119 Charing Cross Rd., WC2 (0171/439-8501).

BREAKDOWNS   A membership in one of the two major auto clubs in England can be helpful: the **Automobile Association,** Fanum House, Basingstoke, Hampshire RG21 2EA (☎ 01256/20123 for information), and the **Royal Automobile Club,** P.O. Box 700, Spectrum, Bond Street, Bristol, Avon BS99 1RB (☎ 01272/232340 for information). Membership in one of these clubs is usually handled by a car-rental agent. In London, the 24-hour number to call for breakdown service is 01800/887766 for the AA and 01800/828282 for the RAC. Members in either club are entitled to free legal and technical advice on motoring matters, as well as a range of discounts on motor-related products and services. All motorways are provided with special emergency phones connected to police traffic units. The police can also contact an automobile club on your behalf.

GASOLINE   Gasoline, called "petrol" by the British, is usually sold by the liter, with 4.5 liters making an imperial gallon. Prices, incidentally, will be much higher than you are accustomed to paying, and you'll probably have to serve yourself. In some remote areas, stations are few and far between, and many are closed on Sunday.

BY BICYCLE

You can rent bicycles by the day or week from a number of firms. One is **On Your Bike,** 52–54 Tooley St., SE1 (☎ 0171/378-6669; tube: London Bridge). It is open Monday through Friday from 9am to 6pm and Saturday from 9:30am to 5:30pm. There's an inventory of some 60 bikes, rented by day or week. The 10-speed sports bikes, with high seats and low-slung handlebars, cost £8 ($12.65) per day or £25 ($39.50) per week and require a £50 ($79) deposit. Also popular are 18-gear mountain bikes, with straight handlebars and oversize gears. Designed for rough terrain, they are useful on the roads of "backstreet London." These cost £14 ($22.10) per day or £55 ($86.90) per week and require a £200 ($316) deposit. MasterCard and VISA accepted.

ON FOOT

London is too vast and sprawling to explore entirely on foot, but if you use public transportation for the long distances and your feet for the narrow crooked lanes, you should do fine. Remember that cars drive on the left. Always look both ways before stepping off a curb. Unlike in some countries, vehicles in London have right of way over pedestrians.

FAST FACTS: London

American Express   The main Amex office is 6 Haymarket, SW1 (☎ 0171/930-4411; tube: Piccadilly Circus). Full services are available from 9am to 5:30pm on Monday through Friday and from 9am to 4pm on Saturday. At other times—Saturday from 9am to 6pm and Sunday from 10am to 4pm—only the foreign-exchange bureau is open.

Area Code   London has two telephone area codes—0171 and 0181. The 0171 area code is for central London within a four-mile radius of Charing Cross (including the City, Knightsbridge, Oxford Street, and as far south as Brixton). The 0181 area code is for outer London (including Heathrow Airport, Wimbledon, and Greenwich). Within London, you will need to dial the area code when calling from one section of the city to the other, but not within a section. The country code for England is 44.

Babysitters   Your hotel may be able to recommend someone, and advertised in the yellow pages are organizations that provide registered nurses and carefully screened mothers, as well as trained nannies, as sitters. One such is Childminders, 9 Paddington St., London W1M 3LA (☎ 0171/935-3000; tube: Baker Street). You pay £4.40 ($6.95) per hour in the daytime and £3.15 to £4.05 ($5 to $6.40) per hour at night. There is a four-hour minimum, and hotel guests pay a £5 ($7.90) booking fee each time they use a sitter. You must also pay reasonable transportation costs. Another company is Universal Aunts, P.O. Box 304, London SW4 ONN (☎ 0171/738-8937), established in 1921 and providing such services as child care, mother's helpers, proxy parents, and nannies. Interviews can be arranged in the Clapham or Fulham-Chelsea area. You must call first for an appointment or a booking.

Business Hours   Banks are usually open Monday through Friday from 9:30am to 3:30pm. Business offices are open Monday through Friday from 9am to 5pm; the lunch break lasts an hour, but most places stay open during that time. Pubs and bars are allowed to stay open from 11am to 11pm on Monday through Saturday and noon to 3pm and 7 to 10:30pm or 11pm on Sunday. Many pubs observe these extended hours; others prefer to close from 3 to 5:30pm. London stores generally open at 9am and close at 5:30pm, staying open until 7pm on Wednesday or Thursday. Most central shops close on Saturday around 1pm. They do not close for lunch earlier.

Car Rentals   See "Getting Around" in this chapter.

Climate See "When to Go" in Chapter 2.

Currency   See "Visitor Information and Entry Requirements" in Chapter 2.

Currency Exchange   In general, banks in London provide the best exchange rates, and you're likely to get a better rate for traveler's checks than for cash. There are branches of the main banks at London's airports, but they charge a small fee. There are also bureaux de change at the airports and around London that charge a fee for cashing traveler's checks and personal U.K. checks, and for changing foreign currency into pounds sterling. Some travel agencies, such as American Express and Thomas Cook, also have currency-exchange services.

Dentists   For dental emergencies, call Emergency Dental Service (☎ 0171/677-8383). The service is available 24 hours a day.

Doctors   In an emergency, contact Doctor's Call at 0181/900-1000. Some hotels also have physicians on call. Medical Express, 117A Harley St., W1 (☎ 0171/499-1991; tube: Regent's Park), is a private British clinic; it is not part of the free British medical establishment. For filling the British equivalent of a U.S. prescription, there is sometimes a surcharge of £20 ($31.60) on top of the cost of the medications; a British doctor must validate the U.S. prescription. In cases where there is a British equivalent of a mixture, and a chemist does not have to prepare a special medication, there is usually no surcharge. The clinic is open Monday through Friday from 9am to 6pm and Saturday from 9:30am to 2:30pm.

Documents Required   See "Visitor Information & Entry Requirements" in Chapter 2.

Driving Rules   See "Getting Around" earlier in this chapter.

Drugstores   In Britain they're called "chemist shops." Every police station in the country has a list of emergency chemists (dial "0" and ask the operator for the local police). One of the most centrally located chemists, keeping long hours, is Bliss the Chemist, 5 Marble Arch, W1 (☎ 0171/723-6116; tube: Marble Arch). It is open daily from 9am to midnight. Every London neighborhood has a branch of the ubiquitous Boots, the leading pharmacist of Britain.

Electricity   British current is 240 volts, AC cycle, roughly twice the voltage of North American current, which is 115–120 volts, AC cycle. You will probably not be able to plug the flat pins of your appliance's plugs into the holes of British wall outlets without suitable converters or adapters. Some (but not all) hotels will supply them for guests. Experienced travelers bring their own transformers. An electrical supply shop will also have what you need. Be forewarned that you will destroy the inner workings of your appliance (and possibly start a fire as well) if you plug an American appliance directly into a European electrical outlet without a transformer.

Embassies and High Commissions   I hope you'll not need such services; but in case you lose your passport or have some other emergency, here's a list of addresses and phone numbers:

- **Australia** The high commission is at Australia House, Strand, WC2 (☎ 0171/379-4334; tube: Charing Cross or Aldwych); it's open Monday through Friday from 10am to 4pm.

- **Canada** The high commission is located at MacDonald House, 38 Grosvenor Sq., W1 (☎ 0171/629-9492; tube: Bond Street), handles visa and passport problems for Canada. Hours are Monday through Friday from 8:45am to 2pm.
- **Ireland** The embassy is at 17 Grosvenor Place, SW1 (☎ 0171/235-2171; tube: Hyde Park Corner); it's open Monday through Friday from 9:30am to 5pm.
- **New Zealand** The high commission is at New Zealand House, 80 Haymarket at Pall Mall, SW1 (☎ 0171/930-8422; tube: Charing Cross or Piccadilly Circus); it's open Monday through Friday from 10am to noon and 2 to 4pm.
- **The United States** The embassy is located at 24 Grosvenor Sq., W1 (☎ 0171/499-9000; tube: Bond Street). However, for passport and visa information go to the U.S. Passport & Citizenship Unit, 55–56 Upper Brook St., W1 (☎ 0171/499-9000, ext. 2563; tube: Marble Arch). Hours are 8:30am to noon and from 2 to 4pm.

Emergencies In London, for police, fire, or an ambulance, dial 999.

Etiquette Be normal, be quiet. The British don't like hearing other people's conversations. In pubs you are not expected to buy a round of drinks unless someone has bought you a drink. Don't talk religion in pubs, and it's best to avoid the subject of politics, especially questions dealing with "the Irish issue."

Eyeglasses If your glasses are lost or broken, try Selfridges Opticians on the street level of Selfridges department store, 400 Oxford St., W1 (☎ 0171/629-1234, ext. 3353; tube: Bond Street or Marble Arch), open Monday through Saturday from 9:30am to 7pm and Thursday until 8pm. Contact lenses are also available on the same day, in most cases. Multifocal lenses sometimes take three to five working days to complete. It's always wise to carry a copy of your eyeglass prescription when you travel.

Hairdressers/Barbers Hairdressers and hairstylists crop up on most major London street corners (a slight exaggeration), and they range from grandly imperial refuges of English dowagers to punk-rock citadels of purple hair and chartreuse mascara. One of the most visible—and one of the best—is a branch of Vidal Sassoon, Whiteleys of Bayswater, 151 Queensway, W2 (☎ 0171/792-2741; tube: Bayswater). Unlike some other Sassoon outlets, this one caters to both men and women. The shop is open Monday through Friday from 10am to 7:45pm and Saturday from 9am to 6:15pm.

Holidays See "When to Go" in Chapter 2.

Hospitals The following offer emergency care in London 24 hours a day, with the first treatment free under the National Health Service: Royal Free Hospital, Pond Street, NW3 (☎ 0171/794-0500; tube: Belsize Park), and University College Hospital, Gower Street, WC1 (☎ 0171/387-9300; tube: Warren Street). Many other London hospitals also have accident and emergency departments.

Hot Lines   For police or medical emergencies, dial 999 (no coins required). If you're in some sort of legal emergency, call Release at 0171/729-9904, 24 hours a day. The Rape Crisis Line is 0171/837-1600, also in service 24 hours a day. Samaritans, 46 Marshall St., W1 (☎ 0171/734-2800; tube: Oxford Circus), maintains a 24-hour crisis hot line that helps with all kinds of trouble, even threatened suicides. Alcoholics Anonymous (☎ 0171/352-3001) answers its hot line daily from 10am to 10pm. The AIDS 24-hour hot line is toll free 01800/567-123.

Information   See "Visitor Information & Entry Requirements" in Chapter 2 and "Orientation" earlier in this chapter.

Laundry/Dry Cleaning   Danish Express Laundry, 16 Hinde St., W1 (☎ 0171/935-6306; tube: Bond Street)—open Monday through Friday from 8:30am to 5:30pm and Saturday from 9:30am to 12:30pm—will clean, repair, or alter clothes, even repair shoes. It's one of the best places in London for such services. One of the leading dry-cleaning establishments of London is Sketchley, 49 Maddox St., W1 (☎ 0171/629-1292), with more than three dozen branches. Sketchley does dry cleaning for pickup the same day, and laundry for pickup within five working days. And if you're in the vicinity of the Bloomsbury B&Bs, you may choose Red and White Laundries, 78 Marchmont St., WC1 (☎ 0171/387-3667; tube: Russell Square), open daily from 6:30am to 8:30pm.

Libraries   Westminster Reference Library, 35 St. Martin's St., WC2 (☎ 0171/798-2036; tube: Leicester Square), is one of London's best general reference public libraries, specializing in business, art and design, official publications, maps, performing arts, and periodicals. Open Monday through Friday 10am to 7pm and Saturday 10am to 5pm.

Liquor Laws   No alcohol is served to anyone under the age of 18. Children under 16 aren't allowed in pubs, except in certain rooms, and then only when accompanied by a parent or guardian. Don't drink and drive; penalties for drunk driving are stiff, even if you are an overseas visitor. Restaurants are allowed to serve liquor during the same hours as pubs; however, only people who are eating a meal on the premises can be served a drink. A meal, incidentally, is defined as "substantial refreshment." And you have to eat and drink sitting down. In hotels, liquor may be served from 11am to 11pm to both residents and nonresidents; after 11pm, only residents may be served.

Lost Property   To find lost property, first report to the police and they will advise you where to apply for its return. Taxi drivers are required to hand over property left in their vehicles to the nearest police station. The property may also be turned over to the Taxi Lost Property Office, 15 Penton St., N1 (☎ 0171/833-0996; tube: Angel Station), open Monday through Friday from 9am to 4pm. London Transport's Lost Property Office will try to assist visitors only at their office at 200 Baker St., NW1 (☎ 0171/486-2496), open from 9:30am to 2pm Monday through Friday. For items lost on British Rail, report the loss as soon as possible to the station on the line where the loss occurred. For lost passports, credit cards, or money, report the loss and circumstances immediately to the nearest police station. For lost passports, you should go directly to your embassy or high commission. The address will be in the telephone book, or see "Embassies and High Commissions," above. For lost credit cards, also report to the appropriate organization; the same holds true for lost traveler's checks.

Luggage Storage/Lockers Places for renting lockers or storing luggage are widely available in London. Lockers can be rented at airports such as Heathrow or Gatwick and at all major rail stations, including Victoria Station. In addition, there are dozens of independently operated storage companies in the London area. Check the yellow pages in your directory for the closest establishment. Excess Baggage Company (☎ 0181/965-3344) operates the left-baggage facilities at both Heathrow and Gatwick, accepting even sports equipment such as canoes and Windsurfers, as well as bikes. The charge is £2 ($3.15) per item up to 12 hours and £3 ($4.75) per item up to 24 hours. Long-term deposit rates are available starting at £8 ($12.65) per week. All baggage is security screened.

Mail Letters and parcels may, as a rule, be addressed to you at any post office except a town suboffice. The words "To Be Called For" or "Poste Restante" must appear in the address. When claiming your mail, always carry some sort of identification, preferably your passport. Poste Restante service is provided solely for the convenience of travelers, and it may not be used in the same town for more than three months. It can be redirected, upon request, for up to three months. An airmail letter to North America costs 39p (60¢) and postcards require a 35p (55¢) stamp. Letters generally take 7 to 10 days to arrive from the United States.

Maps See "Street Maps" under "Orientation" earlier in this chapter.

Money See "Visitor Information & Entry Requirements" in Chapter 2.

Newspapers/Magazines *The Times* is tops, then the *Telegraph,* the *Daily Mail,* and the *Guardian,* all London dailies carrying the latest news. The *International Herald Tribune,* published in Paris, and an international edition of *USA Today,* beamed via satellite, are available daily. Copies of *Time* and *Newsweek* are also sold at most newsstands. Small magazines, such as *Time Out* and *City Limits,* contain much useful data about the latest happenings in London, including theatrical and cultural events.

Photographic Needs The Flash Centre, 54 Brunswick Centre, WC1 (☎ 0171/837-6163; tube: Russell Square), is considered the best professional photographic equipment supplier in London. You can purchase your film next door at Leeds Film and Hire, which has a wide-ranging stock. Kodachrome is accepted for 48-hour processing.

Police   In an emergency, dial 999 (no coin required). You can also go to one of the local police branches in central London, including New Scotland Yard, Broadway (without number), SW1 (☎ 0171/ 230-1212; tube: St. James's Park).

Post Office   Post offices and subpost offices are centrally located and open Monday through Friday from 9am to 5:30pm and on Saturday from 9:30am to noon. The main post office, at King Edward Street, EC1A 1AA, near St. Paul's Cathedral (☎ 0171/239-5047; tube: St. Paul's), is open Monday through Friday 8:30am to 6:30pm. The Trafalgar Square Post Office, 24–28 William IV St., WC2N 4DL (☎ 0171/930-9580; tube: Charing Cross), operates as three separate businesses: inland and international postal service and banking, open Monday through Saturday from 8:30am to 8pm; philatelic postage stamp sales, open Monday through Friday from 10am to 7pm and Saturday from 10am to 4:30pm; and the post shop, selling greeting cards and stationery, open Monday through Friday from 9am to 6:30pm and Saturday from 9:30am to 5pm. Other post offices and subpost offices are open Monday through Friday from 9am to 5:30pm and Saturday from 9am to 12:30pm. Many subpost offices and some main post offices close for an hour at lunchtime.

Radio   There are 24-hour radio channels operating throughout the United Kingdom, including London. They offer mostly pop music and "chat shows" during the night. Some "pirate" radio stations add more spice. So-called legal FM stations are BBC1 (104.8); BBC2 (89.1), BBC3 (between 90 and 92), and the classical station, BBC4 (95). There is also the BBC Greater London Radio (94.9) station, with lots of rock, plus LBC Crown (97.3), with much news and reports of "what's on" in London. Pop/rock U.S. style is heard on Capital FM (95.8), and if you like jazz, Jamaican reggae, or salsa, tune in to Choice FM (96.9). Jazz FM (102.2) also offers blues and big-band music.

Religious Services   Service times are posted outside places of worship. Almost every creed is represented in London. The American Church in London is at 79A Tottenham Court Rd., W1 (☎ 0171/580-2791; tube: Goodge Street). A Sunday School for all ages is conducted Sunday 10 to 10:50am, and a worship service follows beginning at 11am and lasting till noon. The London Tourist Board has a fairly complete list of various churches. Protestants might want to attend a Sunday morning service at either Westminster Abbey (☎ 0171/222-5152), or St. Paul's Cathedral (☎ 0171/248-2705). Sunday service times at St. Paul's are 8, 9:30, and 10:15am, and 3:15pm and on alternate Sundays at 11am. At Westminster Abbey, Sunday services are at 8, 10, and 11:15am and 3, 5:45, and 6:30pm. Roman Catholics gravitate to Westminster Cathedral (not to be confused with Westminster Abbey),

Ashley Place (without number), SW1 (☎ 0171/798-9055). Masses are conducted here Sunday at 7, 8, 9, and 10:30am and noon and 5:30 and 7pm. St. Anne's Lutheran Church, Gresham Street, EC2 (☎ 0171/606-4986; tube: St. Paul's), is one of the smaller Wren churches that has an extensive music program (some 100 concerts a year), in addition to its regular services. The Liberal Jewish Synagogue, 28 St. John's Wood, NW8 (☎ 0171/286-5181; tube: St. John's Wood), conducts services Friday at 6:30pm and again on Saturday at 11am.

Restrooms They are usually found at signs saying PUBLIC TOILETS. Women should expect to pay from 5p (10¢); men usually pay nothing. The English often call toilets "loos." Automatic toilets, found on many streets, are sterilized after each use and cost around 10p (15¢).

Safety Theft here is not as big a problem, perhaps, as in U.S. cities like Miami, Los Angeles, and New York. Muggings mainly occur in poor areas. As for murder and assault, most are reported within families and kin groups. The best advice is to use discretion and a little common sense and keep to well-lit areas.

Shoe Repair Most major Underground stations, including centrally located Piccadilly Circus, have "heel bars"—British for shoe-repair centers. Mostly, these are for quickie jobs. For major repairs, go to one of the major department stores (see "Department Stores" under "Shopping A to Z," in Chapter 8). Otherwise, patronize Jeeves Snob Shop, 8–10 Pont St., SW1 (☎ 0171/235-1101; tube: Knightsbridge).

Smoking Most U.S. cigarette brands are available in London. Antismoking laws are tougher than ever. Smoking is strictly forbidden in the Underground, including the cars and the platforms. Smoking is not permitted on buses and is increasingly frowned upon in many other places.

Taxes As part of an energy-saving program, the British government has added a special 25% tax on gasoline (petrol). There is no local sales tax in cities and towns, but a $17^1/2$% value-added tax (VAT) is added to all hotel and restaurant bills. The VAT is also included in the cost of many of the items you purchase to take home with you. At shops that participate in the Retail Export Scheme, it is possible to get a refund sent to you at home for the amount of the VAT on your purchases. Ask the salesperson for a Retail Export Scheme form (Form VAT 407) and a stamped preaddressed envelope to return it in; to be eligible, you must have your passport with you when you make the purchase. Save the VAT forms along with your sales receipts to show at British Customs when you leave. You may also have to show the actual purchases to Customs officials at airports or other ports of departure. After the form has been stamped by Customs, mail it back to the shop in the envelope provided—before you leave the United Kingdom.

Here are three organizing tips to help you through the Customs procedures: (1) keep your VAT forms with your passport, as Customs is often located near Passport Control; (2) pack your purchases in a carry-on bag so that you will have them handy after you've checked your other luggage; (3) and allow yourself enough time at your departure point to find a mailbox.

Warning: Several readers have reported a scam regarding VAT refunds. Some merchants allegedly tell customers they can get a refund form at the airport on their way out of the country. This is not true. The refund forms must be obtained from and completed by the retailer at the time of your purchase—don't leave the store without a completed Form VAT 407.

In October 1994, Britain imposed a departure tax: £10 ($15.80) for passengers flying worldwide, including the United States, and £5 ($7.90) for flights within Britain and the European Union.

Taxis   See "Getting Around" earlier in this chapter.

Telephone/Telex/Fax   For directory assistance for London, dial 142; for the rest of Britain, 192. To call London from the United States, dial 011 (international code), 44 (Britain's country code), 0171 or 0181 (London's area codes), and the seven-digit local telephone number.

British Tele-Com is carrying out a massive improvement program of its public pay-phone service. During the transitional period, you could encounter four types of pay phones. The old-style (gray) pay phone is being phased out, but there are many still in use. You will need 10p (15¢) coins to operate such phones, but you should not use this type for overseas calls. Its replacement is a blue-and-silver push-button model that accepts coins of any denomination. The other two types of phones require cards instead of coins to operate. The Cardphone takes distinctive green cards specially designed for it. These cards are available in four values—£2 ($3.15), £4 ($6.30), £10 ($15.80), and £20 ($31.60)—and are reusable until the total value has expired. Cards can be purchased from newsstands and post offices. Finally, the credit-call pay phone operates on credit cards—Access (MasterCard), VISA, American Express, and Diners Club—and is most common at airports and large railway stations.

Phone numbers in Britain outside of the major cities consist of an exchange name plus telephone number. In order to dial the number, you will need the code of the exchange being called. Information sheets on call-box walls give the codes in most instances. If your code is not there, however, call the operator by dialing 100. In major cities, phone numbers consist of the exchange code and number (seven digits or more). These digits are all you need to dial if you are calling from within the same city. If you are calling from elsewhere, you will need to prefix them with the dialing code for the city. Again, you will find these codes on the call-box information sheets. If you do not have the telephone number, call directory assistance (see the numbers above).

Telex and fax are restricted mostly to business premises and hotels. If your hotel has a telex or fax, they will send a message for you but you may have to arrange in advance for the receipt of a reply. Otherwise, go to Chesham Executive Centre, 150 Regent St., W1 (☎ 0171/439-6288; tube: Piccadilly Circus). They rent offices by the hour and have secretarial and stenographic services; they also accept walk-in business and will send fax messages. The cost of sending a one-page fax from London to anywhere in the world is from £2.50 ($3.95), plus VAT. Hours are 8:45am to 6pm on Monday through Friday and 9am to noon on Saturday. See also "Area Code," above.

Television TV starts around 6am with breakfast and educational programs. Lighter entertainment begins around 4 to 5pm, after the children's programs, and continues until around midnight. There are four television channels—two commercial and two BBC without commercials.

Time England follows Greenwich mean time (five hours ahead of ET), with British summer time lasting (roughly) from the end of March to the end of October.

Tipping In restaurants, service charges in the 15% to 20% range are usually added to the bill. Sometimes this is clearly marked; at other times it isn't. When in doubt, always ask. If service is not included, it is customary to add 15% to the bill. Sommeliers (wine stewards) get about £1 ($1.60) per bottle of wine served. Tipping in pubs is not common, although in cocktail bars the server usually gets about 75p ($1.20) per round of drinks. Hotels, like restaurants, often add a service charge of 10% to 15% to most bills. In smaller B&Bs, the tip is not likely to be included. Therefore, tip for special service, such as for the person who served you breakfast. If several persons have served you in a B&B, many guests ask that 10% or 15% be added to the bill and divided among the staff. Otherwise, for chamber service, give about £1 ($1.60) per day or about £5 ($7.90) per week. Tip porters about 75p ($1.20) per piece of luggage. It's standard to tip taxi drivers 10% to 15% of the fare, although a tip for a taxi driver should never be less than 20p (30¢), even for a short run. Theater ushers are not tipped.

Transit Information Phone 0171/222-1234, 24 hours a day.

Water Tap water in London is considered safe to drink. However, because the water is different, you might still experience a stomach upset. If in doubt, order bottled water.

Weather Phone 01891/500-401.

Yellow Pages The yellow pages in London are in English, but certainly not American English. Therefore, you'll find drugstores listed under "Chemists" or "Pharmacies."

4

Accommodations

London boasts some of the most famous hotels in the world. These include such hallowed temples of luxury as Claridge's and the Ritz (where the slang term "ritzy" for smart originated), Park Lane Hotel, the Savoy, and their recent-vintage rivals, the Four Seasons Hotel and the London Hilton on Park Lane.

All these establishments are superlative, but nobody would call them budget hotels. It is in this bracket that you get the most fantastic contrasts, both in terms of architecture and comfort. Many of London's hotels were built around the turn of the century, which gives them a rather curlicued appearance. But whereas some have gone to no end of pain to modernize their interiors, others have remained at Boer War level, complete with built-in drafts and wallpaper with floral prints, usually daisies.

In between, however, you come across up-to-the-minute structures that seem to have been shifted bodily from Los Angeles. These aren't necessarily superior, for what the others lack in streamlining they frequently make up in personal service and spaciousness.

In the late '80s and early '90s, the opening of new hotels generated a lot of excitement, as each one seemed to outdazzle the one before. Many charming small-scale hotels emerged—known as *bijou* (jewel) or boutique hotels because of their small size and attention to detail. These hotels continue today to pose major competition to the larger, stately establishments built by the Victorians or Edwardians.

By the mid-'90s this excitement had died down as these new hotels have emerged as a fact of life or fixture on the London hotel scene. The recession and rising inflation have taken their toll on the hotel scene. None of the hotels that made our "best" list have faced serious competition. This is in complete contrast to the outburst of new and exciting restaurants (see Chapter 5).

The problem (and it's a serious one) with London hotels is that there are too many expensive ones and not enough moderately priced establishments so typical of other European capitals including Berlin, Rome, and Paris. The prices charged are often astronomical, so resign yourself to paying a lot more in London for a good hotel room than you would in many other places of the world. You can almost always get a room at a deluxe hotel if you're willing to pay the price. But during certain peak booking periods, including the tourist season (roughly April through October), and during certain trade shows, seasonal events, or what are known as "royal occasions," rooms in the most desirable and most value-oriented hotels may be grabbed up by the person who makes early-bird reservations.

My task is to pick the raisins out of the pudding, so to speak. To select those hotels that combine maximum comfort with good value, in all price categories.

RATES   All hotels, motels, inns, and guesthouses in Britain with four bedrooms or more (including self-catering accommodations) are required to display notices showing minimum and maximum overnight charges. The notice must be displayed in a prominent position in the reception area or at the entrance. The prices shown must include any service charge and may include VAT, and it must be made clear whether or not these items are included; if VAT is not included, then it must be shown separately. If meals are provided with the accommodation, this must be made clear, too. If prices are not standard for all rooms, then only the lowest and highest prices need be given.

PRICE CATEGORIES   Classifying London hotels into a rigid price category is a bit tricky. For example, sometimes it's possible to find a moderately priced room in an otherwise "very expensive" hotel or an expensive room in an otherwise inexpensive property. That's because most hotel rooms—at least the older properties—are not standardized; therefore, the range of rooms goes from superdeluxe suites to the "maid's pantry," now converted into a small bedroom. At some hotels, in fact, you'll find rooms that are "moderate," "expensive," and "very expensive." To complicate matters even more, at some hotels rated "inexpensive," a few special deluxe rooms might fall into the "expensive" or "moderate" category.

The following price categories are only for a quick general reference, and note that there will be many exceptions to this quick rule of thumb. It should also be noted that London is one of the most expensive cities in the world for hotels. Therefore, what might be viewed as expensive in your hometown could very likely be classified as "inexpensive" in London.

In general, hotels rated "very expensive" charge from a low of £195 ($308.10) to a high of £325 ($513.50) for a double room. Doubles in "expensive" hotels might begin as low as £130 ($205.40) but climb all the way to £235 ($371.30) for certain special rooms, which would qualify as "very expensive." "Moderate" hotels offer doubles beginning at £85 ($134.30) but, as mentioned, some rooms in these hotels might climb as high as £175 ($276.50), making them "expensive." In general, hotels considered "inexpensive" ask from £49 to £95 ($77.40 to $150.10) for their doubles, the latter putting a few special rooms in the "moderate" category.

A Note About Prices: Unless otherwise noted, prices are for rooms with private bath, breakfast (often continental instead of English), $17^{1}/_{2}$% VAT, and a 10% to 15% service charge. (VAT and service charges are always included in the prices quoted in this guide, unless otherwise indicated in the write-ups.) Parking rates are per night.

RESERVATIONS Most hotels require at least a night's deposit before they will reserve a room. Preferably, this can be accomplished with an international money order or, if agreed to in advance, with a personal check. You can usually cancel a room reservation one week ahead of time and receive a full refund. A few hotels will return money three days before the reservation date, but some will take a deposit and never return it, even if you cancel far in advance. Many budget hotel owners operate on such a narrow profit margin that they find just buying stamps for airmail replies too expensive by their standards. Therefore, it's most important that you should enclose a prepaid International Reply Coupon with your payment, especially if you're writing to a budget hotel. Better yet, call and speak to the hotel of your choice, or send a fax.

If you're booking at a chain hotel, such as a Hilton, you can call toll free in North America and easily make reservations over the phone. Whenever such a service is available, toll-free 800 numbers are indicated in the individual hotel write-ups.

If you arrive without a reservation, begin your search for a room as early in the day as possible. If you arrive late at night, you may have to take what you can get, often in a much higher price range than you'd like to pay.

A FEW REMINDERS Elevators are called "lifts," and some of them predate Teddy Roosevelt's Rough Riders and act it. They are, however, regularly inspected and completely safe.

Hotel rooms are somewhat cooler than you're accustomed to. It's supposed to be more healthful that way.

What is termed continental breakfast consists of coffee or tea and some sort of roll or pastry. An English breakfast is a fairly lavish meal of tea or coffee, cereal, eggs, bacon, ham or sausages, toast, and jam.

If you want to remain undisturbed, don't forget to hang the DO NOT DISTURB sign on your doorknob. English hotel service personnel—most of whom aren't English—have a disconcerting habit of bursting in simultaneously with their knock.

1 Best Bets

BEST HISTORIC HOTEL Brown's Hotel *(see page 73)* Founded by the former manservant to Lord Byron, this stylish hotel dates back to Victorian times. It's one of London's most genteel hotels, from its legendary afternoon tea to its centenary *Times* clock in the reception area.

BEST FOR BUSINESS TRAVELERS Sheraton Park Tower *(see page 85)* For wheeling and dealing in Knightsbridge, this place has a lively business center operating 24 hours a day. While enjoying a panoramic view of Hyde Park, the business client can keep those fax machines ringing.

BEST FOR A ROMANTIC GETAWAY Blake's Hotel *(see page 94)* This elegant place will make lovers happy. It's one of the best adresses in London for an off-the-record weekend.

BEST TRENDY HOTEL   The Lanesborough *(see page 90)* This is a sumptuous temple of luxury—1.7 million was spent on each guest room. It attracts the see-and-must-be-seen hedonist.

BEST LOBBY FOR PRETENDING THAT YOU'RE RICH   The Dorchester *(see page 69)* This citadel of luxury has a long Promenade with London's largest floral display and rows of faux- marble columns with ornate gilt capitals. Even if you can't afford to stay here, enjoy a traditional English afternoon tea there and pretend you're the Sultan of Brunei, the owner.

BEST FOR FAMILIES   Camelot Hotel *(see page 104)* For the family on a budget, we recommend this pair of 1850 town houses in Paddington on an old tree-filled square. This simple hotel has sheltered thousands of families from all over the world, welcoming all to its homelike environment.

BEST BUDGET HOTEL   Abbey House *(see page 95)* This Kensington hotel was built in the 1860s on a Victorian square; it's refurbished annually yet it's one of the best values in London.

BEST B&B   Claverley Hotel *(see page 89)* Tranquil and in Knightsbridge, close to Harrods for that special buy, this hotel has won awards as the best B&B in London. The awards are deserved. For breakfast, try the fresh salmon kedgeree—it's the cook's special.

BEST SERVICE   Four Seasons Hotel *(see page 70)* The staff here is picked carefully for their efficiency and discretion, and they're always smiling.

BEST LOCATION   Le Meridien Piccadilly *(see page 75)* Here you'll find a haven of peace and quiet, even though the bustle—and convenience—of Piccadilly is right outside your door.

BEST HEALTH CLUB   Hyatt Carlton Tower *(see page 92)* Recently renovated, the hotel's Peak Health Club is spacious and bright. Its state-of-the art equipment will make fitness buffs sweat.

BEST HOTEL POOL   Le Meridien Piccadilly *(see page 75)* Guests can do laps at the spectacular indoor pool at the in-house Champneys Health Club. You can also dip into the plunge pools here, too. Indulge yourself in a spa bath, the Turkish bath, sauna, or solarium.

BEST VIEW   London Hilton on Park Lane *(see page 72)* This was London's first skyscraper hotel. Panoramic views over London are possible from many vantage points, especially the Windows Roof restaurant and cocktail bar on the 28th floor. It's not true that you can see Queen Elizabeth II changing for dinner in her dressing room at Buckingham Palace, as rumor first had it.

BEST OF THE NEW HOTELS   The Lanesborough *(see page 90)* It's new but it's old. The hotel was originally built in the classical Greek Revival style of Portland stone in 1829; then Texas billionaire Caroline Rose Hunt, of Rosewood Hotels, poured money into the decrepit old place to the tune of $1.7 million on *each* of the guest rooms. She created this hedonistic temple of luxury even during one of Britain's worst recessions.

BEST GRAND OLD HOTEL   The Park Lane Hotel *(see page 74)* is English to the core. The suites still have their 1920s decor and art deco bathrooms. No wonder the producers of *Brideshead Revisited* chose the hotel as a site for filming their series. It evokes memories of the grand days of the debutante balls.

BEST FOR OPULENCE   The Dorchester *(see page 69)* It's owned by the world's richest man, the Sultan of Brunei, and multimillion-pound opulence was the order of the day here—from luxurious bathrooms done in white Italian marble to the marble pillared Promenade, one of the finest places for afternoon tea in London. Before jetting off, the sultan left instructions to turn "the Dorch" into the world's greatest hotel, and so they did.

BEST SHABBY GENTILITY   Wilbraham Hotel *(see page 93)* Not afraid to be old fashioned, this hotel remains true to itself—floral-print wallpaper, olde-world English politeness, and stately Victoriana. They're so old-timey here they still call their lounge "the Bar and Buttery."

BEST DISCREET ADDRESS   Brown's Hotel *(see page 73)* If Henry James were alive today, he'd check in here. It's quintessentially "Jamesian" and the site of two famous honeymoons—at least: that of Theodore Roosevelt and Edith Carow in 1886 and that of Franklin D. Roosevelt and Eleanor in 1905.

BEST FOR SHOWING OFF   Blake's Hotel *(see page 94)* Anouska Hempel's small luxury hotel is personalized, elegant, but also fun. Beautiful bathrooms in marble, opulent accessories, and a restaurant often filled with London glitterati, this is the place to show off and spend some money, perhaps worry about how much you spent later.

BEST ENGLISH AMBIENCE   Dukes Hotel *(see page 77)* In a gaslit courtyard in back of St. James's Palace, this hotel has the dignity of an elderly duke. From the bread and butter pudding served in the clubby dining room to the staff's impeccably correct politeness, it's the epitome of what England used to be.

BEST CLUBLIKE ATMOSPHERE   Durrants Hotel *(see page 102)* For 200 years, through wars and the London Blitz, this hotel has endured. It's traditional, clublike, and intimate. There's even an authentic "smoking room." Sit by an open fireplace in a Windsor chair, enjoy a pint, then sample some French or traditional cuisine, and the night is yours.

BEST FOOTMEN   Claridge's *(see page 68)* If you want your footmen in scarlet breeches, white hosiery, and gold-braided tailcoats, you've come to the right address. There's nothing in London more refined than sitting in The Reading Room, taking afternoon tea, as the eagle eye of the founder, Mrs. William Claridge, stares down at you, making sure you behave properly.

BEST COUNTRY HOUSE DECOR   Dorset Square Hotel *(see page 100)* Tim and Kit—the Kemps, that is—are hoteliers of charm, taste, and sophistication. They were never better than when they combined two Georgian town houses, creating an English country house–look with antiques and mahogany bathrooms, right in the heart of London. Gilt-framed paintings and tapestry cushions make you feel warm, cozy, and elegantly refined.

BEST SMALL HOTEL   The Beaufort *(see page 88)* This is a hotel that will charm; it's 200 yards from Harrods on a tree-lined cul-de-sac. Personal service and rural peace combine to make for a winning choice.

BEST VALUE   Aston's Budget Studios *(see page 97)* Ms. Shelagh King is a scream and also a delight. This hostess welcomes the world to her accommodations that range widely in price—and well they should, these run the gamut from budget lodgings to designer suites. Regardless of how much or how little you pay, Ms. King has a deal for you. Readers love this one.

2 Mayfair

VERY EXPENSIVE

✪ Claridge's

Brook St. (without number), London W1A 2JQ. ☎ **0171/629-8860,** or toll free 800/223-6800 in the U.S. and Canada. Fax 0171/499-2210. 109 rms, 56 suites. A/C TV TEL. £185–£220 ($292.30–$347.60) single; £255–£295 ($402.90–$466.10) double; from £550 ($869) suite. Continental breakfast £12.25 ($19.35) extra. AE, DC, MC, V. Tube: Bond Street.

Claridge's has been known from the mid-Victorian era under its present name, although an earlier "lodging house" complex occupied much of the hotel's present area as far back as the reign of George IV. It has cocooned royal visitors in an ambience of discreet elegance since the time of the Battle of Waterloo. Queen Victoria visited Empress Eugénie of France here, and thereafter Claridge's lent respectability to the idea of ladies dining out in public. The hotel took on its present modest exterior in 1898. Inside, art deco decor was added in the 1930s, much of it still existing agreeably along with antiques and TVs. The guest rooms are spacious, many having generous-size baths complete with dressing rooms and numerous amenities. Suites can be connected by private foyers closed away from the main corridors, providing large self-contained units suitable for a sultan and his entourage.

Dining/Entertainment: Excellent food is stylishly served in the intimacy of the Causerie, renowned for its lunchtime smörgàsbord and pretheater suppers, and in the more formal The Restaurant, with its English and French specialties. From The Restaurant, the strains of the Hungarian Quartet, a Claridge's institution since 1902, can be heard in the adjacent foyer during lunch and dinner. Both the Causerie and The Restaurant are open daily from noon to 3pm. The Causerie serves evening meals from 5:30 to 11pm, with dinner offered in The Restaurant from 7:30pm to 1am.

Services: 24-hour room service, valet, laundry, babysitting.

Facilities: Hairdresser, car-rental agent, travel and theater desk. Men have use of nearby Bath and Racquets Club (health club) and women can use Berkeley Hotel's Health Club with a rooftop pool and gym. Guests of the hotel with a recognized golf handicap (30 for women, 20 for men) may play unlimited golf (complimentary) at Berkshire's Wentworth Golf Club. Tennis provided at Vanderbilt Club in West London.

✪ The Dorchester

53 Park Lane, London W1A 2HJ. ☎ **0171/629-8888,** or toll free 800/727-9820 in the U.S. Fax 0171/409-0114. 192 rms, 52 suites. A/C MINIBAR TV TEL. £210–£235 ($331.80–$371.30) single; £235–£265 ($371.30–$418.70) double; from £350 ($553) suite. VAT extra. Continental breakfast £12.50 ($19.75) extra. AE, DC, MC, V. Tube: Hyde Park Corner.

In 1929, with an increased demand for hotel space in the expensive Park Lane district, a famous mansion—whose inhabitants had been known for everything from great debauchery to great aesthetic skills— was torn down. In its place was erected the finest hotel London had seen in many years. Breaking from the neoclassical tradition, the most ambitious architects of the era designed a building of reinforced concrete clothed in terrazzo slabs. Throughout the hotel, completely restored in 1990, you'll find a 1930s interpretation of Regency motifs. The flower arrangements and the elegance of the gilded-cage Prom- enade seem appropriate for a diplomatic reception, yet they convey a kind of sophisticated comfort in which guests from all over the world feel at ease. Those guests used to include Gen. Dwight D. Eisenhower, Marlene Dietrich, and Bing Crosby; today's roster is likely to list Michael J. Fox, Cher, Tom Cruise, or Michael Jackson.

Owned by Brunei Investment Agency, which invested $192 million in its makeover, the Dorchester boasts guest rooms featuring linen sheets, all the electronic gadgetry you'd expect from a world-class hotel, and double- and triple-glazed windows to keep out noise. The rooms are filled with plump armchairs, cherrywood furnishings, and, in many cases, four-poster beds. Done in mottled gray Italian marble and having Lalique-style sconces, the bathrooms are stylish, too. The best rooms open onto views of Hyde Park.

Dining/Entertainment: Two of the hotel's restaurants—The Ter- race and The Grill Room—are considered among the finest dining establishments in London, and the Dorchester Bar is legendary. The pink-and-green Terrace is a historic room outfitted in a Regency motif with an overlay of chinoiserie—a combination that is especially sumptuous. When referring to its soaring columns capped with gilded palm fronds and mammoth swaths of filigree curtains, one English reviewer referred to it as "pure Cecil B. de Mille." With a set menu at £38 ($60) that changes every week, the Terrace, open Friday and Saturday nights only, still features dancing, a tradition that goes back to the 1930s, when London's "bright young things" patronized the place. Today, unlike yesterday, there is a health-conscious *menu léger* to keep waistlines thin. In addition, the hotel also offers Cantonese cuisine in its Asian restaurant, The Oriental, London's most exclusive and expensive Chinese restaurant, which has been awarded a Michelin star for three years running.

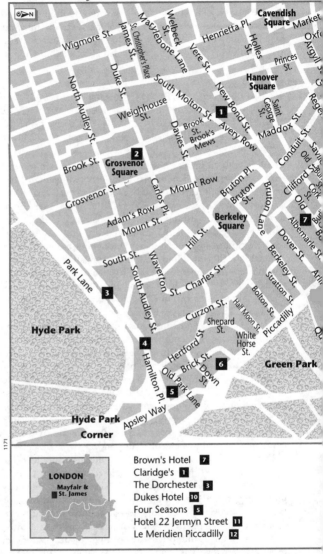

Brown's Hotel **7**
Claridge's **1**
The Dorchester **3**
Dukes Hotel **10**
Four Seasons **5**
Hotel 22 Jermyn Street **11**
Le Meridien Piccadilly **12**

Services: 24-hour room service, laundry, dry cleaning, medical service.

Facilities: One of the best-outfitted health clubs in London, the Dorchester Spa; exclusive nightclub; barbershop; hairdresser.

✪ Four Seasons Hotel

Hamilton Place (without number), Park Lane, London W1A 1AZ. ☎ **0171/499-0888,** or toll free 800/332-3442. Fax 0171/493-1895. 227 rms, 26 suites. A/C MINIBAR TV TEL. £210 ($331.80) single; £255–£265 ($402.90–$418.70)

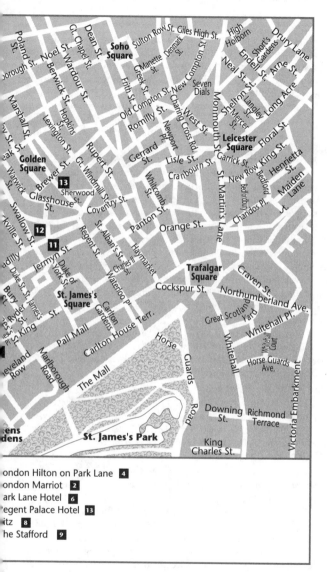

London Hilton on Park Lane **4**
London Marriot **2**
Park Lane Hotel **6**
Regent Palace Hotel **13**
Ritz **8**
The Stafford **9**

double; £330–£355 ($521.40–$560.90) conservatory; from £405 ($639.90) suite. English breakfast £15.50 ($24.50) extra. VAT extra. AE, DC, MC, V. Parking £14 ($22.10). Tube: Hyde Park Corner.

This deluxe hostelry, a member of the Four Seasons group, has captured the imagination of the glamourmongers of the world ever since it was inaugurated by Princess Alexandra in 1970. With its smallish triangular garden and located amid one of the most expensive neighborhoods in the world, it sits behind a tastefully modern facade. Its clientele includes heads of state, superstars, and business executives.

(Eccentric Howard Hughes, who could afford anything, chose it as a retreat.) As you enter the reception area, you'll find that the acres of superbly crafted paneling and opulently conservative decor create the impression that the hotel is far older than it is. A gently inclined grand stairway leads to a symmetrical grouping of Chinese and European antiques flanked by cascades of fresh flowers.

The guest rooms are large and beautifully outfitted with well-chosen chintz patterns, reproduction antiques, and plush upholstery, along with dozens of well-concealed electronic extras. Fourteen of the largest rooms contain private conservatories.

Dining/Entertainment: The Cocktail Bar—a piano bar—serves drinks in a room where Wellington might have felt at home. Both restaurants create a most alluring rendezvous, especially the highly acclaimed Four Seasons, which is both elegant and stylish, with views opening onto Park Lane. The finest wines and continental specialties dazzle guests at lunch and at dinner, with the last order at 10:30pm. The alternative dining choice is the less expensive Lanes Restaurant, rather popular with many members of London's business community. Although without windows, Lanes is nevertheless considered one of the more stylish restaurants in London, with a light contemporary decor that offers a central buffet. A set lunch is offered for £24.75 ($39.10). The lounge, where refreshments and light snacks are served, is open from 9am to 1am.

Services: 24-hour room service, valet, laundry, babysitting.

Facilities: Quality shops, theater-reservations desk, Conservatory fitness club, with all the latest equipment, garden, car-rental agency, business services available around the clock.

London Hilton on Park Lane

22 Park Lane, London W1Y 4BE. ☎ **0171/493-8000,** or toll free 800/445-8667 in the U.S. and Canada. Fax 0171/493-4957. 396 rms, 50 suites. A/C MINIBAR TV TEL. £195–£285 ($308.10–$450.30) single or double; from £350 ($553) suite. VAT extra. Continental breakfast £7–£14 ($11.05–$22.10) extra. AE, DC, MC, V. Parking £13.50 ($21.35). Tube: Hyde Park Corner.

The tallest building along Park Lane, and indeed one of the tallest structures in London, this hotel created an uproar when it was constructed in 1963. Allegations persisted that residents of its uppermost floors could spy on the boudoirs of faraway Buckingham Palace.

Now considered a linchpin of the London hotel scene and currently owned by Britain's Ladbroke chain, the Hilton is stylish and sophisticated. Graced with large picture windows overlooking London and Hyde Park, the guest rooms are decorated in tastefully restful colors, with fine copies of Georgian furniture. Six Executive Floors offer private check-in and a complimentary continental breakfast.

Dining/Entertainment: The 28th-floor Windows on the World restaurant features French/international cuisine and offers panoramic views over London; reservations are needed far in advance for a window table. There is dancing to a live band every night. Food is also served in the hotel's Café-Brasserie, and you can order Polynesian food at Trader Vic's downstairs. Victorian-themed St. George's Bar is a fashionable rendezvous.

Services: 24-hour room service, valet, laundry, babysitting, concierge.

Facilities: Solarium, massage, business center, Hertz Rent-a-Car desk, keep-fit equipment, theater-ticket booking desk.

London Marriott

Grosvenor Sq. (without number), London W1A 4AW. ☎ **0171/493-1232**, or toll free 800/228-9290 in the U.S. and Canada. Fax 0171/491-3201. 223 rms, 17 suites. A/C MINIBAR TV TEL. £210 ($331.80) single; £220 ($347.60) double; from £300 ($474) suite. Children up to 12 stay free in parents' room. English breakfast £12.25 ($19.35) extra. AE, DC, MC, V. Parking £25 ($39.50). Tube: Bond Street.

This hotel was first built in a grander era as the very conservative Hotel Europa with a redbrick Georgian facade. After Marriott poured millions into its refurbishment—only the very best materials, of course —much of the tradition remained. This triumph of the decorator's art sits proudly on one of the most distinguished squares in London, Grosvenor Square. Its battalions of polite porters, doormen, and receptionists wait near the entrance along a side street (Duke Street). The U.S. embassy is just a few doors away.

Throughout the carefully crafted interior, combinations of rose, ivory, and green are consistently in evidence. The breakfast room is filled with a cluster of Chippendale antiques and the kind of chintz that goes perfectly with masses of seasonal flowers. The accommodations, decorated in the Georgian style, contain all the electronic extras you'd expect.

Dining/Entertainment: Guests enjoy the Regent Lounge, which is outfitted in English country style. In the Diplomat, meals are served in an elegant yet comfortable setting. Chef Simon Traynor, one of London's hottest young chefs, serves traditional British cuisine with a modern twist such as pan-fried Cornish crab and prawn cakes on a chive and lemongrass sauce with crispy cabbage.

Services: 24-hour room service, valet, laundry, concierge, babysitting.

Facilities: Rooms for nonsmokers, fitness center, business center.

EXPENSIVE

Brown's Hotel

29–34 Albemarle St., London W1A 4SW. ☎ **0171/493-6020,** or toll free 800/225-5843 in the U.S. and Canada. Fax 0171/493-9381. 110 rms, 6 suites. A/C MINIBAR TV TEL. £185–£225 ($292.30–$355.50) single; £205–£255 ($323.90–$402.90) double; from £320 ($505.60) suite. Continental breakfast £11.75 ($18.55) extra. AE, DC, MC, V. Tube: Green Park.

Brown's is highly recommended for those who want a fine hotel from the best of the traditional choices. This upper-crust prestigious establishment was created by James Brown, a former manservant of Lord Byron's. He and his wife, Sarah, who had been Lady Byron's personal maid, wanted to go into business for themselves. Brown knew the tastes of gentlemen of breeding and wanted to create a dignified clublike place for them. His dream came true when he opened a hotel at a former town house at 23 Dover St. in 1837, the year Queen Victoria ascended the throne.

Today, Brown's Hotel occupies some 12 historic houses on two streets just off Berkeley Square. Old-fashioned comfort is dispensed with courtesy. A liveried doorman ushers you to an antique reception desk, where you check in. The street-floor lounges are inviting, including the Roosevelt Room (Theodore Roosevelt spent his honeymoon at Brown's in 1886), the Rudyard Kipling Room (the famous author was a frequent visitor), and the paneled St. George's Bar (for the drinking of "spirits").

The guest rooms vary considerably and are a tangible record of the history of England, showing restrained taste in decoration and appointments. Even the washbasins are semiantiques.

Dining/Entertainment: Afternoon tea is served in the Albemarle Room. Men are required to wear jackets and ties in the dining room, which has a quiet dignity and unmatched service. Most meals are à la carte, although there is also a set luncheon menu at £21.50 to £24.50 ($33.95 to $38.70) and a fixed-price dinner at £29 ($45.80)—including service and VAT.

Old-time guests wouldn't recognize today's cuisine, under the direction of chef Aidan McCormack, who has brought a more modern British touch to the food. Dover sole has always appeared on the menu but today you are also likely to get poached red snapper on a bed of crisp cabbage leaves with a saffron sauce.

Services: 24-hour room service, laundry, dry cleaning, babysitting.

Facilities: Men's hairdresser, car-rental agency.

✪ Park Lane Hotel

Piccadilly (without number), London W1Y 8BX. ☎ **0171/499-6321**, or toll free 800/223-5652 in the U.S. and Canada. Fax 0171/499-1965. 310 rms, 48 suites. MINIBAR TV TEL. £165–£185 ($260.70–$292.30) single; £185–£210 ($292.30–$331.80) double; from £230 ($363.40) suite. Continental breakfast £10.95 ($17.30) extra. AE, DC, MC, V. Parking £25 ($39.50). Tube: Hyde Park Corner or Green Park.

One of the long-established Park Lane hotels that has its own loyal clients and keeps winning new converts, this hotel is now the last of this breed to be privately owned by an English family. It was begun in 1913 by an enterprising former member of the Life Guards, who used advanced engineering techniques to construct the foundations and an intricately detailed iron skeleton. When its creator was tragically killed in World War I, residents mockingly referred to the empty shell of the uncompleted hotel as "the bird cage." Then, in 1924, one of London's leading hoteliers, Bracewell Smith finished the structure, and a short time later the Park Lane became one of Europe's leading hotels.

Today you'll enter an intensely English hotel behind a discreet stone-block facade. One of its gateways, the Silver Entrance, is considered such an art deco marvel that its soaring columns have been used in many films, including *Shanghai Surprise,* the U.S. miniseries *The Winds of War,* and the British miniseries *Brideshead Revisited,* P. G. Woodhouse's *Jeeves and Wooster,* and Danielle Steel's *Jewels* to name a few. Designed in a U shape, with a view overlooking Green Park, the Park Lane Hotel offers luxurious accommodations with double-glazed windows; the rooms are among the least expensive offered by the major Park Lane competitors. Many of the suites have marble fireplaces and the original marble-sheathed bathrooms. Rooms have benefited from an impressive refurbishment—they're larger and the decor is lighter in tone. The chic decor was designed by the chairman's wife.

Dining/Entertainment: The hotel's moderate restaurant, Bracewells, is recommended in Chapter 5. A less expensive dining choice is the Brasserie on the Park, serving French cuisine (also recommended in Chapter 5). With its decor of Chinese cinnabar lacquer, Bracewells Bar is one of London's most popular cocktail hangouts. A trio plays 1920s-style music in The Palm Court Lounge every Sunday.

Services: 24-hour room service, concierge, valet, laundry, dry cleaning, babysitting.

Facilities: Fitness center, business center, safety-deposit boxes, gift and newspaper shop, barbershop, women's hairdresser, and Daniele Ryman Aromatherapy Shop.

3 St. James's & Piccadilly Circus

ST. JAMES'S
VERY EXPENSIVE

Le Meridien Piccadilly

21 Piccadilly, London W1V 0BH. ☎ **0171/734-8000,** or toll free 800/543-4300 in the U.S. Fax 0171/437-3574. 231 rms, 35 suites. A/C MINIBAR TV TEL. £215–£235 ($339.70–$371.30) single; £235–£255 ($371.30–$402.90) double; from £325 ($513.50) suite. English breakfast £12.75 ($20.15) extra. AE, DC, MC, V. Parking £25 ($39.50). Tube: Piccadilly Circus.

At the time of the hotel's 1908 opening, the Ionic arcade capping its arched neoclassical facade was considered the height of Edwardian extravagance. Le Méridien was instantly pronounced the grandest hotel in London, with such guests as Mary Pickford, but its huge expenses bankrupted its creator. New owners continued to maintain it as one of the world's most stylish. After World War II, however, the hotel sank into a kind of musty obscurity until its lavish refurbishment during the revitalization of the Piccadilly theater district.

Today, enjoying its reincarnation, the hotel is run by the Forte chain. Elaborately detailed plasterwork, stained glass, and limed-oak paneling are notable design elements. Except for the intricate beauty of the skylit reception area, the centerpiece of the hotel is the grand, soaring Oak Room Lounge, where gilded carvings and chandeliers of shimmering Venetian glass re-create Edwardian styles. The guest rooms are tasteful, exuding quality, comfort, and style.

Dining/Entertainment: The formal and very elegant Oak Room is recommended in Chapter 5. The Terrace Restaurant is less formal, a sun-flooded eyrie under the greenhouse walls of the facade's massive Ionic portico. There is, as well, a very British bar sheathed in hardwoods and filled with live piano music.

Services: 24-hour room service, laundry, hairdresser, babysitting.

Facilities: Champney's health club with large pool, saunas, steambaths, aerobic workshops, squash courts; business center.

Ritz

150 Piccadilly, London W1V 9DG. ☎ **0171/493-8181,** or toll free 800/544-7570 in the U.S. Fax 0171/493-2687. 120 rms, 10 suites. MINIBAR TV TEL. £155 ($244.90) single; £190–£265 ($300.20–$418.70) double; from £495 ($782.10) suite. Children up to 14 stay free in parents' room. English breakfast £15 ($23.70) extra. AE, DC, MC, V. Parking £37 ($58.45). Tube: Green Park.

Built in the French Renaissance style and opened by César Ritz in 1906, the Ritz is synonymous with luxury. It overlooks the landscapes of Green Park. The original color scheme of apricot, cream, and dusty rose enhances the gold-leafed molding, marble columns, and potted palms. The gold-leafed statue *La Source* adorns the fountain of the oval-shaped Palm Court.

The guest rooms, each with its own character, are spacious and comfortable; most are air-conditioned. Many have marble fireplaces, elaborate gilded plasterwork, and a decor of soft pastel hues. All have radios and an availability of in-house films.

Dining/Entertainment: The Ritz is still the most fashionable place in London to meet for afternoon tea, at which a selection of finger sandwiches—including cucumber and smoked salmon—and specially made scones, cakes, and French pastries are served. The Ritz Restaurant, one of the loveliest dining rooms in the world, has been faithfully restored to its original splendor. Service is efficient yet unobtrusive, and the tables are spaced to allow the most private of conversations—perhaps the reason Edward and Mrs. Simpson dined here so frequently before they married.

Services: 24-hour room service, valet, laundry, babysitting.

Facilities: News kiosk, boutiques, access to nearby St. James's Health Club.

The Stafford

16–18 St. James's Place, London SW1A 1NJ. ☎ **0171/493-0111,** or toll free 800/525-4800 in the U.S. and Canada. Fax 0171/493-7121. 67 rms, 7 suites. TV TEL. £184 ($290.70) single; £200–£245 ($316–$387.10) double; from £290 ($458.20) suite. English breakfast £13 ($20.55) extra. AE, DC, MC, V. Tube: Green Park.

Famous for its American Bar, its clubland address, and the warmth of its Edwardian decor, the Stafford was built in the late 19th century on a cul-de-sac off one of London's most centrally located and busiest neighborhoods. It can be entered by St. James's Place or by a cobble-covered courtyard originally designed as a mews and known today as the Blue Ball Yard. The Stafford has retained a country-house atmosphere, with touches of antique charm and modern amenities.

All of the guest rooms are individually decorated, reflecting the hotel's origins as a private home. Many singles contain queen-size beds. A handful of the hotel's newest and plushest accommodations in a historically restored stable mews require a walk across the Blue Ball Yard.

Dining/Entertainment: The Stafford Restaurant is an elegant dining room lit with handsome chandeliers and wall sconces and accented with flowers, candles, and white napery. Classic international dishes are made from select fresh ingredients. Lunch costs from £19.50 ($30.80), dinner from £25 ($39.50). The previously mentioned American Bar (actually more like the memento-packed library of an English country house) is an especially cozy attraction. The bar is known for its collection of American university or club ties, badges, and caps.

Services: 24-hour room service, babysitting, concierge, secretarial service, laundry.

EXPENSIVE

Dukes Hotel

35 St. James's Place, London SW1A 1NY. ☎ **0171/491-4840.** Fax 0171/493-1264. 72 rms, 12 suites. A/C TV TEL. £125–£145 ($197.50–$229.10) single; £160–£185 ($252.80–$292.30) double; from £210 ($331.80) suite. English breakfast £12.50 ($19.75) extra. AE, DC, MC, V. Parking £37 ($58.45). Tube: Green Park.

The Dukes provides elegance without ostentation. A hotel since 1908, it stands in a quiet courtyard off St. James's Street with its turn-of-the-century gas lamps. A short walk away are Buckingham Palace, St. James's Palace, and the Houses of Parliament. Shoppers will be near Bond Street and Piccadilly, and literature buffs will be interested to note that Oscar Wilde lived and wrote at St. Jame's Place for a time.

Each well-furnished guest room is decorated in the style of a particular English period, ranging from Regency to Edwardian. All rooms are equipped with en suite marble bathrooms, telephones, satellite television, private bar, and air conditioning. Their most recent renovation occurred in 1994.

Dining/Entertainment: Dukes' Restaurant is small, tasteful, and elegant, combining both classic British and continental cuisine. The hotel also has a clublike bar, which is known for its rare collection of vintage ports, Armagnacs, and cognacs.

✪ Hotel 22 Jermyn Street

22 Jermyn St., London SW1Y 6HL. ☎ **0171/734-2353**, or toll free 800/682-7808 in the U.S. Fax 0171/734-0750. 5 rms, 13 suites. MINIBAR TV TEL. £170 ($268.60) single or double; from £220 ($347.60) suite. English breakfast £13 ($20.55) extra. AE, DC, MC, V. Valet Parking, £25 ($39.50). Tube: Piccadilly Circus.

🏨 Family-Friendly Hotels

Blandford Hotel   *(see page 102)* For families on a budget, this hotel near Baker Street (of Sherlock Holmes fame) has a number of triple and family rooms (suitable for four to five people). Kids can walk to Madame Tussaud's waxworks.

Hart House Hotel   *(see page 103)* This is a small family-run B&B right in the center of the West End near Hyde Park. Many of its rooms are triples. Special family suites, with connecting rooms, can be arranged.

Sandringham Hotel   *(see page 106)* Out in Hampstead, where children have plenty of room to play on the heath, this hotel offers both triple and family rooms for four to five people.

Set behind a facade of gray stone with neoclassical embellishment, this structure was originally built in 1870 as an apartment house for English gentlemen doing business in London. It's only 50 yards from Piccadilly. Since 1915, it has been administrated by three generations of the Togna family, whose most recent scion closed it for a radical restoration in 1990. Now reveling in its new role as a chic and upscale boutique hotel, under the direction of Annette M. Foster, it offers an interior with many plants and the kind of art you might find in an elegant private home. The guest rooms, done in traditional English style, have masses of fresh flowers and lots of chintz fabrics.

Services include 24-hour room service, a concierge, babysitting, laundry and dry cleaning, secretarial services, and fax machines and videophones. Included among the amenities are a CD-ROM library, access to the Internet for patrons, and a weekly newsletter that keeps guests up to date with restaurants, theater, and exhibitions. There is a health club nearby, and the general manager will take you on her morning run.

PICCADILLY CIRCUS
INEXPENSIVE

Regent Palace Hotel
12 Sherwood St., near Piccadilly Circus, London W1A 4BZ. ☎ **0171-734-7000.** Fax 0171/734-6435. 950 rms (none with bath). TV TEL. £49 ($77.40) single; £77 ($121.65) double. For stays of two or more nights, £32–£35 ($50.55–$55.30) per person depending on the time of year. (Rates include English breakfast.) AE, DC, MC, V. Tube: Piccadilly Circus.

Considered a major focal point since it was built in 1915 at the edge of Piccadilly Circus, this is one of the largest hotels in Europe. Today, it's known for staunch loyalty to its original design: None of the rooms contains a private bath. (Shared facilities in the hallways are adequate, and each room has a sink with hot and cold running water. Some clients believe that this huge hotel's design reflects British life from another era.)

The hotel's Original Carvery makes a good place to dine, and The Dome bistro is open for pretheater meals. Drinks are served in the Half Sovereign and the Planters bars. Coffee, sandwiches, and snacks are available in Antonio's Coffee Bar. Included among the facilities are souvenir and gift shops, a bureau de change, and a theater-booking agency.

4　Bloomsbury

MODERATE

Hotel Russell
Russell Sq. (without number), London WC1 B5BE. ☎ **0171/837-6470,** or toll free 800/435-4542 in the U.S. Fax 0171/837-2857. 328 rms, 19 suites. TV TEL. £115 ($181.70) single; £125 ($197.50) double; from £150 ($237) suite. English breakfast £10.50 ($16.60) extra. AE, DC, MC, V. Tube: Russell Square.

Hotels: Bloomsbury to the Strand

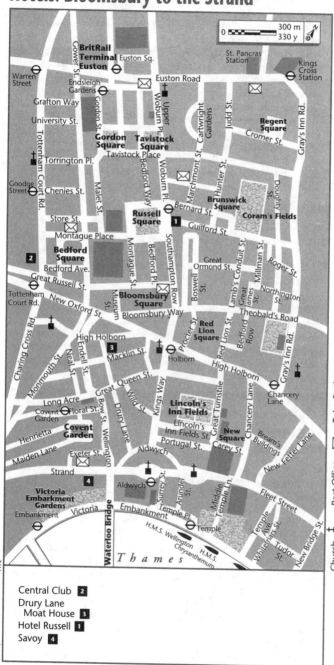

Central Club **2**
Drury Lane
  Moat House **3**
Hotel Russell **1**
Savoy **4**

A late-Victorian hotel facing the garden of this famous square and within easy reach of theaters and shopping, the Russell is run by Forte Hotels. In striking contrast to the ornate belle époque facade, the bedrooms are done in a rather sterile modern although generally well-maintained. An executive floor with 24 rooms has its own lounge reserved exclusively for guests on this floor.

The public rooms have been refurbished and include a main restaurant serving traditional English food. The Virginia Woolf's offers grills, pastas, burgers, and salads in a relaxed informal atmosphere. All the dining establishments offer good value. The Kings Bar serves cocktails in the atmosphere of a London club, and you can enjoy draft beer in the country-pub ambience of the Benjamin's Bar. There are also 24-hour room service, a laundry, and a theater-ticket agent.

INEXPENSIVE

Central Club

16–22 Great Russell St., London WC1B 3LR. ☎ **0171/636-7512.** Fax 0171/636-5278. 109 rms. TV TEL. £33 ($52.15) single; £60.25 ($95.20) double; £18.50 ($29.25) per person in triple or quad. MC, V. Tube: Tottenham Court Road.

This large and attractive building was designed by the famous architect Sir Edwin Lutyens (1869–1944). Erected around 1932 as a YWCA, it now functions as a hotel that accepts men, women, families, and groups traveling together; it still has some vague affiliations with the YWCA. Each simple but comfortable guest room contains a radio and beverage-making facilities. Included in the rate is use of the lounges, coin-operated laundry facilities, hair salon, gym, and solarium. There's a coffee shop.

5 The Strand & Covent Garden

THE STRAND
VERY EXPENSIVE

Savoy

The Strand (without number), London WC2R 0EU. ☎ **0171/836-4343,** or toll free 800/223-6800 in the U.S. and Canada. Fax 0171/240-6040. 154 rms, 48 suites. A/C MINIBAR TV TEL. £180 ($284.40) single; £205–£275 ($323.90–$434.50) double; from £365 ($576.70) suite. English breakfast £16.25 ($25.70) extra. VAT extra. AE, DC, MC, V. Parking £22 ($34.75). Tube: Charing Cross.

The Savoy is a London landmark, its eight stories of glazed tiles rising majestically between the Strand and the Thames. The hotel was built in 1889 by impresario Richard D'Oyly Carte as an annex to his nearby theater, where many Gilbert and Sullivan operettas were first performed. Today, one of the most vivid memories retained by many guests is of the sculpted frieze surrounding the upper reaches of the soaring lobby.

Through the Savoy's portals have passed famous personages of yesterday and today, everybody from royalty to stars of stage, screen, TV, and rock. Nowadays the hotel has regained the impeccable hospitality, service, and splendor of its early years.

Each guest room has a unique decor, with color-coordinated accessories, solid and comfortable furniture, and large closets. The units—48 with their own sitting rooms—contain an eclectic blend of antiques, such as gilt mirrors, Queen Anne chairs, and Victorian sofas. Guests find fresh flowers and fruit in their rooms on arrival. The river-view suites are the most sought after.

Dining/Entertainment: The world-famous Savoy Grill has long been popular with a theatrical clientele, with Sarah Bernhardt among its most celebrated former customers. The even more elegant River Restaurant is in a prime position, with tables overlooking the Thames; a four-person band plays in the evening for dancing. Also included is the establishment, Upstairs, specializing in champagne, Chablis, and seafood. Try fricassée of monkfish with wild rice or salmon kedgeree.

Services: 24-hour room service, nightly turndown, limousine service, same-day laundry and dry cleaning, babysitting.

Facilities: Hairdresser, news kiosk, unique health club with swimming pool built atop historic Savoy Theatre. Guests also granted temporary membership in the exclusive Wentworth Club, a golf and country club lying on the outskirts of London (proof of handicap required).

COVENT GARDEN
EXPENSIVE

Drury Lane Moat House

10 Drury Lane, High Holborn, London WC2B 5RE. ☎ **0171/836-6666.** Fax 0171/831-1548. 153 rms, 7 suites. A/C TV TEL. £119 ($188) single; £139 ($219.60) double; from £197 ($311.25) suite. English breakfast from £10.25 ($16.20) extra. AE, DC, MC, V. Parking £15 ($23.70). Tube: Holborn or Covent Garden.

A steel-and-glass structure, built in 1978, and enlarged in the 1980s, this Covent Garden hotel has terraced gardens and its own plaza. It's furnished in a contemporary style. The guest rooms—many for nonsmokers—have hairdryers, in-house videos, trouser presses, tea/coffee makers, and individually controlled central heating.

Dining/Entertainment: Maudie's Bar makes a good pretheater rendezvous. Specializing in French cuisine, Maudie's Restaurant is open daily for lunch and dinner. Who was the original Maudie? She's Sir Osbert Lancaster's famous cartoon character Maudie Littlehampton, an arbiter of chic.

Services: 24-hour room service, babysitting, laundry.

6 Westminster & Victoria

WESTMINSTER
MODERATE

Stakis St. Ermins Hotel

Caxton St. (without number), London SW1H 0QW. ☎ **0171/222-7888.** Fax 0171/222-6914. 290 rms, 7 suites. MINIBAR TV TEL. £119–£139 ($188–$219.60) single; £129–£159 ($203.80–$251.20) double; from £275 ($434.50) suite. Children up to 16 stay free in Parents' room. Continental breakfast £7.50 ($11.85) extra. AE, DC, MC, V. Tube: St. James's Park.

A turn-of-the-century red-brick building, enlarged with a modern wing, this hotel is ideally located in the heart of Westminster. It's only a few minutes' walk from Buckingham Palace, the Houses of Parliament, and Westminster Abbey. Many guest rooms are quite sumptuous, with luxurious furnishings that are often elegant and ornate. Other rooms are modernized, tastefully furnished, but often rather compact. Some 55 bedrooms are reserved for nonsmokers.

Dining/Entertainment: The hotel has two restaurants. The Caxton Grill offers an excellent-value à la carte menu. The Carving Table has a fixed-price lunch and dinner, serving a selection of roast meats, salads, and international dishes. Lunch costs £14.50 ($22.90), dinner costs £16.50 ($26.05). The lounge bar serves light snacks 24 hours a day, as well as an afternoon tea every day from 3 to 5:30pm.

Services: 24-hour room service, laundry, guide services.

Facilities: Nearby Queen Mother Sports Centre.

VICTORIA
EXPENSIVE

Goring Hotel

15 Beeston Place, Grosvenor Gardens, London SW1W 0JW. ☎ **0171/396-9000.** Fax 0171/834-4393. 75 rms, 5 suites. TV TEL. £125 ($197.50) single; £155–£185 ($244.90–$292.30) double; from £220 ($347.60) suite. English breakfast £12 ($19) extra. AE, DC, MC, V. Parking £15 ($23.70). Tube: Victoria Station.

Built in 1910 by O. R. Goring, this was the first hotel in the world to have central heating and a private bath in every guest room. Located just behind Buckingham Palace, it lies within easy reach of the royal parks, Victoria Station, the West London air terminals, Westminster Abbey, and the Houses of Parliament.

Top-quality service is still provided, nowadays by the founding father's grandson, George Goring. The charm of a traditional English country hotel is evoked in the paneled drawing room, where fires burn in the ornate fireplaces on nippy evenings. Adjoining is a bar overlooking the gardens in the rear. All the well-furnished guest rooms have been refurbished with marble baths and many have air-conditioning. At the hotel's restaurant, three-course luncheons cost £21 ($33.20) and dinner is £26 ($41.10). Some of the chef's specialties are calves' liver with bacon, roast boned lamb, salmon fish cakes, and grilled Dover sole. Chef Tony Elliott prefers classic English recipes England and uses only the freshest ingredients.

Services include 24-hour room service, a laundry, valet service, and free use of local health club.

MODERATE

Tophams Ebury Court

28 Ebury St., London SW1W 0LU. ☎ **0171/730-8147.** Fax 0171/823-5966. 42 rms (23 with bath). TV TEL. £70 ($110.60) single without bath, £100 ($158) single with bath; £95 ($150.10) double without bath, £115 ($181.70) double with bath. AE, DC, MC, V. Tube: Victoria Station.

Only a three-minute walk from Victoria Station, Tophams was created in 1937 when five small row houses were interconnected. With its

Hotels: Westminster & Victoria

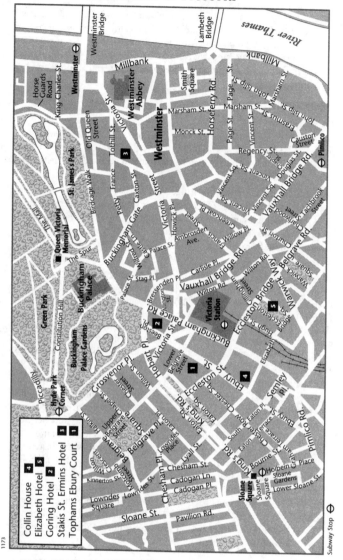

River Thames

Westminster Bridge

Lambeth Bridge

Millbank

Horse Guards Road

King Charles St.

Westminster

Old Queen Street

Tothill St.

Victoria St.

Westminster Abbey

Smith Square

Millbank

Page St.

John Islip St.

Marsham St.

Horseferry Rd.

Marsham St.

Erasmus St.

Vincent St.

John Islip St.

Westminster

Monck St.

Regency St.

Causton Street

Pimlico

Vincent Sq.

Douglas St.

St. James's Park

The Mall

Queen Victoria Memorial

Bridge-cage Walk

France

Petty France

Caxton St.

Buckingham Gate

Palace St.

Victoria Pl.

Howick Pl.

Francis St.

Ambrosden Ave.

Willow Pl.

Carlisle Pl.

Greencoat Pl.

Vincent Sq.

Vincent Sq.

Vauxhall Bridge Rd.

Tachbrook Street

Charlwood Street

The Spur

Green Park

Buckingham Palace

Buckingham Palace Gardens

Constitution Hill

Piccadilly

Hyde Park Corner

Grosvenor Pl.

Chester Street

Wilton St.

Upper Belgrave Street

Belgrave Street

Belgrave Square

Wilton Crescent

Kinnerton St.

Lowndes St.

Lowndes St.

Lowndes Square

Sloane St.

Chesham Pl.

Chesham St.

Cadogan Ln.

Cadogan Pl.

Pavilion Rd.

The Spur

Palace St.

Stag Pl.

Bressenden Pl.

Allington St.

Buckingham Palace Rd.

Beeston Pl.

Hobart Pl.

Lower Belgrave Street

Victoria St.

Warwick Way

Belgrave Rd.

Eccleston Bridge

Hugh St.

Elizabeth Bridge

Wilton Rd.

Gillingham St.

Eccleston St.

Victoria Station

Eccleston St.

Ebury St.

Semley Pl.

Ebury St.

Pimlico Rd.

Eaton Pl.

Eaton Sq.

Lyall St.

Eaton Terrace

Chester Row

South Eaton Pl.

Chester Square

King's Rd.

Eaton Terrace

Bourne St.

Graham Terrace

Holbein Pl.

Sloane Gardens

Lower Sloane St.

Sloane Square

Eccleston Sq.

Warwick Way

Ebury Sq.

Collin House 4
Elizabeth Hotel 5
Goring Hotel 2
Stakis St. Ermins Hotel 3
Tophams Ebury Court 1

Subway Stop ⊖

---

flower-filled windowboxes, the place has a country-house flavor, even though it's situated in the heart of Belgravia. The little reception rooms are informal and decorated with flowery chintzes and nice antiques. All rooms have facilities for making coffee and tea, hairdryers, and satellite TVs. The best accommodations are luxuriously appointed with en suite bathrooms and four-poster beds.

Specializing in traditional English food, Tophams Restaurant offers both lunch and dinner. Walls are decorated with paintings inherited from the owners' ancestors. Both traditional English and modern cooking is combined here, meaning you can order everything from steak-and-kidney pie to tagliatelle with a creamy olive and mushroom sauce. Lunches are served Monday through Friday from noon to 2:30pm and dinner Monday through Saturday from 6 to 10pm. Services include 24-hour porter service, babysitting, and laundry and dry cleaning.

INEXPENSIVE

Collin House

104 Ebury St., London SW1W 9QD. ☎ and **fax 0171/730-8031.** 13 rms (8 with bath). £36 ($56.90) single with bath; £48–£50 ($75.85–$79) double without bath, £60 ($94.80) double with bath. (Rates include English breakfast.) No credit cards. Tube: Victoria Station.

Collin House is a good, clean B&B under the watchful eye of its proprietors, Mr. and Mrs. D. L. Thomas. Everything is well maintained in this mid-Victorian town house. There are a number of family rooms. The main bus, rail, and Underground terminals all lie about a five-minute walk from the hotel.

⊙ Elizabeth Hotel

37 Eccleston Sq., London SW1V 1PB. ☎ **0171/828-6812.** 38 rms (32 with bath or shower), 5 studios and apartments. £36 ($56.90) single without bath, £55 ($86.90) single with bath or shower; £60 ($94.80) double without bath, £70–£80 ($110.60–$126.40) double with bath or shower; £75 ($118.50) triple without bath, £90 ($142.20) triple with bath or shower; £85 ($134.30) quad without bath, £100 ($158) quad with bath or shower; from £195 ($308.10) weekly studio; from £325 ($513.50) weekly two-bedroom apartment. (Rates include English breakfast.) No credit cards. Tube: Victoria Station.

The Elizabeth, a friendly, privately owned establishment overlooking the gardens of Eccleston Square, was built by Thomas Cubitt, Queen Victoria's favorite architect. It was a former residence of Princess Victoria of Hesse (a granddaughter of Queen Victoria) and her husband, Prince Louis of Battenberg. Located behind Victoria Station, it's an excellent place to stay, convenient to Belgravia and Westminster, not far from Buckingham Palace, and just a few doors away from a house where Sir Winston Churchill once lived. Most of the accommodations are reached by elevator, and each is individually decorated in a Victorian motif; many rooms have TVs. The original atmosphere has been carefully preserved, as reflected in the furnishings and framed prints. If you're going to be in London for a minimum of three months, ask about leasing an apartment.

7 Knightsbridge & Belgravia

KNIGHTSBRIDGE
VERY EXPENSIVE

The Capital

22–24 Basil St., London SW3 1AT. ☎ **0171/589-5171,** or toll free 800/926-3199 in the U.S. Fax 0171/225-0011. 40 rms, 8 suites. A/C MINIBAR TV TEL. £167

($263.85) single; £197–£250 ($311.25–$395) double; from £290 ($458.20) suite. AE, DC, MC, V. Parking £15 ($23.70). Tube: Knightsbridge.

One of the most personalized hotels in the West End, this small modern place is a stone's throw from Harrods. The owner, David Levin, has created a warm town-house ambience, the result of extensive refurbishment. The elegant fin-de-siècle decoration is matched by the courtesy and professionalism of the staff. The corridors and staircase are all treated as an art gallery, with original oil paintings. The guest rooms are tastefully decorated, often with Ralph Lauren home furnishings.

Dining/Entertainment: The Capital Restaurant, refurbished in the early 1990s with David Linley panels for the windows, is among the finest in London (Linley is Princess Margaret's son), offering exquisitely prepared main dishes. It is decorated in a vaguely French style and looks out onto a tree-lined street. A set lunch costs £21.50 to £25 ($33.95 to $39.50), a set dinner begins at £25 ($39.50); you can also order à la carte.

Services: 24-hour room service, laundry.

Sheraton Park Tower

101 Knightsbridge, London SW1X 7RN. ☎ **0171/235-8050**, or toll free 800/ 325-3535 in the U.S. Fax 0171/235-8231. 295 rms, 25 suites. A/C MINIBAR TV TEL. £200 ($316) single; £210 ($331.80) double; from £375 ($592.50) suite. VAT extra. English breakfast £14.50 ($22.90) extra. AE, DC, MC, V. Parking £9 ($14.20). Tube: Knightsbridge.

Sheraton Park Tower is not only one of the most convenient hotels in London (virtually at the doorstep of Harrods), but it's also one of the best. Its unusual circular architecture provides a stark but interesting contrast to the well-heeled 19th-century neighborhood around it. From its windows guests have a panoramic view of Hyde Park. The main door is discreetly placed in the rear, where taxis can deposit guests more conveniently.

The travertine-covered lobby bustles with scores of international businesspeople, diplomats (the French embassy is across the street), and military delegations who congregate on the well-upholstered sofas or amid the Edwardian comfort of the hideaway bar. Back in your room, you'll find such comforts as central heating, soundproof windows, in-house movies, a radio, viewbill, voicemail, and in all the executive rooms, fax machines.

Dining/Entertainment: In the Knightsbridge Lounge, near the ground-floor kiosks, afternoon tea is served. The champagne bar offers you the choice of either a glass or a silver tankard filled with bubbly, along with lobster, club sandwiches, or "bangers and mash." The Restaurant 101, with its own entrance onto Knightsbridge, is open daily from 7am to 11pm, offering good food; it's ideal for after-theater supper. You can dine on such dishes as crab-and-salmon ragoût, breast of pheasant, or brochette of tiger prawns and scallops.

Services: 24-hour room service, laundry, babysitting.

Facilities: 24-hour business center, news kiosk, free access to nearby health club.

Hotels: Kensington to Belgravia

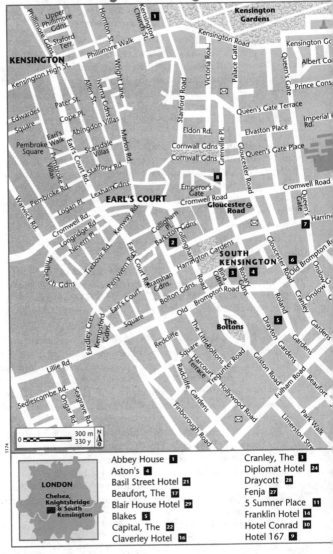

LONDON
Chelsea,
Knightsbridge
& South
Kensington

Abbey House **1**
Aston's **4**
Basil Street Hotel **21**
Beaufort, The **17**
Blair House Hotel **29**
Blakes **5**
Capital, The **22**
Claverley Hotel **16**

Cranley, The **3**
Diplomat Hotel **24**
Draycott **28**
Fenja **27**
5 Sumner Place **11**
Franklin Hotel **14**
Hotel Conrad **30**
Hotel 167 **9**

EXPENSIVE

Basil Street Hotel

8 Basil St., London SW3 1AH. ☎ **0171/581-3311.** Fax 0171/581-3693. 90 rms (80 with bath or shower), 1 suite. TV TEL. £65 ($102.70) single without bath, £120 ($189.60) single with bath; £100 ($158) double without bath, £175 ($276.50) double with bath; £265 ($418.70) suite. Children under 16 stay free in parents' room. English breakfast £11.50 ($18.15) extra. AE, DC, MC, V. Parking £23 ($36.35) at 24-hour lot nearby. Tube: Knightsbridge.

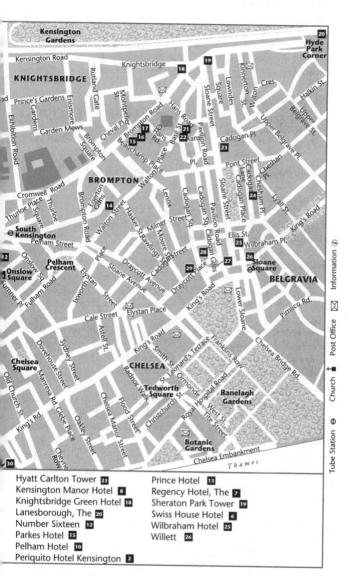

Key		
Information	ⓘ	
Post Office	✉	
Church	✝■	
Tube Station	⊖	

Hyatt Carlton Tower **23**
Kensington Manor Hotel **8**
Knightsbridge Green Hotel **18**
Lanesborough, The **20**
Number Sixteen **12**
Parkes Hotel **15**
Pelham Hotel **10**
Periquito Hotel Kensington **2**

Prince Hotel **13**
Regency Hotel, The **7**
Sheraton Park Tower **19**
Swiss House Hotel **6**
Wilbraham Hotel **25**
Willett **26**

The Basil, an Edwardian charmer totally unmarred by modernization, has long been a favorite little hotel for those discerning British who make an annual pilgrimage to London to shop at Harrods ("just 191 steps away") and perhaps attend the Chelsea Flower Show. Several spacious and comfortable lounges are appropriately furnished with 18th- and 19th-century decorative accessories. Off the many rambling corridors are smaller sitting rooms. At the hotel's restaurant, a three-course table d'hôte luncheon costs £15 ($23.70); dinner is £20

($31.60). Candlelight and piano music re-create the atmosphere of a bygone era. The Upstairs Restaurant serves lighter meals and snacks, and the Downstairs Wine Bar offers an excellent selection of wines and inexpensive food. Ideal for a light lunch or afternoon tea, the Parrot Club is a rendezvous reserved only for women.

The Beaufort

33 Beaufort Gardens, London SW3 1PP. ☎ **0171/584-5252,** or 212/682-9191 in New York. Fax 0171/589-2834. 21 rms, 7 junior suites. TV TEL. £110–£130 ($173.80–$205.40) single; £150–£215 ($237–$339.70) double; £240 ($379.20) junior suite for two. AE, DC, MC, V. Free parking overnight on street. Tube: Knightsbridge.

The Beaufort, only 200 yards from Harrods, sits behind two Victorian porticoes and an iron fence. The owner combined a pair of adjacent houses from the 1870s, ripped out the old decor, and created a stylishly updated ambience of merit and grace. You register at a small desk extending off a bay-windowed parlor, then climb the stairway used by the queen of Sweden during her stay.

Each guest room is decorated by several well-chosen paintings by London artists. They're done in a thoughtfully modern color scheme and have carpeting, as well as earphone radios, flowers, and a selection of books. An advantage of this place is the helpful staff. The owner, Diana Wallis, a television producer, has created the feeling of a private house in the heart of London.

Dining/Entertainment: Light meals are available from room service. There's a 24-hour honor bar.

Services: Theater tickets, car rental, sightseeing, babysitting.

Facilities: Access to nearby health club at a nominal charge.

Franklin Hotel

28 Egerton Gardens, London SW3 2DB. ☎ **0171/584-5533.** Fax 0171/584-5449. 36 rms, 4 suites. TV TEL. £120 ($189.60) single; £145–£210 ($229.10–$331.80) double; £180 ($284.40) suite. (Rates include breakfast.) AE, DC, MC, V. Tube: Knightsbridge.

This gem opened in 1992 and immediately attracted an audience even drawing discriminating patrons away from Claridge's and The Dorchester. Of course, it doesn't have the services and facilities of those hotel giants, but it is intimate and charming, the creation of David Naylor-Leyland who first attracted attention with another little charmer, the Egerton House, down the street.

The hotel lies on a quiet Knightsbridge street halfway between Harrods and the center of South Kensington. Preferred are its "Garden Rooms," opening onto a row of redbrick Victorian town houses across a lawn. These rooms are air-conditioned. Floral prints, canopy beds, antiques, and paintings characterize the bedroom decor. Bathrooms are lined with marble, and several also offer a bidet along with such thoughtful extras as toiletries from Floris. An honor bar is decorated in dark red, most elegant, and a series of parlors constitute the lobby. "Private but not so snobbish" is the motto here. Breakfast only is served, and a limited room service menu is offered.

MODERATE

ⓢ Claverley Hotel

13–14 Beaufort Gardens, London SW3 1PS. ☎ **0171/589-8541.** Fax 0171/ 584-3410. 32 rms (29 with bath). TV TEL. £50–£60 ($79–$94.80) single without bath, £65–£100 ($102.70–$158) single with bath; £95–£175 ($150.10–$276.50) double with bath. (Rates include English breakfast.) AE, MC, V. Free parking on street (6:30pm–8:30am). Tube: Knightsbridge.

Set on a quiet cul-de-sac in Knightsbridge, a few blocks from Harrods, this small, cozy tasteful place is accented with Georgian-era accessories. It's been called "the best bed and breakfast" in London. The appealing lounge contains 19th-century oil portraits, a Regency fireplace, and a collection of elegant antiques and leather-covered sofas—much like the ensemble you'd find in a private country house. Here in the lounge, the hotel serves complimentary tea, coffee, hot chocolate, and cookies 24 hours a day. Awarded the British Tourist Authority's Certificate of Distinction for Bed-and-Breakfast Hotels in 1988, the Claverley continues to maintain the high standards that won it the award. Most guest rooms have Victorian-inspired wallpaper, wall-to-wall carpeting, and upholstered armchairs, along with marble bathrooms with power showers. The full English breakfast is outstanding, with bacon, tomato, eggs, and Cumberland sausage, as well as homemade waffles with maple syrup and the cook's specialty, fresh salmon kedgeree.

Knightsbridge Green Hotel

159 Knightsbridge, London SW1X 7PD. ☎ **0171/584-6274.** Fax 0171/225-1635. 13 rms, 12 suites. TV TEL. £80 ($126.40) single; £110 ($173.80) double; £125 ($197.50) suite. English breakfast £9.50 ($15) extra. AE, MC, V. Tube: Knightsbridge.

In 1966, when this dignified 1890s structure just around the corner from Harrods was converted into a hotel, the developers were careful to retain its wide baseboards, cove moldings, high ceilings, and spacious proportions. None of the accommodations has a kitchen; nonetheless, they come close to apartment-style living. The suites are well furnished, with access to an upstairs "club room," where coffee and pastries are available throughout the day. Rooms contain trouser presses and hairdryers. Many return guests from around the world view this hotel as their "home away from home." Coffee or tea is available all day.

Parkes Hotel

41–43 Beaufort Gardens, London SW3 1PW. ☎ **0171/581-9944.** Fax 0171/ 581-1999. 6 rms, 27 suites. MINIBAR TV TEL. £98 ($154.85) single or double; £135– £215 ($213.30–$339.70) suite; £300 ($474) two-bedroom suite. VAT extra. (Rates include English breakfast.) AE, DC, MC, V. Free parking on street; £12 ($18.95 at nearby garage). Tube: Knightsbridge.

A classy Edwardian-style town house, the Parkes stands in one of the most desirable locations in London, close to Harrods. Facing a quiet and stately square, this place very much resembles a private house, with plenty of charm and style. Except for four standard rooms, each accommodation is a suite, complete with kitchenette. Each unit is individually decorated, sometimes in themes of blue and yellow.

BELGRAVIA
VERY EXPENSIVE
✪ The Lanesborough

1 Lanesborough Place, Hyde Park Corner, London SW1X 7TA. ☎ **0171/259-5599**, or toll free 800/999-1828. Fax 0171/259-5606. 49 rms, 46 suites. A/C MINIBAR TV TEL. £175–£205 ($276.50–$323.90) single; £245–£310 ($387.10–$489.80) double; from £240–£385 ($379.20–$608.30) suite. English breakfast £16 ($25.30) extra. AE, DC, MC, V. Parking £3 ($4.75) per hour. Tube: Hyde Park Corner.

Only a handful of other locations in London have elicited the kind of curiosity and loyalty as The Lanesborough. In 1719, when the neighborhood was relatively uncrowded, a country house for the second Viscount Lanesborough was built here; it was demolished in 1827. Soon after, the neoclassical style St. George's Hospital was constructed on the site; Florence Nightingale crusaded for its improvement and enlargement. During the darkest days of World War II, St. George's was one of the most visible beacons of hope as bombs fell on London, and many of today's older Londoners were born or "patched up" in the hospital's severe and medicinal-smelling wards.

By 1987, the historic hospital had become an inefficient medical an-tique. The medical facilities were moved to newly built quarters in South London, and the grueling task of redefining the building began. Rosewood Hotels and Resorts (known for managing top hotels like the Bel-Air in Los Angeles and The Mansion on Turtle Creek in Dallas) received permission from the London Planning Board to upgrade the building into a luxury hotel. Most Georgian details were retained, and the tacked-on machinery necessary for the hospital was demolished. Into the echoing interior were added acres of Regency and neo-Gothic details, ornate plasterwork reminiscent of some of the finest buildings in Britain, and yards of mahogany paneling. All this formed a discreet and well-polished aura similar to what you might expect in a sumptuously decorated country house. The guest rooms are as opulent and antique-drenched. Each contains electronic sensors to alert the staff as to when a resident is in or out, a CD player and VCR, a personal safe, a fax machine, a 24-channel satellite TV, a bathroom with every conceivable amenity, triple soundproofing, and the services of a personal butler. Security is tight, with the installation of at least 35 surveillance cameras.

Dining/Entertainment: The Conservatory, an elegant restaurant whose decor was inspired by the Chinese, Indian, and Gothic motifs of the Brighton Pavilion, is open daily from 7am to midnight. The Library Bar—which opens into a Regency hideaway, charmingly named "The Withdrawing Room"—re-creates the atmosphere of an elegant private London club.

Services: Personal butlers, concierges.

Facilities: Car rental, exercise room, and equipment (Stairmasters, exercise bicycles) delivered directly to your room.

MODERATE

Diplomat Hotel

2 Chesham St., London SW1X 3DT. ☎ **0171/235-1544.** Fax 0171/259-6153. 27 rms. TV TEL. £70 ($110.60) single; £105–£140 ($165.90–$221.20) double. (Rates include English buffet breakfast.) AE, DC, MC, V. Tube: Sloan Square, Knightsbridge, or Victoria Station.

Part of the Diplomat's multifaceted allure lies in its status as a small, reasonably priced hotel in an otherwise prohibitively expensive neighborhood filled with privately owned Victorian homes and high-rise first-class hotels. It's located on a wedge-shaped street corner near the site of today's Belgravia Sheraton. The registration desk is framed by the sweep of a partially gilded circular staircase, and above it cherubs gaze down from a Regency-era chandelier.

All of the high-ceilinged guest rooms boast tasteful wallpaper in Victorian color schemes. The staff is very helpful. Each accommodation is named after one of the famous streets in this posh district. Amenities include a massage service, a business center, afternoon tea, and a snack menu offered from noon until 9pm.

8 Chelsea & Chelsea Harbour

CHELSEA
VERY EXPENSIVE

✪ Draycott

24–26 Cadogan Gardens, London SW3 2RP. ☎ **0171/730-6466.** Fax 0171/730-0236. 24 rms, 5 junior suites. MINIBAR TV TEL. £100–£150 ($158–$237) single; £195 ($308.10) double; £250 ($395) junior suite for two. English breakfast £10.50 ($16.60) extra. AE, DC, MC, V. Tube: Sloane Square.

Located near Sloane Square in the heart of Chelsea, the Draycott, composed of a pair of red-brick Victorian town houses, opened in 1988. It's remained a well-kept secret among the fanciers of small but elegant hotels around the world. Here you can rest comfortably in a four-poster bed on fresh linen as your champagne cools in a silver bucket. Out back, the view opens onto a well-tended English garden; inside, the tone is set by antiques, chintz, and a blaze in the fireplace.

The main allure of the place is its beautifully furnished guest rooms, decorated with paintings (usually of the English countryside) and porcelain. Rooms are also outfitted with video players, minibars, and satellite TVs. Penhaligon toiletries are found in the immaculately maintained bathrooms. In your room, you are likely to find a copy of *An Innkeeper's Diary* by John Fothergill, but the Draycott doesn't take all his advice seriously—that is, his belief that boring clients should pay a higher tariff. Although the hotel has no restaurant, the 24-hour room service provides perfectly cooked breakfasts and light lunches and suppers. Guests are given a complimentary pass to use a health club nearby, as well as access to Cadogan Gardens.

Hyatt Carlton Tower

2 Cadogan Place, London SW1 X9PY. ☎ **0171/235-1234,** or toll free 800/
228-9000 in the U.S. Fax 0171/235-9129. 164 rms, 60 suites. A/C MINIBAR TV TEL.
£270 ($426.60) single or double; £375 ($592.50) suite. One child up to 18 free in
parents' room. English breakfast £14.50 ($22.90) extra. AE, DC, MC, V. Parking £20
($31.60). Tube: Knightsbridge.

Its location and height made this luxurious hotel a landmark even
before Hyatt's decorators, painters, and antiques dealers transformed
it into its European flagship. It's one of the most plushly decorated and
best-maintained hotels in London. Overlooking one of the city's most
civilized gardens, it's surrounded by Regency-era town houses. The
comfortable and conservatively modern guest rooms feature marble
baths, artwork, and in-house movies. Many open onto panoramic views
over the rooftops of the neighborhood.

Dining/Entertainment: After the publicity it once received as
"Britain's Tea Place of the Year," the hotel has remained one of the
most fashionable spots to enjoy a midafternoon pick-me-up. Scones,
Devonshire clotted cream, pastries, delicate sandwiches, and music are
all part of the experience. The Rib Room, known for its Aberdeen
Angus beef, offers relatively informal meals in a warmly atmospheric
setting. The Chelsea Room, considered one of the great restaurants of
London, is described separately in Chapter 5.

Services: 24-hour room service, valet, laundry, hair salon,
babysitting.

Facilities: Health club with exercise equipment, aerobics studio,
beauty experts, masseurs, sauna, and solariums.

EXPENSIVE

Fenja

69 Cadogan Gardens, London SW3 2RB. ☎ **0171/589-7333,** or toll free 800/525-
4800 in the U.S. Fax 0171/581-4958. 12 rms. MINIBAR TV TEL. £130–£195
($205.40– $308.10) single or double. English breakfast £11.75 ($18.60) extra. AE,
DC, MC, V. Free parking overnight on street; £7 ($11.10) at nearby garage. Tube:
Sloane Square.

Fenja is one of the most luxurious B&Bs in London, located near the
Peter Jones Department Store and the fashionable boutiques of King's
Road. It was built during the 19th century as a private house and purchased from the estate of Lord Cadogan after World War II. From
1985 to 1987 the building was completely restored and converted into
a hotel. Rooms are named after famous writers and painters who lived
in the neighborhood—such as the Turner Room—and are decorated
in a traditional English style and furnished in part with antiques.

Light meals are available from the room-service menu, which
includes a carefully selected wine list. Drinks can be ordered in the
drawing room. Services include same-day laundry and dry cleaning.

MODERATE

⑤ Blair House Hotel

34 Draycott Place, Sloan Sq., Chelsea, London SW3 2SA. ☎ **0171/581-2323.** Fax
0171/823-7752. 16 rms (all with shower). TV TEL. £70 ($110.60) single; £90–£98

($142.20–$154.80) double. (Rates including continental breakfast.) AE, DC, MC, V. Tube: Sloane Square.

This comfortable hotel is a good choice in the heart of Chelsea near Sloan Square. An older building of some architectural interest, it's been completely refurbished inside. The quieter bedrooms open onto the rear. Breakfast is the only meal served. All the rooms sport tea- and coffee-making equipment. Babysitting and laundry can be arranged.

INEXPENSIVE

Wilbraham Hotel

1–5 Wilbraham Place, off Sloane St., London SW1X 9AE. ☎ **0171/730-8296.** Fax 0171/730-6815. 53 rms (40 with bath), 4 suites. TV TEL. £39 ($61.60) single without bath, £54 ($85.30) single with bath; £54 ($85.30) double without bath, £66–£72 ($104.30–$113.80) double with bath; from £78 ($123.20) suite. English breakfast £5.50 ($8.70) extra. No credit cards. Parking £18 ($28.40) nearby. Tube: Sloane Square.

This is a dyed-in-the-wool British hotel set on a quiet residential street just a few hundred yards from Sloane Square. It occupies three Victorian town houses that are joined. The well-maintained guest rooms are furnished in a rather Spartan fashion and are quite small. On the premises is an old-fashioned lounge, The Bar and Buttery, where you can order drinks, a simple lunch, and dinner.

Willett

32 Sloane Gardens, Sloane Sq., London SW1W 8DJ. ☎ **0171/824-8415.** Fax 0171/730-4830. 19 rms. TV TEL. £61 ($96.40) single; £78–£85 ($123.20–$134.30) double. VAT extra. (Rates include English buffet breakfast.) AE, DC, MC, V. Tube: Sloane Square.

The Willett has rapidly become a favorite among English people who prefer to stay in a 19th-century town house located close to the restaurants, attractions, and shops of Chelsea. Its architectural touches include a mansard roof and bay windows. The hotel opens onto gardens. Retaining its traditional charm, the hotel has been fully renovated, with new furnishings in all the well-equipped guest rooms and in the public lounge areas. All the rooms have private bathrooms; the larger doubles contain small refrigerators. The breakfast room is especially inviting.

CHELSEA HARBOUR
VERY EXPENSIVE

Hotel Conrad

Chelsea Harbour, London SW10 0XG. ☎ **0171/823-3000,** or toll free 800/HILTONS in the U.S., 800/268-9275 in Canada. Fax 0171/351-6525. 160 suites. A/C MINIBAR TV TEL. £195–£260 ($308.10–$410.80) single; £210–£275 ($331.80–$434.50) double. AE, DC, MC, V. Parking £10 ($15.80). Transportation: Chelsea Harbour Hoppa Bus C3 from Earl's Court and Kensington High St. Mon–Sat.

One of London's major five-star deluxe hotels and perhaps the first all-suite hotel in Europe, the Conrad is a stunning modern architectural achievement. It's located in a marina complex of boutiques, restaurants, and some of the most desirable apartments in London. Each elegant suite, decorated by the famous designer David Hicks, contains hypoallergenic pillows, a full line of toiletries, a hairdryer, and three phones with two-line capability.

Dining/Entertainment: The hotel's facilities include the Brasserie, whose stylish and cozy interior overlooks the Thames. It's not really a brasserie but a deluxe hotel dining room with formal service. The Lounge offers breakfast, light snacks, afternoon tea, and champagne by the glass in the evening (to the accompaniment of live piano music). Drakes Bar, as richly nautical as its name would imply, offers a view of the dozens of neatly moored yachts in the nearby marina.

Services: 24-hour room service, laundry, babysitting, luggage storage.

Facilities: Health club (heated pool, sauna), electronic safety locks, fax machines, personal computers.

9 Kensington & South Kensington

KENSINGTON
VERY EXPENSIVE

Blake's Hotel

33 Roland Gardens, London SW7 3PF. ☎ **0171/370-6701,** or toll free 800/ 926-3173 in the U.S. Fax 0171/373-0442. 41 rms, 9 suites. MINIBAR TV TEL. £125 ($197.50) single; £150–£300 ($237–$474) double; from £495 ($782.10) suite. English breakfast £16.50 ($26.10) extra. AE, DC, MC, V. Parking £18 ($28.40). Tube: South Kensington or Gloucester Road.

One of the best small hotels of London, Blakes was created by converting a row of Victorian town houses, with seemingly no expense spared. Opulent, highly individual, it is Oriental nights down in old Kensington—everything from the Empress Joséphine's daybed to swaggered draperies, Venetian glassware, walls covered with cloth wallpaper, draped curtains, and bedrooms that rich clients from the Middle East might call home.It is certainly sophisticated (guests might even see Princess Margaret dining in its basement restaurant). The creation of actress Anouska Hempel Weinberg, the hotel's richly appointed lobby boasts Victorian-era furniture, possibly hailing from India. The guest rooms are individually decorated and of various sizes, some with antiques.

Dining/Entertainment: The hotel's restaurant is one of the best in town, with reservations strictly observed. It is furnished with black and white pieces along with Thai costumes and jewelry. Peter Thornley's cuisine blends the best of East and West, ranging from his filet of beef marinated in teriyaki sauce to his chicken and crab shaped like a large delectable egg of the Fabergé variety.

Services: 24-hour room service, laundry, babysitting.

Facilities: Free access to nearby health club, arrange-anything concierge.

INEXPENSIVE

✪ Abbey House

11 Vicarage Gate, London W8 4AG. ☎ **0171/727-2594.** 16 rms (none with bath). TV. £34 ($53.70) single; £55 ($86.90) double; £66 ($104.30) triple; £76 ($120.10) quad. (Rates include English breakfast.) No credit cards. Tube: Kensington High Street.

Some hotel critics have rated this among the best B&Bs in London. Thanks to renovations, Abbey House, built about 1860 on a typical Victorian square, is modern, though many original features have been retained. The spacious guest rooms have central heating, electrical outlets for shavers, vanity lights, and hot- and cold-water basins. Baths are shared by two units. The rooms are refurbished annually. Guests can enjoy free tea or coffee 24 hours a day in a tearoom.

SOUTH KENSINGTON
EXPENSIVE

✪ Pelham Hotel

15 Cromwell Place, London SW7 2LA. ☎ **0171/589-8288.** Fax 0171/584-8444. 35 rms, 2 suites. A/C MINIBAR TV TEL. £120 ($189.60) single; £140–£165 ($221.20–$260.70) double; from £220 ($347.60) suite. English breakfast from £10 ($15.80) extra. AE, MC, V. Tube: South Kensington.

Privately owned and small, the Pelham is suitable for everyone from a visiting movie star to a discerning traveler. Kit and Tim Kemp, hoteliers extraordinaire, preside over one of the most stunningly decorated establishments in London. It's formed from part of a row of early 19th-century terrace houses and has a white portico facade. In the drawing room, 18th-century paneling, high ceilings, and fine moldings create a suitable backdrop for a collection of antiques and Victorian oil paintings. An honor bar in this room creates a clublike atmosphere. Needlepoint, rugs, and cushions create a homelike warmth. Kemps is one of the finest restaurants in South Kensington (see Chapter 5). Services include 24-hour room service and theater-ticket arrangements.

MODERATE
The Cranley

10–12 Bina Gardens, London SW5 OLA. ☎ **0171/373-0123,** or toll free 800/553-2582 in the U.S. Fax 0171/373-9497. 27 rms, 5 suites. A/C TV TEL. £120–£140 ($189.60–$221.20) single or double; £150–£200 ($237–$316) suite. English breakfast £11 ($17.40) extra. (Rates include continental breakfast.) AE, DC, MC, V. Tube: Gloucester Road.

A trio of adjacent 1875 town houses became the Cranley Hotel when the Michigan-based owners upgraded the buildings into one of the most charming hotels in South Kensington. Today, all the high-ceilinged guest rooms have enormous windows, much of the original plasterwork, a scattering of antiques and plush upholstery—adding up to a vivid sense of the 19th century. The public rooms have been described as a stage set for an ultra-English country house. There is no restaurant on the premises, although light meals are served in rooms on request. A continental breakfast is served in a public room. All but one of the accommodations contain tiny kitchenettes.

5 Sumner Place

5 Sumner Place, London SW7 3EE. ☎ **0171/584-7586.** Fax 0171/823-9962. 14 rms. MINIBAR TV TEL. £62–£79 ($98–$124.80) single; £85–£95 ($134.30–$150.10) double. (Rates include English breakfast.) AE, DC, MC, V. Tube: South Kensington.

Winner of the British Tourist Authority Best B&B in Central London award in 1991, this carefully restored 1850s Victorian town house is delightful. The experience here is more like staying with friends in a London home than at a hotel. Some of the traditionally furnished rooms contain minibars. Each is immaculately maintained and refreshingly uncluttered. A breakfast buffet is served in a 19th-century conservatory overlooking a sun terrace. The owners, John and Barbara Palgan, provide the attention that makes visitors want to return.

Number Sixteen

16 Sumner Place, London SW7 3EG. ☎ **0171/589-5232.** Fax 0171/584-8615. 36 rms (34 with bath). MINIBAR TV TEL. £65 ($102.70) single without bath, £78–£98 ($123.20–$154.80) single with bath; £90 ($142.20) double without bath, £130–£155 ($205.40–$244.90) double with bath; £180 ($284.40) triple with bath. (Rates include continental breakfast.) AE, DC, MC, V. Tube: South Kensington.

This is an elegant and luxurious pension, composed of four early-Victorian town houses linked to form a dramatically organized whole. The front and rear gardens of each of the four houses are scrupulously maintained, creating swaths of greenery that today contribute to one of the most idyllic spots on the street. The hotel was the winner of four garden awards during 1994. In 1992, the establishment was awarded a trophy as the best B&B in London.

The rooms are decorated with an eclectic mix of English antiques and modern paintings. There's an honor-system bar in the library. On cold days a blazing fire is lit in the drawing room's fireplace to warm the chill. Breakfast is served in the privacy of the bedrooms, and a tea/coffee service is available 7:30am to 10pm. The hotel has an elevator.

The Regency Hotel

100 Queen's Gate, London SW7 5AG. ☎ **0171/370-4595,** or toll free 800/328-9898 in the U.S. Fax 0171/370-5555. 198 rms, 11 suites. A/C MINIBAR TV TEL. £85–£99 ($134.30–$156.40) single; £105–£120 ($165.90–$189.60) double; £179 ($282.80) luxury suite for two; £199 ($314.40) double suite with Jacuzzi. English breakfast £12.50 ($19.80) extra. AE, DC, MC, V. Tube: Gloucester Road or South Kensington.

The Regency—close to museums, Kensington, and Knightsbridge—takes its name from the historical period of the Prince Regent, later George IV. Located on a street lined with Doric porticoes, six Victorian terrace houses were converted into one stylish, seamless whole by an army of construction engineers and decorators. A Chippendale fireplace, flanked by wing chairs, greets guests near the polished hardwood of the reception area. One of the building's main stairwells contains what could be London's most unusual lighting fixture: five Empire chandeliers suspended vertically, one on top of the other. Since its opening, the hotel has hosted everyone from the late Margot Fonteyn to members of the British royal family. The modernized guest rooms are tasteful and elegant.

The Pavilion Restaurant is described in Chapter 5. Hotel services include 24-hour room service, laundry, and babysitting. At your disposal are the Regency Health Club (with steamrooms, saunas, and a sensory-deprivation tank) and a business center.

INEXPENSIVE

✪ Aston's Budget Studios and Aston's Designer Studios and Suites

39 Rosary Gardens, London SW7 4NQ. ☎ **0171/370-0737,** or toll free 800/ 525-2810 in the U.S. Fax 0171/835-1419. 60 studios and apartments (38 with bath). A/C TV TEL. Budget Studios £35–£39 ($55.30–$61.60) single; £49–£56 ($77.40– $88.50) double; £70–£85 ($110.60–$134.30) triple; £85–£95 ($134.30–$150.10) quad. Designer Studios £85–£110 ($134.30–$173.80) single or double; £120–£160 ($189.60–$252.80) two-room suite for two or four. AE, MC, V. Tube: Gloucester Road.

A carefully restored row of interconnected Victorian town houses, this establishment offers comfortably furnished studios and suites. Weekly rentals are preferred, but daily rentals are also accepted. Heavy oak doors and 18th-century hunting pictures give Aston's foyer a rich traditional atmosphere.

Accommodations range in size and from budget to designer suites. Regardless of its price, however, each unit has a compact but complete kitchenette concealed behind doors. The Budget Studios have fully serviced bathrooms, which are shared with only a handful of other guests. The air-conditioned Designer Studios and two-room Designer Suites are lavishly decorated with rich fabrics and furnishings and contain marble-sheathed private showers and bathrooms. Telephones have answering machines, and there are a host of other electronic accessories suited for doing business in London. Considering its amenities, Aston's is an excellent value for the cost. It's under the personal management of Ms. Shelagh King.

Services include laundry, secretarial service, guests' message line, fax machines, private catering on request, car and limousine, and daily maid service in the Designer Studios and Suites.

Hotel 167

167 Old Brompton Rd., London SW5 OAN. ☎ **0171/373-0672.** Fax 0171/ 373-3360. 18 rms. MINIBAR TV TEL. £54 ($85.30) single; £68–£75 ($107.40– $118.50) double. Extra bed in room £12 ($20.50). (Rates include continental breakfast.) AE, DC, MC, V. Tube: South Kensington.

Hotel 167 is one of the more fashionable guesthouses in the area. It occupies a once-private three-story Victorian town house. The decor is quite stylish, with Scandinavian modern and Japanese accents. Some guest rooms are in the basement; these have large windows for illumination.

Kensington Manor Hotel

8 Emperor's Gate, London SW7 4HH. ☎ **0171/370-7516.** Fax 0171/373-3163. 15 rms, 1 suite. MINIBAR TV TEL. £60 ($94.80) single; £75–£94 ($118.50–$148.50) double; £120 ($189.60) suite for four. (Rates include VAT and English breakfast.) AE, DC, MC, V. Tube: Gloucester Road.

Located on a cul-de-sac, this hotel offers warmth and comfort in a stately late-Victorian building. Personal service of a high standard is the keynote of this place, including room service, laundry service, and dry cleaning. The guest rooms in this small lodging are individually decorated, each named after a county of England. A buffet breakfast is served.

Ⓢ Prince Hotel

6 Sumner Place, London SW7 3AB. ☎ **0171/589-6488.** Fax 0171/581-0824. 20 rms (all with shower; 15 with toilet). TV TEL. £47 ($74.30) single with shower (no toilet), £59 ($93.20) single with shower and toilet; £59 ($93.20) double with shower (no toilet), £72 ($113.80) double with shower and toilet. AE, DC, MC, V. Tube: South Kensington.

The Prince Hotel was successfully converted from an early-Victorian terrace house of about 1850. Decorated and restored in a classic English style, it opens onto a greenhouse-style conservatory and garden in the rear. All the guest rooms are individually designed.

10　Earl's Court & Notting Hill Gate

EARL'S COURT
INEXPENSIVE

Periquito Hotel Kensington

34–44 Barkston Gardens, London SW5 OEW. ☎ **0171/373-7851.** Fax 0171/370-6570. 75 rms. TV TEL. Sun–Thurs £69 ($109) single or double; Fri–Sat £64 ($101.10) single or double. Breakfast £5–£7 ($7.90–$11.10) extra. AE, DC, MC, V. Parking £8.50–£10 ($13.40–$15.80). Tube: Earl's Court.

When it was first established in 1905 in one town house, this hotel offered B&B at 5p (8¢) per person; it rapidly expanded to eventually include six adjoining town houses. In 1993, the hotel was bought and radically renovated by a well-recommended British chain, Periquito, noted for its cost-conscious prices. Bedrooms are comfortably contemporary and done in bright primary colors. Each contains cable-connected TV, a coffee maker, and a hairdryer. On the premises is a bar and a restaurant, Bistro, decorated in a French country-style.

Swiss House Hotel

171 Old Brompton Rd., London SW5 OAN. ☎ **0171/373-2769.** Fax 0171/373-4983. 16 rms (14 with bath). TV TEL. £34 ($53.70) single without bath, £50 ($79) single with bath; £64 ($101.10) double with bath, £74 ($116.90) triple with bath; £84 ($132.70) quad with bath. (Rates include continental breakfast.) AE, DC, MC, V. Tube: Gloucester Road.

Swiss House is one of the more desirable B&Bs in the Earl's Court area. It's in a Victorian row house, with a portico festooned with flowers and vines. The rear bedrooms overlook a communal garden and have a view of the London skyline. Its guest rooms are individually designed in "country-style"; some have fireplaces. Traffic is heavy outside, but windows are double-glazed. Babysitting services are available, and there's room service.

NOTTING HILL GATE
MODERATE

The Abbey Court

20 Pembridge Gardens, London W2 4DU. ☎ **0171/221-7518.** Fax 0171/792-0858. 22 rms, 3 suites. TV TEL. £80 ($126.40) single; £130 ($205.40) double or twin; £160 ($252.80) suite with four-poster bed. AE, DC, MC, V. Tube: Notting Hill Gate.

The Abbey Court is a small and rather luxurious choice. In a white-fronted mid-Victorian town house, it has a patio with lots of flowers in front and a conservatory in back. The lobby is graciously decorated and has a sunny bay window, floral draperies, and a comfortable sofa and chairs. You'll find fresh flowers in the reception area and the hallways. Each room offers carefully coordinated fabrics and fine furnishings, mostly 18th- and 19th-century country antiques. Done in Italian marble, bathrooms are equipped with a Jacuzzi bath, shower, and heated towel racks. Light snacks and drinks are available from room service 24 hours a day. Kensington Gardens is a short walk away, as are the antiques stores along Portobello Road and Kensington Church Street.

11 Marylebone

VERY EXPENSIVE

The Langham Hilton

1 Portland Place, London W1N 3AA. ☎ **0171/636-1000,** or toll free 800/445-8667 in the U.S. and Canada. Fax 0171/323-2340. 360 rms, 20 suites. A/C MINIBAR TV TEL. £190–£220 ($300.20–$347.60) single; £210–£230 ($331.80–$363.40) double; £260–£280 ($410.80–$442.40) executive room (include English breakfast); £320 ($505.60) suite. English breakfast £15.20 ($24) extra. AE, DC, MC, V. Parking £19.50 ($30.80). Tube: Oxford Circus.

When this extremely well-located hotel was inaugurated in 1865 by the Prince of Wales, its accommodations were considered a suitable London address for dozens of aristocratic squires seeking respite from their country estates. (Its guests included Antonin Dvořák, Arturo Toscanini, Oscar Wilde, Mark Twain, and Arnold Bennett.) After it was bombed in the second world war, it languished as dusty office space for the BBC until the early 1990s, when Hilton International took it over.

Today, the Langham's public rooms reflect the power and majesty of the British Empire during its 19th-century apex. Its restoration was painstaking, and Hilton now considers this its European flagship. Guest rooms are somewhat less opulent than public rooms; they feature French provincial furniture and red oak trim. It's a cozy enclave from the restaurants, cinemas, and commercial bustle of nearby Leicester Square.

Hotels: Notting Hill Gate to Marylebone

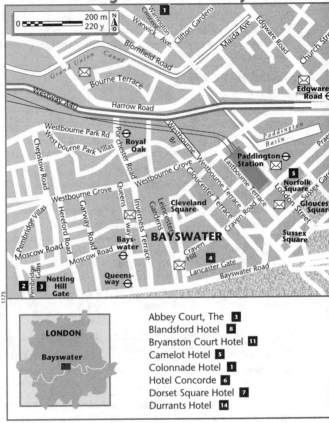

Abbey Court, The **3**
Blandsford Hotel **8**
Bryanston Court Hotel **11**
Camelot Hotel **5**
Colonnade Hotel **1**
Hotel Concorde **6**
Dorset Square Hotel **7**
Durrants Hotel **14**

Dining/Entertainment: Afternoon tea is served amid the potted palms of the Edwardian-style Palm Court. Vodka, caviar, and champagne flow liberally amid the red velvet of the Tsar's Russian Bar and Restaurant, while drinks are served in the Chukka Bar, a green-toned re-creation of a polo-playing private club. The most upscale restaurant is a high-ceilinged Victorian fantasy, Memories of the Empire, serving patriotic nostalgia and cuisine from the far corners of the British Commonwealth.

Services: 24-hour room service, concierge.

Facilities: Health club (saunas), business office.

MODERATE

✪ Dorset Square Hotel

39–40 Dorset Sq., London NW1 6QN. ☎ **0171/723-7874,** or toll free 800/543-4138 in the U.S. Fax 0171/724-3328. 35 rms, 2 junior suites. MINIBAR TV TEL. £85–£95 ($134.30–$150.10) single; £110–150 ($173.80–$237) double; £160 ($252.80) junior suite. English breakfast £10 ($15.80) extra. AE, MC, V. Tube: Baker Street or Marylebone.

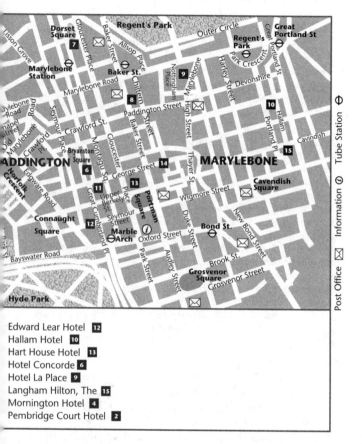

Dorset Square is made up of two Georgian Regency town houses. Hotelier Tim Kemp and his wife, Kit, have designed the interior so that the public rooms, luxurious guest rooms, and baths will make you feel that you're in an elegant private home. The rooms are decorated with chintz-upholstered furniture; it's a mix of antiques and reproductions. Half of the rooms are air-conditioned.

The menu of the hotel's restaurant, the Potting Shed, changes seasonally and features the best of English cuisine. Services include 24-hour room service, laundry, and babysitting.

Bryanston Court Hotel

56–60 Great Cumberland Place, Marble Arch, London W1H 7FD. ☎ **0171/262-3141**, or toll free 800/528-1234 in the U.S. Fax 0171/262-7248. 54 rms. TV TEL. £73 ($115.30) single; £90 ($142.20) double; £105 ($165.90) triple. Continental breakfast £6.50 ($10.30) extra. AE, DC, MC, V. Parking £14 ($22.10). Tube: Marble Arch.

Three individual houses were joined to form Bryanston about two centuries ago. Today this is one of the most elegant hotels on the street

102   Accommodations

thanks partly to the decorating efforts of its owners, the Theodore family. The bedrooms are comfortable. A gas fire burns in the Chesterfield-style bar.

Durrants Hotel

George St. (without number), London W1H 6BJ. ☎ **0171/935-8131.** Fax 0171/487-3510. 96 rms, 3 suites. TV TEL. £65–£87 ($102.70–$137.50) single; £90–£148 ($142.20–$233.80) double; from £200 ($316) suite. English breakfast £8.75 ($13.80) extra. AE, MC, V. Tube: Bond Street.

Established in 1789 off Manchester Square, this historic hotel brown-brick facade ornamented with Georgian details. During the hundred years of its ownership by the Miller family, several neighboring houses were incorporated into the original structure. A walk through the pine-and-mahogany-paneled public rooms is like stepping back into another century. You'll find an 18th-century letter-writing room. Its pub, a neighborhood favorite, has Windsor chairs, an open fireplace, and a decor that probably hasn't changed very much in two centuries. Accommodations have elaborate cove moldings and very comfortable furnishings; they exude an aura of solidity.

The in-house restaurant serves full afternoon teas and a satisfying French or traditional English cuisine in one of the most beautiful Georgian rooms in the neighborhood. The less formal breakfast room is ringed with 19th-century political cartoons by a noted Victorian artist. Services include 24-hour room service, laundry, and babysitting.

INEXPENSIVE

Blandford Hotel

80 Chiltern St., London W1M 1PS. ☎ **0171/486-3103.** Fax 0171/487-2786. 33 rms. TV TEL. £60 ($94.80) single; £75 ($118.50) double; £145 ($229.10) triple. (Rates including English breakfast.) AE, DC, MC, V. Tube: Baker Street.

Located only a minute's walk from the tube, this family-run hotel is something of a find and definitely one of London's better B&Bs for the price. Each room has a hairdryer and coffee-making equipment. Five rooms rented as triples are suitable for families.

☉ Edward Lear Hotel

28–30 Seymour St., London W1H 5WD. ☎ **0171/402-5401.** Fax 0171/706-3766. 31 rms (8 with bath), 4 suites. TV TEL. £39.50 ($62.40) single without bath, £47.50 ($75.10) single with bath; £49.50 ($78.20) double without bath, £62.50 ($98.80) double with bath; from £72.50 ($114.6) suite. (Rates include English breakfast.) MC, V. Tube: Marble Arch.

This popular hotel is made all the more desirable by the bouquets of fresh flowers in the public rooms. It's one block from Marble Arch, occupying a pair of brick town houses, both of which date from 1780. The western house was the London home of the 19th-century artist and poet Edward Lear, whose illustrated limericks adorn the walls of one of the sitting rooms. Steep stairs lead up to the cozy rooms, which are fairly small but comfortable.

Hallam Hotel

12 Hallam St., Portland Place, London W1N 5LF. ☎ **0171/580-1166.** Fax 0171/
323-4527. 25 rms. TV TEL. £50–£62 ($79–$98) single; £65–£75 ($102.70–$118.50)
double. (Rates include English breakfast.) AE, DC, MC, V. Tube: Oxford Circus.

The Hallam is a heavily ornamented stone-and-brick Victorian house,
one of the few on the street to escape the blitz. Today, it's the property of the Baker family, brothers Grant and David, who maintain it
well. The guest rooms are comfortably furnished, each with tea- or
coffee-making facilities. Some singles are quite small. It has a bar for
residents and a bright breakfast room, which overlooks a pleasant patio.

⊛ Hart House Hotel

51 Gloucester Place, Portman Sq., London W1H 3PE. ☎ **0171/935-2288.** Fax
0171/935-8516. 16 rms (10 with bath). TV TEL. £45 ($71.10) single without bath,
£53 ($83.70) single with bath; £63 ($99.50) double or twin without bath, £79
($124.80) double or twin with bath; £80 ($126.40) triple without bath, £89
($140.60) triple with bath; £95 ($150.10) quad with bath. (Rates include English
breakfast.) AE, MC, V. Tube: Marble Arch or Baker Street.

This is a well-preserved historic building, one of a group of Georgian
mansions occupied by members of the French nobility living in exile
during the French Revolution. In the heart of the West End, it lies
within easy walking distance of many different theaters, as well as some
of the most sought-after pockets of shops and public parks in London.
Cozy and convenient, the hotel is run by Mr. and Mrs. Bowden and
son Andrew. All guest rooms are clean and comfortable.

Hotel Concorde

50 Great Cumberland Place, London W1H 7FD. ☎ **0171/402-6169.** Fax 0171/
724-1184. 28 rms. TV TEL. £62 ($98) single; £72 ($113.80) double; £85 ($134.30)
triple. (Rates include continental breakfast,) AE, DC, MC, V. Parking £18 ($28.40).
Tube: Marble Arch.

Owned and run by the Theodore family, the Concorde was converted
into a small and stylish hotel from an 1850s private home. Its reception desk, nearby chairs, and a section of the tiny bar area were taken
from a London church. The guest rooms are well maintained. The
relatively quiet neighborhood is convenient to the attractions and
traffic arteries of Marble Arch.

   The owners also maintain 10 apartments in buildings next door and
across the street. Each has a kitchen and from one to three bedrooms;
in all cases, there is only one bathroom. Most of these—but not all—
have somewhat dowdy furniture. One-bedroom apartments cost £85
($134.30), two-bedroom apartments rent for £95 ($150.10), and a
three-bedroom apartment goes for £105 ($165.90)—always with
breakfast included.

Hotel La Place

17 Nottingham Place, London W1M 3FB. ☎ **0171/486-2323.** Fax 0171/486-4335.
24 rms, 4 suites. MINIBAR TV TEL. £62–£72 ($98–$113.80) single; £75–£95
($118.50–$150.10) double; from £97 ($153.30) suite. (Rates include English
breakfast.) DC, MC, V. Parking £7.50 ($11.90). Tube: Baker Street.

The La Place is a refurbished 4 Crown "Commended" hotel—one of the best of its kind in the area. *Eyewitness Guide* says it's a safe haven for women travelers. The guest rooms are clean and comfortable, with traditional styling. On the premises, doing a healthy neighborhood business, is a chic little wine bar and restaurant with a piano.

12 Paddington, Bayswater & Maida Vale

PADDINGTON
MODERATE

Mornington Hotel

12 Lancaster Gate, London W2 3LG. ☎ **0171/262-7361,** or toll free 800/528-1234 in the U.S. Fax 0171/706-1028. 68 rms. TV TEL. £83 ($131.10) single; £93–£113 ($146.90–$178.50) double. (Rates include Scandinavian buffet breakfast.) AE, DC, MC, V. Tube: Lancaster Gate.

The Mornington brings a touch of northern European hospitality to the center of London. Just north of Hyde Park and Kensington Gardens, the hotel has a Victorian exterior and a Scandinavian-inspired decor. It features a genuine Finnish sauna. The modernized guest rooms are tastefully conceived and comfortable. All include coffee/tea facilities. You can wind down in the library, entertaining your friends or making new ones. From the well-stocked bar, you can order snacks or afternoon tea.

INEXPENSIVE

Camelot Hotel

45–47 Norfolk Sq., London W2 1RX. ☎ **0171/723-9118.** Fax 0171/402-3412. 44 rms (40 with bath or shower). TV TEL. £37 ($58.50) single without bath, £45 ($71.10) single with bath; £71 ($112.20) double with bath; £85 ($134.30) triple with bath; £114 ($180.10) quad with bath. (Rates include English breakfast.) DC, MC, V. Tube: Paddington.

In a pair of adjacent town houses from 1850, this simple but comfortable hotel stands at the center of an old tree-filled square, about two minutes from Paddington Station. Refurbished in the late 1980s, the hotel now has an elevator. Framed prints, floral-print curtains and matching bedspreads create a homelike setting. Families with children are welcome.

BAYSWATER
MODERATE

Pembridge Court Hotel

34 Pembridge Gardens, London W2 4DX. ☎ **0171/229-9977.** Fax 0171/727-4982. 25 rms. TV TEL. £95–£120 ($150.10–$189.60) single; £115–£155 ($181.70–$244.90) double. (Rates include English breakfast.) AE, DC, MC, V. Tube: Notting Hill Gate.

In an 1852 private home, this hotel presents an elegant cream-colored neoclassical facade to a residential neighborhood that has grown increasingly fashionable. Most guest rooms contain at least one antique, as well as 19th-century engravings and plenty of warm-toned floral fabrics. Some of the largest and most stylish rooms are on the top floor, with baths tiled in Italian marble. Three deluxe rooms overlook Portobello Road. The Spencer and Churchill rooms, for example, are decorated in blues and yellows, while the Windsor room has a contrasting array of tartans.

In Caps, the hotel's brick-lined restaurant, good French, Thai, and English food and drink, along with a well-chosen array of wines, is served. It's open only in the evening. Services include 24-hour room service, laundry, same-day dry cleaning, and babysitting. A car-rental agency is on the premises. A day membership in a nearby health club is available for £15 ($23.70).

MAIDA VALE
MODERATE

Colonnade Hotel

2 Warrington Crescent, London W9 1ER. ☎ **0171/289-2167.** Fax 0171/286-1057. 47 rms. TV TEL. £66–£95 ($104.30–$150.10) single; £90–£120 ($142.20–$189.60) double. (Rates include English breakfast.) AE, MC, V. Parking £10 ($15.80). Tube: Warwick Avenue.

The Georgian-style Colonnade has been a landmark in the neighborhood since 1938. For about half a century, it's been run by the Richards family, who maintain its charm and special atmosphere. All rooms have en suite bathrooms and range from standard singles to large doubles (16 in all) with four-poster beds. Every bathroom, bedroom, and corridor is centrally heated 24 hours a day from the first chilly breeze of autumn until the last retreating wind of winter. Forty percent of the rooms are air-conditioned. The hotel also has a highly rated restaurant and bar, Cascades, which is especially known for its fondues, made only in the winter months.

13 Holland Park

VERY EXPENSIVE

✪ Halcyon Hotel

81 Holland Park Ave., London W11 3RZ. ☎ **0171/727-7288,** or toll free 800/457-4000 in the U.S., 800/668-8355 in Canada. 43 rms, 19 suites. A/C MINIBAR TV TEL. £165 ($260.70) single; £235 ($371.30) double; from £275 ($434.50) suite. English breakfast £12.50 ($19.80) extra. AE, DC, MC, V. Tube: Holland Park.

Only a small brass plaque distinguishes the aptly named Halcyon from other buildings on its street. Called "by far the grandest of London's small hotels," it was formed in 1985 by uniting a pair of Victorian mansions from 1860. Today, they constitute a hotel of charm, urban sophistication, and much comfort. The clientele includes a bevy of international film and recording stars who like the privacy and anonymity provided by this place: the Rolling Stones, Bruce Willis, Sigourney Weaver.

Nearly half the accommodations are suites, lavishly outfitted like an Edwardian country house. Several accommodations boast such whimsical touches as tended ceilings. All contain the modern luxuries. The public rooms are inviting oases, with trompe l'oeil paintings against backgrounds of turquoise. The designer of the hotel was an American, Barbara Thornhill.

Dining/Entertainment: The hotel's superb restaurant, The Room at the Halcyon, is recommended separately in Chapter 5.

Services: 24-hour room service, 1-hour pressing service, message-paging system (for which beepers are provided) that extends 20 miles from the hotel, complimentary limousine service, babysitting, night safes.

Facilities: Business center, membership to Vanderbilt Tennis Club and Lambton Place Health Club.

14 Hampstead

INEXPENSIVE

⑤ Sandringham Hotel

3 Holford Rd., London NW3 1AD. ☎ **0171/435-1569.** Fax 0171/431-5932. 15 rms (all with bath or shower). TEL. £56–£66 ($88.50–$104.30) single; £74–£85 ($116.90–$134.30) double; £97 ($153.30) triple. (Rates include English breakfast.) MC, V. Free parking. Tube: Hampstead.

The Sandringham stands on a residential street in one of the best parts of London. The Sandringham Hotel was refurbished in the early 1990s by the energetic American couple who own and operate it. The main lounge is elegant, featuring a Victorian fireplace and a serve-yourself honor bar. The formal dining room overlooks a Japanese garden where in the summer months afternoon tea is served.

Bedrooms are all individually decorated with lovely antique furnishings and luxurious fabrics; some contain working fireplaces. From the upper rooms, you have a panoramic view over Hampstead Heath to the center of London. Laundry service, babysitting, and room service are available.

15 Near the Airports

NEAR GATWICK
EXPENSIVE

Gatwick Hilton International Hotel

Gatwick Airport, Gatwick, West Sussex RH6 0LL. ☎ **0129/351-8080,** or toll free 800/HILTONS in the U.S. Fax 01293/528980. 550 rms, 18 suites. A/C TV TEL. £140–£145 ($221.20–$229.10) single or double; from £165 ($260.70) suite. Breakfast £12 ($19) extra. AE, DC, MC, V. Parking £5 ($7.90).

Gatwick's most convenient resting place, this deluxe five-floor hotel is linked to the airport terminal with a covered walkway. An electric buggy service transports people back and forth from the hotel and the airport. The most impressive part of the hotel is the first-floor lobby; its glass-covered portico rises four floors and contains a scale replica of the de Havilland Gypsy Moth airplane *Jason,* used by Amy Johnson on her solo flight from England to Australia in 1930. The reception desk is nearby, in an area with a lobby bar and lots of greenery. Rooms are equipped with soundproofing triple-glazed windows.

Dining/Entertainment: The American-themed restaurant Amy's serves buffet breakfasts, lunches, and dinners. The Garden Restaurant, outfitted in an English outdoor theme, serves drinks and full meals. There's also the Lobby Bar, open 24 hours a day, plus a watering hole with a polo-playing theme, The Jockey Bar.

Services: Same-day laundry and dry cleaning, up-to-date flight information channel, 24-hour room service, hairdresser, bank, giftshop.

Facilities: Health club (sauna, steamroom, massage room, swimming pool, gymnasium), Jacuzzi.

NEAR LONDON HEATHROW
EXPENSIVE

Sheraton Skyline

A-4 Bath Rd. (without number), Hayes, Middlesex UB3 5BP. ☎ **0181/759-2535,** or toll free 800/325-3535 in the U.S. Fax 081/750-9150. 352 rms, 5 suites. A/C MINIBAR TV TEL. £120–£160 ($189.60–$252.80) single; £130–£170 ($205.40–$268.60) double; from £320 ($505.60) suite. English breakfast buffet £12 ($19) extra. AE, DC, MC, V. Parking £5 ($7.90) per day.

More of a miniature village than a hotel, the Sheraton Skyline was voted the world's best airport hotel in the 1980s, and its standards have remained high. The hotel surrounds an atrium where tropical plants and towering palms thrive beneath a translucent roof. The foundations of a cabana bar are set into the temperature-controlled waters of a pool. Each guest room sports a color TV with in-house pay/free movie channels and a massage-style shower.

Dining/Entertainment: A fireplace flickers late into the night in the Edwardian Colony Bar and in the adjacent well-upholstered restaurant, the Colony Room, where well-prepared food is served beneath massive ceiling timbers and heavy brass chandeliers. A French café offers light meals and full buffet breakfasts. Diamond Lil's, a Montana-style cabaret, features showgirls, charbroiled steaks, and generous drinks.

Services: 24-hour room service, shuttle service to and from four terminals at Heathrow Airport (running every five minutes between 6am and 11:30pm), and verification and confirmation of departures from Heathrow.

Facilities: Business center, heated pool, fitness center.

5

Dining

George Mikes, Britain's famous Hungarian-born humorist, once wrote about the culinary prowess of his adopted country: "The Continentals have good food. The English have good table manners."

Quite a lot has happened since.

London has now emerged as one of the great food capitals of the world. Chefs, both young and old, have fanned out around the globe seeking new dishes and culinary ideas, and they have returned to their London kitchens with innovative items never seen before—or at least not to Londoners at such unprecedented rates. These chefs are pioneering the new style of cooking called "Modern British," which is forever changing, forever innovative.

"A city of foodies," that's how a London magazine described the city's population. Dining out is commonplace, despite the great expense involved. Food columns in newspapers are now almost as avidly read as the astrology column or the latest scandalous stories spinning around the House of Windsor.

Traditional food has made a comeback, too. Those dishes one's mother back in Northampton served have become fashionable again. Yes, we're talking British soul food like faggots, bangers and mash, Norfolk dumplings, and Devizes pie. Perhaps this is a direct result of the minimalist excesses of nouvelle cuisine of the 1980s. The pig's nose with parsley and onion sauce you may want to skip, though, Simpson's is now serving it for breakfast.

In the upper brackets, London has always boasted magnificent restaurants, several of which have achieved world renown. These were the preserve of the middling wealthy. If you want to splurge in a big way, you have the London "greats" at your disposal: gourmet havens such as La Tante Claire, Le Gavroche, Chez Nico at Ninety Park Lane, or half a dozen others. Usually these restaurants serve French cuisine or at least French-inspired cuisine. Many of their chefs also create remarkable and inventive English dishes with the fresh produce available in the country. Wine tends to be pricey in these establishments.

If star eateries are too expensive for you, there are moderately priced and budget restaurants. Among the latter are public houses. The English public house—also known as the "local," the "watering hole," the "boozer," and the pub—is such a significant national institution that it could merit a separate chapter. Far more than a place in which to drink, the pub is also the regular lunchtime rendezvous for millions of English people. For an even larger number, it also doubles as a club, front parlor, betting office, debating chamber, television lounge, or refuge from the family. It is not, by and large, a good "pickup" spot, but it's very nearly everything else.

There are some 5,000 to 6,000 pubs in metropolitan London, so our suggestions represent no more than a few random samplings. Perhaps you could try an exploration of your own, moving on to another establishment after one drink. If repeated at length, the process becomes a "pub crawl," possibly Britain's most popular national pastime.

Although our pub selections are fine for both women and men, choose other pubs with care. Some pubs are what the English call "downright grotty"—dirty, often tough drinking places that attract soccer-loving "lager louts." If you're well dressed, a safer bet would be a hotel bar or cocktail lounge.

What may astonish you is the profusion of international restaurants. London offers a fantastic array of Italian, Indian, Chinese, Thai, French, German, Swiss, Greek, Russian, Jewish, Scandinavian, Turkish, and Middle Eastern dineries, which probably outnumber the native establishments. You'll find them all represented in my list.

Once upon a time London had two traditional areas: Soho for Italian and Chinese fare, Mayfair and Belgravia for French cuisine.

Today the gastronomical legions have conquered the entire heart of the metropolis, and you're liable to find any type of eatery anywhere, from Chelsea to Hampstead. The majority of my selections are in the West End region, but only because this happens to be the handiest for visitors.

SOME DINING NOTES

HOURS Restaurants in London keep varied hours, but in general, lunch is offered from noon to 2pm and dinner is served from 7:30 to 9:30pm. Of course, many restaurants open earlier, and others stay open later. Sunday is the typical closing day for London restaurants, but there are many exceptions to that rule.

RESERVATIONS Nearly all places, except pubs, cafeterias, and fast-food places (often chain-run), prefer or require reservations. Almost invariably, you get a better table if you book in advance. For a few of the really famous places, you might need to reserve a table weeks in advance, even before leaving home, and such reservations should always be confirmed when you land in London.

RATES All restaurants and cafés in Britain are required to display the prices of the food and drink they offer, in a place visible from outside the establishment. Charges for service, as well as any minimum charge or cover charge, must also be made clear. The prices shown must include $17^1/_2$% VAT. Most of the restaurants add a 10% to 15% service charge to your bill, but you'll have to check to make sure of that. If nothing has been added to your bill, leave a 12% to 15% tip.

PRICE CATEGORIES In this guide restaurants that serve dinner for one without wine that costs roughly £45 ($71.10) and up are listed as very expensive. Those charging about £35 to £45 ($55.30 to $71.10) are grouped as expensive; those charging about £15 to £35 ($23.70 to $55.30) as moderate; those charging less than about £15 ($23.70) as inexpensive.

1 Best Bets

BEST STEAK, KIDNEY & OYSTER PIE   Oak Room *(see page 116)* Some pubs serve a horrid version of this dish—one that even Boswell and Johnson would have turned down—but chef Allen Macheral has adapted this classical dish and made it sublime. It's made *à la française* with braised beef cheeks, kidneys, and oysters topped with puff pastry.

BEST BURGER IN TOWN   Hard Rock Café *(see page 122)* Although such an authority as Linda McCartney (Paul's wife, of course) has approved of this café's veggie dishes, most rockers show up for the juicy burgers. If you wish, you can still get them medium rare here. Burgers arrive in a fresh sesame bun with a heap of fries and a salad with such Yankee favorites as Thousand Island or honey mustard. Compare this offering to that served at the highly touted Planet Hollywood, 13 Coventry St., W1, where my burger arrived all pink and watery inside.

BEST JAPANESE RESTAURANT   Suntory *(see page 124)* It's still the most famous and still outclasses the vast array of imitators that have arrived on the scene. One culinary preparation tells it all. Chefs gently "stroke" the fish for any irregularities or bruises; if any are found, the fish is discarded. How many kitchens would do that?

BEST BRITISH CUISINE   Wiltons *(see page 125)* As one reviewer put it, this restaurant has "offered a trough for the toffs since the 18th century." Even the royal family has come here to feast on its renowned poached turbot; those English savouries such as angels on horseback (oysters with bacon); whitebait; gull's eggs; and what is reputed to be London's finest game dishes, including grouse and widgeon.

BEST CONTINENTAL CUISINE   Le Gavroche *(see page 115)* This restaurant was the forerunner of the modern French approach to cuisine in London, or Britain for that matter. The creation of the Roux brothers, the restaurant has lost none of its appeal over the years. If you want to know why, order pigeonneau de Bresse en vessie aux deux celeris. Enclosed in a pig's bladder, the whole bird is presented at your table. Skillfully opened, the pigeon is then carved and served on a bed of braised fennel and celery.

BEST AFTER-THEATER CHOICE   The Ivy *(see page 132)* Popular for both pre- and *après*-theater dining, this traditional restaurant is opposite the Ambassador Theatre. The brasserie-type food reflects both English and modern continental influences. You can try longtime favorites such as potted shrimp, tripe and onions, steak frites, or else some more imaginative dishes such as butternut pumpkin salad or a wild mushroom risotto.

BEST AMERICAN CUISINE   Joe Allen's   *(see page 140)* Like a private club, this place has only a small brass plaque indicating its entrance, the food here is familiar: Maryland crab cakes, spinach salad, burgers, black bean soup, barbecue ribs, chili, Caesar salad, and that famous pecan pie. On our last visit, we spotted movie legend Lauren Bacall digging into a sirloin steak (rare) with sautéed red onions and steak frites—just like she used to cook for Bogie.

BEST ENGLISH ROAST BEEF   Simpson's-in-the-Strand   *(see page 140)* It may not be good for your health but roast Scottish beef (they call it "Scotch" here) with Yorkshire pudding is the single most famous English dish served in the old days of the Empire. A time-honored custom since Henry VIII, this dish is the traditional Sunday lunch in Britain. Simpson's serves it all week and it's a robust affair. Chefs circulate throughout the dining room pushing silver carving wagons, ever ready to cut your choice—rare, medium, or (God forbid) well done.

BEST ATMOSPHERIC PUB   Grenadier   *(see page 154)* The Duke of Wellington's officers on leave from fighting Napoléon downed many a pint of lager here. Complete with a ghost, allegedly that of an officer flogged to death for cheating at cards, the pub is also a very British restaurant. Bloody Marys are a tradition here on Sundays.

BEST INDIAN CUISINE   Bombay Brasserie   *(see page 163)* Offering dishes from throughout the subcontinent, this cosmopolitan restaurant tempts with every dish—some fiery hot—ranging from Tandoori kitchens to the best of Punjabi fare. Even Goan cuisine is featured. Raj pictures and paddle fans evoke the old days of the British Empire, making it the most glamourous Indian restaurant in London. Try the mango Bellini to get you going on the road to Bombay.

BEST FOR AFTERNOON TEA   Palm Court   *(see page 140)* in the Waldorf Hotel. While everyone else is donning their fancy hats and fine apparel and heading for the Ritz for tea (where, chances are, they won't be able to get a table), you should retreat to this grand 1908 hotel. Sunday tea dances here at the heart of the hotel are legendary. Originating with the famous "Tango Teas" of the '20s and '30s, they've been going strong ever since, interrupted by war and a few other inconveniences.

BEST ENGLISH BREAKFAST   Fox and Anchor   *(see page 145)* After the "full house" breakfast at this longtime favorite Smithfield market pub (EC1), you won't be able to eat until the following morning. It's known for attracting early morning pub crawlers who fancy a pint to get them going for the day. One local called the array of breakfast goodies here "gut-busting"—everything from black pudding to fried bread and baked beans.

BEST PICNIC FARE   If you'd like to do what the queen of England, herself, might do if she were inviting guests for a picnic, go to **Fortnum & Mason**, 181 Piccadilly, W1 (☎ 0171/734-8040; tube:

Piccadilly Circus or Green Park). Here at the world's most famous grocery store, you'll find a wide array of foodstuffs to take away to your favorite park. See "Parks/Gardens" in Chapter 6 to decide where you'd like to enjoy your repast.

2 Restaurants by Cuisine

AFTERNOON TEA
Brown's Hotel (Mayfair)
Oak Room Lounge (Mayfair)
Palm Court (Covent Garden)
Palm Court Lounge (Mayfair)
Ritz Palm Court (Mayfair)

AMERICAN
Chicago Pizza Factory
  (Mayfair, I)
Christopher's (Covent
  Garden, M)
Hard Rock Café (Mayfair, I)
Joe Allen's (The Strand, M)

FOR BREAKFAST
Fox and Anchor (Barbican)

BRITISH
Alastair Little (Soho, M)
Antelope (Belgravia, P)
Bill Bentley's (Knightsbridge,
  P)
Bow Wine Vaults (The City,
  WB)
Boaters Wine Bar (Chelsea
  Harbour, WB)
Bracewells (Mayfair, M)
Bubbles (St. James's, VE)
Butler's Wharf Chop House
  (Away from the Center:
  Butler's Wharf, M)
Chapter 11 (West Brompton, I)
Cheshire Cheese (Fleet Street, P)
Cittie of Yorke (Holborn, P)
Clarke's (Notting Hill, E)
Daniel's Bar (Cafe Royal Grill)
  (Piccadilly, WB)
Dickens Inn by the Tower
  (Away from the Center:
  St. Katharine's Dock, I)
English Garden (Chelsea, M)
English House (Chelsea, M)

Georgian Restaurant
  (Knightsbridge, M)
Gilbert's (South Kensington, M)
Grenadier (Belgravia, P)
Fifth Floor at Harvey Nichols
  (Knightsbridge, M)
Fox and Anchor (Barbican, BF)
Ivy, The (Soho, M)
Jamaica Wine House, The
  (The City, WB)
Hispanola, The (On the
  Harbor, I)
King's Head and Eight Bells
  (Chelsea, P)
Langan's Bistro (St. Marylebone,
  I)
Langan's Brasserie (Mayfair, M)
Launceston Place (Kensington, M)
Lindsay House (Soho, M)
Museum Street Cafe
  (Bloomsbury, M)
Museum Tavern (Bloomsbury, P)
Nag's Head (Belgravia, P)
Nag's Head (Covent Garden, P)
Old Coffee House (Soho, P)
Olde Wine Shades (The City,
  WB)
Porter's English Restaurant
  (Covent Garden, I)
Red Lion (St. James's)
Rules (Covent Garden, M)
Salisbury (Leicester Square, WB)
Shampers (St. James's)
Sherlock Holmes (Trafalgar
  Square, P)
Shepherd's (Westminster, M)
Shepherd's Tavern (Mayfair, I)
Simpson's-in-the-Strand (The
  Strand, M)
Star Tavern (Belgravia, P)
Tate Gallery Restaurant
  (Westminster, M)

Veronica's (Bayswater, I)
Wiltons (Piccadilly, E)
Ye Olde Watling (The City, P)
Ye Olde Cock Tavern (Fleet
  Street, P)

CHINESE

Chuen Cheng Ku (Soho, I)
Ken Lo's Memories of China
  (Chelsea Harbour, M)
Ken Lo's Memories of China
  (Victoria, M)
Poons in the City (The City, M)

FRENCH

Arcadia (Kensington, M)
Aubergine (Chelsea, E)
Au Jardin des Gourmets
  (Soho, M)
Bibendum/The Oyster Bar
  (South Kensington, E)
Brasserie on the Park
  (Mayfair, I)
Chelsea Room (Chelsea, M)
Chez Nico at Ninety Park Lane
  (Mayfair, VE)
Gavroche, Le (Mayfair, VE)
Gilbert's (South Kensington, M)
Hilaire (South Kensington, M)
Hispanola, The (On the Harbor,
  I)
Kemps (South Kensington, M)
Langan's Bistro (Marylebone, I)
Langan's Brasserie (Mayfair, M)
Nico Central (Fitzrovia, M)
Oak Room (Mayfair, E)
Pelican (Leicester Square, I)
Saveurs, Les (Mayfair, E)
Simply Nico (Victoria, M)
St. Quentin (South
  Kensington, M)
Tante Claire, La (Chelsea, VE)

HUNGARIAN

Gay Hussar (Soho, M)

INDIAN

Bombay Brasserie (South
  Kensington, M)

Gaylord International India
  Restaurant (Mayfair, M)
Veeraswamy (Mayfair, M)

INTERNATIONAL

Bistro Bruno (Soho, M)
Bubbles (St. James's, VE)
Canteen (Chelsea Harbour, I)
Cork & Bottle Wine Bar
  (Leicester Square, WB)
Deal's Restaurant and Diner
  (Chelsea Harbour, I)
Ebury Wine Bar (Victoria, WB)
Front Page (Chelsea, P)
Joe's (Kensington, M)
Metro, Le (Knightsbridge, WB)
Odin's (Marylebone, M)
Pavilion Restaurant (South
  Kensington, M)
Pelican (Leicester Square, I)
Pied-à-Terre (Fitzrovia, M)
Pont de la Tour, Le (Away from
  the Center: Butlers Wharf, E)
Room at the Halcyon, The
  (Holland Park, M)
Quaglino's (Mayfair, M)
Turner's (Kensington, E)
Waltons of Walton Street
  (South Kensington, E)

ITALIAN

Neal Street Restaurant (Covent
  Garden, M)
Room at the Halcyon, The
  (Holland Park, M)
San Lorenzo (Knightsbridge, M)

JAPANESE

Suntory (St. James's, VE)

LEBANESE

Phoenicia (Kensington, I)

MEDITERRANEAN

Bibendum/The Oyster Bar
  (South Kensington, E)
Bistro 190 (South Kensington,
  M)

PAKISTANI/MUGHLAI

Salloos (Belgravia, M)

PERSIAN

Persepolis (Kensington, I)

PUBS/WINE BARS

Antelope (Belgravia)
Bill Bentley's (Knightsbridge)
Boaters Wine Bar (Chelsea
  Harbour)
Bow Wine Vaults (The City)
Bubbles (St. James's)
Cheshire Cheese (Fleet Street)
Cittie of York (Holborn)
Cork & Bottle Wine Bar
  (Leicester Square)
Daniel's Bar (Piccadilly)
Ebury Wine Bar (Victoria)
Front Page (Chelsea)
Grenadier (Belgravia)
Jamaica Wine House, The
  (The City)
King's Head and Eight Bells
  (Chelsea)
Metro, Le (Knightsbridge)
Museum Tavern (Bloomsbury)
Nag's Head (Belgravia)
Nag's Head (Covent Garden)

Old Coffee House (Soho)
Olde Wine Shades (The City)
Red Lion (St. James's)
Salisbury (Leicester Square)
Shampers (St. James's)
Sherlock Holmes (Trafalgar
  Square)
Shepherd's Tavern (Mayfair)
Star Tavern (Belgravia)
Ye Olde Cock Tavern (Fleet
  Street)
Ye Olde Watling (The City)

SEAFOOD

Greens Restaurant and Oyster
  Bar (Piccadilly, M)
Scotts (Mayfair, M)
Sheekeys (Leicester Square,
  M)

SWEDISH

Garbo's (Marylebone, I)

THAI

Blue Elephant (West Brompton,
  M)

3 Mayfair & St. James's

MAYFAIR
VERY EXPENSIVE

✪ Chez Nico at Ninety Park Lane

90 Park Lane, W1. ☎ **0171/409-1290** Reservations required (2 days in advance for lunch, 10 days for dinner). Fixed-price lunch £25 ($39.50) for three courses; à la carte £48 ($75.85) for two courses, £57 ($90.05) for three courses. AE, DC, MC, V. Lunch Mon–Fri noon–2pm; dinner Mon–Sat 7–11pm. Closed 10 days around Christmas/New Year's. Tube: Marble Arch. FRENCH.

No great restaurant of London has changed locations as often as this one, but dedicated habitués from around the world continue to seek out chef Nico Ladenis, wherever he cooks. Now in Grosvenor House, more impressive and stylish than ever before, chef Nico remains one of the most talked about chefs of Great Britain—the only one who is a former oil company executive, an economist, and a self-taught cook.

As befits any three-star Michelin restaurant, dinners are memorable in the very best gastronomic tradition of "post nouvelle cuisine," in which the tenets of classical cuisine are creatively and flexibly adapted to local fresh ingredients.

The menu, written in English, changes frequently, following the inspiration of Mr. Ladenis. Specialties include a warm salad of foie gras on toasted brioche with caramelized orange, char-grilled sea bass with a basil purée, filet of Scottish beef with truffles and foie gras, or Bresse pigeon. Desserts are sumptuous.

✪ Le Gavroche

43 Upper Brook St., W1. ☎ **0171/408-0881** Reservations required. Appetizers £12.50–£30 ($19.75–$47.40); main courses £12.60–£63 ($19.90–$99.55); fixed-price lunch £37 ($58.45); fixed-price dinner £55 ($86.90). AE, DC, MC, V. Lunch Mon–Fri noon–2pm; dinner Mon–Fri 7–11pm. Tube: Marble Arch. FRENCH.

Le Gavroche has long been at the apogee of London's grand French restaurants. It's the creation of two Burgundy-born brothers, Michel and Albert Roux. Michel, son of Albert, is the chef today and he's truly followed in his father's footsteps. He has changed the menu to reflect his own imaginative and personal style, but "in deference to my father," he continues with the signature dishes. Service is faultless, the ambience chic and formal without being stuffy.

Their wine cellar is among the most interesting in London, with many quality Burgundies and Bordeaux. While you wait, you can enjoy an apéritif upstairs as you peruse the menu and enjoy the delectable canapés. Dishes are always changing, but specialties include rabbit with herb risotto, papillotte of smoked salmon, and tournedos gratiné aux poivres. You might begin with scallops perfumed with ginger or a mousseline of lobster with champagne. A duck pot-au-feu is served for two. Desserts, usually called sublime by diners, range from a sablé of pears and chocolate to an omelette Rothschild. Most main courses are served on silver trays covered with domes, which are lifted with great flourish.

EXPENSIVE

Les Saveurs

37A Curzon St., W1. ☎ **0171/491-8919.** Reservations required. Set-price lunch £22.50–f42 ($35.55–$66.35); set-price dinner £36–£42 ($56.90–$66.35). AE, DC, MC, V. Lunch Mon–Fri noon–2:15pm; dinner Mon–Fri 7–10:15pm. Tube: Green Park. FRENCH.

This restaurant upholds a rigorous set of French standards for a clientele of business directors and residents of its surrounding upscale neighborhood. The dining room is paneled almost entirely in maple; the staff, perfectly trained. Dishes change with the seasons, but are likely to include a terrine of foie gras with eggplant; filet of sea bass with a *salmis* sauce (derived from liver and fish); a *pastilla* of sea bass served with semolina and cardamom-flavored butter; oysters in aspic with horseradish cream; deliberately undercooked breast of pigeon served on a bed of herb-infused couscous with chanterelles; and red mullet on a bed of cubed and creamed celeriac. All these dishes are the creation of Joël Antunès, one of the hot new chefs of London today. He's cooked with the masters: Bocuse, Robuchon, and Troisgros. The savvy diner leaves room for one of the chef's delicately flavored soufflés, such as the lime soufflé flavored with acacia honey, a sublime choice. One restaurant reviewer called the fixed-price menus "the great haute cuisine bargains" of London.

Restaurants: Mayfair, St. James's & Piccadill

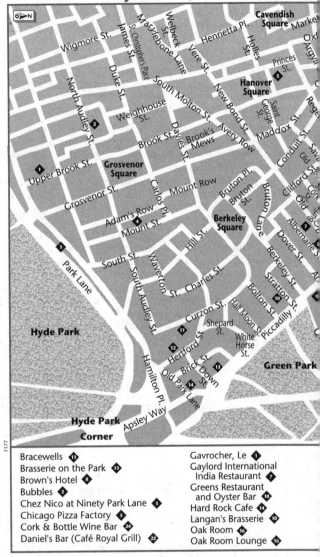

Bracewells 🔸⑮
Brasserie on the Park 🔸⑲
Brown's Hotel 🔸⑧
Bubbles 🔸②
Chez Nico at Ninety Park Lane 🔸③
Chicago Pizza Factory 🔸⑤
Cork & Bottle Wine Bar 🔸㉔
Daniel's Bar (Café Royal Grill) 🔸㉓

Gavrocher, Le 🔸①
Gaylord International
  India Restaurant 🔸⑦
Greens Restaurant
  and Oyster Bar 🔸⑱
Hard Rock Cafe 🔸⑭
Langan's Brasserie 🔸⑩
Oak Room 🔸⑯
Oak Room Lounge 🔸⑯

✪ Oak Room

In Le Méridien Piccadilly, 21 Piccadilly, W1. ☎ **0171/734-8000.** Reservations required. Appetizers £12–£16 ($18.95–$25.30); main courses £22–£39 ($34.75–$61.60); set business lunch £24.50 ($38.70); "menu gourmand" £46 ($72.70). AE, DC, MC, V. Lunch Mon–Fri noon–2:30pm; dinner Mon–Sat 7–10:30pm. Tube: Piccadilly Circus. FRENCH.

The Oak Room, one of the city's finest restaurants, has received numerous culinary awards. The setting alone—said to be the most beautiful dining room in the center of London—is worth the trip.

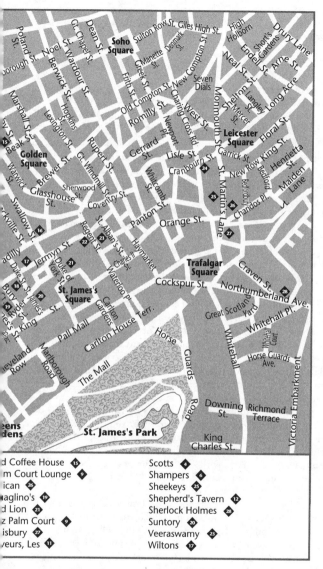

Lavish in its appointments, this grand yet warm and inviting period room has been restored to all its gilded splendor, including the ceiling and the original oak paneling. It's no wonder that luminaries continue to dine here.

The decor notwithstanding, the main draw here is the refined cuisine. The menu is the creation of French consultant chef Michel Lorain and resident executive chef Allen Macheral. You can select from "Cuisine Creative" or "Cuisine Traditionelle" menus, enjoying such dishes as terrine of poached oysters with a confit of shallots cooked in red wine or cold lasagne of crabmeat with a pumpkin and horseradish cream.

MODERATE

✪ Bracewells

In the Park Lane Hotel, Piccadilly, W1. ☎ **0171/499-6321.** Reservations required. Appetizers £6–£12 ($9.50–$18.95); main courses £14–£23 ($22.10–$36.35); three-course set lunch menu £19.50 ($30.80). AE, DC, MC, V. Lunch Mon–Fri 12:30–2:30pm; dinner Mon–Sat 7–10:30pm. Tube: Hyde Park Corner or Green Park. BRITISH.

Sheltered by the thick fortresslike walls of this previously recommended hotel, Bracewells is fast becoming one of London's most popular and award-winning restaurants for truly classic British fare. The cuisine, prepared by the highly acclaimed British-born Andrew Bennett, is among the best in the capital, and the decor and the five-star service are worthy of its distinguished clientele. Amid the gilded torchères and comfortable armchairs of Bracewells Bar, you might begin with a drink and canapés of lobster, foie gras, and caviar in the evening. Later, you will be ushered into an intimately illuminated room, whose Louis XVI paneling was long ago removed from the London home of the American banker and philanthropist Pierpont Morgan.

The specialties are made with the freshest ingredients. Throughout the year, the menu features an array of such dishes as smoked duck and preserved chicken served with apples, or Dublin Bay prawns and asparagus salad with a roast vegetable purée. In addition to traditional grills, such as liver and bacon, dishes prepared at your table include saddle of hare Doivrade (two courses). Fish dishes featured are lobster with noodles and winter vegetables, and the meat choice might include roast partridge with savoy cabbage and duck liver. A baked artichoke and goat cheese soufflé is one of several vegetarian dishes. Linger over the array of offerings on the dessert trolley or you can always opt for fruit salad that includes an abundance of exotic fruits. It is also reassuring to see traditional hot "puddings" on the menu, including hot cabinet pudding scented with kirsch. An impressive selection of British cheeses ranges from your classic Stilton from Nottinghamshire to a Cerney Ash from Gloucestershire.

The table d'hôte represents good value. It may, for instance, feature starters such as crackington clam pasta followed by braised oxtail and a selection of both hot desserts and those off the trolley. An intelligent selection of wines is recommended to accompany the menu, each of which is available by the glass. The full wine list is a good reflection on the vastness of the hotel's cellars. The sommelier is most helpful.

Gaylord International India Restaurant

16 Albemarle St., W1. ☎ **0171/629-9802.** Reservations not required. Appetizers £7–£11 ($11.05–$17.40); main courses £8.25–£10.95 ($13.05–$17.30); dinner with meat £18.95 ($29.95); vegetarian fixed-price lunch or dinner £16.95 ($26.80). AE, DC, MC, V. Lunch daily noon–3pm; dinner Mon–Sat 6–11pm. Tube: Green Park. INDIAN.

Actually, London has two Gaylords, but this is the newer one. Offering a dazzling variety of several regional cooking styles, this Gaylord has established an enviable reputation among local connoisseurs of Indian cuisine. You can feast on Kashmiri and Mughlai as well as the usual tandoori delicacies. To sample this variety, it's best to order as many of the smaller dishes as you can, so go with friends. Try the *keema nan* (leavened bread stuffed with delicately flavored minced meat) and certainly the spiced vegetable pastries known as samosas. For a main course, you might choose *goshtaba* (lamb balls cooked in cream and cardamom) or *murg musallam* (diced chicken sautéed herbs, onions, and tomatoes). If you don't like curry, the staff will help you select a meal of any size totally devoid of that spice, but flavored with a great many others. You'll find the manager helpful in guiding you through the less familiar Kashmiri dishes.

Langan's Brasserie

Stratton St. (without number), W1. ☎ **0171/493-6437.** Reservations recommended. Appetizers £2.95–£8.50 ($4.65–$13.45); main courses £9.50–£13.95 ($15–$22.05). AE, DC, MC, V. Lunch Mon–Fri 12:15–2:45pm; dinner Mon–Fri 7–11:30pm, Sat 8pm–12:45am. Tube: Green Park. FRENCH/BRITISH.

Since its heyday in the early 1980s, when it was among the most hip restaurants in London, this upscale brasserie has welcomed an average of 700 diners a day. The 1976 brainchild of the late restaurateur Peter Langan, in partnership with actor Michael Caine and chef de cuisine Richard Shepherd, it was the first of at least four other restaurants launched by these entrepreneurs. The restaurant sprawls over two noisy, very see-and-be-seen floors, each filled with potted plants and spinning ceiling fans that create a 1930s kind of continental atmosphere. The menu is defined as "mostly French with a dash of English," and includes a spinach soufflé with anchovy sauce, salad of oyster mushrooms, croustade of quail eggs in a pastry case served with a duxelle of mushrooms and hollandaise sauce, Langan's seafood salad, baked filet of sea bass with walnut oil dressing, and roast crispy duck with applesauce and sage-lemon stuffing. In addition, the menu always features a small, bemused selection of English food prepared as the English would, including sausages with mashed potatoes ("bangers and mash") with a white onion sauce.

Quaglino's

16 Bury St., SW1. ☎ **0171/930-6767.** Reservations recommended. Appetizers £4.95–£9.95 ($7.80–$15.70); main courses £8.95–£22.50 ($14.15–$35.55); set-price three-course menu (available only at lunch and for dinner between 5:30 and 6:30pm.) £12.95 ($20.45). AE, DC, MC, V. Lunch daily noon–3pm; dinner daily 5:30pm–midnight (last order; till 1am Fri–Sat). Tube: Green Park. INTERNATIONAL.

It's vast, it's convivial, it's fun, and it was voted best restaurant of the year (1994) by London's *Time Out* magazine. It occupies the premises of a restaurant originally established in 1929 by Giovanni Quaglino from Italy's Piedmont district. Personalities who paraded through these premises in ermine and pearls could fill a between-the-wars roster of Who's Who for virtually every country of Europe.

On Valentine's Day of 1993, Sir Terence Conran, noted restaurateur and industrialist, brought the place into the postmodern age with a vital new decor. It's been likened to a stylishly decorated rail-station waiting room. Eight artists were commissioned to decorate the octet of massive columns supporting the soaring ceiling. My favorite is the one inspired by the music of The Moody Blues; my least favorite, the one outfitted in a mélange of smoldering grays. A mezzanine with a bar features live jazz every Friday and Saturday nights, and an "altar" at the restaurant's back is devoted to what might be the most impressive display of crustaceans and shellfish in Britain.

Everything seems to be served in bowls. Menu items have been criticized for their quick preparation and standardized format—not as marvelously subtle as what you might expect in more manageably sized eateries. But considering that on some nights up to 800 people might show up here for food, laughter, and gossip, the marvel is that the place functions as well as it does. Come for fun, not for culinary finesse. And consider that the portions are huge, and the *plateau des fruits de mer*, the most expensive dish on the menu—priced at £22.50 ($35.55) per person, with an £11 ($17.40) supplement if you want it garnished with lobster—is worth writing home about. Other choices include chicken soup with cannellini and bacon; parfait of chicken livers; foie gras; tartlet of crab with saffron; seared salmon with potato pancakes; and grilled rabbit with herb jus, pancetta, and char-grilled vegetables. There's a short list of reasonably priced wines, as well as a much longer and more sophisticated list made available if you ask for it.

Scotts

20 Mount St., W1. ☎ **0171/629-5248.** Reservations required. Appetizers £3.25–£9.50 ($5.15–$15); main courses £8.50–£27.55 ($13.45–$43.55); fixed-price two-course lunch or dinner £15 ($23.70); fixed-price three-course lunch or dinner £18.50 ($29.25). AE, DC, MC, V. Lunch Mon–Fri noon–2:45pm; dinner Mon–Sat 6–10:45pm. Tube: Green Park. SEAFOOD.

In addition to its spacious dining room and cocktail bar, Scotts has a widely noted oyster, lobster, and caviar bar. Its origins were humble, dating back to a fishmonger's in Coventry Street in 1851. However, its fame rests on its heyday, when the proprietors often entertained Edward VII and his guests in private dining rooms. Scotts has been at its present location since 1967, enjoying a chic address in the neighborhood of the swank Connaught Hotel and Berkeley Square.

Its chef, who believes in British produce, handles the kitchen with consummate skill and authority. You get top-notch quality and ingredients. Lobster, crab, and oysters are featured along with grilled English red mullets with ginger, garlic, and fresh tomato. Dover sole is prepared a variety of ways, although the English prefer it "on the bone," considering filleted fish food for sissies. Starters include home-spiced beef with poached leek salad and mustard dressing, oak-smoked salmon with brown soda bread, and a fish soup sporting chunks of Atlantic fish and shellfish served in their own stock. More down-to-earth dishes, such as fish cakes, appear regularly on the luncheon menu.

Veeraswamy

99–101 Regent St., W1. ☎ **0171/734-1401.** Reservations recommended. Appetizers £3–£6.95 ($4.75–$11); main courses £10.50–£16.50 ($16.60–$26.05); lunch buffet £12.95 ($20.45); set menu £20.95–£28.95 ($33.10 –$45.75). AE, DC, MC, V.

Lunch Mon–Sat noon–2:30pm; dinner Mon–Sat 6–11:30pm. Tube: Piccadilly Circus. INDIAN.

When it was established in 1927 as the first Indian restaurant in Europe, Veeraswamy attracted every socialite in London with its exotic cuisine. Founder Edward Palmer, who made a fortune trading spices, was born in 1860 in India. Beautifully refurbished in the mid-1980s, it is still one of London's leading choices for Indian cuisine.

In the kitchen, each chef specializes in a particular region of the subcontinent. Whether from Gujarat or Goa (try the fiery coconut-flavored chicken), the cuisine is often mouth-tingling. Vegetarians appreciate the thalis, the home-baked breads, and the array of well-seasoned vegetables that some diners order in combinations as a meal. The Regent Street business crowd usually opts for the all-you-can-eat lunchtime buffet, while the evening crowd opts for pre- or posttheater dinners.

INEXPENSIVE

Brasserie on the Park

In the Park Lane Hotel, Piccadilly, W1. ☎ **0171/499-6321**. Reservations recommended. Appetizers £3.50–£7 ($5.55–$11.05); main courses £4.50–£14.50 ($7.10–$22.90); fixed-price menu £10.95 ($17.30) for two courses. AE, DC, MC, V. Lunch Mon–Fri noon–3pm; dinner Mon–Fri 6–11pm; Sat–Sun and public holidays noon–11pm. Tube: Hyde Park Corner or Green Park. FRENCH.

The Brasserie on the Park in the Park Lane Hotel is bright and breezy, decorated in art deco style to match the hotel's famous ballroom. The menu is unapologetically French and includes a menu du jour that easily equals the à la carte in terms of quality and quantity.

The standard menu features appetizers such as a salad of duck confit, green lentils, lardons of bacon and onions, or oysters served on crushed ice. The main courses feature classic brasserie dishes such as a choice of omelets to more exotic dishes such as poached brill with seaweed, eggplant confit and saffron potatoes, or beef cooked in a broth of winter vegetables and bone marrow. The special fixed-price menu changes twice weekly (for instance, dishes may include a starter of fish parfait with crabmeat followed by roast wild duck with lemon and honey). Popular dishes include such favorites as wild mushroom and herb risotto or tender rump or sirloin steaks. The Brasserie has also introduced the idea of offering a choice of wines, available by the glass, that have been carefully selected to "marry" with your food. During the year the Brasserie frequently holds special festivals of foods and wines from different regions of France—Alsace, Provence, or Bordeaux, for example.

⊘ Chicago Pizza Factory

17 Hanover Sq., W1. ☎ **0171/629-2669**. Reservations recommended for lunch. Appetizers £1.75–£3.10 ($2.75–$4.90); main courses £5.25–£12 ($8.30–$18.95); pizza for two £8.95–£11.50 ($14.15–$18.15). AE, MC, V. Mon–Sat 11:45am–11:30pm. Sun noon–10:30pm. Tube: Oxford Circus. AMERICAN.

This restaurant was introduced to London by former advertising executive Bob Payton, an ex-Chicagoan, and is one of the few establishments that provides doggy bags. The 275-seat restaurant is full of authentic Chicago memorabilia, and the waitresses wear *Chicago Sun-Times* newspaper-sellers' aprons. There is a large bar with a wide choice of U.S. beers and cocktails, including a specialty known as St. Valentine's Day Massacre. A television over the bar shows American baseball, football, and basketball games.

The specialty here is deep-dish pizza with toppings in all possible combinations. The regular-size pizza is enough for two or three, and the large one is suitable for four or five. The menu also includes stuffed mushrooms, garlic bread, salads, and homemade cheesecakes. Dress is casual.

Hard Rock Café

150 Old Park Lane, W1. ☎ **0171/629-0382.** Reservations not accepted. Appetizers £2.45–£5.25 ($3.85–$8.30); main courses £5.55–£13.95 ($8.75–$22.05). AE, MC, V. Sun–Thurs 11:30am–12:30am, Fri–Sat 11:30am–1am. Tube: Green Park or Hyde Park Corner. AMERICAN.

This is a southern-cum-midwestern American roadside diner with good food, taped music, and service with a smile. It was established on June 14, 1971, and since then more than 12 million people have eaten here. Almost every night there's a line waiting: young people, visiting rock and film stars, and tennis players from America. The portions are generous, and the price of a main dish includes not only a salad but also fries or baked potatoes. Specialties include smokehouse steak, filet mignon, and a T-bone special, along with charbroiled burgers and hot chili. The equally tempting dessert menu lists homemade apple pie and thick shakes. There's also a good selection of beer.

A PUB

Shepherd's Tavern

50 Hertford St., W1. ☎ **0171/499-3017.** Reservations recommended. Appetizers £3.25–£4.25 ($5.15–$6.70); main courses £6.95–£10.95 ($11–$17.30). AE, DC, MC, V. Restaurant lunch daily noon–3pm; dinner Mon–Sat 6–10pm, Sun 7–10:30pm. Bar Mon–Sat 11am–11pm; Sun noon–3pm and 7–10:30pm. Tube: Green Park. BRITISH.

Set amid a warren of narrow, cobble-covered streets behind Park Lane, an 18th-century town house very similar to many of its neighbors, this pub is one of the focal points of the all-pedestrian shopping zone of Shepherd's Market. The bar on the street level is cramped but congenial. There are many luxurious touches, including a collection of memorabilia and antique furniture, chief among which is a sedan chair that once belonged to the son of George III, the duke of Cumberland. Many of the regular habitués recall this tavern's popularity with the pilots of the Battle of Britain. Bar snacks include simple platters of shepherd's pie and fish pie with vegetables. More formal dining is available upstairs in the cozy, Georgian-style restaurant whose walls are lined with cedar. Menu choices include such classic British dishes as roast beef with Yorkshire pudding, steak-and-kidney pie, and Oxford ham.

You can visit just for drinks, of course, with lager prices beginning at £1.98 ($3.15) and wine by the glass at £2.05 ($3.25).

FOR AFTERNOON TEA

Brown's Hotel

30–34 Albemarle St., W1. ☎ **0171/493-6020.** Reservations not accepted. Afternoon tea £14.95 ($23.60). AE, DC, MC, V. Daily 3–6pm. Tube: Green Park.

Ranking along with the Ritz Hotel as a chic venue for tea in London, Brown's Hotel offers afternoon tea in its drawing room. The room is decorated with English antiques, wall panels, oil paintings, and floral chintz, much like one in a private English country estate. Give your name to the concierge upon arrival. Arrangements will be made for you to be seated on clusters of sofas and settees or at low tables. Afternoon tea includes a choice of 10 teas, sandwiches, and pastries that are rolled around on a trolley for your selection. Scones with jam and clotted cream are also included. All cakes and pastries are made in the hotel kitchens.

Oak Room Lounge

In Le Méridien, 21 Piccadilly, W1. ☎ **0171/734-8000.** Reservations recommended. Average tea from £13.50 ($21.35). AE, DC, MC, V. Daily 3–6pm. Tube: Piccadilly Circus or Green Park.

Restored to its former Edwardian glory, the Oak Room Lounge welcomes nonresidents for the very British tradition of afternoon tea. The soothing elegance of this formal but unstuffy oak-paneled room is augmented by comfortable armchairs and background music by a resident harpist. A complete tea includes a selection of sandwiches and tarts. The menu lists a tempting array of exotic teas, some you may never have tried.

Palm Court Lounge

In the Park Lane Hotel, Piccadilly, W1. ☎ **0171/499-6321.** Reservations not required. Devon cream tea £6.75 ($10.65); afternoon tea £11.25 ($17.80); club sandwich £8.20 ($13). AE, DC, MC, V. Daily 24 hours. Tube: Hyde Park Corner or Green Park.

One of the great favorites of London for tea, it has an atmosphere straight from 1927. Restored to its former charm by John Siddeley, one of the world's leading interior designers, the lounge has a domed yellow-and-white-glass ceiling, torchères, and palms in Compton stoneware jardinières. A delightful afternoon tea of three scones, Devonshire cream and thick jam, sandwiches, a selection of cakes and a long list of different teas is served daily. Many guests come here after the theater for a sandwich and drink, since hot food is served 24 hours a day. During the week a pianist plays every afternoon and evening with a trio that plays '20s music every Sunday afternoon.

✪ Ritz Palm Court

In the Ritz Hotel, Piccadilly (without number), W1. ☎ **0171/493-8181.** Reservations required at least 10 days in advance for weekdays and 8 weeks in advance for weekends. Afternoon tea £16.50 ($26.05). AE, DC, MC, V. Daily 2–6pm. Tube: Green Park.

This is the most fashionable place in London to order afternoon tea and perhaps the hardest to get into without reservations way in advance. With a setting strictly from the 1920s and 1930s, it would be the most appropriate venue for F. Scott Fitzgerald's Gatsby to entertain if he miraculously appeared in London. The atmosphere is one of marble steps and columns, along with a baroque fountain. You have your choice of the widest possible variety of teas, served with those delectable little sandwiches on white bread and luscious pastries. Gentlemen are encouraged to wear jackets and ties, and ladies are encouraged to wear hats. Jeans and sneakers are not acceptable.

ST. JAMES'S
VERY EXPENSIVE

Suntory

72–73 St. James's St., SW1. ☎ **0171/409-0201.** Reservations required. Appetizers £4.70–£15.20 ($7.45–$24); main courses £15–£30 ($23.70–$47.40); set lunch £15–£45 ($23.70–$71.10); fixed-price dinner £49.80–£90 ($78.70–$142.20). AE, DC, MC, V. Lunch Mon–Sat noon–2pm; dinner Mon–Sat 6–10pm. Tube: Green Park. JAPANESE.

Suntory is the most elite, expensive, and best Japanese restaurant in London. Owned and operated by Japanese distillers and brewers, it offers a choice of dining rooms in a setting evocative of a Japanese manor house. First-time visitors seem to prefer the tappanyaki dining room downstairs, where iron grills are set on each table and you watch the mastery of the high-hatted, knife-wielding chef. You can also dine in other rooms on sukiyaki, tempura, and sushi (especially good is the fresh, delicately sliced raw tuna). You may prefer a salad of shellfish and seaweed or a superb squid. Appetizers are artful and delicate, and even the tea is superior. You can be seated in one of the private dining rooms, but only if you are shoeless. Waitresses in traditional dress serve you with all the highly refined ritualistic qualities of the Japanese, including the presentation of hot towels.

PUBS & WINE BARS

Bubbles

41 N. Audley St., W1. ☎ **0171/491-3237.** Reservations recommended. Appetizers £2.50–£3.25 ($3.95–$5.15); main courses £6–£12.50 ($9.50–$19.75); fixed-price dinner £14.50 ($22.90); fixed-price vegetarian menu £7 ($11.05); glass of wine £2 ($3.15). AE, DC, MC, V. Lunch daily noon–6pm; dinner daily 6–10pm. Tube: Marble Arch. BRITISH/INTERNATIONAL VEGETARIAN.

Bubbles is an interesting wine bar lying between Upper Brook Street and Oxford Street (in the vicinity of Selfridges). The owners attach equal importance to their food and to their impressive wine list. Some wine selections are sold by the glass. On the ground floor, guests enjoy not only the fine wines but also draft beer and liquor, along with a limited but well-chosen selection of bar food—mussels marinara and meat and fish salads, for example. Downstairs, an à la carte restaurant serves both English and continental dishes, including an appealing vegetarian selection. You might begin with French onion soup, followed by roast rack of English lamb, Dover sole, or roast duckling with lemon-and-tarragon sauce.

Red Lion

2 Duke of York St. (off Jermyn St.), SW1. ☎ **0171/930-2030.** Reservations not required. Sandwiches £2 ($3.15); fish-and-chips £6 ($9.50). No credit cards. Mon–Sat noon–11pm. Tube: Piccadilly Circus. BRITISH.

This little Victorian pub with its early-1900s decorations is one of London's few remaining gin palaces, with 150-year-old mirrors. Ian Nairn, a noted British writer on architecture, compared the pub's ambience to that of Edouard Manet's painting *A Bar at the Folies-Bergère.* (See the original at the Courtauld Institute galleries.) The menu is composed of a set number of premade sandwiches so once they are gone you're out of luck. The selection usually includes tuna and sweet corn, smoked salmon, and bacon, lettuce, and tomato. On Fridays and Saturdays homemade fish-and-chips is also served. The food is prepared in upstairs kitchens and sent down in a century-old dumbwaiter; orders are placed at the bar. Wash down your meal with Ind Coope's fine ales. The house's special beer is Burton's, an unusual brew made of spring water from the Midlands town of Burton-on-Trent.

Shampers

4 Kingly St., W1. ☎ **0171/437-1692.** Reservations recommended. Appetizers £3.25–£5.95 ($5.15–$9.40); main courses £8–£11.95 ($12.65–$18.90); glass of wine from £2.40 ($3.80). AE, DC, MC, V. Restaurant Mon–Fri noon–3pm; wine bar Mon–Fri 11am–11pm, Sat 11am–3pm. Closed Easter and Christmas. Tube: Oxford Circus. INTERNATIONAL.

For a number of years, this has been a favorite of West End wine-bar aficionados who gravitate to its location between Carnaby Street of 1960s fame and Regent Street of shoppers' fame. The basement is exclusively a restaurant, with the wine bar upstairs. In the restaurant you can order braised leg or breast of guinea fowl, and in the bar you can enjoy food as well. The restaurant is closed in the evening, but the bar serves an extended menu, incorporating not only the luncheon menu but also such dishes as grilled calves' liver, pheasant sausages, pan-fried tiger prawns with garlic and ginger, and free-range chicken served with a cream of Dijon mustard sauce. Salads are especially popular, including tuna and pasta with spicy tomato sauce and chicken with tarragon-cream dressing. A platter of Irish mussels cooked in a cream and tarragon sauce seems to be everyone's favorite.

4 Piccadilly, Leicester Square & Trafalgar Square

PICCADILLY

EXPENSIVE

Wiltons

55 Jermyn St., SW1. ☎ **0171/629-9955.** Reservations required. Appetizers £4.25–£24 ($6.70–$37.90); main courses £11.50–£28.50 ($18.15–$45.05). AE, DC, MC, V. Lunch daily 12:30–2:30pm; dinner Mon–Sat 6:30–10:30pm, Sun 6:30–10pm. Closed three weeks in Aug. Tube: Green Park or Piccadilly Circus. BRITISH.

Wiltons is one of the leading exponents of cookery called "as British as a nanny." In some form or other it has existed since the 18th century, although this version dates from 1941. In spite of its move to new quarters, the restaurant has retained the lush ambience of its original premises. You might be tempted to have an apéritif or a drink at the bar near the entrance, where photos of the royal family alternate with oil portraits of the original owners. One of them, the legendary Jimmy Marks, supposedly used to "strike terror into the hearts of newcomers if he took a dislike to them." However, those days, still fondly recalled by some, are gone forever, and today a wide array of international guests is warmly welcomed.

The thoroughly British menu of this restaurant is known for its fish and game, when in season. You might begin with an oyster cocktail and follow with Dover sole, plaice, salmon, or lobster, prepared in any number of ways. In season, you can choose among such delights as roast partridge, roast pheasant, roast grouse, and roast widgeon, a wild fish-eating river duck. The chef might ask you if you want it "blue" or "black," a reference to roasting times. Game is often accompanied by bread sauce (made of milk thickened with breadcrumbs). To finish, if you want something truly British, order a savory such as Welsh rarebit or soft roes, even anchovies. But if that's too much, try the sherry trifle or syllabub.

MODERATE

Greens Restaurant and Oyster Bar

36 Duke St., SW1. ☎ **0171/930-4566.** Reservations recommended for dinner. Appetizers £3.50–£10 ($5.55–$15.80); main courses £9–£18 ($14.20–$28.45). AE, DC, MC, V. Restaurant lunch daily 12:30–2:45pm; dinner Mon–Sat 6–11pm. Oyster bar lunch Mon–Sat 11:30am–3pm, Sun noon–3pm; dinner Mon–Sat 5:30–11pm. Tube: Piccadilly Circus or Green Park. SEAFOOD.

A busy place, this restaurant is a good choice because of its excellent menu, charming staff, and central location. A cluttered entrance leads to a crowded bar. If the tables are full, you can stand at what the English call "rat-catcher counters" to sip fine wines and (from September to May) enjoy oysters. Other foods include roast woodcock, king prawns, smoked Scottish salmon, "dressed" crab, and baby lobsters. If you choose to go on into the dining room, you can select from a long menu that lists a number of fish dishes and such grilled foods as calves' liver and bacon, kedgeree, and Greens fish cakes with parsley sauce. Desserts include Duke of Cambridge tart, black-currant sorbet, and banana fritters.

A WINE BAR

Daniel's Bar (Café Royal Grill)

68 Regent St., W1. ☎ **0171/437-9090,** ext. 277. Reservations not required. Appetizers £2.50–£6.25 ($3.95–$9.90); main courses £7.95–£13.50 ($12.55–$21.35); glass of wine £2.50–£6 ($3.95–$9.50). AE, DC, MC, V. Lunch Mon–Fri noon–3pm; Mon–Fri 5–11pm open only for drinks and snacks. Tube: Piccadilly Circus. BRITISH.

This deliberately unpretentious annex to the chillingly expensive Café Royal Grill, Daniel's dates from 1865. Both are accessible from the grand café's marble-floored lobby, where the literary greats of

19th-century England have trod, including Oscar Wilde. Despite its opulent design—art nouveau moldings, oaken half-paneling, and abundant framed cartoons and illustrations—the bar is very informal. At lunchtime, a long list of platters and appetizers is available. In the evening, the menu is limited only to a short list of snacks, as most of the clientele comes just to drink.

LEICESTER SQUARE
MODERATE

Sheekeys

28–32 St. Martin's Court, off Charing Cross Rd., WC2. ☎ **0171/240-2565.** Reservations required. Appetizers £4.95–£14.95 ($7.80–$23.60); main courses £9.95–£25.95 ($15.70–$41); fixed-price lunch 15.95–£18.75 ($25.20–$29.65). AE, DC, MC, V. Lunch Mon–Sat 12:30–3pm; dinner Mon–Sat 5:30–11:30pm. Tube: Leicester Square. SEAFOOD.

Since it was established in 1896 by an Irish-born vaudevillian, Sheekeys has always been closely associated with London's theater district. Occupying a series of small, intimate dining rooms, it features walls almost completely covered with photographs of British and North American stage and screen stars, many autographed. A formally dressed staff caters to the culinary needs of a conservative and well-heeled clientele who feel comfortable with the restaurant's sense of tradition and good manners. Seafood is the specialty here, one of the few places in London that almost never (only when specifically required) fries its food. Instead, the delicate fresh ingredients are steamed, grilled, or stewed, then laden with such ingredients as sherry, cream, garlic, lemon, and herbs. The result is usually rich and delicious. Specialties include lobster-and-langoustine bisque, lobster Thermidor, Dover sole prepared in the style of Joseph Sheekey, jellied eels (a British delicacy), fish cakes, and a concoction identified as Sheekeys' fisherman's pie. Desserts include apple tart with calvados.

🔁 Family-Friendly Restaurants

Chicago Pizza Factory   *(see page 121)* If your kids are nostalgic for the food back home, they'll find it here, where regular-size pizzas are big enough for two or three.

Deal's Restaurant and Diner   *(see page 158)* After enjoying the boat ride down to Chelsea Harbour, kids will love the food of North America served here, including Deal's burgers. Reduced-price children's portions are available.

Cheshire Cheese   *(see page 145)* Fleet Street's most famous chophouse, established in 1667, is the eternal family favorite. If "ye famous pudding" turns your kid off, the sandwiches and roast beef will tempt instead.

INEXPENSIVE

Pelican

45 St. Martin's Lane, WC2. ☎ **0171/379-0309.** Reservations recommended on weekdays; required on weekends. In restaurant, pretheater suppers £9.95–£11.95 ($15.70–$18.90); daily 5:30–7:30pm. Appetizers £3.25–£5.95 ($5.15–$9.40); main courses £6.95–£13.95 ($11–$22.05). In brasserie/wine bar, snacks and platters £3.50–£11.95 ($5.55–$18.90); glass of wine from £2.50 ($3.95). AE, DC, MC, V. Daily noon–12:30am. Tube: Charing Cross or Leicester Square. FRENCH/INTERNATIONAL.

More than almost any other restaurant in its neighborhood (adjacent to the English National Opera House), Pelican vibrates with a constant traffic of clients coming and going to one of the nearby theaters. Set within a long and narrow cream-colored room outfitted with mirrors, framed posters, and art deco accessories, Pelican has a bustling brasserie and wine bar in front, and a genial and somewhat more sedate restaurant in back.

Many clients prefer the wine bar and never venture past a position near the front. Here, they enjoy the diversity of vintages, the recorded jazz, and the availability of rapidly but well-prepared specials that change every day. Examples include cream of celery soup, grilled Scotch sirloin steak, and pan-fried veal with Madeira sauce and fresh vegetables.

At the restaurant in back, more elaborate meals might include red mullet in a white wine sauce served with root vegetables; goat cheese mousseline with caramelized shallots; and sliced filet of beef served with a Madeira sauce. Here a pianist adds luster every night after 10pm.

PUBS & WINE BARS

⑤ Cork & Bottle Wine Bar

44–46 Cranbourn St., WC2. ☎ **0171/734-7807.** Reservations recommended. Appetizers £3.25–£8.95 ($5.15–$14.15); main courses £4.95–£8.95 ($7.80–$14.15); glass of wine from £2.30 ($3.65). AE, DC, MC, V. Mon–Sat 11am–midnight, Sun noon–10:30pm. Tube: Leicester Square. INTERNATIONAL.

Cork & Bottle is just off Leicester Square. The most successful dish is a raised cheese-and-ham pie, which has a cream cheese–like filling and crisp well-buttered pastry—not your typical quiche. (In just one week the bar sold 500 portions of this alone.) The kitchen also offers a chicken and apple salad, Lancashire sausage hot pot, Mediterranean prawns with garlic and asparagus, tandoori chicken, and lamb in ale. The expanded wine list features an excellent selection of Beaujolais crus and wines from Alsace, some 30 selections from "Down Under," 30 champagnes, and a good selection of California labels.

✪ Salisbury

90 St. Martin's Lane, WC2. ☎ **0171/836-5863.** Reservations not accepted. Buffet meal £4.50–£6.50 ($7.10–$10.25); pint of lager £2.11–£2.20 ($3.35–$3.50). AE, DC, MC, V. Mon–Sat noon–11pm, Sun noon–3pm and 7–10:30pm. Tube: Leicester Square. BRITISH.

Salisbury's glittering cut-glass mirrors reflect the faces of English stage stars (and hopefuls) sitting around the curved buffet-style bar. A less prominent place to dine is the old-fashioned wall banquette with its copper-topped tables and art nouveau decor. The light fixtures—veiled bronze girls in flowing robes holding up clusters of electric lights concealed in bronze roses—are appropriate. In the saloon, you'll see and hear the Oliviers of yesterday and tomorrow. But do not let this put you off your food. The pub's specialty, an array of homemade meat and vegetable pies set out on a buffet table with salads, is really quite good and inexpensive. Food is served from noon until 7:30pm.

TRAFALGAR SQUARE
A Pub

Sherlock Holmes

10 Northumberland St., WC1. ☎ **0171/930-2644.** Reservations recommended for restaurant. Appetizers £2.75–£5.75 ($4.35–$9.10); main courses £7.75–£13.95 ($12.25–$22.05); fixed-price menus £10.95–£14.95 ($17.30–$23.60); ground-floor snacks £3.25–£4 ($5.15–$6.30). AE, DC, MC, V. Restaurant Mon–Sat noon–10:30pm. Sun lunch noon–3pm and dinner 7–10pm. Pub Mon–Sat 11am–11pm. Sun noon–3:30pm and 7–10:30pm. Tube: Charing Cross or Embankment. BRITISH.

It would be rather strange if the Sherlock Holmes were not the old gathering spot for the Baker Street Irregulars, a once-mighty clan of mystery lovers who met here to honor the genius of Sir Arthur Conan Doyle's most famous fictional character. Upstairs, you'll find a re-creation of the living room at 221B Baker Street and such "Holmesiana" as the serpent of *The Speckled Band* and the head of *The Hound of the Baskervilles.* In the upstairs dining room, you can order complete meals with wine. Main dishes are reliable, including roast beef and Yorkshire pudding as well as The Copper Beeches (grilled butterfly chicken breasts with lemon and herbs). You select dessert from the trolley. The downstairs is mainly for drinking, but there's a good snack bar with cold meats, salads, cheeses, and wine sold by the glass.

5 Soho

MODERATE

Alastair Little

49 Frith St., W1. ☎ **0171/734-5183.** Reservations recommended. Appetizers £6–£15 ($9.50–$23.70); main courses £15–£25 ($23.70–$39.50); fixed-price three-course lunch £25 ($39.50). AE, DC, MC, V. Lunch Mon–Fri noon–3pm; dinner Mon–Sat 6–11:30pm. Tube: Leicester Square. BRITISH.

Tucked in an early 19th-century brick-fronted town house that for a brief period is said to have housed John Constable's art studio, this informal, cozy restaurant serves well-prepared meals. Owned by the British-Danish-Spanish trio of Alastair Little, Kirsten Pedersen, and Andre-Vega, it features such main courses as roasted sea bass with parsley salad, rack of lamb with rosemary, and Tuscan squab. Dessert might consist of a crème brûlée, tarte Tatin with crème fraîche, or a crème caramel. A full complement of wines (most California and Australian) might accompany your meal.

Au Jardin des Gourmets

5 Greek St., W1. ☎ **0171/437-1816.** Reservations required. Appetizers £6.85–£10.50 ($10.80–$16.60); main courses £12.50–£16.50 ($19.75–$26.05); fixed-price three-course lunch or dinner £21.50 ($33.95). AE, DC, MC, V. Lunch Mon–Fri 12:15–2:30pm; dinner Mon–Sat 6:30–11:15pm. Tube: Tottenham Court Road. FRENCH.

Since 1931 this "Ile de France" off Soho Square is where devotees of Gallic cuisine gather to enjoy traditional specialties. The Jardin itself has climbed to a level of hospitality never previously attained, with its new kitchens and wine cellars; lavatories that can be reached without climbing two floors; and, most important of all, air-conditioned restaurant that separates smokers and nonsmokers in the two adjacent rooms on the ground floor. There is a comprehensive à la carte menu with such specialties as poached salmon with thinly sliced beetroot, olive oil and raspberry vinegar dressing, noissettes of lamb topped with a foie gras, truffle and Madeira sauce, and médaillons of venison with juniper berries and sweet-and-sour red onion compote. The masterful selection of vintage Bordeaux and Burgundies is expertly served.

Bistro Bruno

63 Frith St., W1. ☎ **0171/734-4545.** Reservations recommended. Appetizers £4–£6.50 ($6.30–$10.25); main courses £11.50–£17 ($18.15–$26.85). AE, DC, MC, V. Lunch Mon–Fri noon–2:30pm (last order); dinner Mon–Sat 6:15–11:30pm (last order). Tube: Tottenham Court Road. INTERNATIONAL.

Named after its chef and part owner, Bruno Loubet, this is an artfully simple restaurant, with food much more elegant and complicated than its name (bistro) would imply. Within a long and narrow dining room capped with a turquoise ceiling, blue-topped tables, and minimalist accessories, you'll enjoy a menu that changes frequently based on the availability of ingredients and the inspiration of the chef. In many ways, its menu reads like a chic restaurant in France, where combinations of food please the intellect as well as the palate. Menu items include a *boudin blanc* (white sausage) served on a ragoût of broad beans; steamed baby sea bass served on a bed of soy and garlic sauce; confit of duck on a corn pancake with grape-flavored chutney; guinea fowl with rosemary-infused risotto; filet of skate (stingray) with artichoke hearts; and such creative desserts as fresh strawberries served with green peppercorn ice cream. In 1995, this bistro opened a cost-conscious neighbor in the storefront next door, the Café Bruno, (open throughout the afternoon, Monday to Saturday from noon to 11:30pm) where prices are a bit lower and where the menu is less cerebral and more hearty.

Gay Hussar

2 Greek St., W1. ☎ **0171/437-0973.** Reservations recommended. Appetizers £3.40–£4.75 ($5.35–$7.50); main courses £11.50–£15.50 ($18.15–$24.50); fixed-price lunch £16 ($25.30). AE, DC, MC, V. Lunch Mon–Sat 12:30–2:30pm; dinner Mon–Sat 5:30–10:45pm. Tube: Tottenham Court Road. HUNGARIAN.

Gay Hussar has been called "the best Hungarian restaurant in the world." The "last of the great Soho restaurants," it is an intimate place where diners can begin with a chilled wild-cherry soup or a hot, spicy redfish soup in the style of Szeged, located in Hungary's southern Great

Restaurants: Soho

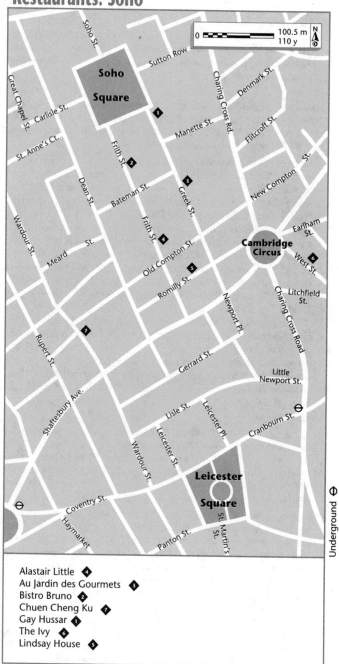

0   100.5 m
     110 y
N

Soho St.

Sutton Row

Soho
Square

Great Chapel St.

Carlisle St.

St. Anne's Ct.

Charing Cross Rd.

Denmark St.

Manette St.

Flitcroft St.

Frith St. **2**

1

Dean St.

Bateman St.

Greek St. **3**

New Compton St.

Wardour St.

Meard St.

Frith St. **4**

Old Compton St.

5

Romilly St.

Cambridge
Circus

Earlham St.

West St. **6**

Litchfield St.

7

Rupert St.

Newport Pl.

Charing Cross Road

Gerrard St.

Little
Newport St.

Shaftesbury Ave.

Lisle St.

Leicester Pl.

Cranbourn St.

Wardour St.

Leicester St.

Leicester
Square

Coventry St.

Haymarket

Panton St.

St. Martin's St.

Underground ⊖

Alastair Little **4**
Au Jardin des Gourmets **3**
Bistro Bruno **2**
Chuen Cheng Ku **7**
Gay Hussar **1**
The Ivy **6**
Lindsay House **5**

Plain. Main courses are likely to include stuffed cabbage; fish dumplings in dill sauce; half a perfectly done chicken served in mild paprika sauce with cucumber salad and noodles; and, of course, veal goulash with egg dumplings. For dessert, select either raspberry-and-chocolate torte or walnut pancakes.

The Ivy

1–5 West St., WC2. ☎ **0171/836-4751.** Reservations required. Appetizers £4.75–£22.75 ($7.50–$35.95); main courses £6.75–£19.75 ($10.65–$31.20); Sat–Sun lunch £14.50 ($22.90). AE, DC, MC, V. Lunch daily noon–3pm; dinner daily 5:30pm–midnight (last order). Tube: Leicester Square. BRITISH.

Effervescent and sophisticated, The Ivy has been intimately associated with the West End theater district since it was established in 1911. Its clientele has included Prime Ministers David Lloyd George and Winston S. Churchill (both of whom knew a lot about viands and wines), Noël Coward, Gracie Fields, Dame Sybil Thorndike, and Rex Harrison. Renovated in the early 1990s, it features near the entrance a tiny bar where guests might be asked to wait until their table is ready; its paneled decor seems deliberately designed to encourage discreet stargazing. Meals are served till very late, a graceful acknowledgment of the allure of after-theater suppers. Most important, the place, with its ersatz-1930s look, is fun—buzzing and throbbing with the energy of London's glamour.

Menu items appear simple, but show a solid appreciation for fresh ingredients and skillful preparation. They include white asparagus with sea kale and truffle butter; seared scallops with spinach, sorrel, and bacon; and corned beef hash with fried egg. Also included in the offerings are Mediterranean fish soup, a great mixed grill, salads, and such English desserts as sticky toffee and caramelized bread-and-butter pudding.

Lindsay House

21 Romilly St., W1. ☎ **0171/439-0450.** Reservations required. Appetizers £4–£12 ($6.30–$18.95); main courses £12–£15 ($18.95–$23.70); fixed-price lunch £14.75 ($23.30). AE, DC, MC, V. Lunch Mon–Sat 12:30–2:30pm, Sun 12:30–2pm; dinner Mon–Sat 6pm–midnight, Sun 7–10pm. Closed Dec 25–26. Tube: Leicester Square or Piccadilly Circus. BRITISH.

Lindsay House bases many of its dishes on 18th-century English recipes, although several platters are designated Tudor or nouvelle. Everyone—from royalty to film stars, from diplomats to regular people—shows up here, including an array of discerning Americans. Since it begins serving dinner early, you might want to consider it for dinner before a stage presentation at a Shaftesbury Avenue theater. Owner Roger Wren, who already runs some of the most fashionable restaurants in London (including Waltons of Walton Street, English House, and the English Garden), decided to open this eating house in the heart of Soho. Fireplaces and fresh flowers give it class and style.

The food lives up to the decor. Appetizers, or "first dishes," include wild mushrooms encased in a pastry with rosemary cream sauce. To follow, you might try roast rack of Southdown lamb or steamed chicken glazed with leek and ginger. Desserts include an apple and cinnamon tart with crème fraîche and a traditional bread pudding. You might also order a floating island, one of England's best 18th-century confections: light poached meringues floating on a rose-scented custard.

INEXPENSIVE

$ Chuen Cheng Ku

17 Wardour St., W1. ☎ **0171/437-1398.** Reservations recommended on weekend afternoons. Appetizers £1.75–£8 ($2.75–$12.65); main courses £6.40–£9 ($10.10–$14.20); fixed-price menus £9.50–£30 ($15–$47.40) per person. AE, DC, MC, V. Daily 11am–midnight. Closed Dec 24–25. Tube: Piccadilly Circus or Leicester Square. CHINESE.

This is one of the finest eateries in Soho's "New China." A large restaurant on several floors, Chuen Cheng Ku is noted for its Cantonese food and is said to have the longest and most interesting menu in London. Specialties are paper-wrapped prawns, rice in lotus leaves, steamed spareribs in black-bean sauce, and shredded pork with cashew nuts—all served in generous portions. Other à la carte dishes include fried oysters with ginger and scallions, sliced duck with chili and black bean sauce, and steamed pork with plum sauce. Dim sum (dumplings) are served from 11am to 5:45pm.

A PUB

Old Coffee House

49 Beak St., W1. ☎ **0171/437-2197.** Reservations not accepted. Main courses £2.20–£3.95 ($3.50–$6.25); beer from £1.95 ($3.10). No credit cards. Restaurant lunch only, Mon–Sat noon–3pm; pub Mon–Sat 11am–11pm, Sun noon–3pm and 7–10:30pm. Tube: Oxford Circus or Piccadilly Circus. BRITISH.

Once honored as Soho Pub of the Year, the Old Coffee House takes its name from the coffeehouse heyday of 18th-century London. Coffee was called "the devil's brew" back then, and the pub still serves pots of filtered coffee. The place is heavily decorated with bric-a-brac, including such items as old musical instruments and World War I recruiting posters. Have a drink at the long, narrow bar, with a lager costing from £1.95 ($3.10), or retreat to the upstairs restaurant, where you can enjoy good pub food at lunch, including the typically English dish of chicken-and-leek pie, steak-and-kidney pie, three vegetarian dishes, and scampi-and-chips. Burgers and fries are always popular.

6 British Cuisine

You don't have to travel around England to experience regional English dishes—you'll find them all over London. On any pub menu you're likely to encounter such dishes as Cornish pasty and shepherd's pie. The first, traditionally made from Sunday-meal leftovers and taken by West Country fishers for Monday lunch, consists of chopped potatoes, carrots, and onions mixed together with seasoning and put into a pastry envelope. The second is a deep dish of chopped cooked beef mixed with onions and seasoning, covered with a layer of mashed potatoes, and served hot. Another version is cottage pie, which is minced beef covered with potatoes and also served hot. The most common pub meal, though, is the ploughman's lunch—traditional farm worker's fare—consisting of a good chunk of local cheese, a hunk of homemade crusty white or brown bread, some butter, and a pickled onion or two, washed down with ale. You will now find such variations as pâté and chutney occasionally replacing the onions and cheese. Or you might find Lancashire hot pot, a stew of mutton, potatoes, kidneys, and onions (sometimes carrots). This concoction was originally put into a deep dish and set on the edge of the stove to cook slowly while the workers spent the day at the local mill.

Among appetizers, called "starters" in England, the most typical are potted shrimp (small buttered shrimp preserved in a jar), prawn cocktail, and smoked salmon. You might also be served pâté or "fish pie," which is very light fish pâté. If you're an oyster lover, try some of the famous Colchester variety. Most menus will feature a variety of soups, including cock-a-leekie (chicken soup flavored with leeks), perhaps a game soup that has been flavored with sherry, and many others.

Among the best-known traditional English dishes is, of course, roast beef and Yorkshire pudding—the pudding made with a flour base and cooked under the joint, allowing the fat from the meat to drop onto it. The beef could easily be a large sirloin (rolled loin), which, so the story goes, was named by James I (not Henry VIII, as some claim) when he was a guest at Houghton Tower, Lancashire. "Arise, Sir Loin," he cried, as he knighted the joint with his dagger. Another dish that makes similar use of a flour base is toad-in-the-hole, in which sausages are cooked in batter. Game is also a staple on English tables, especially pheasant and grouse.

On the west coast, you'll find a not-to-be-missed delicacy called Morecambe Bay shrimp, and on any menu you'll find fresh seafood—cod, haddock, herring, plaice, or the aristocrat of flat fish, Dover sole. Cod and haddock are the most popular fish used in the making of a British tradition, fish-and-chips (chips, of course, are fried potatoes, or thick french fries), which the true Briton covers with salt and vinegar.

The East End of London has quite a few interesting old dishes, among them tripe and onions. Dr. Johnson's favorite tavern, the Cheshire Cheese on Fleet Street, still offers a beefsteak-kidney-mushroom-and-game pudding in a suet case in winter and a pastry case in summer. East Enders can still be seen on Sunday at the Jellied Eel stall by Petticoat Lane, eating either eel or cockles, mussels, whelks, and winkles—all small shellfish eaten with a touch of vinegar. Eel-pie-and-mash shops can still be found in London purveying what is really a minced-beef pie topped with flaky pastry and served with mashed potatoes and a portion of jellied eel.

The British call desserts "sweets" (although some people still refer to any dessert as "pudding"), with trifle perhaps being the most famous. It consists of sponge cake soaked in brandy or sherry, coated with fruit or jam, and topped with a cream custard. A "fool," such as gooseberry fool, is a light cream dessert whipped up from seasonal fruits.

Cheese is traditionally served after dessert as a savory. There are many regional cheeses, the best known being Cheddar, a good, solid, mature cheese, as is Cheshire. Another is the semismooth-textured

Caerphilly from a beautiful part of Wales, and also Stilton, a blue-veined crumbly cheese, often enriched with a glass of port.

London pubs serve a variety of cocktails, but their stock in trade is beer—brown beer, or "bitter"; blond beer, or lager; and very dark beer, or stout. The standard English draft beer is much stronger than American beer and is served "with the chill off," because it doesn't taste good cold. Lager is always chilled, while stout can be served either way.

One of the most significant changes in English drinking habits has been the popularity of wine bars, and you will find many to patronize, some turning into discos late at night. Britain is not known for its wine, although it does produce some medium-sweet fruity whites. Its cider, though, is famous—and very potent in contrast to the American variety.

Whisky (spelled without the *e*) refers to scotch. Canadian and Irish whiskey (spelled with the *e*) are also available, but only the very best-stocked bars have American bourbon and rye. While you're in England, you may want to try the very English drink called Pimm's, a mixture developed by James Pimm, owner of a popular London oyster house in the 1840s. Though it can be consumed on the rocks, it's usually served as a Pimm's Cup—a drink that will have any number and variety of ingredients, depending on which part of the world (or empire) you're in. Here, just for fun, is a typical recipe: Take a very tall glass and fill it with ice. Add a thin slice of lemon (or orange), a cucumber spike (or a curl of cucumber rind), and two ounces of Pimm's liquor. Then finish with a splash of either lemon or club soda, 7-Up, or Tom Collins mix.

7 Bloomsbury & Fitzrovia

BLOOMSBURY
MODERATE

Museum Street Cafe

47 Museum St., WC1. ☎ **0171/405-3211.** Reservations required. Lunch £12 ($18.95) for two courses, £15 ($23.70) for three courses; dinner £17 ($26.85) for two courses, £21 ($33.20) for three courses. MC, V. Lunch Mon–Fri 12:30–2:15pm (last order); dinner Mon–Fri 7:15–9:15pm (last order). Tube: Tottenham Court Road. MODERN BRITISH.

A two-minute walk from the British Museum, this small-scale but charming dining room once contained the neighborhood's "greasy spoon" until it was transformed by Boston-born Gail Koerber and her English partner, Mark Nathan. Today, amid a setting of simple furniture and primitive paintings, you can enjoy such typical dishes as roasted red pepper soup followed by char-grilled pigeon breast with apple and chestnut sauce or char-grilled swordfish with coriander, soy, and ginger. Dessert might be a lemon and almond tart.

A PUB

Museum Tavern

49 Great Russell St., WC1. ☎ **0171/242-8987.** Reservations not accepted. Bar snacks £1.50–£4.95 ($2.35–$7.80); pint of lager £2 ($3.15). AE, DC, MC, V.

Mon–Sat 11am–11pm, Sun noon–10:30pm. Tube: Holborn or Tottenham Court Road. BRITISH.

On a corner opposite the British Museum, Museum Tavern is a pub dating from 1703. However, its Victorian trappings—velvet, oak paneling, and cut glass—are from 1855. It's right in the center of the London University area, very crowded at lunchtime, and frequented by writers and publishers as well as researchers at the museum. It's said that Karl Marx wrote in the pub over his meals. At lunch you can order such authentic low-cost English food as shepherd's pie and beef in beer with two vegetables. There's also a cold buffet, including smoked mackerel, turkey and ham pies, a selection of salads, and English cheeses.

FITZROVIA
MODERATE

Nico Central

35 Great Portland St., W1. ☎ **0171/436-8846.** Reservations required. Lunch appetizers £6.90–£12.20 ($10.90–$19.30); lunch main courses £8–£12 ($12.65–$18.95); fixed-price three-course dinner £26 ($41.10). AE, DC, MC, V. Lunch Mon–Fri noon–2pm; dinner Mon–Sat 7–11pm. Tube: Oxford Circus. FRENCH.

This brasserie—founded and inspired by London's most legendary chef, Nico Ladenis, who now cooks at Chez Nico at Ninety Park Lane (see above)—delivers earthy French cuisine. Of course, everything is handled with considerable culinary urbanity. Guests sit on bentwood chairs at linen-covered tables. Nearly a dozen appetizers—called "starters," the pride of the chef—will tempt you. The menu changes seasonally and according to the inspiration of the chef, but might include risotto with cèpes and parmesan; charlotte of goat cheese with a fondue of red peppers; pan-fried foie gras served with brioche and a caramelized orange; braised knuckle of veal; and baked filet of brill with assorted vegetables.

Pied-à-Terre

34 Charlotte St., W1. ☎ **0171/636-1178.** Reservations recommended. Appetizers £13.50 ($21.35); main courses £23 ($36.35); fixed-price two-course lunch £16.50 ($26.05). AE, DC, MC, V. Lunch Mon–Fri 12:15–2pm (last order); dinner Mon–Sat 7:15–10:30pm. Tube: Goodge Street. INTERNATIONAL.

Considered a gastronomic restaurant of great desirability, with a subtle and very sophisticated cuisine, this restaurant has deliberately understated its decor in favor of a more intense focus on the food. You'll dine within a strictly (some say rigidly) minimalist decor, where gray and pale-pink walls alternate with metal furniture and focused lighting. At least some of the staff members might be French, as will be the wine list and the inspiration for some, but not all, of the cuisine. Menu items change with the seasons, but might include an oyster-and-mushroom broth soup; snails wrapped in a casing of chicken mousse; red mullet with almond sauce; roasted scallops with puréed ginger; filet of trout with morels and mashed potatoes; sea bass with Provençal vegetables floating on a bed of bouillabaisse; filet of John Dory with peas, covered with foie gras sauce; and filet of sea bass served with a

Restaurants: Bloomsbury to the Strand

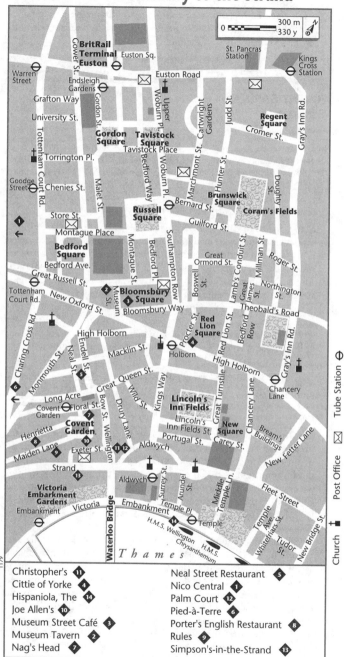

Christopher's	🔶11	Neal Street Restaurant	🔶5
Cittie of Yorke	🔶4	Nico Central	🔶1
Hispaniola, The	🔶14	Palm Court	🔶12
Joe Allen's	🔶10	Pied-à-Terre	🔶6
Museum Street Café	🔶3	Porter's English Restaurant	🔶8
Museum Tavern	🔶2	Rules	🔶9
Nag's Head	🔶7	Simpson's-in-the-Strand	🔶13

caviar-flavored hollandaise. Food is beautifully presented, on hand-painted plates, each combining into lush patterns and textures that off-set the stylish starkness of the minimalist setting.

8 Covent Garden, the Strand & Holborn

COVENT GARDEN
MODERATE

Christopher's

18 Wellington St., WC2. ☎ **0171/240-4222.** Reservations recommended. In upstairs restaurant, appetizers £5–£12 ($7.90–$18.95); main courses £8–£19 ($12.65–$30). In street-level brasserie, appetizers £4.50–£9 ($7.10–$14.20); main courses £5–£12 ($7.90–$18.95). AE, DC, MC, V. Restaurant lunch Mon–Fri noon–3pm; dinner Mon–Sat 6–11:30pm. Brasserie Mon–Sat noon–midnight and Sun noon–3:30pm. Tube: Covent Garden. AMERICAN.

Many visitors to Christopher's are tempted to remain in its street-level brasserie, where steaks, hamburgers, oysters, and fresh salads are served in a bistro-style setting. Serious drinkers descend into the basement, where a bar awaits, serving pints of lager for around £2.50 ($3.95) each. The establishment's real showcase, however, is the restaurant, one floor above street level. Beneath a lavishly frescoed ceiling, an elaborate corkscrew-shaped stone staircase ascends to a pair of Italianate dining rooms. There, flavorful and modern American-inspired dishes are served—including smoked tomato soup with fresh pesto, rack of lamb, grilled breast of chicken, and stewed red cabbage with onions.

Neal Street Restaurant

26 Neal St., WC2. ☎ **0171/836-8368.** Reservations recommended. Appetizers £5.50–£14 ($8.70–$22.10); main courses £7–£20 ($11.05–$31.60). AE, DC, MC, V. Lunch Mon–Sat 12:30–2:30pm; dinner Mon–Sat 7:30–11pm. Tube: Covent Garden. ITALIAN.

Hip and stylish, this restaurant has one of Britain's most extravagant inventories of mushrooms, truffles, and *funghi*. It's operated by Turin-born Antonio Carluccio, a noted author on the use of culinary mushrooms from around the world. Surrounded by the brick walls of what was originally a turn-of-the-century warehouse for the storage and ripening of bananas, the restaurant operates an apéritif bar in the cellar, where prospective diners sometimes wait until a table becomes available.

On the walls hang the works of such artists as Frank Stella and David Hockney, as well as those of many lesser luminaries. Available at any time are between 10 and 20 of the world's most exotic mushrooms—including a highly desirable assortment of truffles. Imported according to season from China, Tibet, Japan, and such less exotic regions as France and California, they pop up in such recipes as the truffled endive salad, wild mushroom soup, pappardelle of venison with funghi, tagliolini with truffle sauce, and scacciata of beef with truffle cheese. Equally appealing—but less expensive because they don't con-tain these exotic mushrooms—might be chicken scallopine, angolotti

Piemontese, or black angel-hair pasta with seafood and bottarga. Service is attentive and polite; the ambience agreeable.

Rules

35 Maiden Lane, WC2. ☎ **0171/836-5314.** Reservations recommended. Appetizers £3.50–£5 ($5.55–$7.90); main courses £10–£15.95 ($15.80–$25.20). AE, DC, MC, V. Daily noon–11:30pm. Tube: Covent Garden. BRITISH.

By anyone's estimate, this might be the most quintessentially British restaurant in London. Established in 1798 as an oyster bar and lined with the framed memorabilia of the British Empire at its height, it rambles through a series of Edwardian dining rooms dripping in patriotic nostalgia. In fact, it lays claim to being the oldest restaurant in London still operating on the site of its original premises. Around the turn of the century, Edward VII, then the portly Prince of Wales, used to arrive here very frequently with his mistress, Lillie Langtry, before heading up to a private red-velvet dining room on the second floor. Their signed portraits still embellish the yellowing walls, along with that of Charles Dickens, who crafted several of his novels here. Brilliant writer and curmudgeon Graham Greene made a visit to Rules an unchangeable condition of each of his birthdays, despite his long-term residence in the south of France. Other artists and actors who have appreciated Rules include William Thackeray, John Galsworthy, H. G. Wells, Evelyn Waugh, John Barrymore, Clark Gable, and Lord Olivier.

Today, amid cartoons executed by George Whitelaw in the 1920s, you can order such classic dishes as Irish or Scottish oysters, jugged hare, and Aylesbury duckling in orange sauce. Game dishes are offered year-round. You can also order wild Scottish salmon or wild sea trout; wild Highland red deer; or any of an array of such game birds as grouse, snipe, partridge, pheasant, and woodcock. These might be followed by those unusually British savories called angels on horseback (oysters wrapped in bacon and served on toast).

INEXPENSIVE

⑤ Porter's English Restaurant

17 Henrietta St., WC2. ☎ **0171/836-6466.** Reservations recommended. Main courses £6.95–£8 ($11–$12.65); fixed-price menu £15.75 ($24.90). AE, MC, V. Mon–Sat noon–11:30pm, Sun noon–10:30pm. Tube: Covent Garden. BRITISH.

This place is owned by the current Earl of Bradford, who stops by frequently. It has a friendly, informal, and lively atmosphere in comfortable surroundings on two floors. Porter's specializes in classic English pies, including steak and kidney; lamb and apricot; and ham, leek, and cheese. Main courses are so generous that the menu wisely eliminates appetizers. Traditional roast beef with Yorkshire pudding is offered daily. Served with whipped cream or custard, the puddings come hot or cold, and they include bread-and-butter pudding and steamed-syrup sponge. The English call all desserts "puddings," but at Porter's they are puddings in the American sense. The bar concocts quite a few exotic cocktails, and you can order cider by the half pint as well as English wine. A traditional afternoon tea is also served, costing £3.95 ($6.25) per person.

A PUB

Nag's Head

10 James St., WC2. ☎ **0171/836-4678.** Reservations not accepted. Sandwich platters with salad £2.50–£4.95 ($3.95–$7.80); full meal salads £4.25 ($6.70); main courses £4.95 ($7.80); pint of lager £1.80 ($2.85). AE, DC, MC, V. Mon–Sat 11:30am–11pm, Sun noon–3pm and 7:30–10:30pm. Tube: Covent Garden. BRITISH.

The Nag's Head is one of London's most famous Edwardian pubs. In days of yore, patrons had to make their way through lorries of fruit and flowers for a drink here; elegantly dressed operagoers used to mix with cockney cauliflower peddlers at the bar. With the moving of the market, 300 years of British tradition faded away. Today, the pub is patronized mainly by young people, who seem to fill up all the tables every evening, as well as the drinking space around the bar. Try a draft Guinness for a change of pace. Lunch is typical pub grub: sandwiches, salads, pork cooked in cider, and garlic prawns. The sandwich platters mentioned above are served only during the lunch hour (noon to 3:30pm); however, snacks are available in the afternoon.

FOR AFTERNOON TEA

Palm Court

In the Waldorf Hotel, Aldwych (without number), WC2. ☎ **0171/836-2400.** Reservations required. Afternoon tea £13.25 ($20.95); tea dance £20.50 ($32.40). AE, DC, MC, V. Afternoon tea Mon–Fri 3:30–6pm; tea dance Sat–Sun 3:30–6pm. Tube: Covent Garden.

The Palm Court is aptly compared to a 1920s movie set, which, in fact, it's been several times. You can order tea on a terrace or in a pavilion lit by skylights. On Saturday and Sunday, the Palm Court combines afternoon tea with ballroom dancing. The orchestra leader will conduct such favorites as "Ain't She Sweet" and "Yes, Sir, That's My Baby," while a butler in a cutaway inquires if you want a cucumber sandwich. Men must wear jackets and ties.

THE STRAND
MODERATE

Joe Allen's

13 Exeter St., WC2. ☎ **0171/836-0651.** Reservations required. Appetizers £3.50–£7 ($5.55–$11.05); main courses £5.50–£11 ($8.70–$17.40). No credit cards. Mon–Sat noon–1am, Sun noon–midnight. Tube: Covent Garden or Embankment. AMERICAN.

This fashionable American restaurant, which has branches in New York and Paris, attracts mainly theater crowds. It lies north of the Strand in the vicinity of the Savoy Hotel. The decor is inspired by that of the New York branch, with theater posters and gingham tablecloths in red-and-white check. Specialties are black-bean soup, barbecued ribs with black-eyed peas, chili, and pecan pie.

Simpson's-in-the-Strand

100 The Strand, WC2. ☎ **0171/836-9112.** Reservations required. Appetizers £3.25–£12 ($5.15–$18.95); main courses £14.50 ($22.90); fixed-price lunch £10

($15.80) for two courses; fixed-price dinner £10 ($15.80) for two courses (6–7pm only); set breakfasts £8.50–£10 ($13.45–$15.80). AE, DC, MC, V. Breakfast Mon–Fri 7am–noon; lunch daily noon–2:30pm; dinner daily 6–11pm. Tube: Charing Cross or Embankment. BRITISH.

Simpson's is more of an institution than a restaurant. Located next to the Savoy Hotel, it has been in business since 1828. This very Victorian place features Adam paneling, crystal, and an army of grandly formal waiters hovering about. Men should wear jackets and ties. Most first-time visitors to London should count on seeing the Changing of the Guard, then lunching at Simpson's.

One food critic wrote that "nouvelle cuisine here means anything after Henry VIII." However, there is one point on which most diners agree: Simpson's serves the best roasts (joints) in London. Huge roasts are trolleyed to your table and slabs of beef are carved off and served with traditional Yorkshire pudding. The classic dishes are roast sirloin of beef; roast saddle of mutton with red-currant jelly; roast Aylesbury duckling; and steak, kidney, and mushroom pie. Remember to tip the coat-tailed carver. For a "pudding," you might order the treacle roll and custard or Stilton with vintage port.

Simpsons, to help pay the bills, started serving fixed-price breakfasts and we're talking the "trad British brekky" here: black pud, grilled mushrooms, grilled tomatoes, eggs, bacon, sausage, and such lovelies as salmon kedgeree, pig's nose with parsley and onion sauce, kippers, quail eggs with haddock, fried kidneys, fried liver, baked beans, fried bread, bubble and squeak, along with stewed fruit, orange juice, coffee, and pastries.

HOLBORN
A PUB

Cittie of Yorke

22–23 High Holborn, WC1. ☎ **0171/242-7670.** Reservations not accepted. Appetizers £2.25–£4 ($3.55–$6.30); main courses £4.50–£6 ($7.10–$9.50); glass of wine from £2 ($3.15). AE, MC, V. Mon–Fri 11am–11pm, Sat 11:30am–3pm and 5:30–11pm. Tube: Holborn or Chancery Lane. BRITISH.

Cittie of Yorke stands near the Holborn Bars, the historic entrance to London marked by dragons holding the coat-of-arms of the City between their paws. Persons entering and leaving London were checked and paid tolls here. A pub has stood on this site since 1430. Its principal hall, said to have the longest bar in England, boasts handsome screenwork, comfortable compartments, a row of large vats, and a high trussed roof. The place is popular with barristers, judges, and employees of London's financial district. Lunchtime rituals involve ordering your food at the food counter and carrying your choices back to a table. Dinner involves placing your order at the bar, whereupon someone will carry your choice to your table about 10 minutes later. Lunch bustles a bit more frenetically than dinner, when a wider choice of food is available. At any time, you'll have a choice of five hot platters of the day (goulashes, casseroles, lasagne, ham steaks, rumpsteaks, etc.), plus burgers and sandwiches.

ON THE HARBOR
INEXPENSIVE

The Hispaniola
Victoria Embankment (without number), Charing Cross, WC2. ☎ **0171/839-3011.**
Reservations recommended. Appetizers £2.75–£5.75 ($4.35–$9.10); main courses
£6.50–£18.50 ($10.25–$29.25). AE, DC, MC, V. Lunch Mon–Fri noon–2pm; dinner
Mon–Sat 6:30–10pm (last order). Closed Mon in Jan–Apr. Tube: Embankment.
BRITISH/FRENCH.

This large, comfortably outfitted ship was originally built in 1953 to
haul passengers around the islands of Scotland. Stripped of its engine
in 1976, the ship is permanently moored to a quay beside the Thames,
a few steps from the Embankment Underground station. Good food
and views of the passing river traffic are part of the waterborne
experience on board. Tables are set up on two different levels, and
throughout, a certain elegance prevails. A harpist or an automated
piano provides evening music. The menu changes frequently, but
might include such dishes as queen scallops with chili and sherry
dressing, honey roasted pork tenderloin with apple and thyme crumble,
salmon steak in a leek and green peppercorn sauce, and several vegetarian dishes.

9   The City, Fleet Street & Barbican

THE CITY
MODERATE

Poons in the City
2 Minster Pavement, Minster Court, Mincing Lane, EC3. ☎ **0171/626-0126.**
Reservations recommended. Set lunch £20.80–£27.80 ($32.85–$43.90) per person;
appetizers £2.60–£6.20 ($4.10–$9.80); main courses £5.80–£8.80 ($9.15–$13.90).
AE, DC, MC, V. Mon–Fri noon–11pm. Tube: Monument. CHINESE.

In 1992, Poons opened this branch restaurant in the City, less than a
five-minute walk from the Tower of London and close to other City
attractions. It is modeled on the Luk Yew Tree House in Hong Kong.
The rosewood furniture and all the accessories were imported from
China.

The menu tempts you with both hot and cold hors d'oeuvres, ranging from chicken satay to crispy soft-shell crab to Cantonese chicken.
Poons famous Lap Yuk Soom contains finely chopped wind-dried
bacon. Main courses feature crispy aromatic duck, prawns with cashew
nuts, and barbecued pork. Special dishes can be ordered on 24-hour
notice. At the end of the L-shaped restaurant is an 80-seat fast-food area
and take-out counter—accessible from Mark Lane—which becomes a
relaxing cocktail bar in the evening. The menu here changes every two
weeks, and set lunches cost £12.60 ($19.90) per person (minimum of
two), with plats du jour such as stir-fried sliced beef or sweet-and-sour
chicken for £4.60 ($7.25).

Restaurants: The City, Fleet St. & Barbican

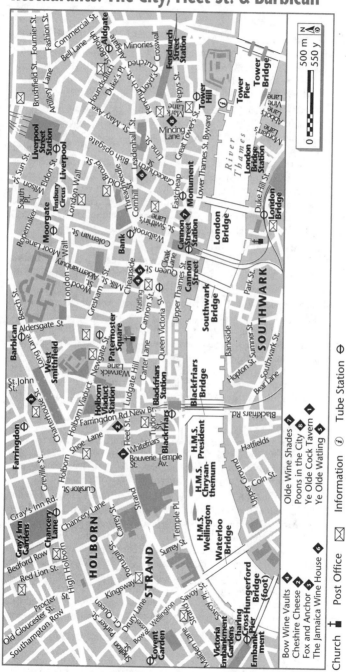

Bow Wine Vaults ◆ 4
Cheshire Cheese ◆ 2
Fox and Anchor ◆ 3
The Jamaica Wine House ◆ 6

Olde Wine Shades ◆ 7
Poons in the City ◆ 8
Ye Olde Cock Tavern ◆ 1
Ye Olde Watling ◆ 5

Church ▪   Post Office ⊠   Information ⓘ   Tube Station ⊖

PUBS & WINE BARS

Bow Wine Vaults

10 Bow Churchyard, EC4 ☎ **0171/248-1121.** Reservations recommended. Appetizers £2.50–£4 ($3.95–$6.30); main courses £6.50–£7.95 ($10.25–$12.55); glass of wine from £2.50 ($3.95). AE, DC, MC, V. The Restaurant and Grill Bar Mon–Fri 11am–2:45pm; pub Mon–Fri 11am–11pm. Tube: Bank or St. Paul's. BRITISH.

Bow Wine Vaults existed long before the current wine-bar fad that began in the 1970s and is now firmly entrenched in London. It attracts cost-conscious diners and drinkers from the financial district, who head for its vaulted cellars. Menu choices in the Grill Bar, as it's called, include such traditional fare as deep-fried Camembert, chicken Kiev, and a mixed grill, along with fish. More elegant meals are served in the street-level dining room, called The Restaurant, which offers an English-inspired menu, including mussels in cider sauce, English wild mushrooms in puff pastry, and beef Wellington. Try the steak with brown-butter sauce.

The Jamaica Wine House

St. Michael's Alley (without number; off Cornhill), EC3. ☎ **0171/626-9496.** Reservations not accepted. Bar snacks £1–£4 ($1.60–$6.30); lager £1.55–£2 ($2.45–$3.15). AE, DC, MC, V. Mon–Fri 11am–8pm. Tube: Bank. BRITISH.

The Jamaica Wine House was one of the first coffeehouses opened in England and, reputedly, in the Western world. For years, London merchants and daring sea captains came here to transact deals over rum and coffee. Nowadays, the two-level house dispenses beer, ale, lager, and fine wine, among them a variety of ports. The oak-paneled bar is on the street level, attracting a jacket-and-tie crowd of investment brokers. You can order game and baked potatoes, toasted sandwiches, and such old English favorites as Lancashire hot pot and shepherd's pie. The basement bar is an even cozier retreat.

Olde Wine Shades

6 Martin Lane, Cannon St., EC4. ☎ **0171/626-6876.** Reservations not required. Appetizers £3–£4.40 ($4.75–$6.95); main courses £6–£14 ($9.50–$22.10); glass of wine from £1.90 ($3). AE, MC, V. Lunch Mon–Fri 11:30am–3pm; dinner Mon–Fri 5–8pm. Closed bank holidays. Tube: Cannon Street. BRITISH.

Dating from 1663 and a survivor of both the Great Fire of 1666 and Hitler's bombs, this is the oldest wine house in the City. Located near the Monument (a famous London landmark designed by Christopher Wren to commemorate the Great Fire of 1666), Olde Wine Shades is decorated with oil paintings and 19th-century political cartoons. It is also one of the many London bars that Dickens used to patronize. There is a restaurant downstairs, but you can also order light meals upstairs, including Breton pâté, French bread with ham "off the bone," jacket potatoes filled with cheese, venison pie with salad garnish, or a large beef salad. The simple fare notwithstanding, men must wear jackets, collars, and ties.

Ye Olde Watling

29 Watling St., EC4. ☎ **0171/248-6252.** Reservations not accepted. Lunch £2.50–£4.95 ($3.95–$7.80); bar snacks from £1.95 ($3.10); beer from £1.70 ($2.70).

AE, MC, V. Restaurant Mon–Fri noon–2:30pm; pub Mon–Fri 11am–10pm. Tube: Mansion House. BRITISH.

Ye Olde Watling was built after the Great Fire of 1666. On the ground level is a mellow pub, and upstairs is an intimate restaurant where, under oak beams and at trestle tables, you can dine on English main dishes for lunch. The menu varies daily, with such choices as fish-and-chips, steak-and-kidney pudding, lamb satay, lasagne, fish cakes, and usually a vegetarian dish. All are served with two vegetables or salad, plus rice or potatoes.

FLEET STREET
PUBS

Cheshire Cheese

Wine Office Court, 145 Fleet St., EC4. ☎ **0171/353-6170.** Reservations not required. Appetizers £2.95–£5 ($4.65–$7.90); main courses £7–£15 ($11.05–$23.70). AE, DC, MC, V. Lunch daily noon–2:30pm; dinner daily 6–9:30pm. Drinks and bar snacks available daily 11:30am–11pm. Tube: St. Paul's. BRITISH.

Set within a remodeled, carefully preserved building whose foundation was laid in the 13th century, this is one of the most famous of the old city chophouses and pubs. Established in 1667, it claims to be the spot where Dr. Samuel Johnson (who lived nearby) entertained admirers with his acerbic wit. Later, many of the inkstained journalists and scandalmongers of 19th- and early 20th-century Fleet Street made its four-story premises their "local."

You'll find six bars and three dining rooms here. The house specialties include "ye famous pudding" (steak, kidney, mushrooms, and game) and Scottish roast beef, with Yorkshire pudding and horseradish sauce. Sandwiches, salads, and standby favorites like steak-and-kidney pie are also available.

Ye Olde Cock Tavern

22 Fleet St., EC4. ☎ **0171/353-8570.** Reservations recommended. Appetizers £3–£5.75 ($4.75–$9.10); main courses £8–£12 ($12.65–$18.95); fixed-price two-course lunch £9.95 ($15.70). AE, DC, MC, V. Carvery lunch Mon–Fri noon–3pm; pub Mon–Fri 11am–11pm. Tube: Temple or Chancery Lane. BRITISH.

Dating back to 1549, this tavern boasts a long line of literary patrons. Samuel Pepys mentioned the pub in one of his diaries. Dickens frequented it, and Tennyson referred to it in one of his poems, a copy of which is framed and proudly displayed near the front entrance. It is one of the few buildings in London to have survived the Great Fire of 1666. At street level, you can order a pint as well as snack-bar food. You can also order steak-and-kidney pie or a cold chicken-and-beef plate with salad. At the Carvery upstairs, a meal includes a choice of appetizers, followed by roast beef, lamb, pork, or turkey.

BARBICAN
FOR AN ENGLISH BREAKFAST

Fox and Anchor

115 Charterhouse St., EC1. ☎ **0171/253-4838.** Reservations required. "Full house" breakfast £6.95 ($11); steak breakfast £4.60–£9.60 ($7.25–$15.15). AE, DC, MC, V.

Breakfast Mon–Fri 7–10:30am; lunch Mon–Fri noon–2:15pm. Tube: Farringdon or Barbican. BRITISH.

For a breakfast at its best, try this place that has been serving traders from the nearby famous Smithfield meat market since the pub was built in 1898. Breakfasts are gargantuan, especially if you order the "full house," which provides at least eight items on your plate, including sausage, bacon, mushrooms, kidneys, eggs, beans, white pudding, and fried slice of bread, to mention just a few, along with unlimited tea or coffee, toast, and jam. If you want a more substantial meal, you can have a filet steak with mushrooms, chips, tomatoes, and salad. Add a Black Velvet (champagne with Guinness) and the day is yours. Of course, in the modern British view, Guinness ruins champagne, but some people order it anyway—just to be traditional. More fashionable is a Bucks fizz, with orange juice and champagne. The Fox and Anchor is noted for its range of fine English ales, all available at breakfast. Butchers from the meat market, spotted with blood, still appear, as do nurses getting off their shifts and clerks and tycoons from the City who have been working at bookkeeping chores all night.

10 Westminster & Victoria

WESTMINSTER
MODERATE

Shepherd's

Marsham Court, Marsham St. (without number), at the corner of Page St., SW1. ☎ **0171/834-9552.** Reservations recommended. Set meals £18.95 ($29.95) for two courses, £22.95 ($36.25) for three courses. AE, DC, MC, V. Lunch Mon–Fri 12:30–2:45pm; dinner Mon–Fri 6:30–11:30pm. Tube: Westminster or Pimlico. BRITISH.

Some observers of London's political landscape claim that many of the inner workings of the British government operate from the precincts of this conservative and likable restaurant. Set within the shadow of the House of Parliament, two blocks north of the Tate Gallery, it enjoys a regular clientele of barristers, members of Parliament, and many of their constituents from the far-flung districts of the British Isles. Since the business of government seems to go on throughout the day and evening, don't imagine that most of the intrigue here occurs at lunchtime; evenings seem just as ripe an hour for parliamentary negotiations, particularly over the restaurant's perennial specialty of roast rib of Scottish beef served with (what else?) Yorkshire pudding. So synchronized is this establishment to the goings-on at Parliament that a Division Bell rings in the dining room, calling MPs back to the House of Commons when it's time to vote.

Ironically, even the decor of the restaurant seems to duplicate that of Parliament, with leather banquettes, sober 19th-century accessories, and a worthy collection of English portraits and landscape paintings.

Menu items reflect many years of British culinary tradition, but are made intelligently and with fresh ingredients. They include a cream-based mussel stew, hot salmon and potato salad with dill dressing, black pudding with bubble and squeak, roast leg of lamb with

Restaurants: Westminster & Victoria

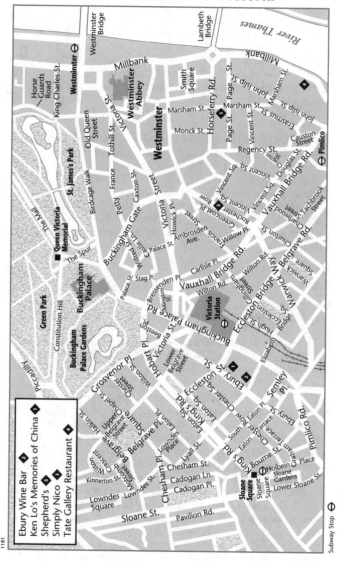

mint sauce, filet of salmon with tarragon and chive butter sauce, a changing array of daily specials based on relatively modern inspiration, and a dessert specialty of crème brûlée that this very English restaurant appropriately identifies as burnt Cambridge cream.

Tate Gallery Restaurant

Millbank, SW1. ☎ **0171/887-8877.** Reservations recommended. Appetizers £3.50–£6 ($5.55–$9.50); main courses £8–£16 ($12.65–$25.30). MC, V. Lunch Mon–Sat noon–3pm. Tube: Pimlico. Bus 77 or 88. BRITISH.

This restaurant is particularly attractive to wine fanciers, offering what may be the best bargains for superior wines anywhere in Britain. Bordeaux and Burgundies are in abundance, and the management keeps the markup between 40% and 65%, rather than the 100% to 200% added to the wholesale price in other restaurants. In fact, the prices here are even lower than they are in most retail wine shops. Wine begins at £10 ($15.80) per bottle or £2.95 ($4.65) per glass. Wine connoisseurs frequently come for lunch, heedless of the museum's paintings.

The restaurant specializes in an English menu that changes about every month. Menu items might include seafood crêpe; roasted duck with spiced apricots; roast English sirloin of beef with Yorkshire pudding; steak, kidney, and mushroom pie; and a selection of vegetarian dishes. At rare intervals, the restaurant also offers dishes inspired by English cuisine of the 17th century, including "hindle wakes" (cold stuffed chicken with prunes) and "pye with fruyt ryfshews" (fruit tart topped with meringue). Access to the restaurant is through the museum's main entrance on Millbank.

VICTORIA
MODERATE

Ken Lo's Memories of China
67–69 Ebury St., SW1. ☎ **0171/730-7734.** Reservations recommended. Appetizers £4.25–£9.75 ($6.70–$15.40); main courses £9.80–£29.50 ($15.50–$46.60); fixed-price lunch £15–£29.50 ($23.70–$46.60); fixed-price dinner £20.50–£29.50 ($32.40–$46.60). AE, DC, MC, V. Lunch Mon–Sat noon–2:30pm; dinner daily 7–11:15pm. Tube: Victoria Station. CHINESE.

Considered the finest Chinese eatery in London by many food critics, this restaurant was founded by Ken Lo, whose grandfather was the Chinese ambassador to the Court of St. James's (he was knighted by Queen Victoria in 1880). Mr. Lo has written more than 30 cookbooks and a well-known autobiography, and once was the main figure in his own TV cooking show. His restaurant, which is impeccably staffed and outfitted with an appealing minimalist decor of white with mahogany trim, has been called "a gastronomic bridge between London and China." Menu items derive from broadly divergent regions of China, and might include Cantonese quick-fried beef in oyster sauce, lobster with handmade noodles, pomegranate prawn balls, and "bang-bang chicken" (a Szechuan dish), among many others. This restaurant is not to be confused with its less expensive branch restaurant of the same name in Chelsea Harbour, which is also recommended (see Section 12, below).

ⓢ Simply Nico
48A Rochester Row, SW1. ☎ **0171/630-8061.** Reservations required. Two-course set lunch £20 ($31.60); three-course set lunch £23.50 ($37.15); three-course fixed-price dinner £25 ($39.50). AE, DC, MC, V. Lunch Mon–Fri 12:30–2pm; dinner Mon–Sat 6:45–11:15pm. Tube: Victoria Station. FRENCH.

This place was created in a moment of whimsy by Nico Ladenis, owner of the grander and more expensive Chez Nico at Ninety Park Lane (see above). Run by his sous-chef, Simply Nico is, in the words of Nico, "cheap and cheerful." Wood floors seem to reverberate the din of contented diners, who pack in here daily at snug tables. The food is often simply prepared and invariably French inspired, with fresh ingredients handled deftly in the kitchen. The set menu changes frequently. The options might include starters such as goat cheese with roasted red peppers or poached egg tartlet with hollandaise sauce with marinated puréed mushrooms and main courses such as grilled Scottish beef with horseradish sauce and crispy duck with plum sauce.

A WINE BAR

Ebury Wine Bar

139 Ebury St., SW1. ☎ **0171/730-5447.** Reservations recommended. Appetizers £2–£4.50 ($3.15–$7.10); main courses £6.95–£13.50 ($11–$21.35); fixed-price Sun lunch £9 ($14.20); glass of wine from £2.60 ($4.10). AE, DC, MC, V. Lunch Mon–Sat noon–2:45pm, Sun noon–3pm; dinner Mon–Sat 6–10:30pm, Sun 7–10pm. Tube: Victoria Station or Sloane Square. INTERNATIONAL.

Convenient for dining or drinking, this wine bar and bistro attracts a youthful clientele to its often-crowded though always atmospheric precincts. Wine is sold either by the glass or by the bottle. You can always get an enticing plat du jour, such as traditional beef Wellington or one of the grilled filet steaks.

11 Knightsbridge & Belgravia

KNIGHTSBRIDGE
MODERATE

Fifth Floor at Harvey Nichols

Corner of Knightsbridge at Sloane St., SW1. ☎ **0171/235-5250.** Reservations recommended. Set price menus £17.50 ($27.65) for two courses, £21.50 ($33.95) for three courses; appetizers £4.95–£12.50 ($7.80–$19.75); main courses £9.75–£26.50 ($15.40–$41.85). À la carte dishes available at dinner only. AE, DC, MC, V. Lunch Mon–Sat noon–3pm; dinner Mon–Sat 6:30–11:30pm (last order). Tube: Knightsbridge. BRITISH.

Set on the fifth floor of the flagship store of a chain of clothing emporiums scattered across Britain, this restaurant is probably the most carefully orchestrated of any eatery in any of the large department stores of London. There's a simple café near the entrance, which tends to be the domain of shoppers laden with packages looking for a cuppa tea and a salad, but serious diners (many from the upscale neighborhoods nearby), usually head directly into the high-ceilinged blue-and-white restaurant. There, big windows overlook the red-brick Edwardian walls of the Hyde Park Hotel, across the street, and waiters imbue any meal with a polite kind of formality. Menu items are appropriately fashionable, and include such dishes as pan-fried calves' liver with lentils and wild mushrooms, black pudding with mustard and parsley sauce, a salad of marinated grilled leeks and mushrooms with tapenade croutons, fish cakes of haddock with tartare sauce, shredded duck confit, and roulade of fresh figs.

Restaurants: Kensington to Belgravia

Antelope 28
Arcadia 1
Aubergine 5
Bibendum/
  The Oyster Bar 12
Bill Bentley's 16
Bistro 190 4
Bombay Brasserie 6
Chelsea Room 26

English Garden 29
English House 27
Fifth Floor at Harvey Nichols 24
Front Page 32
Georgian Restaurant 19
Gilbert's 11
Grenadier 22
Hilaire 7
Joe's 13

LONDON
Chelsea,
Knightsbridge
& South
Kensington

Incidentally, there's a glamorous food emporium (open till 8pm Monday to Saturday) set just outside the restaurant's entrance, where ingredients and their variety hint at the culinary splendors of the restaurant. Although the department store closes at 6pm, a pair of elevators continue to haul restaurant clients up to the fifth floor even after closing hours of "Harvey Nic's."

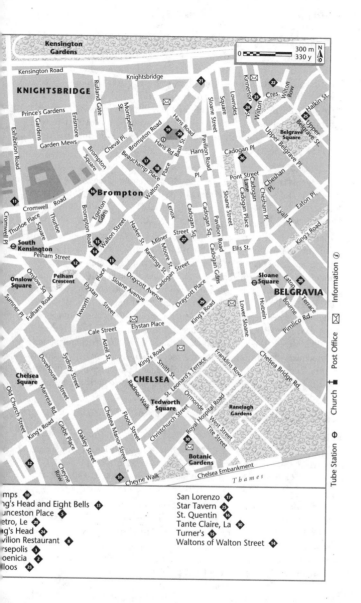

Ⓢ Georgian Restaurant

In Harrods Department Store, 87–135 Brompton Rd., SW1. ☎ **0171/581-1656.**
Reservations recommended but accepted only for lunch. Appetizers £4.50–£15
($7.10–$23.70); main courses £14.75–£16.50 ($23.30–$26.05); set lunch £18.75–
£22 ($29.65–$34.75); sandwiches and pastries at teatime £11.50 ($18.15). AE, DC,
MC, V. Lunch Mon–Sat noon–3pm; tea Mon–Sat 3:45–5:15pm. Tube: Knightsbridge.
BRITISH.

The Georgian Restaurant, lying atop London's fabled emporium, under elaborate ceilings and belle époque skylights, is one of the neighborhood's most appealing places for lunch and afternoon tea. One of the rooms, big enough for a ballroom, features a pianist, whose music trills among the crystal of the chandeliers. A lunchtime buffet features cold meats and an array of fresh salads. Guests who want a hot meal can head for the carvery section, where a uniformed crew of chefs dishes out such offerings as roast beef with Yorkshire pudding, poultry, fish, and pork.

San Lorenzo

22 Beauchamp Place, SW3. ☎ **0171/584-1074.** Reservations required. Appetizers £3.50–£9.50 ($5.55–$15); main courses £12.50–£18.50 ($19.75–$29.25). No credit cards. Lunch Mon–Sat 12:30–3pm; dinner Mon–Sat 7:30–11:30pm. Tube: Knightsbridge. ITALIAN.

Opened in 1987, this is a fashionable restaurant specializing in the cuisines of Tuscany and the Piedmont region of Italy. Well known for attracting a clientele of painters, writers, photographers, and fashion models, it quickly gained a reputation as one of the favorite dining spots of Princess Diana (business soared as a result). Inside, a series of dining rooms includes paintings by, among others, Jonathan Routh, whose tongue-in-cheek depictions of Queen Victoria visiting her colonies have provoked many an amused commentary throughout the West Indies.

Reliability is the keynote of the cuisine, which includes homemade fettuccine with salmon, carpaccio, risotto with fresh asparagus, bollito misto, fried calamari, veal piccata, grouse, and partridge in white-wine sauce. Regional offerings, which are sometimes presented, might include salt cod with polenta.

PUBS & WINE BARS

Bill Bentley's

31 Beauchamp Place, SW3. ☎ **0171/589-5080.** Reservations recommended. Appetizers £2.95–£10 ($4.65–$15.80); main courses £7.50–£16.90 ($11.85–$26.70); glass of wine £2 ($3.15). MC, V. Lunch Mon–Sat noon–2:30pm; dinner Mon–Sat 6–10:30pm. Tube: Knightsbridge. BRITISH.

Bill Bentley's stands on a fashionable restaurant- and boutique-lined block. Its wine list is varied and reasonable, including a good selection of Bordeaux. Many visitors come here just to sample the wines, including some "New World" choices along with popular French selections. In summer, a garden patio is used. If you don't prefer the formality of the restaurant, you can order from the wine-bar menu that begins with half a dozen oysters, or you can enjoy the chef's fish soup with croutons and rouille. Main dishes include Bill Bentley's famous fish cakes, served with tomato sauce, and the day's specialties are written on a chalkboard. In keeping with contemporary trends in London dining, the menu has been simplified and is rather less expensive than before. The carte is changed frequently, but typical dishes might include avocado, crab, and prawn salad as an appetizer, followed by pan-fried calves' liver or a poached stuffed salmon.

Le Metro

28 Basil St., SW3. ☎ **0171/589-6286.** Reservations: Accepted only for large parties. Appetizers £3–£4.75 ($4.75–$7.50); main courses £6–£8.95 ($9.50–$14.15); glass of wine £2 ($3.15). AE, DC, MC, V. Mon–Sat 7:30am–10:30pm. Tube: Knightsbridge. INTERNATIONAL.

Located around the corner from Harrods, Le Metro draws a fashionable crowd to its basement precincts. You can order special wines by the glass instead of by the bottle. Owned by David and Margaret Levin, the place serves good, solid, and reliable food prepared with flair. The frequently changed menu might include spinach gnocchi, calves' liver served with creamed potatoes and caramelized onions, or confit of duck.

BELGRAVIA
MODERATE

Salloos

62–64 Kinnerton St., SW1. ☎ **0171/235-4444.** Reservations recommended. Appetizers £3.50–£5 ($5.55–$7.90); main courses £9.50–£12.50 ($15–$19.75); three-course set lunch £16 ($25.30); four-course set dinner £25 ($39.50). AE, DC, MC, V. Lunch Mon–Sat noon–2:30pm; dinner Mon–Sat 7–11:30pm. Tube: Hyde Park Corner. PAKISTANI/MUGHLAI.

Considered one of London's most elegant Pakistani restaurants, this small hideaway is located in one of London's most fashionably expensive neighborhoods. It has only about 60 seats. Trimmed with elegant cornices, its interior is done in shades of terra-cotta. The lighting is dim and soothing; spotlights focus on Pakistani embroideries. The cosmopolitan clientele appreciates such dishes as lamb chops grilled in a tandoori oven, chicken shish kebabs, chicken karahi (spicy, with curry), chicken korma (moderately spicy and served with yogurt sauce), and a house specialty of *haleem akbari* (shredded lamb cooked in wheat germ with lentils and spices). Most of these specialties were developed during the reign of North India's Moghul emperors. The restaurant gets its name from its owner, Muhammad Salahuddin; his nickname is Salloos. He's assisted by his charming and articulate daughter, Farizeh, who greets customers near the door.

PUBS

Antelope

22 Eaton Terrace, SW1. ☎ **0171/730-7781.** Reservations recommended for upstairs dining room. Appetizers £2.25–£3 ($3.55–$4.75); main courses £7.50–£10 ($11.85–$15.80); glass of wine £2.25 ($3.55). MC, V. Lunch daily noon–2:30pm; pub Mon–Sat 11am–11pm, Sun noon–3pm and 7:30–10:30pm. Tube: Sloane Square. BRITISH.

Located on the fringe of Belgravia, at the gateway of Chelsea, this eatery caters to a hodgepodge of clients, aptly described as "people of all classes, colours, and creeds." It is also a base for English rugby aficionados (not to be confused with those who follow soccer). At lunchtime, the ground-floor bar provides hot and cold pub food, but in the evening, only drinks are served there. On the second floor (British first floor), the lunch menu includes principally English dishes—steak-and-kidney pie, jugged hare, and the like. Steaks are also served.

Grenadier

18 Wilton Row, SW1. ☎ **0171/235-3074.** Reservations recommended. Appetizers £3.50–£8.25 ($5.55–$13.05); main courses £11.15–£18.95 ($17.60–$29.95); glass of wine £2 ($3.15). AE, DC, MC, V. Lunch daily noon–3pm; dinner Mon–Sat 6–11pm, Sun 7–10:30pm. Closed Dec 25–26 and Jan 1. Tube: Hyde Park Corner. BRITISH.

Tucked away in a mews, Grenadier is one of London's numerous reputedly haunted pubs. Apart from the poltergeist, the basement houses the original bar and skittles alley used by the Duke of Wellington's officers on leave from fighting Napoléon. The scarlet front door of the one-time officers' mess is guarded by a scarlet sentry box and shaded by a vine. The bar is nearly always crowded. Luncheons and dinners are offered daily—even on Sunday, when it is a tradition to drink Bloody Marys here. In the stalls along the side, you can order good-tasting fare based on seasonal ingredients. Filet of beef Wellington is a specialty; other good dishes include pork Grenadier and chicken and Stilton roulade. Snacks are available at the bar if you don't want a full meal.

Nag's Head

53 Kinnerton St., SW1. ☎ **0171/235-1135.** Reservations not required. Main courses £3.75–£4.25 ($5.95–$6.70); beer from £1.80 ($2.85). No credit cards. Mon–Sat 11am–11pm, Sun noon–3pm and 7–11pm. Tube: Knightsbridge. BRITISH.

Nag's Head, snuggled on a "back street," is a short walk from the deluxe Berkeley Hotel. Previously a jail dating from 1780, it is said to be the smallest pub in London, although others also claim that distinction. In 1921, it was sold for £12 and 6p.

Have a drink up front or wander to the tiny little bar in the rear. For food, you might enjoy "real ale sausage" (made with pork and ale), shepherd's pie, steak-and-mushroom pie, or even the quiche of the day. This warm and cozy pub, with a welcoming staff, is patronized by a cosmopolitan clientele—newspaper people, musicians, and curious tourists.

Star Tavern

6 Belgrave Mews West, SW1. ☎ **0171/235-3019.** Reservations not accepted. Lunch pub snacks £2.50–£5 ($4–$7.90); dinner pub snacks £3.50–£5.90 ($5.55–$9.30); glass of wine £2.05 ($3.25). No credit cards. Lunch Mon–Fri noon–2:30pm, dinner Mon–Fri 6:30–8:45pm; pub Mon–Thurs 11:30am–3pm and 5–11pm, Fri 11:30am–11pm, Sat 11:30am–3pm and 6:30–11pm, Sun noon–3pm and 7–10:30pm. Closed Dec. 25. Tube: Knightsbridge or Hyde Park. BRITISH.

Set in a Georgian mews behind a picture-postcard facade, Star Tavern is one of the most colorful pubs in the West End. Inside are Victorian walls and banquettes beneath 19th-century Victorian moldings. In winter it's one of the coziest havens around, with two fireplaces going. Groups of office workers descend after work, staking out their territory. You can order baby spring chicken, sirloin steak, or vegetable quiche. There is no waitress service; patrons place their orders at the bar.

12 Chelsea & Chelsea Harbour

CHELSEA
VERY EXPENSIVE

✪ La Tante Claire

68–69 Royal Hospital Rd., SW3. ☎ **0171/352-6045.** Reservations required. Appetizers £19–£25 ($30–$39.50); main courses £24.50–£35 ($38.70–$55.30); fixed-price lunch £25 ($39.50); minimum charge £60 ($94.80) per person. AE, DC, MC, V. Lunch Mon–Fri 12:30–2pm; dinner Mon–Fri 7–11pm. Closed Dec 25 and Jan 1. Tube: Sloane Square. FRENCH.

The quality of its cuisine is so legendary that La Tante Claire has become, in the eyes of many critics, the leading choice among the capital's gaggle of French restaurants. The ring of a doorbell set discreetly into the facade of Aegean blue and white prompts an employee to usher you politely inside. There, bouquets of flowers, a modernized, vaguely Hellenistic decor, and birchwood-and-chrome trim complement an array of paintings that might have been inspired by Jean Cocteau.

Pierre Koffman is the celebrated chef, creating such specialties as ravioli stuffed with frog meat. Every gastronome in London talks about the pig's trotters stuffed with morels and the exquisite sauces that complement many of the dishes. These include grilled scallops served on a bed of squid-ink sauce, baked filet of turbot with cabbage and fresh vegetables cooked in consommé with preserved duck, and duck in red-wine sauce and confit. For dessert, try a caramelized ice-cream soufflé with hazelnut and raspberry coulis or the pistachio soufflé.

EXPENSIVE

Aubergine

11 Park Walk, SW10. ☎ **0171/352-3449.** Reservations required. Three-course fixed-price lunch £18–£34 ($28.45–$53.70); fixed-price dinner £34–£44 ($53.70–$69.50). AE, DC, MC, V. Lunch Mon–Sat noon–2:30pm; dinner Mon–Sat 7–11pm. Tube: South Kensington. FRENCH.

"The Eggplant" is luring savvy diners down to Chelsea, its lower reaches, where Gordon Ramsay, the owner and chef, continues to create excitement. The decor evokes a summer's day, and tables are placed far enough apart so that you don't have to listen to your fellow diners' conversation. Aubergine is so popular that reservations as far in advance as possible are needed. Even though a visiting movie star or an overpaid decorator might show up, the place is not all hype and publicity. It genuinely delivers a most satisfying menu.

Ramsay has worked with the biggest chefs in London or Paris, including Guy Savoy, Albert Roux, Joël Robuchon, and Marco Pierre White, yet has forged his own style. Begin with—say, cappuccino of haricot blancs with truffle oil, or else a parfait of duck foie gras with a toasted brioche. The watercress soup might be served with poached oysters, and salad of roast wood pigeons is flavored with wild mushrooms. A specialty is red mullet built upon a foundation of eggplant caviar. The filet of sea bass emerges with braised fennel hearts flavored with tarragon. Guinea fowl *en cocotte* was never lovelier or better tasting than when presented with caramelized sweetbreads, a leek tagliatelle, and a turnip confit. The food has been called "jewel like" to the eye. An assiette of lusciously tempting desserts—offered for at least two diners—gives you an opportunity to sample them in miniature, a taste of this, a taste of that. Most of the wine comes from France, although some bottles come from what some critics in Britain still call "the New World." End with coffee and a selection of delectable *petits fours.*

MODERATE

Chelsea Room

In the Hyatt Carlton Tower, 2 Cadogan Place, SW1. ☎ **0171/235-1234.** Reservations required. Appetizers £4.50–£15 ($7.10–$23.70); main courses £12.50–£28 ($19.75–$44.25); fixed-price lunch £22.50 ($35.55); fixed-price dinner £29.50 ($46.60). AE, DC, MC, V. Lunch Mon–Sat 12:30–2:45pm; dinner Mon–Sat 7–11pm, Sun 7–10pm. Tube: Sloane Square. FRENCH.

The superb Chelsea Room, one of the best restaurants in London, is in one of Hyatt's finest international properties. The dining room's combination of haute cuisine, stylish clientele, and elegant decor make it a much-sought-after place for lunch or dinner. Wedgwood plates with the restaurant's cockerel motif adorn each place setting. The color scheme is tasteful and subdued, in grays, beiges, and soft greens.

The kitchen is run by maître cuisinier de France Bernard Gaume, who has pleased palates at some of the leading hotels of Europe, including L'Abbaye in Talloires in the French Alps, the Savoy in London, and the Hotel des Bergues in Geneva. His portions are large and satisfying, and their presentation shows his extraordinary flair. Highly professional dishes, original offerings, as well as time-tested classics and very fresh ingredients are his forte. The menu changes, but here is an idea of the fare you are likely to be served: sautéed scallops with seafood stock, diced lobster and truffles; filet of lamb tossed in butter served with eggplant purée, basil, and tomato; or two small filets of beef, one with bordelaise and one with shallot sauce. His desserts require a separate menu, ranging from light chestnut mousse with ginger sauce to chilled hazelnut parfait in light Cointreau sauce.

English Garden

10 Lincoln St., SW3. ☎ **0171/584-7272.** Reservations required. Appetizers £3.75–£9.95 ($5.95–$15.70); main courses £7.25–£16.75 ($11.45–$26.45); fixed-price set lunch £14.75 ($23.30). AE, DC, MC, V. Lunch Mon–Sat 12:30–2:30pm, Sun 12:30–2pm; dinner Mon–Sat 7:30–11:30pm, Sun 7–10:30pm. Closed Dec 25–26. Tube: Sloane Square. BRITISH.

The decor is pretty and lighthearted in this historic Chelsea town house. The Garden Room on the ground floor is whitewashed brick, with panels of large stylish flowers. Attractive pelmets, in vivid flower colors, contrast with stark-white curtains; rattan chairs in a Gothic theme and candy-pink napery complete the scene. With the domed conservatory roof and banks of plants, the atmosphere is relaxing.

The menu includes plenty of salads and fish—offering a checkerboard of freshwater fish, including a steamed fish of the day—or roast rack of Welsh lamb with roasted garlic. The chef's daily specials are included in a separate luncheon menu. A comprehensive wine list is available, with an excellent French house wine always obtainable.

English House

3 Milner St., SW3. ☎ **0171/584-3002.** Reservations required. Appetizers £3.75–£9.95 ($5.95–$15.70); main courses £8.50–£15.50 ($13.45–$24.50); fixed-price set lunch £14.75 ($23.30). AE, DC, MC, V. Lunch Mon–Sat 12:30–2:30pm, Sun 12:30–2pm; dinner Mon–Sat 7:30–11:15pm, Sun 7–10pm. Closed Dec 25–26. Tube: Sloane Square. BRITISH.

This restaurant is another design creation of Roger Wren, who did the English Garden, described above. The English House is a tiny place in the heart of Chelsea where diners feel like a guest in an elegant private home. The decor provides both spectacle and atmosphere. Shades of blue and terra-cotta predominate, and the walls are clad in a printed cotton depicting a traditional English design of autumn leaves and black currants. The fireplace creates a homelike environment, with a collection of interesting, beautiful furniture adding to the background. Attention has been paid to detail, and even the saltcellars are Victorian in origin.

The food is British, with such succulent offerings as chicken, leek, and lemon pie; poached halibut with orange cream sauce; and grilled filet of beef with celeriac pancake and port sauce. Summer berries (in season) predominate on the "pudding" menu, including a bowl of fresh berries laced with elderflower syrup. Another offering is a "A Phrase of Apples," the chef's adaptation of a 17th-century recipe for a delectable apple pancake.

PUBS

Front Page

35 Old Church St., SW3. ☎ **0171/352-0648.** Reservations not required. Main courses £2.50–£8 ($3.95–$12.65). MC, V. Restaurant lunch daily noon–2:30pm; dinner Mon–Sat 7–10pm, Sun 7–9:30pm; pub Mon–Sat 11am–3pm and 5:30–11pm, Sun noon–3pm and 7–11pm. Tube: Sloane Square. INTERNATIONAL.

Front Page is favored by young professionals who like the mellow atmosphere provided by its wood paneling, wooden tables, and pews and benches. In one section an open fire burns on cold nights. The pub stands in an expensive residential section of Chelsea and is a good place to go for a drink, with lager costing from £2 ($3.15). You can also order bottled Budweiser. Check the chalkboard for a listing of the daily specials, which might include hot chicken salad, fish cakes, and smoked salmon and cream cheese bagel. You might begin with homemade soup du jour.

King's Head and Eight Bells

50 Cheyne Walk, SW3. ☎ **0171/352-1820.** Reservations not accepted. Appetizers £2–£4 ($3.15–$6.30); main courses £3.50–£7.50 ($5.55–$11.85). MC, V. Mon–Sat 11am–11pm, Sun noon–3pm and 7–10:30pm. Tube: Sloane Square. BRITISH.

Many distinguished personalities once lived near this historic Thames-side pub, and a short stroll will take you to the former homes of such personages as Carlyle, Swinburne, and George Eliot. In other days, press gangs used to roam these parts of Chelsea seeking lone travelers to abduct for a life at sea. Today, it's popular with stage and TV celebrities as well as writers.

The best English beers are served here, as well as a good selection of reasonably priced wine. A refrigerated display case holds cold dishes and salads, and a hot counter features the homemade specials of the day, including at least one vegetable main dish.

CHELSEA HARBOUR
MODERATE

Ken Lo's Memories of China

Harbour Yard (without number), Chelsea Harbour, SW10. ☎ **0171/352-4953.** Reservations recommended. Appetizers £3.50–£9.75 ($5.55–$15.40); main courses £4.50–£29.95 ($7.10–$47.30); fixed-price dinner £13.50–£29.60 ($21.35–$46.75) Mon–Sat; Sun brunch £15 ($23.70). AE, DC, MC, V. Lunch Sun–Fri noon–3pm; dinner daily 7pm–midnight. Directions: Chelsea Harbour Hoppa Bus C3 from Earl's Court Mon–Sat. On Sun, take a taxi. CHINESE.

This restaurant is a slightly less expensive branch of a famous Chinese restaurant with the same name near Victoria Station. Decorated in shades of beige, the restaurant offers a cuisine that wanders from region to region of China, with an emphasis on fish and seafood. Specialties include Peking duck, steamed sea bass, Mongolian-style barbecued lamb, and chicken in hot black-bean sauce. Especially popular on weekends, it offers a Sunday brunch with live jazz.

INEXPENSIVE

Deal's Restaurant and Diner

Harbour Yard (without number), Chelsea Harbour, SW10. ☎ 0171/352-5887. Reservations recommended. Appetizers £3.10–£4.95 ($4.90–7.80); main courses £5.25–10.95 ($8.30–$17.30). MC, V. Mon–Fri noon–3:30pm and 6–11pm, Sat–Sun noon–11:30pm. Directions: Chelsea Harbour Hoppa Bus C3 from Earl's Court. On Sun, take a taxi. INTERNATIONAL.

After the Queen Mother arrived here on a barge to order a Deal's burger, the success of this place was assured. Deal's is co-owned by Princess Margaret's son, Viscount Linley, and Lord Lichfield. The early 1900s atmosphere includes ceiling fans and bentwood banquettes. The food is American diner–style with a strong Eastern influence: Try teriyaki burgers, prawn curry, spareribs, or a vegetarian dish and finish with New England apple pie.

Canteen

Unit G4, Harbour Yard, Chelsea Harbour, SW10. ☎ **0171/351-7330.** Cover charge £1 ($1.60) per person. Reservations recommended. Appetizers £6.50 ($10.25); main courses £11.50 ($18.15). Three-course set lunch (Sat–Sun only) £17.50 ($27.65). MC, V. Lunch Mon–Sat noon–3pm, Sun noon–3:30pm; dinner Mon–Sat 6:30pm–midnight (last order), Sun 6:30–10:30pm (last order). Directions: Chelsea Harbour Hoppa Bus C3 from Earl's Court. On Sun, take a taxi. INTERNATIONAL.

Set on the ground floor of a three-story building devoted to offices, some visitors call this the most viable and popular of the several restaurants in the Chelsea Harbour Complex, the multimillion-dollar development of what used to be abandoned piers and wharves southwest of the center of London. You'll dine in a setting influenced by the themes of *Alice in Wonderland,* with a whimsical decor based on depictions of playing cards and harlequins—all very fantastical and the kind of thing that children as well as adults seem to appreciate. Even more attractive are the low prices, where all appetizers and main courses cost the same (see above), although three or four concocted from more expensive raw ingredients are garnished with a small supplement. Menu items include smoked haddock with poached eggs; gazpacho of crab; savoy cabbage prepared in the style of Alsace; artichokes stuffed with exotic mushrooms; a papillotte of smoked salmon; guinea fowl *en cocotte;* risotto in squid ink; confit of duck in the style of Toulouse; and roast rump of lamb niçoise.

A WINE BAR

Boaters Wine Bar

Harbour Yard (without number), Chelsea Harbour, SW10. ☎ 0171/352-3687. Reservations not required. Main courses £2.20–£4.75 ($3.50–$7.50). AE, DC, MC, V. Mon–Fri 11am–11pm, Sat 6:30–11pm, Sun noon–3pm. Directions: Chelsea Harbour Hoppa Bus C3 from Earl's Court Mon–Sat. On Sun, take a taxi. BRITISH.

Well-heeled locals who own the soaringly expensive apartments in the Chelsea Harbour complex often come here to drink champagne by the bottle while munching complimentary bowls of popcorn on the long wooden bar counter. Visitors from all over the world pour in here as well. Most of the emphasis at the bar is on an impressive array of bottled beer, beer on tap, and wine by either bottle or glass; only a minimum array of liquor is available. Sandwiches, cheese plates, and salads are available throughout the day. An impressive carte offers wine by the glass, costing from £1.85 ($2.90) for the house version.

13 Kensington & South Kensington

KENSINGTON
EXPENSIVE

Turner's

87–89 Walton St., SW3. ☎ **0171/584-6711.** Reservations required. Weekday set lunch £9.95–£13.50 ($15.70–$21.35); Sun fixed-price lunch £19.50 ($30.80); set dinner £26.50 ($41.90). AE, DC, MC, V. Lunch Mon–Fri and Sun 12:30–2:30pm; dinner Mon–Sat 7:30–11:15pm, Sun 7:30–10pm. Closed One week at Christmas. Tube: Knightsbridge. INTERNATIONAL.

This restaurant is named after a native of Yorkshire, Brian J. Turner, the accomplished London chef who gained fame at a number of establishments he didn't own, including the Capital Hotel, before achieving his own place in the culinary sun. As one critic has aptly put it, his food comes not only fresh from the market each day but also "from the heart." He doesn't seem to imitate anyone but sets his own goals and standards. The establishment's set menus change every day; its à la carte listings, at least every season. Examples of cuisine—which may or may not be listed by the time of your visit—include creamy crab soup, fine chicken liver pâté with foie gras, a terrine of fresh salmon with a dill sauce, Scotch smoked salmon with artichokes, cucumber and horseradish dressing, roast rack of lamb with herb crust, smoked and roast breast of duck in a port and green peppercorn sauce, or sea bass on a bed of stewed leeks with a bacon dressing.

MODERATE

Arcadia

35 Kensington High St., W8. ☎0171/937-4294. Reservations recommended. Appetizers £3–£5 ($4.75–$7.90); main courses £8.50–£13 ($13.45–$20.55); fixed-price lunch £13.95 ($22.05). AE, DC, MC, V. Lunch Sun–Fri noon–2:30pm; dinner daily 7–11:30pm. Tube: Kensington High Street. FRENCH PROVENÇAL.

In a cobbled passageway off Kensington High Street, Vincent Quiros took over this restaurant in December of 1994. Previously it was known as the Ark, whose passing one reviewer called "unlamented." The two-floor restaurant has a color scheme of green and buttermilk, relieved with French cartoons and landscape paintings.

Starters include escargot cooked in a garlic and butter sauce; a seafood mousse crêpe; mussels cooked in a parsley and butter sauce; and avocado mousse wrapped in smoked salmon. Main courses include filet of steak caramelized with Dijon mustard; roasted lamb with green peppers or mustard greens; Dover sole with lobster and truffles; roasted duck with black-currant sauce; chicken with creamed mushrooms and port wine sauce; and veal tongue with prawns or caper sauce.

Joe's

126 Draycott Ave., SW3. ☎ **0171/225-2217.** Reservations recommended. Appetizers £4.50–£9.50 ($7.10–$15); main courses £11.95–£13.95 ($18.90–$22.05). AE, DC, MC, V. Lunch Mon–Sat noon–3pm; dinner Mon–Sat 7–11pm; Sun 10am–5pm. Tube: South Kensington. INTERNATIONAL.

This is one of five London restaurants established by fashion designer Joseph Ettedgui, and partly because of its sense of glamor and fun, is often filled with well-known names in the roster of the British fashion, music, and entertainment industries. (Two fashion-industry names associated with the upper dining room include Vivian West and Al McPherson.) Amid a split-level decor of pale ashwood paneling and a monochromatic color scheme of beige and honey, you can enjoy such dishes as leek and onion tart with Gorgonzola and mixed greens; filet of John Dory with celeriac mash and red wine sauce; ricotta tarts; grilled tuna, an eggplant and mussel soup, grilled chicken with onion and pumpkin fritters, and oxtail stew. No one will mind if your meal is composed exclusively of one or more appetizers (the menu is well suited for everyone from slim anorexics, of which there seem to be many, and for heartier appetites as well.) There's a bar near the entrance, a cluster of tables for quick meals near the door, and more leisurely (and gossipy) dining available in an area a few steps up from the bar and entrance level.

Launceston Place

1A Launceston Place, W8. ☎ **0171/937-6912.** Reservations required. Appetizers £4.50–£9.50 ($7.10–$15); main courses £9–£18 ($14.20–$28.45); set menu £13.50 ($21.35) for two courses, £16.50 ($26.05) for three-courses. MC, V. Lunch Mon–Sat 12:30–2:30pm, Sun 12:30–3pm; dinner Mon–Sat 7–11:30pm. Tube: Gloucester. MODERN BRITISH.

Launceston Place is situated in an affluent, almost villagelike neighborhood where many Londoners would like to live if only they could afford it. The architecturally stylish restaurant is a series of uncluttered Victorian parlors illuminated by a rear skylight and decorated with Victorian oils and watercolors, plus contemporary paintings. Since its opening in spring 1986, it has been known for its new British cuisine. The menu changes frequently but you are likely to be served such appetizers as stir-fried squid with lemon, garlic, ginger, and coriander or seared foie gras with grilled sourdough bread and chutney. For a main dish, perhaps it'll be poached smoked haddock with parsley sauce, médaillons of pork with mustard sauce, or filet steak with bordelaise sauce, garlic, and shallot marmalade.

INEXPENSIVE

Persepolis

39 Kensington High St., W8. ☎ **0171/937-3555.** Reservations not required. Appetizers £2.10–£3.15 ($3.30–$5); main courses £6.30–£10.50 ($10–$16.60). AE, DC, MC, V. Daily noon–11pm. Tube: High Street Kensington. PERSIAN.

Persepolis offers Iranian cooking, which in some culinary circles is still called Persian. The restaurant is sleek and modern, without the slightest touch of Asian kitsch. The only distinctive Persian features are wall friezes showing winged lions and spade-bearded ancient kings. A small, subtly lit place, it features picture windows with a view of the street. Appetizers include homemade creamy yogurt with either chopped mint-flavored cucumber or chopped spinach flavored with fried onions. For a main dish, you might choose a quarter of chicken cooked with grated walnuts and served with pomegranate purée or finely chopped lamb, eggplant, and split peas cooked with tomato purée. Baklava and *halva shekari* (a sesame-seed concoction) are among the desserts.

✪ Phoenicia

11–13 Abingdon Rd., W8. ☎ **0171/937-0120.** Reservations required. Appetizers £2.60–£4.95 ($4.10–$7.80); main courses £7.50–£9.50 ($11.85–$15); buffet lunch £9.95 ($15.70); fixed-price dinner £15.30–£28.30 ($24.15–$44.70). AE, DC, MC, V. Daily noon–midnight; buffet lunch Mon–Sat 12:15–2:30pm. Tube: High Street Kensington. LEBANESE.

Phoenicia is highly regarded for the quality of its Lebanese cuisine—outstanding in presentation and freshness—and for its moderate prices. For the best value, go for lunch, when you can enjoy a buffet of more than two dozen *meze* (appetizers), presented in little pottery dishes. Each day, also at lunch, the chef prepares two or three home-cooked dishes to tempt your taste buds, including chicken in garlic sauce or stuffed lamb with vegetables. Many Lebanese patrons begin their meal with the apéritif arak, a liqueur some have compared to ouzo. You can select as an appetizer such classic Middle Eastern dishes as hummus or stuffed vine leaves. In a clay oven the kitchen staff bakes its own bread and makes two types of pizza. Minced lamb, spicy and well flavored, is the eternal favorite. Various charcoal-grilled dishes are also offered.

SOUTH KENSINGTON
EXPENSIVE

✪ Bibendum/The Oyster Bar

81 Fulham Rd., SW3. ☎ **0171/581-5817.** Reservations required in Bibendum; not accepted in The Oyster Bar. Appetizers £4.75–£12 ($7.50–$18.95); main courses £12–£20 ($18.95–$31.60); three-course fixed-price lunch £27 ($42.65); cold shell-fish platter in Oyster Bar £22 ($34.75) per person. AE, MC, V. Bibendum lunch Mon–Fri noon–2:30pm, Sat–Sun noon–3pm; dinner Mon–Sat 7–11:15pm, Sun 7–10:15pm. Oyster Bar Mon–Sat noon–11pm, Sun noon–3pm and 7–10pm. Tube: South Kensington. MODERN FRENCH/MEDITERRANEAN.

Considered a top London restaurant, this fashionable eating place occupies two floors of a building that's an art deco masterpiece. Built in 1911, it housed the British headquarters of Michelin Tire. Bibendum, the more visible eatery, lies one floor above street level in a white-tiled art deco room whose stained-glass windows, streaming sunlight, and chic clientele make meals extremely pleasant. Menu items are carefully planned interpretations of seasonal ingredients. The menu might include red pepper and basil risotto, sautéed squid with aioli and salsa, poached cod with lobster sauce and chives, or breast of duck with garlic and sherry cream sauce. Simpler meals and cocktails are available at street level, in the Oyster Bar. The bar-style menu and 1930s decor stress fresh shellfish presented in the traditional French style, on ice-covered platters occasionally adorned with strands of seaweed.

Waltons of Walton Street

121 Walton St., SW5. ☎ **0171/584-0204.** Reservations recommended. Appetizers £4.75–£14 ($7.50–$22.10); main courses £12–£16.75 ($18.95–$26.45); "Simply Waltons" fixed-price lunch £14.95 ($23.60); late-night fixed-price supper £21 ($33.20). AE, DC, MC, V. Lunch Mon–Sat 12:30–2:30pm, Sun 12:30–2:30pm; dinner Mon–Sat 7:30–11:30pm, Sun 7–10:30pm; late-night supper Mon–Sat from 10pm. Tube: South Kensington or Knightsbridge. INTERNATIONAL.

A posh and intimate rendezvous, Waltons offers the best-quality fresh produce from local and European markets and serves it with flair amid silk walls and floral decorations. Its chefs prepare a refined international cuisine, featuring such dishes as roast breast of Norfolk duck served pink, prime filet of Scottish beef, and rack of lamb with an herb crust served on a leek purée with a rosemary gravy. Specialties include terrine of squab and grilled pepper with baby spinach and tomato and coriander chutney and raspberry millefeuille, wafers of puff pastry layered with brandy cream and fresh raspberries. Walton's, long a favorite with the Harrods shopping crowd, also has special-value fixed-price menus. The wide-ranging wine list, encompassing vintages from Australia to California, features the best champagnes in London.

MODERATE

Bistro 190

In the Gore Hotel, 190 Queen's Gate, SW7. ☎ **0171/581-8172.** Reservations recommended. Appetizers £2.65–£6.95 ($4.20–$11); main courses £6.95–£10.50 ($11–$16.60). AE, DC, MC, V. Mon–Sat noon–12:30am, Sun noon–11pm. Tube: Gloucester Road. MEDITERRANEAN.

Set in the airy front room of a hotel, this restaurant features a light Mediterranean cuisine much appreciated by the hip and stylish crowd that comes here. (Many are in the music industry; many others are well-known faces in entertainment and media.) Within an artfully simple decor of wooden floorboards, potted plants, lots of framed art-works, and a convivial but gossipy roar, which adds a lot to its allure, you can order dishes anytime throughout the afternoon, until the late hours listed above. Service is not particularly fast, the policy on reser-vations is confusing, and in the crush of peak dining hours, your waiter may or may not remember the nuances you expressed while placing your order, but the restaurant is nonetheless memorable. Menu items include such items as lamb grilled over charcoal and served with deep-fried basil; salmon fish cakes with chips; linguine with walnuts and Gorgonzola-flavored cream; a cassoulet of fish with chili toast; Mediterranean chowder with pesto toast, and—if it's available—a des-sert (rhubarb crumble) based loosely on old-fashioned British cuisine.

Bombay Brasserie

Courtfield Close (without number; adjoining Bailey's Hotel), SW7. ☎ **0171/370-4040.** Reservations recommended. Appetizers £3.95–£4.95 ($6.25–$7.80); main courses £11.50–£18 ($18.15–$28.45); buffet lunch £14.95 ($23.60). MC, V. Buffet lunch daily 12:30–3pm; dinner daily 7:30pm–midnight. Closed Dec 25–26. Tube: Gloucester Road. INDIAN.

By anyone's estimation, this is the finest, most popular, and most talked about Indian restaurant in London. Established in 1982, this cavernous trio of rooms is staffed by one of London's most accommo-dating teams of Indian-born waiters, each of whom is very able to advise you on the spice-laden delicacies that thousands of years of Indian culinary tradition have developed. Lattices decorate the windows, dhurrie rugs cover the floors, cooling is by paddle fans, and sepia Raj pictures of imperial Britain at its height adorn the walls.

Before heading in to dinner, you might enjoy a drink amid the wicker chairs of the pink-and-white bar. The bartender's special is a mango Bellini. The restaurant's menu features tandoori trout, fish with mint chutney, chicken tikka (a dish originating from the Hindu Kush mountains), and vegetarian meals. One corner of the menu is reserved for Goan cookery, representing that part of India seized from Portugal in 1961. The cookery of North India is represented by Mughlai specialties, including chicken biryani, the famous Muslim pilaf dish. Under the category "Some Like It Hot," you'll find such main courses as lamb korma Kashmiri style, a favorite of a frequent customer, Faye Dunaway.

Gilbert's

2 Exhibition Rd., SW7. ☎ **0171/589-8947.** Reservations recommended. Fixed-price lunch £11.50–£18.50 ($18.15–$29.25); fixed-price dinner £16–£20 ($25.30–$31.60). AE, DC, MC, V. Lunch Mon–Fri noon–2pm; dinner Mon–Fri 6–10pm. Closed Sat–Sun. Tube: South Kensington. BRITISH/FRENCH.

A small restaurant that opened in 1988, Gilbert's changes its menu every four weeks; the food is based on the fresh ingredients of the season. Virtually everything is prepared on the premises, including fudge with coffee and homemade bread at dinner. The cuisine might be called "new English," for much of it is adaptations of French dishes. The menu is normally limited to five choices per course, and there are often specials. At dinner, there is a two- or three-course fixed-price meal, which includes bread and vegetables, but not service. For dessert, try if featured Mrs. Beeton's lemon tart or chocolate tipsy cake. The wine list also changes frequently.

⑤ Hilaire

68 Old Brompton Rd., SW7. ☎ **0171/584-8993.** Reservations recommended. Two-course fixed-price lunch £16.50 ($26.05); four-course fixed-price dinner £32.50 ($51.35); dinner appetizers £4.50–£16 ($7.10–$25.30); dinner main courses £14.50–£19.50 ($22.90–$30.80). AE, DC, MC, V. Lunch Mon–Fri 12:15–2:30pm; dinner Mon–Sat 6:30–11:30pm. Closed bank holidays. Tube: South Kensington. FRENCH.

Hilaire is a jovially cramped restaurant, housed in what was originally a Victorian storefront. Ceiling fans, lemon-yellow walls, fresh flowers, and twin Corinthian columns provide the setting for the elegant culinary specialties. Chef Bryan Webb prepares a mixture of classical French and cuisine moderne that has made this one of the most stylish restaurants in London. An apéritif bar, extra tables, and a pair of semiprivate alcoves are in the lower dining room. A typical lunch might begin with a red wine risotto with radicchio and sun-dried tomato pesto; then follow with sautéed scallops with creamed chicory; and end with rhubarb sorbet. The menu always reflects the best of the season's offerings, and main courses at dinner might include rack of lamb with tapenade and wild garlic, saddle of rabbit, or grilled tuna with Provençal vegetables.

Kemps

In the Pelham Hotel, 15 Cromwell Place, SW7. ☎ **0171/589-8288.** Reservations required. Appetizers £3–£4.75 ($4.75–$7.50); main courses £8.50–£11.50 ($13.45–$18.15); fixed-price lunch £8.95 ($14.15). AE, MC, V. Lunch Mon–Sat 12:30–2:30pm; dinner Sun–Fri 7–10:30pm. Tube: South Kensington. FRENCH.

Located on the ground floor of this previously recommended elegant hotel (see Chapter 4, Section 9), the Pelham is decorated with a subtle racing motif, accented with subtle lighting, cove moldings, a blue-and-yellow decor, and a large mahogany bar. It provides uniformed and impeccable French service at its limited number of well-attended tables, which are often filled with London luminaries.

Fashion aside, it is the food that attracts diners. The expertly prepared dishes represent an interpretation of modern French cuisine, including salad of char-grilled vegetables and goat cheese on toasted brioche, crab claws served with a poached egg and dandelion greens, and fresh mussels cooked in saffron wine with tagliatelle. For your main course, your selection might be filet steak served with dauphinoise potato and carrot chips or pan-fried sea bass in a soya sauce with artichokes and new potatoes. Desserts are sumptuous, often presented like portrait miniatures, including a dark chocolate mousse with a white chocolate sauce and orange and walnut tartlet served with custard.

Pavilion Restaurant

In the Regency Hotel, 100 Queen's Gate, SW7. ☎ **0171/370-4595.** Reservations not required. Appetizers £3.50–£7.95 ($5.55–$12.55); main courses £6.25–£14.50 ($9.90–$22.90); lunch buffet £16 ($25.30). AE, DC, MC, V. Lunch Mon–Fri noon–2:30pm; dinner daily 5:30–10:15pm. Tube: Gloucester Road or South Kensington. INTERNATIONAL.

The Pavilion is a glamorous but reasonably priced choice if you're staying at one of the many hotels in South Kensington and would like to come here for meals and drinks. Menu selections are modern dishes based on prime seasonal produce and include English lamb cutlets served with tomatoes, mushrooms, and watercress and pan-fried calves' liver with Dubonnet and orange sauce. Cod steak is lightly grilled and served with anchovy butter. Dover sole can be grilled or pan-fried to your request, and you can always order tender steaks from the charcoal grill; vegetarian dishes are also available. Care and attention also go into the appetizers such as the chef's terrine of ham with garlic and parsley or duck salad served with orange dressing.

St. Quentin

243 Brompton Rd., SW3. ☎ **0171/581-5131.** Reservations required. Appetizers £3.20–£11.90 ($5.05–$18.80); main courses £11–£14.80 ($17.40–$23.40); two-course set-price £9 ($14.20). AE, DC, MC, V. Lunch daily noon–3pm; dinner Mon–Sat 7–11pm, Sun 6:30–11pm. Tube: Knightsbridge or South Kensington. FRENCH.

Founded in 1980, St. Quentin is probably the most authentic looking French brasserie in London. Modeled after the famous La Coupole in Paris (with its memories of the Lost Generation), it attracts many members of the French community in London, all of whom seem to talk at once. (This tends to raise the level of noise and conviviality here to a subdued roar.) The decor of mirrors and crystal chandeliers reflects a fashion-and-trend-conscious clientele who enjoy the social hubbub that sometimes accompanies bistro dining. The waiters take it all in stride, usually with seemingly effortless Gallic tact. Try the scallops with chopped artichoke, or the duck confit, foie gras, and smoked goose breast. Look also for chicory and Roquefort cheese salad or Bayonne ham with celeriac.

14 West Brompton

MODERATE

Blue Elephant

4–6 Fulham Broadway, SW6. ☎ **0171/385-6595.** Reservations recommended. Appetizers £5.25–£7.95 ($8.30–$12.55); main courses £6.25–£14.25 ($9.90–$22.50). AE, DC, MC, V. Lunch Sun–Fri noon–2:30pm; dinner Mon–Sat 7pm–12:30am, Sun 7–10:30pm. Tube: Fulham Broadway. THAI.

This is the counterpart of the famous L'Eléphant Bleu in Brussels. Located in a converted factory building, London's Blue Elephant has been all the rage since it opened in 1986. In fact, it is the leading Thai restaurant of London, where the competition is growing.

In an almost magical garden setting of lush tropical foliage, diners are treated to an array of ancient and modern MSG-free Thai food. You can begin with a "floating market" (shellfish in clear broth flavored with chili paste and lemongrass), then go on to a splendid and varied selection of main courses, for which many of the ingredients have been flown in from Thailand. You might try roasted duck curry served in a clay cooking pot. The most popular choices are the Royal Thai banquet at £25 to £28 ($39.50 to $44.25) a head and the Sunday buffet at £14.50 ($22.90) per person.

INEXPENSIVE

Chapter 11

51 Hollywood Rd., SW10. ☎ **0171/351-1683.** Reservations required. Appetizers £2.50–£5 ($3.95–$7.90); main courses £6.50–£11 ($10.25–$17.40). AE, DC, MC, V. Dinner only, Mon–Sat 6–11:30pm. Closed Dec 24–26. Tube: Earl's Court. MODERN BRITISH.

At one time, the best cuisine you could hope to find in this neighborhood was bangers and mash. But today some of the most fashionable members of young London gravitate here, drawn by shops selling some of the most exclusive and costly goods in town. Chapter 11 has a small garden terrace in back, but in bad weather there is a lower-level dining room. The menu, wisely limited, offers well-prepared dishes based on fresh ingredients. You might begin with butternut-pumpkin soup, lobster ricotta ravioli, or a goat cheese soufflé, then follow with Thai prawn curry, grilled tuna steak, grilled rack of lamb with roast garlic and shallots, even a char-grilled hamburger.

15 Notting Hill & Holland Park

NOTTING HILL
EXPENSIVE

✪ Clarke's

124 Kensington Church St., W8. ☎**0171/221-9225.** Reservations recommended. Fixed-price lunch £22–£26 ($34.75–$41.10); fixed-price dinner £37 ($58.45). MC, V. Lunch Mon–Fri 12:30–1:45pm; dinner Mon–Fri 7–10pm. Tube: Notting Hill Gate or High Street Kensington. BRITISH.

Named after its owner, Englishwoman Sally Clarke, one of the finest chefs in London, this is one of the hottest restaurants around. Clarke honed her skills at Michaels in Santa Monica and the West Beach Café in Venice (California). In this excellent restaurant, everything is bright and modern, with wood floors; discreet lighting; and additional space in the basement, where tables are more spacious and private. The fixed-price menu offers no choices, but the food is so well prepared "in the new style" that diners rarely object. The menu is changed daily.

You might begin with an appetizer of apple, Stilton, and celeriac soup, then follow with grilled swordfish with lemon mayonnaise. Desserts are likely to include a baked pear filled with mincemeat, candied orange, and almonds.

HOLLAND PARK
MODERATE

The Room at the Halcyon

In the Halcyon Hotel, 81 Holland Park Ave., W11. ☎ **0171/727-7288.** Reservations required. Appetizers £6–£6.50 ($9.50–$10.25); main courses £14–£18 ($22.10–$28.45); two-course set lunch £18 ($28.45); three-course set dinner £21 ($33.20). AE, DC, MC, V. Lunch Mon–Fri noon–2:30pm, Sun noon–3pm; dinner Mon–Thu 7–10:30pm, Fri–Sat 7–11pm, Sun 7–10pm. Tube: Holland Park. INTERNATIONAL/ITALIAN.

Part of the Halcyon Hotel (see Chapter 4), this restaurant is worth a detour to visit this pocket of posh. Located on the hotel's lower level, the restaurant attracts the rich and famous, including royalty. You might enjoy an apéritif in the pink-tinted bar before heading for a meal in the tastefully uncluttered dining room. Lattices and a garden view create an image of springtime even in winter.

Of the sophisticated and highly individualized menu, one food critic wrote it "reads like a United Nations of cuisine." The daily bill of fare is based on the inspiration of the chef and the freshest ingredients available, along with minimal sauces. You might begin with spicy chicken soup with lemongrass and coconut milk or terrine of foie gras on spinach with hazelnut oil and green bean salad. Main dishes are likely to feature filet of brill with leeks, saffron potatoes, a quenelle of caviar, a steamed oyster, and *beurre blanc;* roasted rack of lamb with herbed breadcrumbs, garlic, and rosemary served with creamy garlic potatoes and carrots; or roasted squab with morel mushroom sausage, broad beans, smoked bacon, and sage. There is also a special vegetarian menu.

16 Marylebone & Bayswater

MARYLEBONE
MODERATE

Odin's

27 Devonshire St., W1. ☎ **0171/935-7296.** Reservations recommended. Two-course set-price lunch or dinner £20.95 ($33.10); three-course set-price lunch or dinner £22.95 ($36.25). AE, DC, MC, V. Lunch Mon–Fri 12:30–2:30pm; dinner Mon–Fri 7–11:30pm. Tube: Regent's Park. INTERNATIONAL.

Odin's is an elegant restaurant, one of at least four in London partially owned by actor Michael Caine. Set adjacent to its slightly less expensive twin, Langan's Bistro (see entry below), it features ample space between tables and an eclectic decor. Amid gilt-edged mirrors, evocative paintings, Japanese screens, and art deco accessories, you'll be offered a choice of menu items that changes with the seasons. Typical fare might include an English goat cheese salad serve with garlic dressing;

pigeon breast with roast new potatoes and onions; grilled Dover sole with a butter sauce; veal with Pommery mustard and tarragon; and filet of beef with a green peppercorn sauce.

INEXPENSIVE

⑤ Garbo's

42 Crawford St., W1. ☎ **0171/262-6582**. Reservations required. Appetizers £2.60–£6.50 ($4.10–$10.25); main courses £5.50–£11.95 ($8.70–$18.90); buffet lunch £8.95 ($14.15). AE, MC, V. Lunch Mon–Fri noon–3pm; dinner daily 6pm–midnight. Tube: Baker Street, Edgware Road, or Marylebone. SWEDISH.

Garbo's is the most engaging and appealing Swedish restaurant in London, taking its theme from that country's celebrated export, the late star herself. Located south of Marylebone Road, it attracts patrons from the Swedish embassy on Montagu Place. The best value—in fact, one of the finest lunchtime values in St. Marylebone—is the "mini-smörgåsbord," which, despite being called "mini," has a range of perfectly prepared hot and cold dishes and is most satisfying and filling. The evening menu might even tempt you to visit Scandinavia. You could begin with gravlax with dill-mustard sauce prepared in the old Viking manner, smoked eel, or Swedish pea soup. Various meat courses are featured, including Swedish meatballs in cream sauce and white cabbage stuffed with beef and pork. Watch also for the specialties of the day. Finish with a dessert from the sweets trolley or ask for crêpe Garbo, filled with vanilla cream and coated with Melba sauce.

Langan's Bistro

26 Devonshire St., W1. ☎ **0171/935-4531**. Reservations recommended. Two-course set-price lunch or dinner £15.95 ($25.20); three-course set-price lunch or dinner £17.95 ($28.35). AE, DC, MC, V. Lunch Mon–Fri 12:30–3:30pm; dinner Mon–Sat 7–11:30pm. Tube: Regent's Park. FRENCH/BRITISH.

This deliberately unpretentious restaurant has been a busy fixture on the London restaurant scene since the mid-1960s, when it was established by actor Michael Caine and a group of investors. Of the several restaurants within its chain, it's the least expensive, provides the least space between its tables, and is probably the most visually appealing. Set behind a brightly colored storefront on a quiet residential street, it contains an interior whose surfaces are richly covered with fanciful clusters of Japanese parasols, rococo mirrors, surrealistic paintings, and old photographs of almost-forgotten subjects.

The French-inspired menu changes with the seasons, and might include salmon and broccoli mousse, snails in a garlic butter sauce, poached salmon encased in pastry served with a watercress sauce, sirloin steak with horseradish sauce, and pan-fried squid. The dessert extravaganza is known as "Langan's chocolate pudding."

BAYSWATER
INEXPENSIVE

Veronica's

3 Hereford Rd., W2. ☎ **0171/229-5079**. Reservations required. Appetizers £4.50–£8.50 ($7.10–$13.45); main courses £8.50–14.50 ($13.45–$22.90); fixed-price meal

Restaurants: Marylebone to Maida Vale

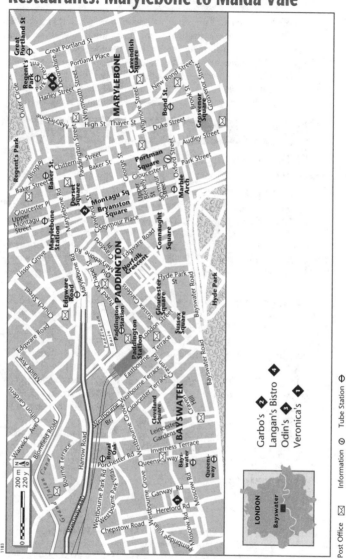

Garbo's ◆ 2
Langan's Bistro ◆ 4
Odin's ◆ 3
Veronica's ◆ 1

Post Office ⊠   Information ⊘   Tube Station ⊖

£11.50 ($18.15). AE, DC, MC, V. Lunch Mon–Fri noon–3pm; dinner Mon–Sat 6:30pm–midnight. Tube: Bayswater or Queensway. BRITISH.

Called the "market leader in café salons," Veronica's offers some of the finest British cuisine in London at tabs you won't mind paying. In fact, it's like a celebration of British food, including some dishes based on recipes used in medieval or Tudor times. For example, your appetizer might be a salad called salmagundy that was enjoyed by Elizabeth I, made with crunchy pickled vegetables. Another concoction might be watersouchy, a medieval stew crammed with mixed seafood. However, each dish is given today's imaginative interpretation by owner Veronica Shaw. One month she'll focus on Scotland, another month on Victorian foods, yet another month on Wales. Many dishes are vegetarian, and everything tastes better when followed with one of the selections of British farmhouse cheeses or a "pudding." The restaurant is brightly and attractively decorated, with service that is warm and ingratiating.

17 Away from the Center

ST. KATHARINE'S DOCK
INEXPENSIVE

Dickens Inn by the Tower

St. Katharine's Way, E1. ☎ **0171/488-2208.** Reservations recommended. In Pickwick Grill, appetizers £2.75–£6.25 ($4.35–$9.90); main courses £8.95–£15.95 ($14.15–$25.20); in Tavern Room, snacks and platters £3.50–£4.95 ($5.55–$7.80); in pizza restaurant, pizzas £4.25–£23 ($6.70–$36.35). AE, DC, MC, V. Restaurant Mon–Sat noon–3:30pm and 6:30–10:30pm, Sun noon–3:30pm and 6:30–9:30pm; bar Mon–Sat 11am–11pm, Sun noon–3pm and 7–10:30pm. Tube: Tower Hill. BRITISH.

This three-floor restaurant is within the solid brick walls of an 1830 structure first used as a warehouse for spices pouring into London from afar. Its main decorative allure derives from massive redwood timbers of its original construction. It is deliberately devoid of carpets, curtains, or anything that might conceal its unusual antique trusses. Large windows afford a sweeping view of the nearby Thames and Tower Bridge.

On the ground level, you'll find a bar and the Tavern Room, serving sandwiches, platters of lasagne or smoked mackerel, steaming bowls of soup or chili, and bar snacks. One floor above you'll find a pizza restaurant, serving four sizes of pizzas, including a much-accessorized 18-inch behemoth known as "The Beast." Above that, you'll find a relatively formal dining room, The Pickwick Grill, serving more elegant meals. Specialties there include roast lamb or roast beef.

BUTLER'S WHARF
EXPENSIVE

Le Pont de la Tour

36d Shad Thames, Butler's Wharf, SE1. ☎ **0171/403-8403.** Reservations: Not accepted in the Bar and Grill; recommended in the Restaurant. Bar and Grill appetizers £2.95–£12.75 ($4.65–$20.15); main courses £8–£14.50 ($12.65–$22.90). Restaurant appetizers £6–£14.50 ($9.50–$22.90); main courses £14.50–£18.50 ($22.90–$29.20); three-course fixed-price lunch £26.50 ($41.85). AE, DC, MC, V. Restaurant lunch Sun–Fri noon–3pm; dinner Mon–Sat 6pm–midnight, Sun 6–11pm. Bar and Grill Mon–Sat noon–midnight, Sun noon–11pm. Tube: Tower Hill or London Bridge. INTERNATIONAL.

Set at the edge of the Thames near Tower Bridge, this commercial complex holds condominiums, rental apartments, offices, and an assortment of food and wine shops collectively known as the Gastrodome. Originally built of brick and sandstone in the mid-19th century as a warehouse, it's known today as the Butlers Wharf Building. From its windows, diners and shoppers enjoy sweeping views of some of the densest river traffic in Europe.

Although visual and gastronomic diversions are scattered throughout the complex, many visitors prefer the brash hubbub of the Bar and Grill. Live piano music (evenings and weekends) and a wide choice of wines, spirits, and cocktails create one of the most lively and convivial places in the area. Although such dishes as chicken liver and foie gras parfait, smoked Irish salmon, and langoustine mayonnaise are featured, the culinary star is a heaping platter of fresh shellfish (*fruits de mer*). It's perfect when consumed with a bottle of wine and shared with a friend.

In bold contrast is the large, more formal room known simply as The Restaurant. Filled with burr oak furniture framed and decorated with framed lithographs by Sem of early 20th century Parisian cafésociety, it offers excellent food and a polite but undeniable English reserve. Menu items include terrine of foie gras with an onion and raisin confit; sauté of scallops with grilled tomatoes and gremolata; braised lamb shank with roast onions and rosemary; and roast saddle of rabbit with bacon and mustard vinaigrette. Both areas of this restaurant offer additional seating on outdoor terraces overlooking the Thames.

MODERATE

Butler's Wharf Chop House

36E Shad Thames, SE1. ☎ **0171/403-3404.** Reservations recommended. Set lunch £22.75 ($35.95); dinner appetizers £3.75–£7.50 ($5.95–$11.85); dinner main courses £9–£14 ($14.20–$22.10). AE, DC, MC, V. Lunch Sun–Fri noon–2:45pm (last order); dinner Mon–Sat 6–10:45pm. Tube: Tower Hill. BRITISH.

This is one of four restaurants set within the renovated warehouse known as Butler's Wharf. Of the four, it's the closest to Tower Bridge, and of the four, it's the one that most aggressively retains its commitment to moderate prices. The complex contains an even cheaper (Italian) restaurant, la Cantina del Ponte, although most diners consider that merely a place for pastas. The complex's more upscale restaurants, Le Pont de la Tour, are separately recommended in this chapter (see above).

The decor of the Chop House was modeled after that of a large boathouse, with russet-colored banquettes, lots of exposed timbers, wood floors, flowers, candles, and big windows overlooking Tower Bridge and the traffic on Britain's mightiest river. Lunchtime crowds include a goodly number of workers from the City's nearby financial district; evening crowds have higher percentages of friends and acquaintances dining together under less pressing circumstances. Menu items are adaptations of British recipes, some (but not all) geared for modern tastes. Examples include Lunesdale breast of duck with pears, cracked pepper, and port wine sauce; a salad of poached codfish with baby spinach; potted crab; roast salmon with a mustard-dill sauce and pickled cucumbers; kidney-and-oyster pudding; and Dublin bay prawns and salmon wrapped in bacon. Dessert might include a double chocolate mousse with Irish coffee sauce or sticky toffee pudding. Drinks might include such stiff-upper-lip choices as Theakston's best bitter, several choices of English wine, and a half-dozen French clarets served by the jug.

6

What to See & Do in London

The moment you have to categorize the marvels of a sightseer's paradise like London, you find yourself in a predicament. What on earth do you put where?

Is Madame Tussaud's a museum or a show, when it happens to be both? Is the Commonwealth Institute educational, cultural, or entertaining, when it's all three?

It's almost as bad as trying to index "Love."

This chapter covers the most interesting attractions in all categories that can be seen in the daytime. Which ones you elect to see depends on what strikes your fancy and the time you have to spend in London.

SUGGESTED ITINERARIES

Obviously this list for the rushed is for the first-time visitor. Presumably, if it's your second or third visit you will want to seek out other treasures that London offers. However, such sights as the British Museum can hardly be covered in one visit in one lifetime. There are actually some people living in London who go there almost every day of their lives, always discovering something not seen before.

If You Have 1 Day

Day 1   Even on the most rushed of itineraries, no first-time visitor should leave London without a visit to Westminster Abbey. Afterward, walk over to see Big Ben and the Houses of Parliament. Also see the Changing of the Guard at Buckingham Palace and walk over to 10 Downing Street, home of the prime minister. Dine at one of the little restaurants in Covent Garden.

For the ultimate English experience in dining, make it Porter's English Restaurant, owned by the earl of Bradford. Try one of their classic English pies such as lamb and apricot. For your nightcap, head over to the Red Lion, 2 Duke of York St. in Mayfair *(see page 125)*. You can enjoy a lager in this ultimate Victorian pub, a place Oscar Wilde might have chosen for a brandy.

If You Have 2 Days

Day 1   Spend Day 1 as above.

Day 2   Devote a good part of the second day exploring the British Museum, considered by many the best in the world. Spend the afternoon visiting the Tower of London and seeing the Crown Jewels (expect slow-moving lines).

Cap your day by taking one of the London Launches (see "For River Thames Buffs," below) which will give you a view and sense of London from the river. Go to some really local place for dinner such as Shepherd's, Marsham Court, Marsham Street *(see page 146)*, where you'll be able to order roast rib of Scottish beef and Yorkshire; dining along with you at these places will be many of the MPs from the House of Commons.

If You Have 3 Days

Days 1–2   Spend Days 1 and 2 as above.

Day 3   In the morning visit the National Gallery, facing Trafalgar Square. For a change of pace in your sightseeing, enjoy an afternoon at Madame Tussaud's waxworks. Take our walking tour of St. James's (see Chapter 7, "Strolling Around London") and try to catch some cultural performance at the South Bank Centre.

If You Have 5 Days

Days 1–3   Spend Days 1 to 3 as above.

Day 4   In the morning, head for the City, the financial district of London in the East End. Your major sightseeing goal here will be St. Paul's Cathedral, designed by Sir Christopher Wren. Take our walking tour of the City (see Chapter 7) and visit such attractions as the Guildhall (city hall). Later in the afternoon, head for King's Road in Chelsea for some boutique hopping and dine at one of Chelsea's many restaurants. Later that evening visit a London nightclub in Soho, such as Ronnie Scott's, 47 Frith St. *(see page 269)*, for some of the best jazz in the city.

Day 5   Explore the Victoria and Albert Museum in the morning, then go to the Tate Gallery for a look at some of its many masterpieces; have lunch at its restaurant. For a historic glimpse of the dark days of the 1940s, visit the Cabinet War Rooms at Clive Steps (see below) where Churchill directed British operations in the war against the Nazis. Attend the theater in the evening. It would be enjoyable to take in as many West End shows as you can on all your evenings in London.

1 The Top Attractions

✪ British Museum

Great Russell St., WC1. ☎ **0171/636-1555.** Admission free. Mon–Sat 10am–5pm, Sun 2:30–6pm. Closed New Year's Day, Good Friday, early May, bank holidays, Dec 24–26. Tube: Holborn or Tottenham Court Rd.; Piccadilly for Museum of Mankind.

Set in scholarly Bloomsbury, this immense museum grew out of a private collection of manuscripts purchased in 1753 with the proceeds of

What's Special About London

Historic Buildings
- The Tower of London, a former palace, prison, mint, and place of execution. A chief attraction today is the Crown Jewels.
- Westminster Abbey, where English monarchs have been crowned since 1066.
- The Houses of Parliament, the imposing neo-Gothic "Mother of Parliaments."
- St. Paul's Cathedral, a beautiful church designed by Sir Christopher Wren.

Museums
- The British Museum, a repository for everything from the Parthenon's Elgin Marbles to an original version of the Magna Carta.
- The Tate Gallery, a fantastic collection of British painting from the 16th to the 20th centuries.
- The National Gallery, possessing an unrivaled collection of European painting, expertly displayed.

Parks
- Hyde Park, some 340 acres of greenery and the famous Speakers' Corner.
- Regent's Park, with an Open Air Theatre.

For the Kids
- Madame Tussaud's lifelike waxwork effigies of famous and infamous characters.

City Spectacle
- The Changing of the Guard, a famous daily ceremony at Buckingham Palace.

Evening Entertainment
- The London theater, a great array of productions from Shakespeare to *Sunset Boulevard.*

a lottery. It grew and grew, fed by legacies, discoveries, and purchases, until it became one of the world's largest museums, containing literally millions of objects. It is utterly impossible to take in this museum in one day. You have to choose a particular section to focus on, then move on to another, preferably on another day.

The Egyptian room, for instance, contains the Rosetta Stone, whose discovery led to the deciphering of hieroglyphs; the Duveen Gallery houses the Elgin Marbles (a priceless series of sculptures from the pediments, metopes, and friezes of the Parthenon in Athens); the Nimrud Gallery has the legendary Black Obelisk, dating from around 860 B.C.

Other museum treasures include the contents of Egyptian royal tombs (including mummies); the oldest land vehicle ever discovered (a Sumerian sledge); fabulous arrays of 2,000-year-old jewelry, cosmetics,

British Museum

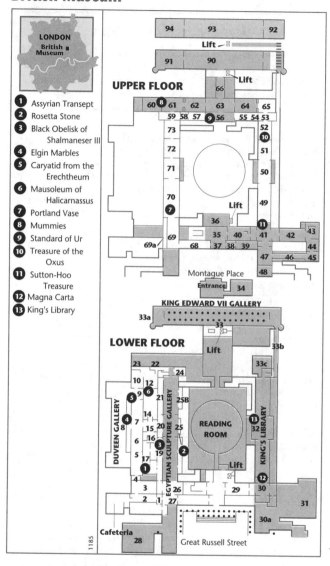

LONDON
British Museum

1. Assyrian Transept
2. Rosetta Stone
3. Black Obelisk of Shalmaneser III
4. Elgin Marbles
5. Caryatid from the Erechtheum
6. Mausoleum of Halicarnassus
7. Portland Vase
8. Mummies
9. Standard of Ur
10. Treasure of the Oxus
11. Sutton-Hoo Treasure
12. Magna Carta
13. King's Library

UPPER FLOOR

Lift

LOWER FLOOR

KING EDWARD VII GALLERY

Montague Place

Entrance

DUVEN GALLERY

EGYPTIAN SCULPTURE GALLERY

READING ROOM

KING'S LIBRARY

Lift

Cafeteria

Great Russell Street

1185

weapons, furniture, and tools; Babylonian astronomical instruments; and winged lions(in the Assyrian Transept) that once guarded Ashurnasirpal's palace at Numrud.

For information on the Museum of Mankind and the British Library, part of the British Museum, see below.

✪ Buckingham Palace

At end of The Mall, on road running from Trafalgar Sq. ☎ **0171/930-4832.** Palace tours £8.50 ($13.40) adults to age 60, £6 ($9.50) adults over 60, £4.50 ($7.10) children under 17. (*Warning:* These ticket prices, or even the possibility of public

A Note About Admission Prices

As a rule, children's prices apply to persons aged 16 and under. For senior citizens to get discounts granted at some attractions, a man or woman must be 60 years of age or older. Students, to get discounted admissions, wherever granted, must have a student ID card.

admission to Buckingham Palace, depend entirely on the whim of the queen, as it is her home.) Changing of the Guard, free. You can avoid the long queues by purchasing tickets through Edwards & Edwards, 1 Times Square Plaza, New York, NY 10036 (☎ 212/944-0290). Physically handicapped visitors can reserve tickets directly through the palace by calling 0171/930-5526. Palace tours, check tourist information offices, local publications. Changing of the Guard, see below. Tube: St. James's Park or Green Park.

This massively graceful building is the official residence of the queen, and you can tell whether Her Majesty is at home by the Royal Standard flying at the masthead. For most of the year you can't visit the palace unless you're officially invited. You can, however, peep through the railings into the front yard. Since 1993 you can also tour much of the palace during an eight-week period in August and September, when the Royal Family usually is vacationing outside London. Elizabeth II agreed to allow visitors to tour the state room; the Grand Staircase, Throne Room, and other areas designed by John Nash (1752–1835) for George IV; and the huge Picture Gallery, which displays masterpieces by Van Dyck (*Charles I on Horseback*), Rembrandt (*Shipbuilder and His Wife*), Rubens (*Farm at Laeken*), and others. There's an admission charge, which will help pay for repairing Windsor Castle, badly damaged by fire in 1992.

The redbrick palace was built as a country house for the notoriously rakish duke of Buckingham. In 1762, it was bought by King George III, who needed room for his 15 children. From then on, the building was expanded, remodeled, faced with Portland stone, and twice bombed (during the blitz). Located in a 40-acre garden, it stands 360 feet long and contains 600 rooms.

Buckingham Palace's most famous spectacle is the **Changing of the Guard.** This ceremony begins (when it begins) at 11:30am and lasts for half an hour. It's been called the finest example of military pageantry extant. The new guard, marching behind a band, comes from either the Wellington or Chelsea Barracks and takes over from the old guard in the forecourt of the palace. When this martial ceremony occurs is the subject of mass confusion, and you should always check locally with the tourist office to see if one of the world's most famous military rituals is likely to be staged at the time of your visit. This ceremony has been cut at the last minute and on short notice, leaving thousands of tourists confused, baffled, and perhaps a little angry, feeling they have missed out on a London "must-see."

Any schedule announced here is not writ in stone. Officials of the ceremony never announce their plans a year in advance, which poses a dilemma for guidebook writers. In theory at least, the guard is changed daily from some time in April to mid-July, at which time it goes on its "winter" schedule—that is, changed every other day. The cutback is said to be because of budget constraints. The ceremony might also be abruptly canceled in "uncertain" weather conditions.

☼ Houses of Parliament

Bridge St. and Parliament Sq., SW1. ☎ **0171/219-4272** (House of Commons), 0171/219-3107 (House of Lords). Admission free. House of Lords, open to public Mon–Thurs from about 9:30am–2:30pm; also some Fridays (check by phone). House of Commons, open to public Mon–Tues and Thurs from 2:30pm, Wed from 10am; and Fri from 9:30am. Join line at St. Stephen's entrance. Tube: Westminster.

The political opposite of the Tower of London, the Houses of Parliament are the stronghold of Britain's democracy, which effectively checked royal power. Both Houses (Commons and Lords) are in the former royal Palace of Westminster, the king's residence until Henry VIII moved to Whitehall.

Although I can't assure you of the oratory of a Charles James Fox or a William Pitt the Elder, the debates are often lively and controversial in the House of Commons (seats are at a premium during crises). The chances of getting into the House of Lords when it's in session are generally better than for the more popular House of Commons, where even the queen isn't allowed. Many political observers maintain that the peerage speak their minds more freely and are less likely to adhere to the party line than their counterparts in the Commons.

The general public is admitted to the Strangers' Gallery in the House of Commons on "sitting days." You have to join a public line outside the St. Stephen's entrance on the day in question, and there is often considerable delay before the public is admitted. You can speed matters up somewhat by applying at the American embassy or the Canadian High Commission for a special pass, but this is too cumbersome for many people. Besides, the embassy has only four tickets for daily distribution, so you might as well stand in line. It's usually easier to get in after about 6pm. Debates often continue into the night.

The present House of Commons was built in 1840, but the chamber was bombed and destroyed by the German air force in 1941. The 320-foot tower that houses Big Ben, however, remained standing, and the celebrated clock continued to strike its chimes, the signature tune of Britain's news broadcasts. Big Ben, incidentally, was named after Sir Benjamin Hall, a cabinet minister distinguished by his long-windedness.

Except for the Strangers' Galleries, the two Houses of Parliament and Westminster Palace are presently closed to the public. Further information is available by telephone.

Kensington Palace

The Broad Walk, Kensington Gardens, W8. ☎ **0171/937-9561.** Admission £4.50 ($7.10) adults, £3 ($4.75) children, £3.40 ($5.35) students and senior citizens. Mon–Sat 9am–5pm, Sun 11am–5pm. Tube: Queensway or Bayswater on north side of gardens; High Street Kensington on south side.

Once the residence of British monarchs, Kensington Palace has not been the official home of reigning kings since the death of George II in 1760, although it is now the London home of the Princess of

The Much-Abused Portland Vase

One of the most famous exhibits in the British Museum (see above) is the Portland Vase. Dating from about 50 B.C., this cameo-cut glass vessel is an early and very fine example of Roman glass-blowing. The vase was discovered in 1582 in a marble sarcophagus in a large burial mound, Monte del Grano, just outside what was the core of ancient Rome. At that time, Cardinal Francesco Maria del Monte, reputed to be a ruthless art collector, seized possession of it.

Upon del Monte's death, his heirs sold the vase to the Barberini family, who christened it Vaso Barberini. Descendants of that fabled family held onto the vase until 1780 when they sold it. After a change or two of ownership in three years, it was purchased by Sir William Hamilton, who in turn sold it to the dowager duchess of Portland in 1784. The vase was loaned to the British Museum in 1810, and finally purchased by the museum from the Portland family in 1945.

During the interim, however, on February 17, 1845, a young man calling himself William Lloyd entered the museum and smashed the vase into 200 fragments. Bow Street police took him into custody; under the Wilful Damage Act, he could only be indicted for damaging an object worth £5 or less. He was therefore charged with breaking the glass case, valued at £3. Upon conviction, he was sentenced to a fine of £3 or two months of hard labor. Two days later, an anonymous donor paid the fine, and Lloyd was released. His motive for breaking the vase was never determined.

The task of repairing the vase fell to John Doubleday, a restorer, who completed the task in September of 1845. He was paid only about 25 guineas (a guinea is a pound and a shilling) for his effort. Doubleday was unable to incorporate 37 small chips, which were set aside.

In 1948, the vase was reconstructed, this time three of the remaining chips were incorporated. In 1985, the vase was found to be in "unstable condition"; it needed to be completely dismantled and reassembled again. For this go-round, restorers employed the most advanced techniques and epoxy resins. Many of Doubleday's unused fragments were incorporated. The vase is now in fine enough shape to last at least until the late 21st century.

Wales and the little princes. (The Prince of Wales now resides at St. James's Palace.) The palace had been acquired in 1689 by William and Mary as an escape from the damp royal rooms along the Thames. Since the end of the 18th century, the palace has been a residence for various other members of the royal family. It was here in 1837 that a young Victoria was roused from her sleep with the news that her uncle, William IV, had died and that she was now queen of England. You can view a nostalgic collection of Victoriana, including some of her memorabilia. Here, too, the late Queen Mary was born.

Attractions: Westminster & Victoria

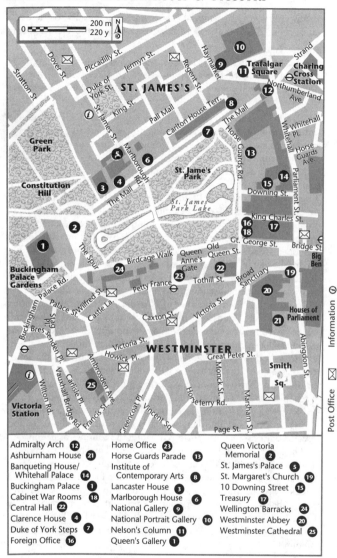

Admiralty Arch ⑫	Home Office ㉓	Queen Victoria Memorial ②
Ashburnham House ㉑	Horse Guards Parade ⑬	St. James's Palace ⑤
Banqueting House/ Whitehall Palace ⑭	Institute of Contemporary Arts ⑧	St. Margaret's Church ⑲
Buckingham Palace ①	Lancaster House ③	10 Downing Street ⑮
Cabinet War Rooms ⑱	Marlborough House ⑥	Treasury ⑰
Central Hall ㉒	National Gallery ⑨	Wellington Barracks ㉔
Clarence House ④	National Portrait Gallery ⑩	Westminster Abbey ⑳
Duke of York Steps ⑦	Nelson's Column ⑪	Westminster Cathedral ㉕
Foreign Office ⑯	Queen's Gallery ①	

In the apartments of Queen Mary II, wife of William III, you can admire a striking piece of furniture, a 17th-century writing cabinet inlaid with tortoiseshell. Paintings from the Royal Collection literally line the walls of the apartments.

A special attraction is the Royal Ceremonial Dress Collection, a series of room settings with the appropriate court attire of the day, from 1760 to 1950.

Kensington Gardens are open daily to the public for leisurely strolls around the Round Pond. One of the most famous sights here is the controversial Albert Memorial, a lasting tribute not only to Victoria's consort but also to the questionable artistic taste of the Victorian era.

Madame Tussaud's

Marylebone Rd. NW1. ☎ **0171/935-6861.** Admission £8.35 ($13.20) adults, £5.25 ($8.30) children under 16. Mon–Fri 10am–5:30pm, Sat–Sun 9:30am–5:30pm. The museum may be closed due to restoration work during the life of this edition. Tube: Baker Street.

Madame Tussaud's is not so much a wax museum as an enclosed entertainment world. A weird, moving, sometimes terrifying collage of exhibitions, panoramas, and stage settings, it manages to be most things to most people, most of the time.

Madame Tussaud attended the court of Versailles and learned her craft in France. She personally took the death masks from the guillotined heads of Louis XVI and Marie Antoinette, which you'll find among the exhibits. Her original museum, founded in Paris, moved to England in 1802. Since then, her exhibition has been imitated in every part of the world, but never with the realism and imagination on hand here. Madame herself molded the features of Benjamin Franklin, whom she met in Paris. All the rest—from George Washington to John F. Kennedy, from Mary Queen of Scots to Sylvester Stallone—are subjects for the same painstaking (and breathtaking) replication.

In the well-known **Chamber of Horrors**—a kind of underground dungeon—there stands a genuine gallows (from Hertford prison) and other instruments of the death penalty, along with figures of their victims. The shadowy presence of Jack the Ripper lurks in the gloom as you walk through a Victorian London street; George Joseph Smith can be seen with the tin bath in which he drowns the last of his three brides; and Christie conceals another murdered body behind his kitchen wall. Dr. Crippen, the poisoner, and his accomplice, Ethel le Neve, stand trial in the dock, and Mrs. Pearcey raises a poker to a crying baby in its pram. Many of their peers are displayed nearby, and present-day criminals are portrayed within the confines of prison.

The latest attraction to open here is called "The Spirit of London," a musical show that depicts 400 years of London's history, using special effects that include Audio-Animatronic figures that move and speak. Visitors take "time-taxis" that allow them to see and hear "Shakespeare" as he writes and speaks lines, to be received by Queen Elizabeth I, and to feel and smell the great fire that started in Pudding Lane in 1666. You'll find a snack bar and gift shops on the premises.

✪ National Gallery

Northwest side of Trafalgar Sq., WC2. ☎ **0171/747-2885.** Admission free. Mon–Sat 10am–6pm, Sun 2–6pm. Tube: Charing Cross, Embankment, or Leicester Square.

This stately neoclassical building contains an unrivaled collection of painting that spans seven centuries and covers every great European school of art. It does not include painting after 1929 (there are other galleries for that), but for sheer skill of display and arrangement, it surpasses counterparts in Paris, New York, Madrid, and Amsterdam.

Attractions: Above Hyde Park

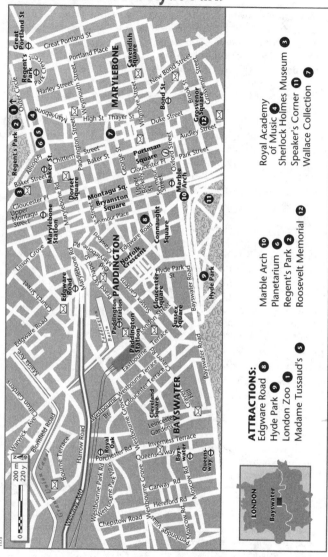

ATTRACTIONS:

Edgware Road ❽
Hyde Park ❾
London Zoo ❶
Madame Tussaud's ❺

Marble Arch ❿
Planetarium ❻
Regent's Park ❷
Roosevelt Memorial ⓬

Royal Academy of Music ❹
Sherlock Holmes Museum ❸
Speaker's Corner ⓫
Wallace Collection ❼

Post Office ☒   Information ⊘   Tube Station ⊖

All the British greats are here—Hogarth, Gainsborough, Reynolds, Constable, Turner—and shown at their finest.

The Italian Renaissance is represented by Leonardo da Vinci's *Virgin of the Rocks;* Titian's *Bacchus and Ariadne;* Giorgione's *Adoration of the Kings;* and unforgettable canvases by Bellini, Veronese, Botticelli, and Tintoretto.

Then there are the Spanish giants: El Greco's *Agony in the Garden,* and portraits by Goya and Velázquez. The Flemish-Dutch school is represented by two Brueghels, Jan van Eyck, Vermeer, and de Hooch; the Rembrandts include two of his immortal self-portraits (at age 34 and 63), while Rubens is represented in adjoining galleries. There is also an immense French collection by late 19th-century impressionists and postimpressionists, including Manet, Monet, Degas, Renoir, and Cézanne. A particularly charming item is the peep-show cabinet by Hoogstraten in one of the Dutch rooms: It's like spying through a keyhole.

The Sainsbury Wing was opened in 1991 by Elizabeth II and designed by noted Philadelphia architects, Robert Venturi and Denise Scott Brown, to house the gallery's Early Renaissance collection. Displayed are such masterpieces as Jan van Eyck's *The Arnolfini Portrait,* along with *The Doge* by Bellini, *Christ Mocked* by Bosch, and *Portrait of a Man* by Antonello da Messina. Botticelli's *Venus and Mars* is eternally enchanting. In addition, the Sainsbury Wing is used for large temporary exhibitions.

The National Gallery contains a computer information center where visitors can design a personal tour map. The computer room, located in the Micro Gallery, includes 12 computer work stations that individuals and families can use. The on-line system lists 2,200 paintings and has background notes for each artwork. The program includes four indexes that are cross-referenced for your convenience. Using a touch-screen computer, you design your own personalized tour by selecting a maximum of 10 paintings that you would like to view. Once you have made your choices, you print a personal tour map with your selections; this map service is free.

✪ St. Paul's Cathedral

St. Paul's Churchyard, EC4. ☎ **0171/236-4128** or 0171/248-2705. Cathedral £3 ($4.75) adults, £2 ($3.15) children 6–16. Galleries £2.50 ($3.95) adults, £1.50 ($2.35) children. Guided tours £3 ($4.75), recorded tours £2.50 ($3.95). Children 5 and under free. Sightseeing Mon–Sat 8:30am–4pm; galleries Mon–Sat 10am–4:15pm. No sightseeing Sun (services only). Tube: St. Paul's.

Partly hidden by nondescript office buildings on Ludgate Hill yet shining through by the sheer power of its beauty, stands London's largest and most famous church. Built by Sir Christopher Wren in place of the cathedral that burned down during the Great Fire of 1666, St. Paul's represents the ultimate masterpiece of this genius.

The golden cross surmounting it is 365 feet above the ground; the golden ball on which the cross rests measures 6 feet in diameter yet looks like a marble from below. Surrounding the interior of the dome is the **Whispering Gallery,** an acoustic marvel in which the faintest whisper can be heard clearly on the opposite side.

Although the interior of the church looks almost bare, it houses a vast number of monuments linked to Britain's history. The Duke of Wellington (of Waterloo fame) is entombed there, as are Lord Nelson and Sir Christopher Wren himself. At the east end of the cathedral is the **American Memorial Chapel,** honoring the 28,000 U.S. service personnel who fell while based in Britain in World War II.

Guided tours last 1½ hours and include parts of the cathedral not open to the general public. They take place Monday through Saturday

St. Paul's Cathedral

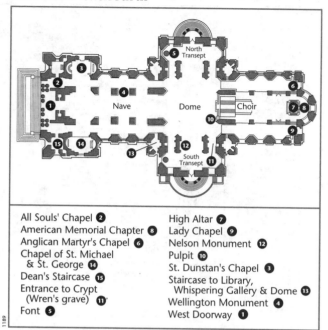

All Souls' Chapel **2**
American Memorial Chapter **8**
Anglican Martyr's Chapel **6**
Chapel of St. Michael
  & St. George **14**
Dean's Staircase **15**
Entrance to Crypt
  (Wren's grave) **11**
Font **5**

High Altar **7**
Lady Chapel **9**
Nelson Monument **12**
Pulpit **10**
St. Dunstan's Chapel **3**
Staircase to Library,
  Whispering Gallery & Dome **13**
Wellington Monument **4**
West Doorway **1**

at 11am, 11:30am, 1:30pm, and 2pm. Recorded tours lasting 45 minutes are available throughout the day.

St. Paul's is an Anglican cathedral with daily services at the following times: matins at 7:30am Monday to Friday, 10am on Saturday, Holy Communion Monday through Saturday at 8am and 12:30pm, and evensong Monday through Saturday at 5pm. On Sunday, there is Holy Communion at 8am and again at 11:30am, matins at 10:30am, and evensong at 3:15pm. Admission charges do not apply if visitors are attending services.

✪ Tate Gallery

Millbank, SW1. ☎ **0171/887-8000.** Admission free, except special exhibitions varying from £3 ($4.70) to £5 ($7.90). Mon–Sat 10am–5:50pm, Sun 2–5:50pm. Tube: Pimlico. Bus 77A, 88 or C10.

Fronting the Thames near Vauxhall Bridge in Pimlico, the Tate looks like a smaller and more graceful relation of the British Museum. Considered by many the most prestigious gallery in Britain, it houses the national collections, covering British art from the 16th century on, plus an international array of moderns. The Tate's holdings are split between the traditional and the contemporary. Because it is difficult to take in all the exhibits, I suggest that you concentrate on whichever section interests you more.

The older works include some of the best of Hogarth, Stubbs, Gainsborough, Reynolds, Blake, and Constable. The Turner Bequest of more than 19,000 watercolors and nearly 300 oils is housed in the adjoining Clore Gallery, which opened in 1987. Among the moderns,

Attractions: The City

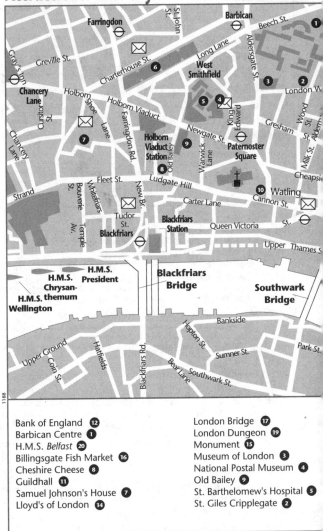

you'll find Picasso, Braque, Matisse, Dalí, Munch, Modigliani, Bacon . . . you name it, it's here. There are also the sculptures—masterpieces by Epstein and Moore.

The wide-ranging exhibits include surrealism and postwar painting in Britain and France, and the most fascinating part of the gallery is frequently the "current exhibition."

Downstairs are a restaurant (see Chapter 5), with murals by Rex Whistler, and a self-service coffee shop.

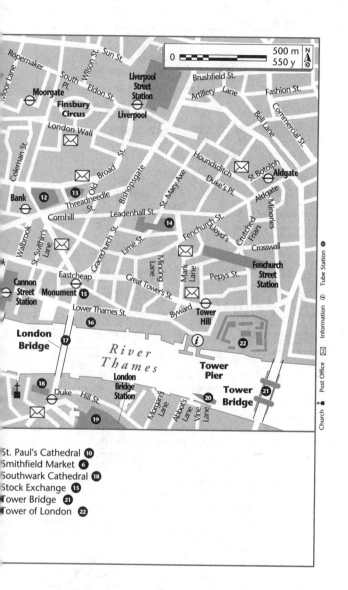

✪ Tower of London

Tower Hill, EC3. ☎ **0171/709-0765**. Admission £7.95 ($12.55) adults, £5.95 ($9.40) students and senior citizens, £5.25 ($8.30) children. Free for children under 5. Family ticket for five (but no more than two adults) £21.95 ($34.70). Gates Mon–Sat year-round 9am, Sun 10am. Gates close 5pm Nov–Feb, 6pm Mar–Oct. Closed Dec 24–26, Jan 1. Tube: Tower Hill. Boats: From Westminster Pier.

This forbidding gray-brown giant could be the stone symbol of London's past. Even today, centuries after the last head rolled on

Tower of London

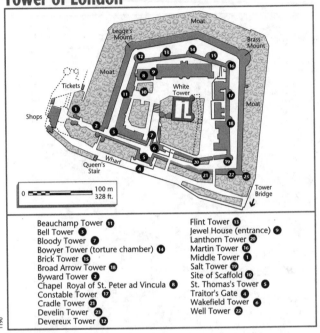

Moat
Legge's Mount
Brass Mount
Moat
Tickets
White Tower
Shops
Wharf
Queen's Stair

0   100 m
       328 ft.

Tower Bridge

Beauchamp Tower ⑪
Bell Tower ③
Bloody Tower ⑦
Bowyer Tower (torture chamber) ⑭
Brick Tower ⑮
Broad Arrow Tower ⑱
Byward Tower ②
Chapel Royal of St. Peter ad Vincula ⑧
Constable Tower ⑰
Cradle Tower ㉑
Develin Tower ㉓
Devereux Tower ⑫

Flint Tower ⑬
Jewel House (entrance) ⑨
Lanthorn Tower ⑳
Martin Tower ⑯
Middle Tower ①
Salt Tower ⑲
Site of Scaffold ⑩
St. Thomas's Tower ⑤
Traitor's Gate ④
Wakefield Tower ⑥
Well Tower ㉒

Tower Hill, a shivery atmosphere of impending doom lingers over the mighty walls. The Tower is actually an intricate pattern of different structures built at various times and for varying purposes, mostly as expressions of royal power.

The oldest is the **White Tower,** begun by William the Conqueror in 1078 to keep the native Saxon population of London in check. Later rulers added other towers, more walls, and fortified gates, until the building became something like a small town within a city. Until the reign of James I, the Tower was also one of the royal residences. But above all, it was a prison for distinguished captives . . . usually their last.

In the **Bloody Tower,** according to the unproved story dramatized by Shakespeare, the two little princes were murdered by the henchmen of Richard III. Here, too, Sir Walter Raleigh spent 13 years before his date with the executioner.

One American was locked in the Tower—a South Carolina merchant named Henry Laurens, who was also president of the Continental Congress. Captured at sea by the British in 1780, Laurens spent 18 months behind those menacing walls, until he was exchanged for the defeated Cornwallis.

Every stone of the Tower tells a story—usually a gory one. On the walls of the **Beauchamp Tower,** you can actually read the last messages scratched by despairing prisoners.

But the Tower, besides being a royal palace, a fortress, and a prison, was also an armory, a treasury, a menagerie, and in 1675 an astronomical observatory.

Attractions: Kensington to Belgravia

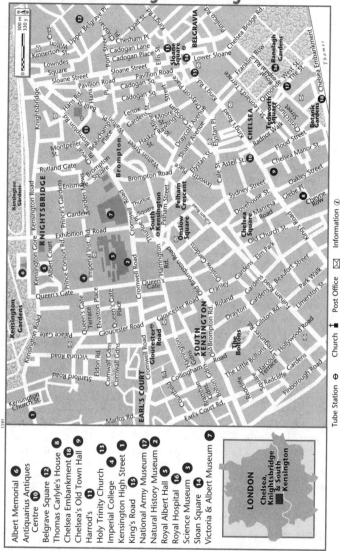

Albert Memorial ⑥
Antiquarius Antiques Centre ⑩
Belgrave Square ⑫
Thomas Carlyle's House ⑧
Chelsea Embankment ⑨
Chelsea's Old Town Hall ⑱
Harrod's ⑪
Holy Trinity Church ⑪
Imperial College ④
Kensington High Street ⑬
King's Road ⑮
National Army Museum ⑰
Natural History Museum ②
Royal Albert Hall ⑯
Royal Hospital ③
Science Museum ③
Sloan Square ⑭
Victoria & Albert Museum ⑦

LONDON

Chelsea, Knightsbridge & South Kensington

⊖ Tube Station ✝ Church ■ Post Office ⊠ Information ⓘ

In the **Jewel House** lie England's Crown Jewels—some of the most precious stones known—set into the robes, sword, scepter, and crowns donned by each monarch at his or her coronation. They've been heavily guarded ever since the daredevil Colonel Blood almost got away with them.

A palace once inhabited by King Edward I in the late 1200s was opened to visitors for the first time in 1993. Above Traitor's Gate, it is the only surviving medieval palace in Britain. Guides are dressed in period costumes. Reproductions of furniture and fittings, including Edward's throne, evoke the era, along with burning incense and candles. Admission to the palace is included in the standard ticket price.

Tours approximately one hour long are given by the Yeoman Warders at frequent intervals, starting at 9:30am from the Middle Tower near the main entrance. The tour includes the Chapel Royal of St. Peter ad Vincula (St. Peter in Chains). The last guided walk starts about 3:30pm in summer, 2:30pm in winter; weather permitting, of course.

✪ Victoria and Albert Museum

Cromwell Rd., SW7. ☎ **0171/938-8500.** Admission free, donation of £4.50 ($7.10) per adult suggested. Mon noon–5:50pm, Tues–Sun 10am–5:50pm. Jazz brunch Sun 11am–3pm. Tube: South Kensington. Bus C1, 14, or 74.

Located in South Kensington, the Victoria and Albert is the greatest museum in the world devoted to the decorative arts. It's named, of course, after that much-beloved 19th-century queen and her consort. On display are seven great cartoons painted by Raphael for Pope Leo in 1516, the world's greatest collection of paintings by Constable, and the largest collection of Italian Renaissance sculpture outside of Italy. A medieval gallery has sculpture done in wood and ivory, silver candlesticks, and enamel caskets. Contemporary design, fashion, and images are showcased in the new 20th-Century Gallery, the sparkling Glass Gallery, and the Dress Collection.

Asian art is represented by stunning carpets from Iran and from every other part of the Muslim world. The museum also has the greatest collection of Indian art outside of India. Recently, it opened Chinese and Japanese galleries, too. In complete contrast to the Eastern art are suites of English furniture, metalwork, and ceramics, dating from the 16th century and earlier. A superb collection of portrait miniatures includes one of Anne of Cleves, done by Hans Holbein the Younger for the benefit of Henry VIII, who was casting about for a suitable new wife.

Other treasures displayed include the Eltenberg Reliquary (Rhenish, latter half of the 12th century); the Gloucester Candlestick (Early English); the Veroli Casket (Byzantine); the Syon Cope (early 14th century); a marble sculpture, *Neptune with Triton,* by Bernini; and another rare portrait miniature by Holbein, this one of Mrs. Pemberton. The museum has a lively program of changing exhibitions and displays, so there's always something new to see.

✪ Westminster Abbey

Broad Sanctuary, SW1. ☎ **0171/222-7110.** Abbey free; £1.35 ($2.15) donation suggested. Royal Chapels, Royal Tombs, Coronation Chair, Henry VII Chapel £4 ($6.30) adults, £1 ($1.60) children. Mon–Fri 9am–4pm, Sat 9:15am–2pm and 4–5pm; Royal Chapels Wed 6–7:45pm. Tube: Westminster or St. James's Park.

With its square twin towers and superb archways, this early English Gothic abbey is one of the greatest examples of ecclesiastical architecture on earth. But it's far more than that: It's the shrine of a nation, the symbol of everything Britain has stood for and stands for, the edifice in which most of its rulers were crowned and where many lie buried, along with the remains of the Unknown Warrior.

King Edward the Confessor, whose grave also lies here, rebuilt the abbey in 1065 just before his death. The next year saw both the last of the Saxon kings, Harold, who died at the Battle of Hastings, and the first of the Normans, William the Conqueror, crowned in the church. Little now remains of Edward the Confessor's abbey, as rebuilding in the Gothic style was started by Henry III and completed shortly before the dissolution of the monasteries by Henry VIII, but it has remained the Coronation Church.

Next to the tomb of Edward III is the Coronation Chair, with the ancient Scottish relic known as the Stone of Scone beneath the seat. Just before Elizabeth II's coronation, some Scottish nationalists kidnapped the stone but were persuaded to return it in time for the crowning.

The entire abbey is crammed with treasures, some truly priceless, some curious. There are the strange waxworks, showing images of important personalities that were carried in their funeral processions, including those of Lord Nelson and the duchess of Richmond (who achieved immortality by posing as the figure of Britannia you see on British pennies).

There is the Poets' Corner, with monuments to the British greats, from Chaucer to Lord Laurence Olivier, and one American, Henry Wadsworth Longfellow. You'll also find the graves of such figures from U.S. history books as Maj. John André and Gen. John Burgoyne. A memorial stone for Sir Winston Churchill was placed in 1965.

Westminster Abbey

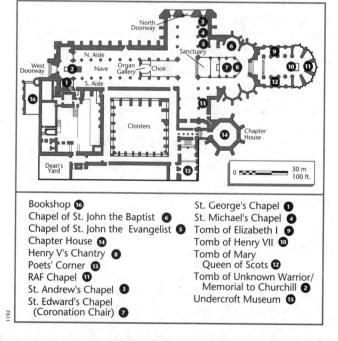

Bookshop ⑯
Chapel of St. John the Baptist ⑥
Chapel of St. John the Evangelist ⑤
Chapter House ⑭
Henry V's Chantry ⑧
Poets' Corner ⑬
RAF Chapel ⑪
St. Andrew's Chapel ③
St. Edward's Chapel (Coronation Chair) ⑦

St. George's Chapel ①
St. Michael's Chapel ④
Tomb of Elizabeth I ⑨
Tomb of Henry VII ⑩
Tomb of Mary Queen of Scots ⑫
Tomb of Unknown Warrior/ Memorial to Churchill ②
Undercroft Museum ⑮

Poets' Corner

When you enter the transept on south south side of the nave in Westminster Abbey (see above) and see a statue of the Bard with one arm resting on a stack of books, you've arrived at Poets' Corner. Shakespeare, himself, is buried at Stratford-upon-Avon, but resting here are Dickens, Chaucer, Ben Jonson, John Dryden, William Wordsworth, Milton, Kipling, Shelley, Goldsmith, Thackeray, Hardy, and Alfred, Lord Tennyson; even an American is interred here, Henry Wadsworth Longfellow. Inscriptions honor Dr. Samuel Johnson, the Brontë sisters, D. H. Lawrence, Lewis Carroll, Edward Lear, Dylan Thomas, and John Masefield.

The only time photography is allowed in the abbey is Wednesday evening in the Royal Chapels. On Sunday, the Royal Chapels are closed, but the rest of the church is open unless a service is being conducted. For times of services, phone the Chapter Office (☎ 0171/222-5152). Up to six supertours of the abbey are conducted by the vergers Monday through Friday, beginning at 10am and costing £7 ($11.05) per person.

2 More Attractions

A CEMETERY OF ROMANTIC RUBBLE

Highgate Cemetery

Swain's Lane, N6 ☎ **0181/340-1834.** Western Cemetery guided tour £3 ($4.75) donation is requested; Eastern Cemetery £1 ($1.60) donation is requested. Western Cemetery Apr–Oct Mon–Fri guided tours only at noon and 2 and 4pm, Sat–Sun hourly 11am–4pm; Nov and Mar Tues–Fri noon and 2 and 3pm, Sat–Sun hourly 11am–4pm; Dec–Feb Sat–Sun 11am–4pm. Eastern Cemetery Apr–Oct Mon–Fri 10am–4:45pm, Sat–Sun 11am–4:45pm; Nov–Mar daily 10am–3:45pm. Tube: Archway, then walk through Waterlow Park.

This 37-acre burial ground is of great interest to tombstone fanciers. Described in the British press as everything from "walled romantic rubble" to "an anthology of horror," it is the ideal setting for a collection of Victorian sculpture as well as the graves of Karl Marx and others.

CHURCHES

St. Martin-in-the-Fields

Trafalgar Sq., WC2. ☎ **0171/437-6023.** Mon–Sat 10am–6pm, Sun noon–6pm. Tube: Charing Cross.

Completed in 1726, and designed by James Gibbs, a disciple of Sir Christopher Wren, this classical temple stands at the northeast corner of Trafalgar Square, opposite the National Gallery. Its spire, added in 1824, towers 185 feet, taller than Nelson's Column, which also rises

The Fall of the House of Windsor

When a racy London tab reported that eyewitnesses saw Princess Di spot a good-looking young stud in Knightsbridge, lunge for him, toss him in her car, and speed off down the pike with her prize, you knew that House of Windsor had lost its awesome prestige. Whether these so-called eyewitnesses saw anything of the sort is highly unlikely, but dissing the dirt on the royals brings millions to Fleet Street coffers.

Contrast this story to the prolonged press silence about the affair of King Edward VIII and the American divorcee, Wallis Warfield Simpson, in the 1930s. The British newspapers eventually published the story—long after the American papers did—but by the time Fleet Street got around to it, everybody in the British Empire had already heard of it by word of mouth.

Although the Windsors, especially the queen, "loathe" today's tabloid coverage, the royals certainly set themselves up for it. If only they'd keep their clothes on in public—Princess Di lounging topless on a beach; Fergie getting her toes sucked by her American "accountant" on the Riviera; "Randy Andy" galloping buck naked through a Canadian stream in view of a photographer. Poor, unfortunate Prince Charles—disrobed in a men's locker room, his royal genitalia was snapped by a photographer. The German press gleefully ran the nude pictures of his royal highness, but London tabs modestly covered up the vital parts when they ran the pix. One audacious German paper ran the cruel picture caption: "No wonder Princess Di is unhappy."

Through it all, the queen remains properly attired at all times in public.

No one is sure whether Prince Charles will ever inherit the throne, much less with Princess Diana as his queen. For the future, even the most devoted monarchists predict a more scaled-down version of the monarch—trimmed in size, power, benefits and (probably) influence.

Jack Straw, the Labor shadow minister and longtime critic of the monarchy (though not an attacker of the queen herself) told me in Shepherd's, a London watering hole of MPs, that he would like to "see the type of monarchy they have in Norway or perhaps Sweden. Let the Royals shop for groceries like the rest of us. Just like the Queen of Denmark. It would signal a classless British society." Even Prince Charles has admitted that a lot of "persons" need to be taken off the royal payroll and the "monarchy scaled back if it is to survive."

Charles didn't help matters, however, when he expressed his desire to be a tampon to his girl friend, Camilla Parker-Bowles. Later, he went on the telly and confessed his infidelity to Britain. Diana joined in the fray by terming herself "the biggest prostitute in the world." No one could imagine Queen Elizabeth ever uttering a phrase like that.

What does Prince Edward have to say about this? Very little, other than to insist repeatedly that "I'm not gay."

on the square. The steeple became the paradigm for those of many churches in colonial America. Since the first year of World War I (1914), the homeless have sought "soup and shelter" at St. Martin, a tradition that continues.

The Academy of St. Martin-in-the-Fields was founded here, and, and lunchtime and evening concerts are staged on Monday, Tuesday, and Friday at 1:15pm, and on Thursday through Saturday at 7:30pm.

In the crypt rests Charles II who was christened here, giving St. Martin a claim as a royal parish church. His mistress, Nell Gwynne, is also interred here, as is the notorious highwayman, Jack Sheppard. The crypt is also London's finest brass-rubbing center. A little restaurant, Café in the Crypt, is still called "Field's" by its devotees. While enjoying a spinach crêpe, you can sometimes hear the music of Bach drifting through the crypt from the concert in the apse above. The floors of the crypt are actually gravestones, and the walls date from the 1500s. In back of the church is a crafts market.

HISTORIC BUILDINGS

Banqueting House

Whitehall Palace, Horse Guards Ave., SW1. ☎ **0171/930-4179.** Admission £3 ($4.75) adults, £2 ($3.15) children, £2.20 ($3.50) senior citizens and students. Mon–Sat 10am–5pm (last admission 4:30pm). Closed Good Friday, Easter, Dec 24–Jan 2. Tube: Westminster.

The feasting chambers in Whitehall Palace are probably the most sumptuous eateries on earth. Unfortunately, you can't dine there unless you happen to be a visiting head of state. Designed by Inigo Jones and decorated with—among other things—original paintings by Rubens, these banqueting halls are dazzling enough to make you forget about food. Among the historic events that took place here was the beheading of King Charles I (the scaffold stood outside). The restoration ceremony of Charles II, which also took place here, marked the return of monarchy after Cromwell's brief Puritan-republican Commonwealth.

Cabinet War Rooms

Clive Steps at end of King Charles St., off Whitehall near Big Ben, SW1. ☎ **0171/930-6961.** Admission £3.90 ($6.15) adults, £1.90 ($3) children. Daily 10am–5:30pm. Closed on certain state occasions. Tube: Westminster or St. James's.

Visitors today can see the bombproof bunker just as it was left by Winston Churchill in September 1945 at the end of World War II. Many objects were removed only for dusting, and the Imperial War Museum studied photographs to replace things exactly as they were, including notepads, files, and typewriters, right down to pencils, pins, and clips.

You can see the **Map Room** with its huge wall maps, the one of the Atlantic Ocean being a mass of pinholes. Each hole represented at least one convoy. Next door is Churchill's bedroom-cum-office, reinforced with stout wood beams; it has a very basic bed and a desk with two BBC microphones on it for those famous broadcasts that stirred the nation. The **Transatlantic Telephone Room,** to give it its full name, is little more than a broom closet, but it contained the Bell Telephone

Company's special scrambler phone called Sig-Saly. From here, Churchill conferred with Roosevelt. The scrambler equipment itself was actually too large to house in the bunker, so it was placed in the basement of Selfridges department store on Oxford Street. All visitors are provided with a step-by-step personal sound guide, providing a detailed account of the function and history of each room.

Horse Guards

Whitehall, SW1. ☎ **0171/414-2396.**

North of Downing Street, on the west side of Whitehall, two much-photographed mounted members of the Household Cavalry keep watch daily from 10am to 4pm. The chief guard rather grandly inspects the troops here Monday through Saturday at 11am and again on Sunday at 10am. The guard, with flair and fanfare, dismounts at 4pm.

The rather uninspired building of the Horse Guards was designed by William Kent, chief architect to George II, as the headquarters for the king's general staff. The site was originally Henry VIII's tiltyard. When Kent died, John Vardy took over and completed the structure in 1758.

The guards, themselves, are drawn from the Cavalry Regiments of the Household Division, and in theory their duty is to protect the sovereign. "Life Guards" wear red tunics and white plumes and the "Blues and Royals" are attired in blue tunics with red plumes. Troopers change duty every two hours.

Some visitors prefer the changing of the guards here to the more famous ceremony at Buckingham Palace. Guards are changed around 10:30am Monday through Saturday or 9:30am on Sunday. A new guard leaves the Hyde Park Barracks, rides down Pall Mall, and arrives at the Horse Guards building all in about 30 minutes. The old guard then returns to the barracks.

If you pass through the arch at Horse Guards you'll find yourself at the Horse Guards Parade, which opens onto St. James's Park. This spacious court provides the best vantage point for viewing the various architectural styles that make up Whitehall. Regrettably, the parade ground is now a parking lot filled with the cars of the movers and shakers of Whitehall.

The military pageant—the most famous in Britain—Trooping the Colour, which celebrates the queen's birthday, takes place in June at the Horse Guards Parade. The "Colour" refers to the flag of the regiment. For devotees of pomp and circumstance, "Beating the Retreat" is staged here three or four evenings a week during the first two weeks of June. It is only a dress rehearsal, though, for Trooping the Colour.

Fenton House

Windmill Hill, NW3. ☎ **0171/435-3471.** Admission £3.50 ($5.55) adults, £1.75 ($2.75) children, £9 ($14.20) family ticket. Mar Sat–Sun 2–5pm; Apr–Oct Sat–Sun 11am–5:30pm, Mon–Wed 2–5:30pm. Closed Good Friday and Nov–Feb. Tube: Hampstead.

A National Trust property, Fenton House is in a village area on the west side of Hampstead Grove, just a little north of Hampstead Village. It was built in 1693, and its paneled rooms contain furniture

London's Most Famous Square

✪ **Trafalgar Square, WC1.**
One of the landmark squares of London, Trafalgar Square honors one of England's great military heroes, Horatio, Viscount Nelson (1758–1805), who died at the Battle of Trafalgar. Although he suffered from seasickness all his life, he went to sea at the age of 12 and was an admiral at the age of 39. Lord Nelson was a hero of the Battle of Calvi in 1794 where he lost an eye, the Battle of Santa Cruz in 1797 where he lost an arm, and the Battle of Trafalgar in 1805 where he lost his life.

The square today is dominated by a 145-foot granite column, the work of E. H. Baily in 1843. The column looks down Whitehall toward the Old Admiralty, where Lord Nelson's body lay in state. The figure of the naval hero towers 17 feet high, not bad for a man who stood 5 feet 4 inches in real life. The capital is of bronze cast from cannons recovered from the wreck of the Royal George. Queen Victoria's favorite animal painter, Sir Edward Landseer, added the four lions at the base of the column in 1868. The pools and fountains were not added until 1939, the last work of Sir Edwin Lutyens. Political demonstrations take place from time to time around the column. The square has the most aggressive pigeons in London; these birds will even land on your head or perform less desirable stunts. Actually, the birds are part of a long feathery tradition, as the site of the square was once used by Edward I (1239–1307) to keep his birds

and pictures; English, German, and French porcelain from the 18th century; and the outstanding Benton-Fletcher collection of early keyboard musical instruments.

A LIBRARY OF TREASURES

British Library
British Museum, Great Russell St., WC1. ☎ **0171/636-1544.** Admission free. Mon–Sat 10am–5pm, Sun 2:30–6pm. Tube: Holborn or Tottenham Court Road.

Some of the treasures from the collections of the British Library, one of the world's greatest libraries, are on display in the exhibition galleries in the east wing of the British Museum building. The Middle Room contains Western illuminated manuscripts. In the Manuscript "Saloon" (yes, that's right), items of historical and literary interest include two of the four surviving copies of King John's Magna Carta (1215). Almost every major author—Dickens, Jane Austen, Charlotte Brontë, Keats—is represented in the section devoted to English literature. Also on display are Nelson's last letter to Lady Hamilton and the journals of Captain Cook.

In the King's Library, the history of the book is illustrated by notable specimens of early printing, including the Diamond Sutra of 868, the first dated example of printing, as well as the Gutenberg Bible, of prey. Called "Longshanks," he came here often before dying of dysentery in 1307. Richard II, who ruled from 1377 to 1399, kept goshawks and falcons here, too. By the time of Henry VII, who ruled from 1485 to 1509, the square was used as the site of the royal stables. Sir Charles Barry, who designed the Houses of Parliament, created the present square in the 1830s.

Much of the world focuses on the square via TV cameras on New Year's Eve. It's a wild and raucous time with revelers jumping into the chilly waters of the fountains. In 1986, five people were crushed to death during the festivities. The giant Christmas tree that goes up here every year in December is an annual gift from Norway to the British people in appreciation of their sheltering the royal family during World War II. Today, street performers, now officially licensed, will entertain you, and hope for a donation for their efforts.

To the southeast of the square, at 36 Craven St., stands a house once occupied by Benjamin Franklin (1757–74) when he was a general of the Philadelphia Academy. On the north side of the square rises the National Gallery, constructed in the 1830s. In front of the building is a copy of a statue of George Washington by J. A. Houdon.

To the left of St. Martin's Place is the National Portrait Gallery, a "who was who" of British greats and not so greats. Everyone from Chaucer and Shakespeare to Captain Hook and Nell Gwynne is represented. Also on the square is the landmark St. Martin-in-the-Fields by James Gibbs, with its towering steeple, a resting place of such greats as Sir Joshua Reynolds, William Hogarth, and Thomas Chippendale.

the first book ever printed from movable type, 1455. In the center of the library is an exhibition of fine book bindings dating from the 16th century. Beneath Roubiliac's 1758 statue of Shakespeare stands a case of documents relating to the Bard, including a mortgage bearing his signature and a copy of the First Folio of 1623. The library's unrivaled collection of philatelic items, including the 1840 Great British Penny Black and the rare 1847 Post Office issues of Mauritius, are also on view.

MUSEUMS/GALLERIES

Commonwealth Institute

Kensington High St., W8. ☎ **0171/603-4535.** Admission £1 ($1.60) adults, 50p (80¢) children. Mon–Sat 10am–5pm, Sun 2–5pm. Closed Jan 1, Good Friday, May Day, Dec 24–26. Tube: High Street Kensington, Earl's Court, or Holland Park. Bus 9, 9A, 10, 27, 28, 31, 49, or C1 Hoppa.

Why come just to London when you can visit the Caribbean, see Canada from a skidoo, climb Mount Kenya, and take a rickshaw across Bangladesh? The history, landscapes, wildlife, and crafts of the Commonwealth of Nations are presented in this tent-shaped building next to Holland Park. Something's always happening here, ranging from special exhibitions to gallery animations. The Commonwealth

Attractions: Mayfair & St. James's

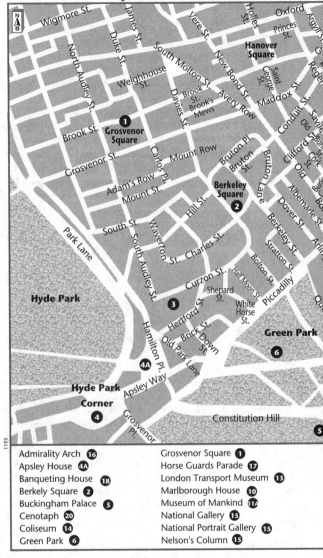

Admirality Arch ⑯
Apsley House ④ⓐ
Banqueting House ⑱
Berkely Square ②
Buckingham Palace ⑤
Cenotaph ⑳
Coliseum ⑭
Green Park ⑥

Grosvenor Square ①
Horse Guards Parade ⑰
London Transport Museum ⑬
Marlborough House ⑩
Museum of Mankind ⑪ⓐ
National Gallery ⑮
National Portrait Gallery ⑮
Nelson's Column ⑮

Shop is a source for gifts and items, including food and wine from around the world, and light refreshments are sold at the Commonwealth Brasserie.

Courtauld Institute Galleries

Somerset House, The Strand, WC2. ☎ **0171/873-2526.** Admission £3 ($4.75) adults, £1.50 ($2.35) children. Mon–Sat 10am–6pm, Sun 2–6pm. Tube: Temple or Embankment.

These galleries contain the following wealth of paintings: the great collection of French impressionist and postimpressionist paintings

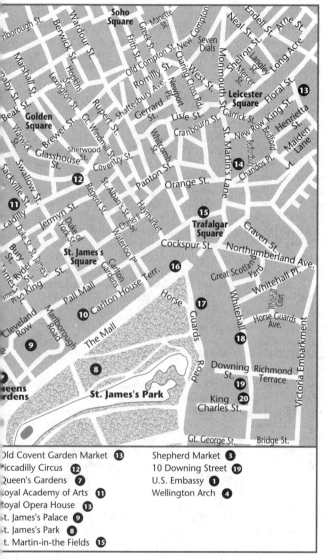

(masterpieces by Monet, Manet, Degas, Renoir, Cézanne, van Gogh, Gauguin) brought together by the late Samuel Courtauld; the Princes Gate collection of superb old-master paintings and drawings, especially those by Rubens, Michelangelo, and Tiepolo; the Gambier-Parry collection of early Italian paintings, ivories, majolica, and other works of art; the Lee collection of old masters; the Roger Fry collection of early 20th-century English and French painting; and the Hunter collection of 20th-century British painting. The galleries are air-conditioned and some of the paintings are displayed without glass.

Institute of Contemporary Arts

Nash House, Duke of York Steps, SW1. ☎ **0171/930-3647.** Admission £1.50 ($2.35) adult membership, £1 ($1.60) for students. Films £4–£6.50 ($6.30–$10.25). Galleries Mon and Wed–Sun noon–7:30pm, Tues noon–9pm. Bookstore daily noon–10pm. Film screenings Mon–Fri 5, 7, and 9pm; Sat–Sun 3, 5, 7, and 9pm. Tube: Piccadilly Circus or Charing Cross.

London's liveliest cultural program takes place in this temple to the avant-garde, launched in 1947. It keeps Londoners and others up-to-date on "the latest" in the world of cinema, theater, photography, painting, sculpture, whatever. Technically you have to be a member, but membership is immediately granted. Foreign or experimental movies are shown, and special tributes are often the order of the day— perhaps a retrospective of the films of Rainer Fassbinder. The classics are frequently dusted off, along with films that enjoy cult status. On Saturday and Sunday at 3pm the cinémathèque offers screenings for the kids. You'll want to browse through the institute's bookstore, which carries fascinating recent publications of art books. Sometimes well- known writers and artists speak here, which makes the low cost of membership even more enticing. Experimental plays are also presented. One we recently saw had not one word of dialogue. The photography galleries, showing the latest from both British and foreign photographers, would not necessarily win the approval of the senator from North Carolina, Jesse Helms.

Apsley House, The Wellington Museum

149 Piccadilly, Hyde Park Corner, W1. ☎ **0171/499-5676.** Admission £3 ($4.75) adults, £1.50 ($2.35) children. Tues–Sun 11am–5pm. Closed Mon, Jan 1, May Day, Dec 24–26. Tube: Hyde Park Corner.

This was the mansion of the Duke of Wellington, one of Britain's greatest generals. The "Iron Duke" defeated Napoléon at Waterloo, but later, for a short period while prime minister, he had to have iron shutters fitted to his windows to protect him from the mob outraged by his autocratic opposition to reform. His unpopularity soon passed, however.

The house is crammed with art treasures; military mementos; and a regal silver, china, and porcelain collection. You can admire the duke's medals, the array of field marshals' batons, the battlefield orders, plus three original Velázquez paintings among a score of other greats. One of the features of the museum is a colossal marble statue of Napoléon by Canova in the vestibule. It was a present from the grateful King George IV, who was then regent.

Freud Museum

20 Maresfield Gardens, NW3. ☎ **0171/435-2002.** Admission £2.50 ($3.95) adults, £1.50 ($2.40) full-time students, children under 12 free. Wed–Sun noon–5pm. Tube: Finchley Road.

This is the spacious house in which the founder of psychoanalysis lived, worked, and died after escaping with his family and possessions from Nazi-occupied Vienna. The rooms contain his furniture (including the famous couch), letters, photographs, paintings, and personal effects, as well as those of his daughter, Anna Freud, also a noted psychoanalyst. Temporary exhibitions and an archive film program are available.

Hayward Gallery

South Bank Centre, ☎ **0171/928-3144**. Admission £5 ($7.90) adults, £3.50 ($5.55) children; family ticket £12 ($18.95). Fee varies according to exhibitions; children are often half price. Thurs–Mon 10am–6pm, Tues–Wed 10am–8pm. Tube: Waterloo Station.

Opened by Elizabeth II in 1968, this gallery presents a changing program of major contemporary and historical exhibitions. It is part of the South Bank Centre, which also includes the Royal Festival Hall, the Queen Elizabeth Hall, the Purcell Room, the National Film Theatre, and the National Theatre. The gallery is closed between exhibitions, so check the listings before crossing the Thames; for recorded information, phone 0171/261-0127.

Imperial War Museum

Lambeth Rd., SE1. ☎ **0171/416-5000**. Admission £4.10 ($6.50) adults, £2.05 ($3.20) children. Free daily 4:30–6pm. Daily 10am–6pm. Closed Dec 24–26. Tube: Lambeth North or Elephant and Castle.

One of the few major sights south of the Thames, this museum occupies one city block the size of an army barracks, greeting you with 15-inch guns from the battleships *Resolution* and *Ramillies*. The large domed building, constructed in 1815, was the former Bethlehem Royal Hospital for the insane, known as Bedlam.

A wide range of weapons and equipment is on display, along with models, decorations, uniforms, posters, photographs, and paintings. You can see a Mark V tank, a Battle of Britain Spitfire, and a German one-man submarine, as well as a rifle carried by Lawrence of Arabia. In the documents room, you can view the famous "peace in our time" agreement that Neville Chamberlain brought back from Munich in 1938. Of his signing the agreement, Hitler later said, "He was a nice old man, so I decided to give him my autograph." Another exhibition is the self-styled "political testament" that Hitler dictated in the chancellery bunker in the closing days of World War II in Europe; it was witnessed by henchmen Joseph Goebbels and Martin Bormann.

Public film shows take place on weekends at 3pm and on certain weekdays during school holidays and on public holidays. Various special exhibitions are displayed at different times.

Kenwood

Hampstead Lane, NW3. ☎ **0181/348-1286**. Admission free. Apr–Sept daily 10am–6pm; Oct–Mar daily 10am–4pm. Closed Dec 24–25. Tube: Golders Green, then bus 210.

This structure was built as a gentleman's country home and later enlarged and decorated by the famous Scottish architect Robert Adam, starting in 1764. The house contains period furniture and paintings by Rembrandt, Vermeer, Gainsborough, and Turner, among others. It is also a venue for special visiting exhibitions, at which time admission might be charged.

London Transport Museum

The Piazza, Covent Garden, WC2. ☎ **0171/379-6344**. Admission £4.25 ($6.70) adults, £2.50 ($3.95) children, £10.50 ($16.60) family ticket. Sat–Thurs 10am–6pm, Fri 11am–6pm (last entrance at 5:15pm). Closed Dec 24–26. Tube: Covent Garden.

A collection of nearly two centuries of historic vehicles is displayed in a splendid Victorian building that formerly housed the Flower Market at Covent Garden. The museum shows how London's transport system evolved, and a representative collection of road vehicles includes a reconstruction of George Shillibeer's omnibus of 1829. A steam locomotive that ran on the world's first underground railway, a knifeboard horse bus, the "B"-type motor bus, London's first trolleybus, and the Feltham tram are also of particular interest. One of the unique and popular features of the museum is the number of participatory exhibits, which allow visitors to operate the controls of a tube train, a tram, a bus, and full-size signaling equipment.

The museum shop sells a range of souvenirs.

MOMI (Museum of the Moving Image)

South Bank underneath Waterloo Bridge, SE1. ☎ **0171/401-2636.** Admission £5.50 ($8.70) adults, £4 ($6.30) children and senior citizens, £4.70 ($7.45) students, £16 ($25.30) family ticket (up to two adults and four children). Daily 10am–6pm (last admission 5pm). Tube: Waterloo or Embankment.

MOMI is also part of the South Bank complex. Tracing the history of cinema and television, it takes the visitor on an incredible journey from cinema's earliest experiments to modern animation, from Charles Chaplin to the operation of a TV studio. There are artifacts to handle, buttons to push, and a cast of actors to tell visitors more. Three to four changing exhibitions are presented yearly. Allow two hours for a visit.

Museum of London

150 London Wall, EC2. ☎ **0171/600-3699.** Admission £3.50 ($5.55) adults, £1.75 ($2.75) children. Tues–Sat 10am–5:50pm, Sun noon–5:50pm. Tube: St. Paul's, Barbican, or Moorgate.

In London's Barbican district near St. Paul's Cathedral, overlooking the city's Roman and medieval walls, the museum allows visitors to trace the history of London from prehistoric times to the present through archeological finds; paintings and prints; and social, industrial, and historical artifacts; as well as costumes, maps, and models. On two floors around a central courtyard, exhibits are arranged so that you can begin and end your chronological stroll through 250,000 years at the main entrance to the museum. You can see the death mask of Oliver Cromwell, but the pièce de résistance is the Lord Mayor's Coach, built in 1757 and weighing in at three tons. This gift-and-red horse-drawn vehicle is like a fairy-tale coach. Visitors can also see the Great Fire of London in living color and sound; reconstructed Roman dining rooms, together with the kitchen and utensils; cell doors from Newgate Prison made famous by Charles Dickens; and most amazing of all, a shop counter with pre–World War II prices.

There is a restaurant overlooking a garden.

Museum of Mankind

6 Burlington Gardens, W1. ☎ **0171/437-2224.** Admission free; charges for specially mounted exhibitions. Mon–Sat 10am–5pm, Sun 2:30–6pm. Tube: Tottenham Court Road. Directions: To get there, take the Burlington Arcade, right next to the Royal Academy; this is a clear path leading up to the museum.

Part of the British Museum, this is considered the finest ethnographic collection in the world. It has it all: Eskimo polar-bear pants, an Amazonian's human-head mascot, a painted skull from Mexico honoring the "Day of the Dead," British Columbian stone carvings, Sioux war bonnets. A chief curiosity is a Hawaiian god with a mohawk, found by Captain Cook and shipped back to London. The Beninese bronzes from "darkest" Africa are stunning, as is the Asante West collection of gold jewelry and ornaments from West Africa. The collection is ever-growing. The building itself, a fine example of "high Victorian" architecture, was constructed by James Pennethorne in 1866; it originally served as the headquarters of London University.

National Army Museum

Royal Hospital Rd., Chelsea, SW3. ☎ **0171/730-0717.** Admission free. Daily 10am–5:30pm. Closed New Year's Day, Good Friday, first Mon in May, Dec 24–26. Tube: Sloane Square.

The National Army Museum occupies a building adjoining the Royal Hospital, a home for retired soldiers, the Chelsea Pensioners. Whereas the Imperial War Museum is concerned only with wars in the 20th century, the National Army Museum tells the colorful story of British armies from 1485 on. Here you'll find the uniforms British soldiers wore in every corner of the world and many of the items they brought back, as well as weapons and other gear, flags, and medals. Even the skeleton of Napoléon's favorite charger is here. Also on display are Florence Nightingale's jewelry, Hitler's telephone exchange (captured in 1945), and T6 Orders and Medals of HRH T6 Duke of Windsor.

National Portrait Gallery

St. Martin's Place, WC2. ☎ **0171/306-0055.** Admission free (a fee is charged for certain temporary exhibitions). Mon–Sat 10am–6pm, Sun noon–6pm. Tube: Charing Cross or Leicester Square.

In a gallery of remarkable and unremarkable pictures, a few paintings tower over the rest, including Sir Joshua Reynolds's first portrait of Samuel Johnson ("a man of most dreadful appearance"). Among the best are Nicholas Hilliard's miniature of a handsome Sir Walter Raleigh and a full-length Elizabeth I (painted to commemorate her visit to Sir Henry Lee at Ditchley in 1592), along with the Holbein cartoon of Henry VIII (sketched for a family portrait that hung, before it was burned, in the Privy Chamber of Whitehall Palace). There is also a portrait of William Shakespeare (with gold earring, no less) by an unknown artist that bears the claim of being the "most authentic contemporary likeness" of its subject. The John Hayls portrait of Samuel Pepys is here, as is a portrait of Whistler, no mean painter in his own right. One of the most famous pictures in the gallery is the group portrait of the Brontë sisters (Charlotte, Emily, and Anne) painted by their brother, Bramwell. An idealized portrait of Lord Byron by Thomas Phillips is also on display, and you can treat yourself to the likeness of the incomparable Aubrey Beardsley. For a finale, Diana, Princess of Wales, is on the Royal Landing. In 1993, this emporium of portraits opened new galleries displaying later 20th-century portraiture, including major works by such artists as Warhol and Hambling. Subjects range from Paul McCartney to Iris Murdoch, from Glenda Jackson to T. S. Eliot, even the Baroness Thatcher.

National Postal Museum

King Edward Building, King Edward St., EC1. ☎ **0171/239-5420.** Admission free. Mon–Fri 9:30am–4:30pm. Tube: St. Paul's or Barbican.

This museum attracts philatelists and many others. Actually part of the Post Office, it features permanent exhibitions of the stamps of Great Britain and the world, as well as special displays of stamps and postal history, changing every few months according to certain themes. On permanent display is the Penny Black, the world's first adhesive postage stamp.

National History Museum

Cromwell Rd., SW7. ☎ **0171/938-9123.** Admission £5 ($7.90) adults, £2.50 ($3.95) children 5–17. Children 4 and under free. Free to everyone Mon–Fri after 4:30pm and Sat–Sun after 5pm. Closed Dec 23–26. Tube: South Kensington.

This is the home of the national collections of living and fossil plants and animals, minerals, rocks, and meteorites, with many magnificent specimens on display. Exciting exhibitions designed to encourage people of all ages to enjoy learning about natural history include "Human Biology—An Exhibition of Ourselves," "Our Place in Evolution," "Introducing Ecology," "Origin of the Species," "British Natural History," and "Discovering Mammals." What attracts the most attention is the 13,000-square-foot dinosaur exhibit, displaying 14 complete skeletons. The center of the show depicts a trio of ripping, clawing, chewing, moving full-size robotic Deinonychus having a freshly killed Tenontosaurus for lunch.

The Geological Museum, which opened in 1935, has now been engulfed by the Natural History Museum. A connecting gallery links the two. Its "Story of Earth" takes you back a billion years and includes erupting volcanoes and the reenactment of an earthquake. Exhibitions offer keen insights into how we obtain light, heat, and power. The mineral collection is stunning and displays diamonds from Siberia, indigo-blue lapis lazuli from Afghanistan, and even a model of the Koh-i-Noor diamond. The sheer scope and drama of the place is so overpowering that one visit will hardly do. You get it all here, from a hunk of the moon collected by Apollo astronauts in 1972 to a model of Stonehenge on the second floor. Entrance to the Geological Museum is included in the overall admission to the Natural History Museum.

Percival David Foundation of Chinese Art

53 Gordon Sq., WC1. ☎ **0171/387-3909.** Admission free; donations accepted; £3 ($4.75) for a guided tour. Mon–Fri 10:30am–5pm. Tube: Russell Square or Euston Square. Bus 7, 8, 10, 14, 18, 19, 24, 25, or 27.

This foundation displays the greatest collection of Chinese ceramics outside of China. More than 1,700 ceramic objects reflect Chinese court taste from the 10th through 18th centuries. Many pieces are not only of exceptional beauty but bear important inscriptions. Several pieces were once owned by Chinese emperors. The foundation possesses an exceptional collection of stonewares from the Song (960–1279) and Yuan (1279–1368) dynasties, including examples of rare Ru and Guan wares. Among the justifiably famous blue and white porcelains are two unique temple vases. A wide variety of polychrome wares is also represented; these include examples of the delicate doucai wares from the Chenghua period (1465–87) as well as a remarkable group of 18th-century porcelains traditionally known as Gu yue xuan.

The foundation also offers a library filled with East Asian and Western books on Chinese art and culture. Both the library and the ceramics were donated to the University of London by Sir Percival David in 1950.

Science Museum

Exhibition Rd., SW7. ☎ **0171/938-8000.** Admission £5 ($7.90) adults, £2.50 ($3.95) children 5–17. Children 4 and under free. Free to everyone Mon–Fri after 4:30pm and Sat–Sun after 5pm. Mon–Sat 10am–5:50pm, Sun 11am–5:50pm. Closed Dec 23–26. Tube: South Kensington.

This museum traces the development of science and industry and their influence on everyday life. The collections are among the largest, most comprehensive, and most significant anywhere. On display is Stephenson's original Rocket, the tiny prototype railroad engine. You can also see Whittle's original jet engine and the Apollo 10 space module. The King George III Collection of scientific instruments is the highlight of a gallery on science in the 18th century.

To help the visitor's understanding of science and technology, there are working models and video displays, including two "hands-on" galleries called Launch Pad and Flight Lab. Health Matters, a permanent gallery on modern medicine, opened in 1994. You can buy souvenirs at the shopping concourse.

Sherlock Holmes Museum

221B Baker St., NW1. ☎ **0171/935-8866.** Admission £5 ($7.90) adults, £3 ($4.75) children. Daily 10am–6pm. Tube: Baker Street.

Where but on Baker Street would there be a museum displaying mementos of this famed fictional detective? Museum officials call it "the world's most famous address," though 10 Downing Street in London is a rival. It was here that mystery writer Sir Arthur Conan Doyle created a residence for Sherlock Holmes and his faithful Doctor Watson. These sleuths "lived" here from 1881 to 1904 at least in the annals of fiction. In Victorian rooms, visitors examine a range of exhibits, including published Holmes adventures and letters written to Holmes. A gift shop is on the premises.

Wallace Collection

Manchester Sq., W1. ☎ **0171/935-0687.** Admission free. Mon–Sat 10am–5pm, Sun 2–5pm. Closed New Year's Day, Good Friday, first Mon in May, Dec 24–26. Tube: Bond Street or Baker Street.

Located in a palatial setting (the modestly described "town house" of the late Lady Wallace), the Wallace Collection is a contrasting array of art and armaments. The former (mostly French) includes Watteau, Boucher, Fragonard, and Greuze, as well as such classics as Frans Hals's *Laughing Cavalier* and Rembrandt's portrait of his son Titus. The paintings of the Dutch, English, Spanish, and Italian schools are outstanding. The collection also contains important 18th-century French works of decorative art, including furniture from a number of royal palaces, Sèvres porcelain, and gold boxes.

The European and Asian armaments, shown on the ground floor, are works of art in their own right: superb inlaid suits of armor, some obviously more for parade than battle, together with more businesslike swords, halberds, and magnificent Persian scimitars. The crescent sabers were reputedly tested by striking the blade against a stone, then examining it for even the most minute dent; if one was found, the sword was rejected.

PARKS/GARDENS

London's parks are the greatest, most advanced system of "green lungs" of any large city on the globe. Although not as rigidly maintained as those of Paris, they are cared for with a loving and lavishly artistic hand that puts their American equivalents to shame.

Battersea Park is a vast patch of woodland, lakes, and lawns on the south bank of the Thames, opposite Chelsea Embankment between Albert Bridge and Chelsea Bridge. Formerly known as Battersea Fields, the present park was laid out between 1852 and 1858 on an old dueling ground. (The most famous duel here was between Lord Winchelsea and the Duke of Wellington in 1829.)

The park, which measures three-quarters of a mile on each of its four sides, has a lake for boating, a deer field with fenced-in deer and wild birds, and areas for tennis and soccer. There's even a children's zoo, open from Easter to late September, daily from 11am to 5pm. The park's architectural highlight is the **Peace Pagoda,** built by Japanese craftspeople in cooperation with British architects, who ensured that it would fit gracefully into its surroundings. Built of stone and wood, the pagoda was constructed in 1986 and donated to the now-defunct Council of Greater London by an order of Japanese monks.

Battersea Park can be visited daily from 7:30am to dusk. Tube: Sloane Square in Chelsea on the Right Bank. From there it is a brisk 15-minute walk. If you prefer to ride the bus, take no. 137 from the Sloane Square station, exiting at the first stop after the bus crosses the Thames.

Hampstead Heath is the traditional playground of the Londoner, the "'Appy 'Ampstead" of cockney legend, the place dedicated "to the use of the public forever" by special Act of Parliament in 1872. Londoners would certainly mount the barricades if Hampstead Heath were imperiled.

Situated on a ridge, Hampstead Heath encompasses 785 acres of wild royal parkland about 4 miles north of the center of London. Its varied landscape encompasses formal parkland, woodland, heath, meadowland, and ponds. There is a wide variety of recreational facilities, ranging from athletics to a small zoo. The heath draws thousands of visitors each year for the walks, views, and traditional bank holiday fairs. Tube: Hampstead.

Hampstead

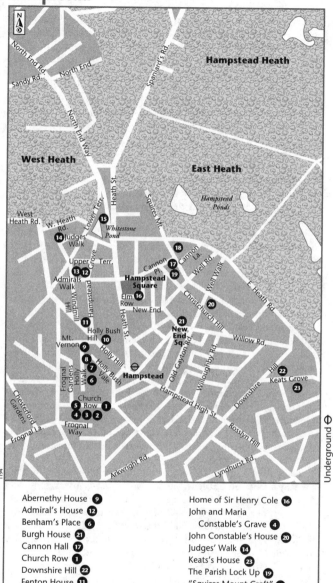

Largest of the central London parks—and one of the biggest in the world—is **Hyde Park.** With the adjoining Kensington Gardens, it covers 615 acres of central London with velvety lawns interspersed with ponds, flowerbeds, and trees. At the northeastern tip, near Marble Arch, is **Speakers' Corner.**

Hyde Park was once a favorite deer-hunting ground of Henry VIII. Running through its width is a 41-acre lake known as The Serpentine, where you can row, sail model boats, or swim, provided you're not accustomed to Florida water temperatures. **Rotten Row,** a 1½-mile sand track, is reserved for horseback riding and on Sunday attracts some skilled equestrians.

Kensington Gardens, blending with Hyde Park and bordering on the grounds of Kensington Palace, contains the famous **statue of Peter Pan,** with the bronze rabbits that toddlers are always trying to kidnap. It also contains the **Albert Memorial,** that Victorian extravaganza.

East of Hyde Park, across Piccadilly, stretch **Green Park** and **St. James's Park,** forming an almost unbroken chain of landscaped beauty. This is an ideal area for picnics, and you'll find it hard to believe that it was once a festering piece of swamp near the leper hospital. There is a romantic lake, stocked with a variety of ducks and some surprising pelicans, descendants of the pair that the Russian ambassador presented to Charles II back in 1662.

Regent's Park covers most of the district of that name, north of Baker Street and Marylebone Road. Designed by the 18th-century genius John Nash to surround a palace for the prince regent that never materialized, this is the most classically beautiful of London's parks. Its core is a **rose garden** planted around a small lake alive with waterfowl and spanned by humped Japanese bridges; in early summer, the rose perfume in the air is as heady as wine. Regent's Park also contains the **Open Air Theatre** and the **London Zoo.** As at all the local parks, there are hundreds of deck chairs on the lawns in which to sunbathe. The deck-chair attendants, who collect a small fee, are mostly college students on summer vacation.

The hub of England's—and perhaps the world's—horticulture are the **Royal Botanic Gardens,** also known as Kew Gardens, at Kew in Surrey (☎ 0181/940-1171; tube: Kew Gardens), next to the Thames southwest of the city. These splendid gardens have been a source of delight to visitors, scientific and otherwise, for more than 200 years. The staff deals annually with thousands of inquiries, covering every aspect of plant science. Immense flowerbeds and equally gigantic hothouses grow species of shrubs, blooms, and trees from every part of the globe, from the Arctic Circle to tropical rain forests. Attractions vary with the seasons. There's also the permanent charm of **Kew Palace,** home of George III and his queen, which was built in 1631 and is open for inspection.

Admission to the gardens is £4 ($6.30) for adults and £2 ($3.15) for children; a family ticket costs £10 ($15.80). Admission to the palace is £1.50 ($2.35) for adults and 80p ($1.25) for children. The gardens may be visited daily, except Christmas and New Year's Day, from

9:30am; closing varies from 4 to 7:30pm on Monday through Saturday, 6:30pm on Sunday and public holidays. The palace is open April to September, daily from 11am to 5:30pm.

Syon Park (☎ 0181/560-0881), is in Brentford, Middlesex, on the north bank of the Thames between Brentford and Isleworth, just nine miles from Piccadilly Circus. On 55 acres of the duke of Northumberland's Thamesside estate, this is one of the most beautiful spots in all of Great Britain. It lies two miles west of Kew Bridge and is signposted from A315/310 at Bush Corner. There's always something in bloom. A nation of green-thumbed gardeners is dazzled here, and the park is also educational, showing amateurs how to get the most out of their gardens. The vast flower- and plant-studded acreage still reflects the influence of "Capability" Brown, who laid out the grounds in the 18th century.

Particular highlights include a six-acre rose garden, a butterfly house, and the **Great Conservatory,** one of the earliest and most famous buildings of its type, built between 1822 and 1829. There is a quarter-mile-long ornamental lake studded with water lilies and surrounded by cypresses and willows, even a large gardening supermarket. The gardens also include a miniature steam railway that costs an additional £1 ($1.60) for adults or 50p (80¢) for children.

The gardens are open all year (except Christmas and Boxing Day). The gates open at 10am and close at 6pm; in winter (after October 31), the gates close at 5pm. Admission is £2.25 ($3.55) for adults and £1.75 ($2.75) for children, students, and senior citizens.

On the grounds is **Syon House,** built in 1431, the original structure incorporated into the duke of Northumberland's present home. From 1762 to 1769, the house was remade to the specifications of the first duke of Northumberland, with interior design by Robert Adam. The battlemented facade, however, is that of the original Tudor mansion. Katherine Howard, Henry VIII's fifth wife, was imprisoned in the house before her scheduled beheading in 1542.

The house is open only on Saturday and Sunday from 11am to 5pm (last entrance at 4:15pm). A combined ticket to the house and gardens costs £5.50 ($8.70) for adults and £4 ($6.30) for children, students, and senior citizens. Tube: Gunnersbury, then bus 237 or 267.

3 Especially for Kids

The attractions that follow are general and universal fun places to which you can take youngsters. And—there's nothing to stop you from going to any of them minus a juvenile escort. Other, previously described attractions that hold great interest for kids include Madame Tussaud's, the Science Museum, the London Transport Museum, the Natural History Museum, the Tower of London, and the Commonwealth Institute.

Kidsline (☎ 0171/222-8000) in theory is a worthy service, computerized information about current events that might interest kids. Only problem is, every parent in London with children is calling for information, and it's almost impossible to get through.

Bethnal Green Museum of Childhood

Cambridge Heath Rd., E2. ☎ **0181/980-2415.** Admission free. Mon–Thurs and Sat 10am–5:50pm, Sun 2:30–5:50pm. Tube: Bethnal Green.

This establishment displays toys from past and present centuries. The variety of dolls alone is staggering, some of them dressed in period costumes of such elaborateness you don't even want to think of the price tags they must have carried. With the dolls go dollhouses, from simple cottages to miniature mansions, complete with fireplaces and grand pianos, furniture, kitchen utensils, household pets, and carriages.

In addition, the museum displays optical toys, toy theaters, marionettes, puppets, and a considerable exhibit of soldiers and warlike toys of both world wars, plus trains and aircraft. There is also a display of children's clothing and furniture relating to the social history of childhood. The museum is a branch of the Victoria and Albert Museum.

Little Angel Theatre

14 Dagmar Passage, N1. ☎ **0171/226-1787.** Admission £5–£6.50 ($7.90–$10.25) adults, £4–£5 ($6.30–$7.90) children. Show times Sat–Sun 11am and 3pm. Tube: Angel Station, Highbury and Islington Station.

This theater, especially constructed for the presentation of puppetry in all its forms, gives between 400 and 500 performances a year. The theater is the focal point of a loosely formed group of about 20 professional puppeteers who work there as occasion demands, sometimes presenting their own shows and often helping with the performances of the resident company.

In the current repertory are 25 programs. These vary in style and content from *The Soldier's Tale,* using eight-foot-high figures, to *The Ugly Duckling* and *Cindermouse,* written especially for the humble glove puppet. Many of the plays, such as Hans Christian Andersen's *The Little Mermaid,* are performed with marionettes (string puppets), but whatever is being presented, you'll be enthralled with the exquisite lighting and the skill with which the puppets are handled. The shows are often accompanied by live music.

The theater is beautifully decorated and well equipped. There are a coffee bar in the foyer and an adjacent workshop where the settings and costumes, as well as the puppets, are made.

London Dungeon

28–34 Tooley St., SE1. ☎ **0171/403-0606.** Admission £6.95 ($11) adults, £5.50 ($8.70) children under 14. Apr–Sept daily 10am–5:30pm; Oct–Mar daily 10am–4:30pm. Closed Dec 24–26. Tube: London Bridge.

The premises simulate a ghoulish atmosphere deliberately designed to chill the blood while reproducing the conditions that existed in the Middle Ages. Set under the arches of London Bridge Station, the dungeon is a series of tableaux that are more grisly than the ones in Madame Tussaud's. The rumble of trains overhead adds to the spine-chilling horror of the place, and tolling bells bring a constant note of melancholy to the background; dripping water and live rats (caged!) make for even more atmosphere. The murder of Thomas à Becket in Canterbury Cathedral is also depicted. Naturally, there's a burning at the stake, as well as a torture chamber with racking, branding, and fingernail extraction.

If you survive, there is a souvenir shop selling certificates that testify you have been through the works.

London Zoo

Regent's Park, NW1. ☎ **0171/722-3333.** Admission £7 ($11.05) adults, £5 ($7.90) children (under 4 free). Mar–Sept daily 10am–5:30pm; Oct–Feb daily 10am–4pm. Tube: Camden Town; then take bus Z2 or 274.

One of the greatest zoos in the world, the London Zoo is more than a century and a half old. Run by the Zoological Society of London, this 36-acre garden houses about 8,000 animals, including some of the rarest species on earth. Separate houses are reserved for various species: the insect house (incredible bird-eating spiders, a cross-sectioned ant colony); the reptile house (huge dragonlike monitor lizards and a fantastic 15-foot python); and other additions such as the Sobell Pavilion for Apes and Monkeys and the Lion Terraces.

Designed for the largest collection of small mammals in the world, the Clore Pavilion has a basement called the Moonlight World, where special lighting effects simulate night for the nocturnal beasties, while rendering them clearly visible to onlookers. You can see all the night rovers in action.

Many families budget almost an entire day to spend with the animals, watching the penguins being fed, enjoying an animal ride in summer, and meeting the elephants on their walks around the zoo. On the grounds are two restaurants, one self-service.

National Maritime Museum

Romney Rd., Greenwich. ☎ **0181/858-4422.** Tickets for all attractions below, £5.50 ($8.70) adults, £3 ($4.70) children 7–16, £4.50 ($7.10) senior citizens and students. Family ticket (two adults and up to five children) £16 ($25.30). Children 6 and under free. Mon–Sat 10am–5pm, Sun noon–5pm. Closed Dec 24–26. Transportation: Thames launch downstream from Westminster Charing Cross, or Tower Piers, or train from Charing Cross Station to Maze Hill.

Down the Thames at Greenwich, about five miles from London, the National Maritime Museum stands in a beautiful royal park along with the Old Royal Observatory. From early seafarers to 20th-century seapower, the building harbors the glory that was Britain at sea. The cannon, relics, ship models, and paintings tell the story of a thousand naval battles and a thousand victories . . . also the price of those battles: Among the exhibits is the uniform that Lord Nelson wore when he was struck by a French musket ball at the very moment of his triumph at the Battle of Trafalgar.

The **Old Royal Observatory,** also part of the museum, designed by Sir Christopher Wren, overlooks Greenwich from a park laid out to the design of Le Nôtre, the French landscaper. Here you can stand at 0° longitude, where the Greenwich meridian, or prime meridian, marks the first of the globe's vertical divisions. See also the big red time-ball used in olden days by ships sailing down the river from London to set their timepieces by. There is a fascinating array of astronomical and navigational instruments, and time and travel become better understood after a visit here. There is a licensed restaurant in the museum's west wing.

You can also visit **Queen's House,** a 17th-century palace designed by Inigo Jones for the wives of James I and Charles I. The house has been restored in the vibrant colors of 1662, when the place was occupied by Henrietta Maria. A fine art collection of Dutch marine paintings and a treasury complement a tour of the royal apartments.

Unicorn Theatre for Children

The Arts Theatre, 6–7 Great Newport St., WC2. ☎ 0171/379-3280; box office **0171/836-3334.** Admission £4.50 ($7.10), £6.50 ($10.25), £7.50 ($11.85) depending on seat locations. Show times Sept–June Sat 11am and 2:30pm; Sun and holidays 2:30pm. Tube: Leicester Square.

Situated in the heart of London's theater district in the West End, the Unicorn is its only theater just for children. Founded in 1947 and going stronger than ever, it presents a season of plays for 4- to 12-year-olds from September to June each year. The schedule includes specially commissioned plays and adaptations of old favorites, all performed by adult actors. You can also become a temporary member while you are in London and join in an exciting program of workshops every weekend.

4 Special-Interest Sightseeing

FOR THE LITERARY ENTHUSIAST

Carlyle's House

24 Cheyne Row, SW3. ☎ **0171/352-7087.** Admission £2.90 ($4.60) adults, £1.45 ($2.30) children. Easter–Oct Wed–Sun 11am–5pm. Tube: Sloane Square. Bus 11, 19, 22, or 39.

From 1834 to 1881, Thomas Carlyle, author of *The French Revolution,* and Jane Baillie Welsh Carlyle, his noted letter-writing wife, resided in this modest 1708 terraced house. Furnished essentially as it was in Carlyle's day, the house is located about three-quarters of a block from the Thames, near the Chelsea Embankment, along King's Road. It was described by his wife as being "of most antique physiognomy, quite to our humour; all wainscotted, carved and queer-looking, roomy, substantial, commodious, with closets to satisfy any Bluebeard." The second floor contains the drawing room of Mrs. Carlyle, but the most interesting chamber is the not-so-soundproof "soundproof" study in the skylit attic. Filled with Carlyle memorabilia—his books, a letter from Disraeli, personal effects, a writing chair, even his death mask—this is where the author labored on his *Frederick the Great* manuscript.

Dickens House

48 Doughty St., WC1. ☎ **0171/405-2127.** Admission £3 ($4.75) adults, £2 ($3.15) students, £1 ($1.60) children, £6 ($9.50) families. Mon–Sat 10am–5pm. Tube: Russell Square.

Here in Bloomsbury stands the simple abode in which Charles Dickens wrote *Oliver Twist* and finished *The Pickwick Papers* (his American readers actually waited at the dock for the ship that brought in each new installment). The place is almost a shrine for a Dickens fan; it

Literary Bloomsbury & Beyond

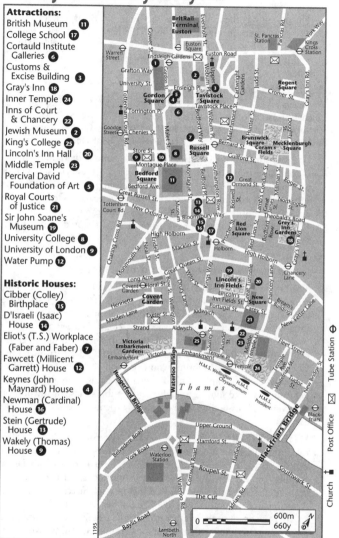

Attractions:
British Museum ⑪
College School ⑰
Cortauld Institute
  Galleries ⑥
Customs &
  Excise Building ③
Gray's Inn ⑱
Inner Temple ㉔
Inns of Court
  & Chancery ㉒
Jewish Museum ②
King's College ㉕
Lincoln's Inn Hall ⑳
Middle Temple ㉓
Percival David
  Foundation of Art ⑤
Royal Courts
  of Justice ㉑
Sir John Soane's
  Museum ⑲
University College ⑧
University of London ⑨
Water Pump ⑫

Historic Houses:
Cibber (Colley)
  Birthplace ⑮
D'Israeli (Isaac)
  House ⑭
Eliot's (T.S.) Workplace
  (Faber and Faber) ⑦
Fawcett (Millicent
  Garrett) House ⑫
Keynes (John
  Maynard) House ④
Newman (Cardinal)
  House ⑯
Stein (Gertrude)
  House ⑬
Wakely (Thomas)
  House ⑨

⊖ Tube Station
⊠ Post Office
✠ Church

contains his study, manuscripts, and personal relics, as well as reconstructed interiors.

Keats's House

Wentworth Place, Keats Grove, NW3. ☎ **0171/435-2062.** Admission free; donations welcome. Apr–Oct Mon–Fri 10am–1pm and 2–6pm, Sat 10am–1pm and 2–5pm, Sun and bank holidays 2–5pm; Nov–Mar Mon–Fri 1–5pm, Sat 10am–1pm and 2–5pm, Sun 2–5pm. Closed New Year's Day, Easter holidays, first Mon in May, Dec 24–26. Tube: Hampstead.

This house was the home of the poet John Keats for only two years. But it was here in Hampstead in 1819 that he wrote two famous poems, "Ode to a Nightingale" and "Ode on a Grecian Urn." This well-preserved Regency house contains some of his manuscripts and letters.

Samuel Johnson's House

17 Gough Sq., EC4. ☎ **0171/353-3745.** Admission £3 ($4.75) adults, £2 ($3.15) students and senior citizens, £1 ($1.60) children. May–Sept Mon–Sat 11am–5:30pm; Oct–Apr Mon–Sat 11am–5pm. Tube: Blackfriars. Directions: Walk up New Bridge St. and turn left onto Fleet. Gough Sq. is tiny and hidden, north of Fleet.

Dr. Johnson and his copyists compiled a famous dictionary in this Queen Anne house, where the lexicographer, poet, essayist, and fiction writer lived from 1748 to 1759. Although Johnson also lived at Staple Inn in Holborn and at a number of other places, the Gough Square house is the only one of his residences remaining in London. The 17th-century building has been painstakingly restored, and it's well worth a visit.

Cheshire Cheese

Wine Court Office Court, 145 Fleet St., EC4. ☎ **0171/353-6170.**

The burly literary figure of G. K. Chesterton, author of *What's Wrong with the World* (1910) and *The Superstition of Divorce* (1920), was a familiar patron at the pub Cheshire Cheese. Flamboyant in manner, he usually swept into the place encased in a cloak. That, along with his swordstick, became his trademarks. Earlier, it's said that Oliver Goldsmith, playwright of *She Stoops to Conquer* (1773), patronized the Chesire Cheese. Dr. Johnson, who lived at 17 Gough Sq., off Fleet Street, where he completed his dictionary, was also a frequent visitor. He must have had some lean nights at the pub, because by the time he had compiled his dictionary, he'd already spent his advance of 1,500 guineas.

WHERE VIRGINIA WOOLF LIVED   Born in London in 1882, the author Virginia Woolf used London as the setting of many of her novels, including *Jacob's Room* (1922). The daughter of Sir Leslie Stephen and his wife, Julia Duckworth, Virginia spent her formative years at 22 Hyde Park Gate, off Kensington High Street, west of Royal Albert Hall. Her mother died in 1895 and her father in 1904.

After the death of their father, the Stephen siblings left Kensington for Bloomsbury and settled in the area around the British Museum. Upper-class Victorians at that time, however, didn't view Bloomsbury as "respectable." From 1905 they lived first at 46 Gordon Sq., east of Gower Street and University College. It was here that the nucleus of the soon-to-be celebrated Bloomsbury Group was created, which would in time embrace Clive Bell (husband of Vanessa) and Leonard Woolf, who was to become Virginia's husband. Later, Virginia went to live at 29 Fitzroy Sq., west of Tottenham Court Road, in a house once occupied by Bernard Shaw. During the next two decades, Virginia resided at several more addresses in Bloomsbury, including on Brunswick Square, Tavistock Square, and Mecklenburgh Square, these homes have either disappeared or else been altered beyond recognition.

During this time, the Bloomsbury Group reached out to include the artists Roger Fry and Duncan Grant, and Virginia became friends with the economist Maynard Keynes and the author E. M. Forster. At Tavistock Square (1924–39) and at Mecklenburg Square (1939–40) she operated Hogarth Press with Leonard. She published her own early work here, as well as T. S. Eliot's *The Waste Land.*

To escape from urban life, Leonard and Virginia purchased Monk's House in the village of Rodmell between Lewes and Newhaven in Sussex. There, they lived until 1941 when Virginia drowned herself in the nearby Ouse. Her ashes were buried in the garden at Monk's House.

FOR VISITING AMERICANS

Despite the historic fact that they fought wars against each other, no two countries have stronger links than the United States and Britain, with the possible exception of the U.S. and Canada. The common heritage cuts right across political and economic conflicts.

In London, mementos of this heritage virtually crowd in on you. Stand in front of the National Gallery and you'll find a bronze **statue of George Washington** gazing at you over Trafalgar Square. Visit **Westminster Abbey** and you'll see a memorial tablet to Pres. Franklin D. Roosevelt, a bust of Longfellow in the Poets' Corner, and the graves of Edward Hyde (Hyde Park, N.Y., was named for him) and James Oglethorpe, who founded the state of Georgia. **Grosvenor Square,** in the heart of the West End, is known as "Little America." Watched over by a statue of FDR, it contains the modern U.S. embassy and the home of John Adams when he was minister to Britain. **Norfolk House,** St. James's Square, was Gen. Dwight D. Eisenhower's headquarters during World War II, the spot from which he directed the Allies' Normandy landing in 1944. At 36 Craven St., just off the Strand, stands **Benjamin Franklin's London residence.** And in **St. Sepulchre's,** at Holborn Viaduct, is the grave of Capt. John Smith of Pocahontas fame—he had been prevented from sailing on the *Mayflower* because the other passengers considered him an "undesirable character."

The most moving reminder of national links is the **American Memorial Chapel in St. Paul's Cathedral.** It commemorates the 28,000 U.S. service personnel who lost their lives while based in Britain during World War II. The Roll of Honor containing their names was handed over by General Eisenhower on July 4, 1951, and the chapel—with the Roll of Honor encased in glass—has become an unofficial pilgrimage place for visiting Americans.

FOR RIVER THAMES BUFFS

There is a row of fascinating attractions lying on, across, and alongside the **River Thames.** All of London's history and development is linked with this winding ribbon of water. The Thames connects the city with the sea, from which it drew its wealth and its power. For centuries the river was London's highway and main street.

Some of the Thames bridges are household names. **London Bridge,** contrary to the nursery rhyme, never fell down, but it has been dismantled and shipped to the United States. When here, it ran from the

Overfed & Oversexed

Rich Relations: The American Occupation of Britain 1942–1945, by David Reynolds (Random House, 1995) is stirring up many wartime memories among older Brits—some painful, some fun. The book lets a younger generation in on what happened on the homefront, too. In 1943, George Orwell, author of *Animal Farm* and *1984,* wrote: "It is difficult to go anywhere in London without having the feeling that Britain is occupied territory." He certainly didn't mean occupied by the Nazis, although that was a real threat at the time.

Following the entry of the United States into World War II through the D-day assault of June 1944 on the beaches of Normandy, and up until the final Nazi surrender, Roosevelt and later Truman sent three million troops to England.

For the most part, GIs were hardly eager to rush off to the war-torn, British Isles. One Kansas City soldier wrote home that, "All of Britain is one gray, dark, muddy swamp."

Even though American troops had arrived to save the English from an attack of Hitler's armies, many Yanks initially found their new hosts "snobbish, cold as their winters, and completely standoffish," according to one report. Black American soldiers, though, were treated more kindly in England than they often were back home; Reynolds confirms this in his research. Blacks from southern states who didn't dare date a white woman there found themselves romantically involved with English roses.

Monument (a tall pillar commemorating the Great Fire of 1666) to Southwark Cathedral, parts of which date back to 1207.

Its neighbor to the east is the still-standing Tower Bridge (without number or road name), SE1 (☎ 0171/407-0922; tube: Tower Hill), one of the city's most celebrated landmarks and possibly the most photographed and painted bridge on earth. Its outward appearance is familiar to Londoners and visitors alike, and it is that same bridge that a certain American thought he'd purchased instead of the one farther up the river.

In spite of its medieval appearance, Tower Bridge was actually built in 1894. In 1993 an exhibition opened inside the bridge to commemorate its century-old history, from its conception, through its construction, and up to the present day. The exhibition takes visitors up the north tower to the high-level walkways between the two towers—a photographer's dream—where views of St. Paul's, the Tower of London, and in the distance, the Houses of Parliament, can be seen. Visitors are then led down the south tower and on to the bridge's original engine room, with its Victorian boilers and steam-pumping engines that used to raise and lower the roadway across the river.

Admission to the bridge is £5 ($7.90) for adults and £3.50 ($5.55) for children. It is open daily from 10am to 6:30pm (to 5:45pm in

The typical wisecrack of the day was: "The Yanks are overpaid, oversexed, overfed, and over here." Another observer expressed it this way: "The Yanks are boisterous, materialistic, and decidedly horny."

When the American troops started arriving, many British soldiers were away fighting on foreign soil, leaving their wives, sweethearts, and gay boyfriends (at least those not already in the army) behind. All of these were eagerly claimed by the invading American troops, as we know from countless wartime memoirs. Out-of-wedlock maternities were commonplace, as was widespread venereal disease.

Many Brits wondered when the Yanks were ever going to fight. In the view of some, they spent all their time in Britain hanging out "gum-chewing and jitterbugging." (Of course, D-day and the incredible courage and strength of the American troops changed that skeptical early view.)

To the recorded tunes of Glenn Miller's orchestra, many Yanks fell in love with British girls—some were left behind at the end of the war, others were taken back to America as war brides. An unprecedented number of British war brides arrived on American shores in 1945.

As that darling old British actress, Hermione Gingold, star of such films as *Gigi* once confided to me: "My dear boy, I knew there was a war going on, and that people were dying. But those war years were something special. You Americans made the warmest bedfellows on those cold, rainy English nights."

winter). Last entry is $1^{1}/_{4}$ hours before closing. Closed: Good Friday, December 24–26, and January 1.

The Thames was London's chief commercial thoroughfare and a royal highway, the only regal one in the days of winding cobblestoned streets. Every royal procession was undertaken by gorgeously painted and gilded barges (which you can still see at the National Maritime Museum in Greenwich; see Section 3 of this chapter). All important state prisoners were delivered to the Tower by water, eliminating the chance of an ambush by their friends in one of those narrow, crooked alleys surrounding the fortress. The royal boats and much of the commercial traffic disappeared when London's streets were widened enough for horse-drawn coaches to maintain a decent pace.

A trip up or down the river today will give you an entirely different view of London from the one you get from dry land. You'll see exactly how the city grew along and around the Thames and how many of its landmarks turn their faces toward the water. It's like Manhattan from a ferry.

Several companies operate motor launches that depart from the Westminster piers, offering panoramic views of one of Europe's most historic waterways en route.

The busiest of the companies concerns itself only with downriver traffic from Westminster Pier to such destinations as Greenwich. Between April and September, the most popular excursion departs for Greenwich (a 50-minute ride) at 30-minute intervals between 10:30am and 4pm. Between October and March, boats depart from Westminster Pier at hourly intervals, daily between 10:30am and 3:30pm. Regardless of the season, one-way fares cost £4.80 ($7.60) for adults, £2.40 ($3.80) for children under 16. Round-trip fares cost £5.80 ($9.15) for adults, £3 ($4.75) for children. For information and ticket sales, contact the Westminster-Greenwich Thames Passenger Boat Service, Westminster Pier, Victoria Embankment, SW1 (☎ 0171/930-4097; tube: Westminster).

A second, completely independent network of companies offers boat trips upriver to as far away as Hampton Court. Passage is offered only between early April and late September, with only a limited number of departures per day on ships operated by several different shipping and passenger lines. Passage between Westminster Pier and Hampton Court requires about four hours each way. For information and reservations, call **Westminster Passenger Service Association** (Upstream Division), Westminster Pier, Victoria Embankment, SW1 (☎ 0171/930-2062).

Since its official opening in 1984, the engineering spectacle known as the **Thames Flood Barrier** has drawn increasing crowds to the site, at a point in the river known as Woolwich Reach (east London), where the Thames is a straight stretch about a third of a mile in width. During the day, visitors can drop in at the **Thames Barrier Visitors Centre,** Unity Way, SE18 (☎ 0181/854-1373), if they're seeking information. The center is open Monday through Friday from 10am to 9:30pm and Saturday and Sunday from 10:30am to 6pm. Admission to the barrier is £2.55 ($4.05) for adults and £1.50 ($2.35) for children. For centuries, the Thames estuary has from time to time brought tidal surges that have caused disastrous flooding at Woolwich, Hammersmith, Whitehall, Westminster, and elsewhere within the river's flood reaches. The flooding peril has increased during this century from a number of natural causes, which led to the construction, beginning in 1975, of a great barrier; when in use, all parts of it make a solid steel wall (about the height of a five-story building) that completely dams the waters of the Thames, keeping the surge tides from passage up the estuary.

London Launches (☎ 0171/930-3373; tube: Waterloo Station to Charleton Station near Thames Flood Barrier; bus: 177 or 180) offers trips up the Thames to the barrier, operating from Westminster Pier to Barrier Pier and back five times daily. Adults pay £5.85 ($9.25) round-trip or £4.15 ($6.55) one-way; children under 14 are charged £2.95 ($4.65) round-trip or £2.40 ($3.80) one-way, and senior citizens pay £4.70 ($7.45) round-trip or £3 ($4.75) one-way. If you wish to go one way by main line, trains make the 15-minute trip every 30 minutes.

What was a dilapidated wasteland in 8 square miles of property surrounded by water—some 55 miles of waterfront acreage within a sailor's cry of London's major attractions—has been reclaimed, restored, and rejuvenated. **London Docklands** is coming into its own as a leisure, residential, and commercial lure. Included in this complex are **Wapping,** the **Isle of Dogs,** the **Surrey and Royal Docks,** and more—all with **Limehouse** at its heart.

The former urban wasteland of deserted warehouses and derelict wharves, and the many facilities already completed, can be visited by taking the **Dockland Light Railway,** which links the Isle of Dogs and London Underground's Tower Hill station, via several new local stations. To see the whole complex, take the railway at the Tower Gateway near Tower Bridge for a short journey through Wapping and the Isle of Dogs. You can get off at **Island Gardens** and then cross through the 100-year-old **Greenwich Tunnel** under the Thames to see attractions at Greenwich.

A visit to the **Exhibition Centre** on the Isle of Dogs gives you an opportunity to see what the Docklands—past, present, and future—include. Already the area has given space to the overflow from the City of London's square mile, and its development is more than promising.

An 11,500-ton cruiser, **HMS** *Belfast,* Morgan's Lane, Tooley Street, SE1 (☎ 0171/407-6434; tube: Monument, Tower Hill, or London Bridge), is a World War II ship now preserved as a floating naval museum. It is moored opposite the Tower of London, between Tower Bridge and the new London Bridge. During the Russian convoy period and on D-day, the *Belfast* saw distinguished service, and in the Korean War it was known as "that straight shootin' ship." Exhibitions both above and below deck show how sailors have lived and fought over the past 50 years. The ship can be explored from the bridge right down to the engine and boiler rooms seven decks below. It's open daily from 10am, with last boarding at 5:15pm in summer, 4:15pm in winter. Admission is £4 ($6.30) for adults and £2 ($3.15) for children. Senior citizens and students pay £3 ($4.75). Refreshments are available. A ferry runs from Tower Pier (limited service in winter).

Two other ships, both world-famous, are at Greenwich, four miles east of London. At Greenwich Pier, now in permanent dry dock, lies the last and ultimate word in sail power—the **Cutty Sark,** King William Walk, Greenwich, SE10 (☎ 0181/858-3445; bus: 1, 177, 180, or 188). Named after the witch in Robert Burns's poem "Tam O'Shanter," it was the greatest of the breed of clipper ships that carried tea from China and wool from Australia in the most exciting ocean races ever sailed. The *Cutty Sark's* record stood at a then-unsurpassed 363 miles in 24 hours. Launched in Scotland in 1869, the sleek black three-master represented the final fighting run of canvas against steam. Although the age of the clippers was brief, they did outpace the steamers as long as there was wind to fill their billowing mountain of sails.

On board the *Cutty Sark* you'll find a museum devoted to clipper lore, plus all the fittings that made it the fastest thing at sea. Admission is £3.25 ($5.15) for adults and £2.25 ($3.55) for children over 7. The vessel may be boarded Monday through Saturday from 10am to 6pm and Sunday (and Good Friday) from noon to 6pm. It closes at 5pm in winter.

Next to the clipper—and looking like a sardine beside a shark—lies the equally famous ***Gipsy Moth IV,*** King William Walk, Greenwich, SE10 (☎ 0181/858-3445; bus: same as above). This, in case you don't remember, was the ridiculously tiny sailing craft in which Sir Francis Chichester circumnavigated the globe . . . solo! You can go on board and marvel at the minuteness of the vessel in which the gray-haired sea dog made his incredible 119-day journey. His chief worry—or so he claimed—was running out of ale before reaching land. The admission to go aboard is 50p (80¢) for adults and 25p (40¢) for children under 16. The *Gipsy Moth IV* keeps the same hours as the Cutty Sark, but it's closed November through March.

5 Organized Tours

ORIENTATION TOURS
BY BUS

For the first-timer, the quickest and most economical way to bring the big city into focus is to take a bus tour. One of the most popular is called **"The Original London Sightseeing Tour,"** taking only 1¹/₂ hours. London unfolds from a traditional double-decker bus, with live commentary by a guide. The sightseeing tour costs £10 ($15.80) for adults, £5 ($7.90) for children under 16. The tour plus admission to Madame Tussaud's goes for £17 ($26.85) for adults, £9 ($14.20) for children, or the tour including the River Thames costs £12.50 ($19.80) for adults and £6.50 ($10.30) for children. Tickets can be purchased on the bus or from any London Transport or London Tourist Board Information Centre, where you can receive a discount. The concierges of most central London or airport hotels also sell these tickets.

Departures are from various convenient points within the city; you can choose your departure point when you purchase your ticket. For information or ticket purchases by phone, call 0181/877-1722. It's also possible to write for tickets: **London Coaches,** Jews Row, London SW18 1TB. You might prefer the **London Plus ticket,** allowing you to hop on and off guided tour buses all day long, spending time going inside various sights that attract you.

The London Plus Hop On/Hop Off ticket costs £10 ($15.80) for adults and £5 ($7.90) for children.

A double-decker air-conditioned coach in the discreet green-and-gold livery of Harrods (☎ 0171/581-3603; tube: Knightsbridge) takes sightseeing tours around London's attractions. The first departure from Door 8 of Harrods, on Brompton Road, is at 10:30am; afternoon tours begin at 1:30 and 4pm. Tea, coffee, and orange juice are served on board. The tour costs £15 ($23.70) for adults and £7 ($11.05) for children under 12. All-day excursion tours to Bath, Windsor, Stratford-upon-Avon, and the outlying areas of London, are available. You can purchase tickets at Harrods, Sightseeing Department, lower ground floor.

The Big Bus Company Ltd., Waterside Way, London SW17 (☎ 0181/944-7810), is an alternative choice, operating since 1991.

This company operates 90-minute tours every 30 minutes departing daily in summer from 9am to 6pm (reduced in the off-season to daily from 9:10am to 3:50pm). Tours cover all the highlights, ranging from the Houses of Parliament and Westminster Abbey to the Tower of London and Buckingham Palace (exterior looks only) Live commentary is provided. Departure points are Marble Arch by Speakers Corner, Green Park by the Ritz Hotel, and Victoria Station (Buckingham Palace Road by the Royal Westminster Hotel). The cost is £8 ($12.65) for adults, £5 ($7.90) for children.

SPECIALTY TOURS
BY BOAT

The London canals were once major highways. Since the Festival of Britain in 1951, some of the traditional painted canal boats have been resurrected for Venetian-style trips through these waterways. One of them is *Jason,* which takes you on a 90-minute trip from Blomfield Road in Little Venice through the long Maida Hill tunnel under Edgware Road; through Regent's Park, passing the Mosque, the London Zoo, and Lord Snowdon's Aviary; past the Pirate's Castle to Camden Lock; and finally back to Little Venice.

The season begins on April 1 and lasts through October. During April, May, and September, the boat runs at 10:30 and 11:30am and 12:30, 1:30, and 3:30pm. In June, July, and August, an additional afternoon trip on weekends is run, but always telephone first; in October, the boat runs at 12:30 and 2:30pm only.

A canalside restaurant/café at *Jason's* moorings offers lunches, dinners, and teas, all freshly made. Take-out food can also be ordered here for the boat trips. The round-trip fare is £5.25 ($8.30) for adults and £3.75 ($5.90) for children. For reservations, contact **Jason's Trip,** opposite 60 Blomfield Rd., Little Venice, London W9 (☎ 0171/ 286-3428). Tube: Warwick Avenue.

ON FOOT

ORGANIZED LONDON WALKS John Wittich, of **J. W. Promotions,** 66 St. Michael's St., W2 (☎ 0171/262-9572), started walking tours of London in 1960. A Freeman of the City of London and a member of two of the ancient guilds of London, he is the author of several books on London walks. All the tours are conducted by Mr. Wittid himself; you'll search out the unusual, the beautiful, and the historic. He'll also arrange personal tours for families and groups who have booked in advance. The cost for a walking tour of 1¹/₂ to 2 hours is £15 ($23.70) for one or two adults with £10 ($15.80) per hour assessed for extended walks. A whole-day guided tour costs £60 ($94.80).

Of the companies operating a daily program of regularly scheduled public walks, **The Original London Walks,** 87 Messina Ave., NW6 (☎ 0171/624-3978 or 0171/794-1764), is the best, hands down. Their hallmarks are a variety of routes, reliability, reasonably sized groups, and—above all—superb guides. The guides include the renowned crime historian Donald Rumbelow ("internationally recognized as the leading authority on Jack the Ripper"), a distinguished

BBC producer, the foremost authority on the Regent's Canal, the author of the classic guidebook London Walks, a London Historical Society officer, and several prominent actors and actresses (including the classical actor Edward Petherbridge). They offer more than 60 walks a week, year-round. Their repertory ranges from Greenwich to Ghost Walks; Beatles to Bloomsbury; Dickens to Docklands; Hampstead to Hidden London; Old Westminster to the Old Jewish Quarter; Legal London to Little Venice to the London Nobody Knows; Covent Garden to Camden Town; Shakespeare to Soho; the Famous Square Mile to the Footsteps of Sherlock Holmes; the "Undiscovered City" to the "Secret Village"; and Aristocratic London to Along the Thames. Walks cost £4 ($6.30) for adults or £3 ($4.75) for students and senior citizens. Children go free. No reservations needed.

6 Outdoor Activities

BICYCLING   Bicycles are forbidden on most highways, trunk roads, and on what the English call "dual carriageways" (two-lane highways). In town or in the country the bike is a great way to get around. If you're interested in a cycling holiday in England, contact the **Cyclists' Tourist Club,** Cotterell House, 69 Meadrow, Godalming, Surrey GU7 3HS (☎ 01483/417217). Club membership costs £25 ($39.50) a year for adults, £12.50 ($19.75) for those 17 and under. A family with three or more members can obtain a membership for £42 ($66.35). There are no specific tours, however, within London.

HEALTH & FITNESS CENTER   The **Jubilee Hall Sports Centre,** 30 The Piazza, Covent Garden, WC2 (☎ 0171/836-4835; tube: Covent Garden), is the result of a radical 1980s makeover of a Victorian-era fish-and-flower market into a modern gym. Today, it's one of the best and most centrally located sports centers in London, with the capital's largest weight room and an avid corps of exercise enthusiasts. It also offers badminton, basketball, aerobics, gymnastics, martial arts, and self-defense training (for women). It's open Monday through Friday from 6:30am to 10pm and Saturday and Sunday from 10am to 5pm. The cost of admission is £6 ($9.50) for use of the weight room and £5 ($7.90) for participation in an aerobics class.

HORSEBACK RIDING LESSONS   The **Ross Nyde Riding School,** 8 Bathurst Mews, W2 (☎ 0171/262-3791; tube: Lancaster Gate), is the only public stable in Hyde Park. The school has 16 horses that are reliable and are not easily disturbed by traffic. It's recommended that you go riding early in the morning to avoid crowds in the park. The stable opens at 7am; rides are given each hour during the week until dark except on Monday when it is closed. On the weekend, scheduled rides are 10 and 11am Saturday and Sunday; 2 and 3pm Saturday; and 1:30 and 2:30pm on Sunday. The cost of a group lesson is £25 ($39.50) and £30 ($47.40) for a private lesson.

ICE SKATING   The **Queen's Ice Skating Club,** 17 Queensway, Bayswater, W2 (☎ 0171/229-0172; tube: Queensway or Bayswater), is London's only serious ice venue. The admission charge is £5 ($7.90) for adults and £3.50 ($5.55) for children. You can rent a pair of skates for £1.50 ($2.35) and lessons cost £5.50 ($8.70) for 15 minutes. The club is open Sunday through Thursday from 10am to 4:30pm and 7:30 to 10:30pm. On Friday and Saturday evenings, it's disco night from 7:30 to 11pm, with a DJ and flashing lights.

SWIMMING   The **Brittania Leisure Centre,** 40 Hyde Rd., N1 (☎ 0171/729-4485; tube: Old Street), is a sports-and-recreation center operated and paid for by the eastern borough of Hackney. One of the most modern sports-and-recreational facilities in London, it contains a swimming pool with a wave machine, fountains, badminton and squash courts, and soccer and volleyball fields. Admission costs 60p (95¢) for adults and 30p (45¢) for children; the complex is open Monday through Friday from 9am to 10pm and Saturday and Sunday from 9am to 6pm.

7   Spectator Sports

London can be as exciting for sports enthusiasts as it is for theater fans.

SOCCER   Association football is the national winter sport, provoking endless debate in offices and pubs throughout the nation. The London-based teams that set British pulses racing—Arsenal, Chelsea, and the Tottenham Hotspurs—sound like so many brands of cheese spread to a Statesider, although with a little research, the names and merits of the various teams become apparent. Various venues and matches are announced in the newspaper, although the country's most visible site of world-class soccer matches is Wembley Stadium, Wembley, Middlesex (☎ 0181/902-8833), about six miles north of London's center. Tube: Wembley Park.

CRICKET   In summer, the national passion turns to cricket, played either at **Lord's,** St. John's Wood Road, NW8 (☎ 0171/289-1611; tube: St. John's Wood), in north London; or at the somewhat less prestigious **Oval Cricket Ground,** The Oval, Kennington, London SE11 (☎ 0171/582-6660; tube: The Oval), in south London. During the international test matches between Britain and Australia, the West Indies, India, or New Zealand (equivalent in importance to the World Series in the U.S.), the country goes into a collective trance, with everyone glued to the nearest radio or TV describing the event.

TENNIS   Fans from around the world focus on Wimbledon for two weeks (beginning around late June).

Here you'll see some of the world's greatest tennis players in action, while enjoying the traditional snack of strawberries and cream. The famous annual championships span roughly the last week in June to the first in July, with matches lasting from about 2pm till dark. (The gates open at 10:30am.) Although the British founded the All England Lawn Tennis & Croquet Club back in 1877, they haven't produced a world champion in ages. Most tickets range in price from a low of £8 to £50 ($12.65 to $79). For information during the tournament, call 0181/944-1066 for recorded information. For details send

Offbeat London or Some Places to Visit in London that You Might Not Have Automatically Thought Of

- **Chelsea Physic Garden,** 66 Royal Hospital Rd., SW3 (☎ 0171/ 352-5646). Founded in 1673 by the Worshipful Society of Apothecaries, this is the second-oldest surviving botanical garden in England. Sir Hans Sloane, doctor to George II , required the apothecaries of the empire to discover 50 plant species a year for presentation to the Royal Society. The objective was to grow plants for medicinal study; plant specimens and even trees arrived at the gardens by barge. Many plants grew here in English soil for the first time. Cotton seeds from this garden launched an industry in the new colony of Georgia. In 1983, this four-acre garden was opened to the public. Some 7,000 plants still grow here, everything from the pomegranate to the willow Pattern tree. Even an exotic cork oak can be viewed. England's earliest rock garden is here, too. Hours are Wednesday through Sunday from 2 to 5pm, late March through October. Tube: Sloane Square.
- **Vidal Sassoon School of Hairdressing,** 56 Davies Mews, W1 (☎ 0171/629-4635). At this internationally famous school of Sassoony, you can be made over. Depending on what you pay, you get the services of one stylist or else "the creative team." Precision cutting and innovative styling—no shaggy perms—are the hallmarks of this frighteningly trendy place. Hours are Monday through Friday from 10am to 3pm. Some appointments can run up to three hours or more. Tube: Bond Street.
- **The Voice Box,** Level 5, Royal Festival Hall, SE1 (☎ 0171/ 921-0906). Part of London's creatively fertile Arts Centre Project, this is a venue for prose and poetry readings presented by the organization's Literature Department. The readings are performed by celebrated writers and are generally held in the evenings around 7:30pm. Attendance at the readings costs from £3.50 to £6 ($5.55 to $9.50), and for students £2 to £3 ($3.15 to $4.75). A complete schedule is listed in the free brochure *Literature Quarterly*. Next door to the Voice Box is the Poetry Library (☎ 0171/921-0943), containing the largest collection of 20th-century poetry in Britain. You can find audio and video recordings here, too; information about workshops and contests is posted on a bulletin board.

a self-addressed stamped envelope (only from September through December) to the **All England Lawn Tennis & Croquet Club,** P.O. Box 98, Church Road, Wimbledon, SW19 5AE. To reach Wimbledon, take the tube to Southfields.

HORSE RACING   Within easy reach of central London, there are **horse-racing** tracks at **Kempton Park, Sandown Park,** and the most famous of them all, **Epsom,** where the Derby is the main feature of the

Although membership is free, you must bring an ID with your current address on it. Hours are from 11am to 8pm daily. Tube: Waterloo.

- **London College of Fashion,** 20 John Princess St., W1 (☎ 0171/514-7400). Feeling in need of some pampering? At this school, you can indulge yourself without overtaxing your wallet. The most expensive treatment costs £5 ($7.90), which covers the cost of the products used. Students in the beauty-therapy department perform facials, body wraps, electrical massages, and cathiodermie. Hours are Monday through Friday from 9am to 8pm, with the last treatment scheduled at 5pm. Some appointments can run up to three hours or more. Tube: Oxford Circus.

- **Porchester Baths,** Queensway, W2 (☎ 0171/792-3980). Looking for a reminder from the relatively recent past, when bathtime was considered a rare event? The Porchester Baths were constructed in 1929 in marble and gold and have been hailed as an art deco masterpiece. In the Porchester Centre, the baths offers a swimming pool, dry-heat saunas, and a steamy Turkish bath. For a visit of up to three hours, you're charged £15.40 ($24.35). It's women's day on Tuesday, Thursday, and Friday, and men only on Monday, Wednesday, and Saturday. Hours are from 10am to 10pm. On Sunday, it's women only from 10am to 4pm, and mixed couples from 4 to 10pm. No nudity is allowed. Tube: Bayswater.

- **College of Psychic Studies,** 16 Queensbury Place, SW7 (☎ 0171/589-3292). London has been the home of some of the most noteworthy eccentrics in Europe, and many of them are deeply interested in psychic phenomena. This college focuses on every aspect of spiritualism, stressing psychic development and healing. On Thursday evenings, you can visit the healing clinic for a half-hour session; it's free, but donations are welcomed. If you would like a sitting with a "sensitive," also a half hour, the cost ranges from £17 to £31 ($26.85 to $49). On the weekends, personal workshops are held for psychic development. Hours are Monday through Thursday 10am to 7:30pm, and on Friday 10am to 4:30pm. The college is closed the last two weeks of August. Tube: South Kensington.

meeting in early June. Racing takes place both midweek and on weekends, but not continuously. Sometimes during the summer, there are evening race meetings, so you should telephone **United Racecourses Ltd.,** Epsom, Surrey (☎ 01372/726311), for information on the next meeting at Epsom, Sandown Park, or Kempton Park. You can drive yourself or, if you want to travel by rail, phone 0171/928-5100 in London for details of train services.

ROYAL TOURNAMENT   Finally, we come to a spectacle for which it is difficult to find a comprehensive tag—the **Royal Tournament,** which some viewers describe as a series of indoor parades paying homage to the traditions and majesty of the British armed forces. Performed every year in late July, usually for a $2^{1}/_{2}$-week run, it's a long-running spectacle that has been viewed enthusiastically by thousands. The show includes massed bands presenting stirring music, the Royal Navy field-gun competition, the Royal Air Force with their dogs, the Royal Marines in action, the King's Troop Royal Horse Artillery, the Household Cavalry, and a series of visiting military-style exhibitions from throughout the British Commonwealth.

There are two performances Tuesday through Saturday, at 2:30 and 7:30pm, at the Earl's Court Exhibition Centre, Warwick Road, SW5. There are no evening performances on Sunday and no matinees on Monday. Seats cost from £5 to £24 ($7.90 to $37.90), with discounts of around 20% for children 5 to 14 and senior citizens over 65. For tickets and other information, write to the Royal Tournament Exhibition Centre, Warwick Road, London SW5 9TA (☎ 0171/373-8141; tube: Earl's Court Station). For any other information, contact the Royal Tournament Horse Guards, Wellington Barracks, Birdcage Walk, London SW1E 6HQ (☎ 0171/799-2323; tube: Westminster).

London Strolls

The best way to discover London is on foot, but unless you are in London for several weeks, it is virtually impossible to visit all of the major attractions. Most people are lucky to see merely the highlights. Your busy itinerary may not allow you to take all of the strolls in this chapter, but try to fit in as many as possible. For additional information on many sights mentioned in the Walking Tours, see Chapter 6.

WALKING TOUR 1
THE CITY

Start: The southern terminus of London Bridge. *Tube:* London Bridge or Monument.
Finish: St. Paul's Cathedral. *Tube:* St. Paul's.
Time: About three hours, excluding interior visits.
Best Times: Weekday mornings, when the financial district is functioning but churches are not crowded.
Worst Times: Weekends when the district is almost deserted, unless you prefer the lack of traffic.

Encompassing only a small patch of urban real estate, the area known as the City offers the densest concentration of historic and cultural monuments in Britain. The City is proud of its role as one of the financial capitals of the world. Our tour begins on the southern edge of the Thames, directly to the west of one of the world's most famous bridges. Facing the Thames rises the bulk of:

1. **Southwark Cathedral.** When it was built in the 1200s, it was an outpost of the faraway diocese of Winchester. Deconsecrated after Henry VIII's Reformation, it later housed bakeries and pigpens. Much of what you'll see is a result of a sorely needed 19th-century rebuilding, but a view of its Gothic interior, with its multiple commemorative plaques, gives an idea of the religious power of London's medieval church. After your visit, walk across the famous:

2. **London Bridge.** Originally designed by Henry de Colechurch under the patronage of Henry II in 1176 but replaced several times since, it's probably the most famous bridge in the world. Until as late 1729, it was the only bridge across the Thames. During the

Middle Ages, it was lined with shops, and houses crowded its edges. It served for centuries as the showplace for the severed heads— preserved in tar—of enemies of the British monarchs. (The most famous of these included the head of Sir Thomas More, the highly vocal lord chancellor.) The bridge built from 1825 to 1831 was moved to the United States. The current bridge was built from 1967 to 1973. From Southwark Cathedral, cross the bridge. At its northern end, notice the first street that descends to the right (east), Monument Street. Detour down it a short distance to read the commemorative plaques attached to the:

3. **Monument.** Commemorating the Great Fire of 1666, this soaring Doric column is appropriately capped with a carved version of a flaming urn. The disaster it memorializes erupted from a bakery in nearby Pudding Lane, raged for four days and nights, and destroyed 80% of the City. A cramped and foreboding set of stairs spirals up to the top's view over the cityscape, so heavily influenced after the fire by architect Sir Christopher Wren.

   Retrace your steps toward London Bridge, but before you actually step onto it, detour to the left (south, toward the river) at Monument Street's first intersection, Fish Hill Street. Set near the edge of the water, the shadow of the bridge, is one of Wren's many churches:

4. **St. Magnus the Martyr.** Completed in 1685 (with a tower added in 1705), it has a particularly magnificent interior, which at one time was devoted to the neighborhood's many fishmongers.

   After your visit, continue walking east along Lower Thames Street. At the corner of Idol Lane (the fifth narrow street on your left), turn left to see the bombed-out remains of another of Sir Christopher Wren's churches:

5. **St. Dunstan-in-the-East.** Its unexpectedly verdant garden, the only part of the complex that regenerated itself after the Nazi blitz of World War II, offers a comforting oasis amid a sea of traffic and masonry. After your visit, continue walking northward. Where Idol Lane dead-ends at Great Tower Street, look straight ahead to the spire of another of Wren's churches, this one in substantially better shape, the church of:

6. **St. Margaret Pattens.** Built between 1684 and 1689, it has much of its original 17th-century paneling and interior fittings, plus a narrow, slender spire that inspired, in one way or another, the form of many later churches. After your visit, walk to the west side of the church and take Rood Lane north one block to Fenchurch. Go left (west) for two blocks, then right on Gracechurch Street, noting your presence in the dusky and narrow streets of Europe's largest financial capital. Within a very short walk, on your right, you'll reach the Victorian arcades of one of the neighborhood's most densely packed shopping centers:

7. **Leadenhall.** Designed in 1881 by Horace Jones, it contains the accoutrements you'd need for either a picnic or a full gourmet

Walking Tour—The City

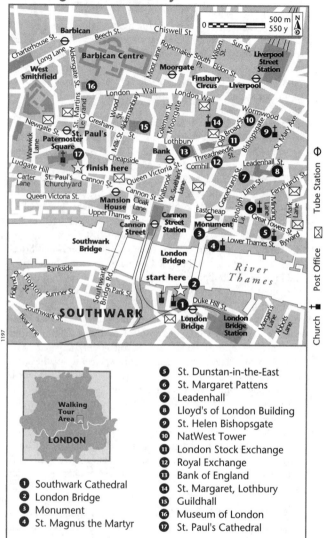

Legend:

- ⊖ Tube Station
- ⊠ Post Office
- ✝ Church

1. Southwark Cathedral
2. London Bridge
3. Monument
4. St. Magnus the Martyr
5. St. Dunstan-in-the-East
6. St. Margaret Pattens
7. Leadenhall
8. Lloyd's of London Building
9. St. Helen Bishopsgate
10. NatWest Tower
11. London Stock Exchange
12. Royal Exchange
13. Bank of England
14. St. Margaret, Lothbury
15. Guildhall
16. Museum of London
17. St. Paul's Cathedral

dinner. Browse at will, but once you've finished, return to Gracechurch Street, walk north about a block, then go right (east) on Leadenhall Street. Take the second right (south) turn on Lime Street, where you can admire the soaring and iconoclastically modern:

8. Lloyd's of London Building. Designed by Richard Rogers in 1986, this is the most recent home of an organization founded in the 1680s as a marine-insurance market. This is the most famous although financially troubled insurer in the world, with a hyper-modern headquarters built atop the heart of the ancient Roman community (Londinium) whose builders launched London's destiny over 2,000 years ago. In the early 1990s Lloyd's survival was threatened by immense underwriting losses. (Within a few blocks of your position are the London Metal Exchange, the London Futures and Options Exchange, and many financial institutions whose clout is felt around the world.)

Emerge from Lime Street back onto Leadenhall, where you turn left, then take the first right on Bishopsgate, then the second right turn into an alleyway known as Great St. Helen's. Near its end, you'll find the largest surviving medieval church in London:

9. **St. Helen Bishopsgate.** Built in the 1400s, it was dedicated to St. Helen, the legendary British mother of the Roman emperor Constantine. It was fashionable during the Elizabethan and Jacobean periods, and its interior monuments, memorials, and grave markers are especially interesting. Exit back onto Bishopsgate, turning right (north). Two blocks later, turn left onto Wormwood Street. Turn at the first left (Old Broad Street). Towering above you— the most visible building on its street—rises the modern bulk of the tallest building in Britain and the second-tallest building in Europe, the:

10. **NatWest Tower.** Housing the headquarters of National Westminster Bank, it was designed in 1981 by Richard Seifert. Built upon massive concrete foundations above a terrain composed mostly of impervious clay, it was designed to sway gently in the wind. Unfortunately, there is no publicly accessible observation tower in the building, so most visitors admire it from afar.

Continue south along Old Broad Street, noticing on your right the bulky headquarters of the:

11. **London Stock Exchange.** The center was built in the early 1960s to replace its outmoded original quarters. Its role has become much quieter since 1986, when the nature of most of the City's financial operations changed from a face-to-face agreement between brokers to a computerized clearinghouse conducted electronically.

☕ **TAKE A BREAK**　Continue southwest along Old Broad Street until it merges with Threadneedle Street. Cross over Threadneedle Street, walk a few paces to your left, and head south along the narrow confines of Finch Lane. Cross the busy traffic of Cornhill to the south side of the street. Follow it east to St. Michael's Alley to **Jamaica Wine House,** St. Michael's Alley, EC3 (☎ 0171/ 626-9496), claims to be one of the first coffeehouses in the Western world. It has been favored by London merchants and the sea captains who imported their goods. From its historic precincts, it today dispenses beer, ale, lager, wine, and other refreshments, including bar snacks and soft drinks.

After you tipple, explore the labyrinth of narrow alleyways that shelter you within an almost medieval maze from the district's roaring weekday traffic. Eventually, however, head for the major boulevard (Cornhill), which lies a few steps north of the site of your earlier refueling stop. There, near the junction of five major streets, rises the:

12. **Royal Exchange.** Designed by William Tite in the early 1840s, its imposing neoclassical pediment is inset with Richard Westmacott's sculpture of *Commerce.* Launched by a partnership of merchants and financiers during the Elizabethan Age, the Royal Exchange's establishment was a direct attempt to lure European banking and trading functions from Antwerp (then the financial capital of northern Europe) to London. Separate markets and auction facilities for raw materials were conducted in frenzied trading here until 1982, when the building became the headquarters of the London International Financial Futures Exchange (LIFFE).

On the opposite side of Threadneedle Street rises the massive bulk of the:

13. **Bank of England.** Originally established "for the Publick Good and Benefit of Our People" in a charter granted in 1694 by William and Mary, it is a treasure trove both of gold bullion, British banknotes, and historical archives. The only part of this massive building open to the public is the Bank of England Museum, whose entrance is on a narrow side street, Bartholomew Lane (☎ 0171/601-4878; open Monday through Friday from 10am to 5pm; admission free).

From the Bank of England, walk northwest along Prince's Street to the intersection of Lothbury. From the northeast corner of the intersection rises another church designed and built by Sir Christopher Wren between 1686 and 1690:

14. **St. Margaret, Lothbury.** Filled with statues of frolicking cupids, elaborately carved screens, and a soaring eagle near the altar, it's worth a visit inside. After you exit, cross Prince's Street and head west on Gresham Street. After traversing a handful of alleyways, you'll see on your right the gardens and the grandly historical facade of the:

15. **Guildhall.** The power base for the lord mayor of London since the 12th century (and rebuilt, adapted, and enlarged many times since), it was the site of endless power negotiations throughout the Middle Ages between the English kings (headquartered outside the City at Westminster) and the guilds, associations, and brotherhoods of the City's merchants and financiers. Today, the rituals associated with the lord mayor are almost as elaborate as those of the monarchy itself. The medieval crypt of the Guildhall is the largest in London, and its east facade was rebuilt by Sir Christopher Wren after the Great Fire of 1666.

After your visit to the Guildhall, continue walking westward on Gresham and take the second right turn onto Wood Street. Walk two blocks north to London Wall, go left for about a block, where you'll see the modern facade of the:

16. **Museum of London.** Located in new quarters built in 1975, it contains an assemblage of London memorabilia gathered from several earlier museums, as well as one of the best collections of period costumes in the world. Built on top of the western gate of the ancient Roman colony of Londinium, it is especially strong on archeological remnants unearthed during centuries of London building. There are also tableaux portraying the Great Fire and Victorian prison cells.

   After your visit to the museum, head south on Aldersgate, whose name is soon changed to St. Martins-le-Grand. After you cross Newgate Street, the enormous and dignified dome of one of Europe's most famous and symbolic churches will slowly loom in front of you:

17. **St. Paul's Cathedral.** Considered the masterpiece of Sir Christopher Wren and the inspiration for the generation of Londoners who survived the bombings of World War II, it was the scene of the state funerals of Nelson, Wellington, and Churchill as well as the wedding celebration of Prince Charles and Princess Diana. It is the only church in England built with a dome, the country's only church in the English baroque style, and the first English cathedral to be designed and built by a single architect.

WALKING TOUR 2
CHELSEA

Start: Chelsea Embankment at Battersea Bridge. *Tube:* Sloane Square.
Finish: Chelsea's Old Town Hall, or any of the nearby pubs. *Tube:* Sloane Square.
Time: About two hours, not counting stops.
Best Times: Almost anytime.
Worst Times: A rainy day.

Historically, Chelsea has been one of the most artistically creative districts of London. Today, it's home to some of the most prosperous residents of the capital and is considered one of the most complete, perfect, and attractively scaled "villages within the city." Its residents have included Baroness Margaret Thatcher, Mick Jagger, Oscar Wilde, Thomas Carlyle, J. M. W. Turner, John Singer Sargent, Henry James, and Henry VIII. Begin your tour above the massive masonry buttresses known as the Chelsea Embankment, at the northern terminus of:

1. **Battersea Bridge.** Although not the most famous bridge in London, it will align and orient you to an understanding of Chelsea's vital link to the Thames. Here begins a beautiful walk eastward through a historic neighborhood marred only by the roar of the riverside traffic. Across the water rises the district of Battersea, a rapidly gentrifying neighborhood.

Walking Tour — Chelsea

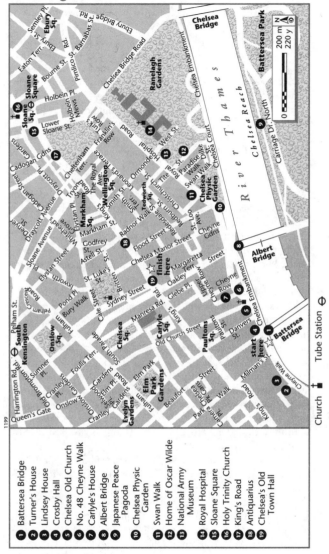

1 Battersea Bridge
2 Turner's House
3 Lindsey House
4 Crosby Hall
5 Chelsea Old Church
6 No. 48 Cheyne Walk
7 Carlyle's House
8 Albert Bridge
9 Japanese Peace Pagoda
10 Chelsea Physic Garden
11 Swan Walk
12 Home of Oscar Wilde
13 National Army Museum
14 Royal Hospital
15 Sloane Square
16 Holy Trinity Church
17 King's Road
18 Antiquarius
19 Chelsea's Old Town Hall

The street that rambles beside the Thames eventually is identified as Cheyne Walk. Rich with Georgian and Victorian architecture (and containing some of the most expensive houses of a very expensive neighborhood), it is considered an architectural treasure house. Although the bulk of your exploration along this street will be eastward, for the moment detour from the base of Battersea Bridge westward to 119 Cheyne Walk, which is:

2. **Turner's House.** Its tall and narrow premises sheltered one of England's greatest painters, J. M. W. Turner (1775–1851), during the last years of his life. His canvases, although predating those of the French impressionists, are distinctly different and uniquely recognizable for the shimmering quality of their colors. When he died in one of the bedrooms of this house, his very appropriate final words were, "God is Light."

Just to the east at nos. 96–100, is a building considered one of Chelsea's most beautiful, completed in the 1670s:

3. **Lindsey House.** Built by the Swiss-born physician to two British kings (James I and Charles II), it became the British headquarters of the Moravian Church around 1750. Later divided and sold as four separate residences, it housed the American-born painter James Whistler (at no. 96 between 1866 and 1879). The gardens of no. 99 and no. 100 were designed by Britain's most celebrated Edwardian architect, Sir Edwin Lutyens (1869–1944).

At this point, retrace your steps eastward to Battersea Bridge and begin what will become a long eastwardly ramble along Cheyne Walk. Midway between the heavy traffic of Beaufort Street and the much quieter Danvers Street, you'll see:

4. **Crosby Hall.** Designated by no identifying street number, its original brick-and-stone construction (resembling a chapel) is prefaced with a modern wing of gray stone added in the 1950s. It was built in the early 1400s and owned successively by both Richard III and Sir Thomas More. It was transported in the early 1900s stone by stone from Bishopsgate, partly under the financial incentive of American-born Lady Nancy Astor. Today, it provides apartments and dining facilities for the British Federation of University Women. Parts of its interior (which contains paintings by Holbein, a trussed roof, and some Jacobean furniture) are open free to the public (Monday through Saturday from 10am to noon and 2:15 to 5pm).

After your visit, continue walking eastward on Cheyne Walk. After crossing both Danvers and Church streets, if you detour a few buildings away from the river onto Old Church Street, you'll reach the parish church of the late Sir Thomas More:

5. **Chelsea Old Church.** Its beauty is diminished only by the masses of traffic outside and the fact that it and its neighborhood were heavily damaged by Nazi bombs during World War II. Gracefully repaired, it contains a chapel partly designed by Hans Holbein; an urn containing the earthly remains of a man who owned most of Chelsea during the 1700s, Sir Hans Sloane; and a plaque commemorating the life of American novelist Henry James, a longtime Chelsea resident who died nearby in 1916. The building's Lawrence Chapel is reputed to have been the scene of Henry VIII's secret marriage to Jane Seymour several days before their official marriage in 1536.

Continue walking eastward along Cheyne Walk. Within about a block, the pavement will branch to form a swath of trees and lawn, behind which stand some of the most expensive and desirable town houses of Chelsea. Occupants of these elegantly proportioned buildings have included some very famous people, including Mick Jagger, who purchased:

6. No. 48 Cheyne Walk. Jagger lived here for a while, brushing elbows with neighbors like guitarist Keith Richards, publishing magnate Lord Weidenfeld, and the grandson of oil industry giant J. Paul Getty. Artistic denizens of an earlier age included George Eliot, who lived for part of her flamboyant life (and later died) at no. 41. The star of the Pre-Raphaelite movement, Dante Gabriel Rossetti, lived in what is considered the street's finest building, no. 16.

Branch inland from the Thames, heading north along Cheyne Row, where, within a short walk, at no. 5, stands:

7. Carlyle's House. Considered one of the most interesting houses in London, particularly to literary enthusiasts, it is one of the neighborhood's few houses open to the public. The former home of "the sage of Chelsea" and his wife, Jane, it offers a fascinating insight into the Victorian decor of its time. Notice the small gravestone in the garden marking the burial place of the author's favorite dog.

After you visit, retrace your steps to Cheyne Walk and continue east. The bridge that looms into view is:

8. Albert Bridge. Matched only by Tower Bridge and Westminster Bridge, this might be the most-photographed bridge in London. Created at the height of the Victorian fascination with cast iron, it was designed in 1873 by R. M. Ordish.

Continue walking eastward beneath the trees of Cheyne Walk, eventually branching inland, away from the river, along Royal Hospital Road. Before you leave the banks of the Thames, however, look on the opposite end of the Thames for the:

9. Japanese Peace Pagoda. Containing a massive statue of Buddha covered in gold leaf and unveiled in 1985, it was crafted by 50 Japanese nuns and monks. Set at the riverside edge of Battersea Park, according to plans by the Buddhist leader Nichidatsu Fugii, it was offered to Britain by the Japanese government.

Continue walking northeast along Royal Hospital Road. The turf on your right (its entrance is at 66 Royal Hospital Rd.) belongs to the oldest surviving botanic garden in Britain, the:

10. Chelsea Physic Garden (also known as Chelsea Botanic Garden). Established in 1673 on four acres of riverfront land that belonged to Charles Cheyne, it was founded by the Worshipful Society of Apothecaries, and later (1722) funded permanently by Sir Hans Sloane, botanist and physician to George II. The germ of what later became international industries began in the earth of these gardens, greenhouses, and botanical laboratories.

Now, continue your walk northeast along Royal Hospital Road, but turn right at the first cross street onto:

11. Swan Walk. Known for its 18th-century row houses, it's a charming and obscure part of Chelsea. Walk down it, turning at the first left onto Dilke Street, and at its dead end, turn left onto Tite Street. (From here, your view of the Japanese Peace Pagoda on the opposite bank of the Thames might be even better than before.) At 34 Tite St., you'll see a plaque commemorating the:

12. Home of Oscar Wilde. Here, Wilde wrote many of his most charming plays, including *The Importance of Being Earnest* and *Lady Windermere's Fan*. After Wilde was arrested and imprisoned, following the most famous trial for homosexuality in British history, the house was sold to pay his debts. The plaque was presented in 1954, a century after Wilde's birthday. A few steps away on the same street are houses that once belonged to two of America's most famous expatriates. No. 31 was the home of John Singer Sargent (and the studio where he painted many of his most famous portraits), and no. 35 was the home of James McNeill Whistler.

At the end of Tite Street, turn right onto Royal Hospital Road. Within a block are the fortresslike premises of the:

13. National Army Museum. Its premises contain galleries devoted to weapons, uniforms, and art, with dioramas of famous battles and such memorabilia as the skeleton of Napoléon's favorite horse.

Next door to the museum, a short distance to the northeast, is the building that contains the world's most famous horticultural exhibition, the Chelsea Flower Show, which is held every year amid the vast premises of the :

14. Royal Hospital. Designed in 1682 in the aftermath of the Great Fire of London by Sir Christopher Wren (and considered, after St. Paul's Cathedral, his masterpiece) it might have been built to compete with Louis XIV's construction of Les Invalides in Paris. Both were designed as a home for wounded or aging soldiers, and both are grandiose.

Pass the Royal Hospital, eventually turning left (northeast) four blocks later at Chelsea Bridge Road. This street will change its name in about a block to Lower Sloane Street, which leads eventually to:

15. Sloane Square. Considered the northernmost gateway to Chelsea, it was laid out in 1780 on land belonging to Sir Hans Sloane. His collection of minerals, fossils, and plant specimens was the core of what eventually became the British Museum. Detour half a block north of Sloane Square (its entrance is on Sloane Street) to visit a church known as a triumph of the late-19th-century's arts-and-crafts movement:

16. Holy Trinity Church. Completed in 1890, it contains windows by William Morris following designs by Sir Edward Burne-Jones and embellishments in the Pre-Raphaelite style.

Exit from Sloane Square's southwestern corner and stroll down one of the most variegated and interesting commercial streets in London:

17. King's Road. Laden with antiques stores, booksellers, both stylish and punk clothiers, restaurants, coffeehouses, tearooms, and die-hard adherents of the 1980s "Sloane Ranger" mystique, it is a delightful area in which to observe the human comedy. Dozens of possibilities for food, sustenance, and companionship exist.

☕ **TAKE A BREAK** **Henry J. Bean's** (But His Friends All Call Him Hank) Bar & Grill, 195–197 King's Rd. (☎ 0171/352-9255), lures the homesick Yankee. It's been compared to a "Cheers"-style bar. Big burgers and meaty dogs are part of the American fare, and you can order such drinks as tequila sunrise. In summer, you can eat and drink in the rose garden in the back. Happy hour with reduced drink prices is daily from 6 to 8pm.

After your refreshment (which can be repeated at any of the neighborhood's other pubs and cafés along the way), continue walking southwest along King's Road. Midway between Shawfield Street and Flood Street lies a warren of antiques sellers, all clustered together into a complex known as:

18. Antiquarius, 135–141 King's Rd., SW3. Browse at will—maybe you'll buy an almost-heirloom or perhaps even something of lasting value.

As you continue down King's Road, oval-shaped blue-and-white plaques will identify buildings of particular interest. One that you should especially watch for is:

19. Chelsea's Old Town Hall. Set on the south side of King's Road, midway between Chelsea Manor and Oakley Street, it's the favorite hangout of everyone from punk rockers to soon-to-be-married couples applying for a marriage license. Many wedding parties are photographed in front of its Georgian grandeur.

The energetic and/or still curious participants in this walking tour might transform its finale into a pub crawl, as the neighborhood is filled with many enticing choices.

8

London Shopping

When Prussian Field Marshal Blücher, Wellington's stout ally at Waterloo, first laid eyes on London, he allegedly slapped his thigh and exclaimed, "Herr Gott, what a city to plunder!" He was gazing at what, for the early 19th century, was a phenomenal mass of shops and stores, overwhelming to Herr Blücher's unsophisticated eyes. Since those days, other cities have drawn level with London as shopping centers, but none has ever surpassed it.

1 The Shopping Scene

London's shopping world today is a superbly balanced mixture of luxury and utility, of small personalized boutiques and giant department stores, of junk-heaped market stalls and breathtakingly elegant specialty shops. As for bargains—that magic word in every traveler's dictionary—they are everywhere.

TAXES & SHIPPING Many London shops will help you beat the shopping value-added tax (VAT) levied on much of England's merchandise. By presenting your passport, you can frequently purchase goods tax free, but only on condition that you either have your purchase sent directly to your home address or have it delivered to the plane you're taking back. Because airlines usually charge a great deal for excess luggage, it's cheaper to have it shipped independently. Try London Baggage Company, which ships by sea, stores luggage, and even sells quality travel products. Its branches are open seven days a week. Locations include Heathrow Airport Terminal 1 (☎ 0181/745-5301), Heathrow Airport Terminal 4 (☎ 0181/745-7460), and London Air Terminal, Victoria Place, Victoria Station, SW1 (☎ 0171/834-2345). There's also a branch at Room 3032 at Gatwick Village South Terminal, Gatwick Airport in Sussex (☎ 01293/543-853). Within Britain, you can call toll free at 01800/378254.

If you don't send goods, you can still have the VAT refunded by filling out a form available at many shops and then either presenting the form and the goods at a Cash VAT Refund desk at a major airport when you leave Great Britain or sending the form to the specified address.

Note: Many stores that assist foreigners in avoiding the VAT display a prominent sign—"TAX FREE Shopping/European VAT Refund

Network." For more information, refer to "Taxes," listed under "Fast Facts: London" in Chapter 3.

BARGAINS   When bargain hunting, zero in on those goods that are manufactured in England and liable to cost much more when exported. These are—above all—men's and women's suits, woolens, tweeds, overcoats, scarves, tartans, bone china, cutlery, and prints, plus specialties such as antiques, rare books, and those magnificent old-world and city maps in most bookstores.

SALES   Some savvy British shoppers don't buy anything until January. After the busy Christmas season, when business lags, stores revive shopping fever by offering a series of sales. Discounts can range from 25% to 50% at leading department stores such as Harrods and Selfridges (see below), along with many other small shops. But let's not paint too rosy a picture: Some shopkeepers deliberately display merchandise of lesser quality so they can discount it heavily just for these sales.

HOURS   London keeps fairly uniform store hours, mostly shorter than American equivalents. The norm is 5:30pm closing, with a late Wednesday or Thursday night, until 7pm. Most central shops close Saturday around 1pm. They don't, however, observe a French-style lunch-hour closing.

MAIN SHOPPING STREETS   London's retail stores tend to cluster in certain areas, a phenomenon that evolved in the era when each guild or craft had its own street. This is what gives a London shopping spree its special flavor: You head in a certain direction to find a certain type of merchandise.

Beauchamp Place (tube: Knightsbridge), pronounced like "Beecham," is a block off Brompton Road, near Harrods department store. Whatever you're looking for—from a pâté de marcassin to a carved pine mantelpiece—you are likely to find it here. Rejects of china, crystal, pottery, secondhand silver, old alligator bags, collages, custom-tailored men's suits—whatever. It's pure fun even if you don't buy anything.

Divided into New and Old, **Bond Street** (tube: Bond Street) connects Piccadilly with Oxford Street and is synonymous with the luxury trade. Here are found the very finest—and most expensive—of antique shops, hatters, jewelers, milliners, tailors, shoe stores, and sporting goods establishments.

Burlington Arcade (tube: Piccadilly Circus), the famous glass-roofed, Regency-style passage leading off Piccadilly, looks like a period exhibition and is lined with intriguing shops and boutiques. Lit by wrought-iron lamps, decorated with clusters of ferns and flowers, the small, smart stores specialize in fashion, jewelry, Irish linen, camera equipment, stationery, pipes and smoking accessories, and model soldiers.

If you linger in the arcade until 5:30pm, you can watch the beadles, those ever-present attendants in their black-and-yellow livery and top hats, ceremoniously put in place the iron grills that block off the arcade until 9 the next morning, at which time they just as ceremoniously remove them to mark the start of a new business day. Also at 5:30pm, a hand bell called the Burlington Bell is sounded, signaling the end of trading. It's rung by one of the beadles. (There are only three of these constables remaining, the last London representatives of Britain's oldest police force.)

Just off Regent, **Carnaby Street** (tube: Oxford Circus) no longer dominates the world of pacesetting fashion as it did in the 1960s, but it is still visited by the young, especially punks, and some of its shops display claptrap and quick-quid merchandise.

Kensington High Street (tube: High Street Kensington) has been called "the Oxford Street of West London." Stretching for about $1^{1}/_{2}$ miles, it includes numerous shops. Many establishments are on adjacent side streets, including Earl's Court and Abington roads. Thackeray and Victoria streets retain some of the old village atmosphere. From Kensington High Street, you can walk up Kensington Church Street, which, like Portobello Road, is one of the city's main shopping avenues, selling everything from antique furniture to impressionist paintings.

King's Road (tube: Sloane Square), the main street of Chelsea, which starts at Sloane Square, will forever remain a symbol of London in the "swinging sixties." Today, the street is still frequented by young people, but perhaps there are fewer Mohican haircuts, "Bovver boots," and Edwardian ballgowns than before. More and more in the 1990s, King's Road is a lineup of markets and "multistores," large or small conglomerations of in- and outdoor stands, stalls, and booths within one building or enclosure. They spring up so fast that it's impossible to keep them tabulated, but few thorough shopping strollers in London can afford to omit King's Road from their itineraries.

Together with Kensington and Brompton roads, **Knightsbridge** (tube: Knightsbridge) forms an extremely busy shopping district south of Hyde Park. It's patronized for furniture, antiques, jewelry, and Harrods department store.

Oxford Street (tube: Tottenham Court Road), the main shopping artery of London, runs from St. Giles Circus to Marble Arch. It's an endless, faceless, totally uninspiring but utility-crammed strip of stores, stores, and yet more stores. It contains six of London's major department stores, along with just about every kind of retailing establishment under the sun.

Unlike the circus, the street **Piccadilly** (tube: Piccadilly Circus) is distinctly in the upper bracket, specializing in elegant automobile showrooms, travel offices, and art galleries, plus London's poshest grocery store, Fortnum & Mason.

If you like one-stop shopping, you may be drawn to the **Princes Arcade** (tube: Piccadilly Circus), opened by Edward VII in 1883, when he was still Prince of Wales. Situated between Jermyn Street and Piccadilly in the heart of London, the arcade has been restored. Wrought-iron lamps light your way as you search through some 20 bow-fronted shops, looking for that special curio (say, a 16th-century nightcap) or a pair of shoes made by people who have been satisfying royal tastes since 1847. A small sign hanging from a metal rod indicates what kind of merchandise a particular store sells.

Curving down elegantly from Oxford Circus to Piccadilly Circus, **Regent Street** (tube: Piccadilly Circus) is crammed with fashionable stores selling everything from silks to silverware. This stylish thoroughfare has both department stores and boutiques, but the accent is on the medium-size establishment in the upper-medium price range.

Saint Christopher's Place (tube: Bond Street), one of London's most interesting shopping streets (and lesser known to the foreign visitor), lies just off Oxford Street; walk down Oxford Street from Selfridges toward Oxford Circus, ducking north along Gees Court across Barrett Street. There you'll be surrounded by antiques markets and shops for women's clothing and accessories.

Stately, broad, and dignified, **The Strand** (tube: Charing Cross Station) runs from Trafalgar Square into Fleet Street. It's lined with hotels and theaters, and a selection of specialty stores you could spend a whole day peeking into.

STREET MARKETS

Markets are considerably more ancient than shops as a retailing medium. Most of the old world's large cities began as market towns, and in London you still have a few thriving survivors of the open-air trading tradition. They're great fun to visit, even if you don't plan on buying anything. But you'll probably go home with something.

Berwick Street Market (tube: Oxford Circus or Tottenham Court Road) may be the only street market in the world that is flanked by two rows of strip clubs, porno stores, and adult-movie dens. Don't let that put you off, however. Humming six days a week in the scarlet heart of Soho, this array of stalls and booths sells probably the best and cheapest fruit and vegetables in town. It also sells ancient records that may turn out to be collectors' items, tapes, books, and old magazines. It's open Monday to Saturday from 8am to 5pm.

After four centuries **Covent Garden Market** (☎ 0171/836-9136), the most famous market in all England—possibly all Europe—has gone suburban. It followed the lead of Les Halles in Paris and shifted to more contemporary but less colorful quarters south of the River Thames. The move relieves some of the wild congestion it generated, but a lot of memories have been left behind. Today's Covent Garden (tube: Covent Garden) has developed into an impressive array of shops, pubs, and other attractions, such as smaller markets where you can buy just about anything.

Covent Garden Market offers one of the best shopping opportunities in London. The specialty shops that fill the building sell fashions and herbs, gifts and toys, books and personalized dollhouses, hand-rolled cigars, automata, and much, much more.

Also within the Covent Garden Market building restaurants, wine bars, public houses, coffee shops, and cafés abound, many with chairs outside on the piazza offering an al fresco experience unique in London. What better way to relax than to take in this vibrant area's rich and cosmopolitan atmosphere and watch the famous street entertainers?

Jubilee Market Hall, Covent Garden Piazza, WC2, is open seven days a week, offering antiques and bric-a-brac on Monday from 7am to 5pm. General goods (not necessarily antique) are featured Tuesday through Friday from 9am to 5pm. Items range from perfumes to household goods. London's largest craft market is held here every Saturday and Sunday, usually from 9am to 5pm.

The **Apple Market,** Covent Garden Piazza, WC2, almost qualifies as street entertainment. A fun, bustling place, it is filled with traders selling . . . well, everything. Much is what the English call "collectible nostalgia." Some items are generally worthless (of the type you capriciously give to "the man who has everything"), while other pieces are genuinely worthy, such as interesting brass door knockers. Wander through the market and keep your sales resistance up. Some of the vendors are mighty persuasive. The Apple Market stalls from Tuesday to Saturday are home to a selection of the best of British craftspeople, with the stallholders themselves having made the crafts on display. On Monday and alternate Sundays the stalls are occupied by specialists in antiques and "collectibles," and on alternate Sundays arts and crafts traders display their works.

Off Neal Street runs a narrow road leading to **Neal's Yard** (tube: Covent Garden), a mews of warehouses that seem to retain some of the old London atmosphere. The open warehouses display such goods as vegetables, health foods, fresh-baked breads, cakes, sandwiches, and, in an immaculate dairy, the largest variety of flavored cream cheeses you are likely to encounter.

While in the area, you can pick up a copy of *In and Around Covent Garden,* which not only has a map but also will help you quickly locate the type of merchandise you might be seeking—everything from crafts to herbalists, from fashion to antique watches. Beauty salons, hairdressers, health clubs, chemists, and the like are listed here, along with a selection of restaurants and news of special exhibitions.

Open Monday through Friday from 11am to 5pm, the lively **Leather Lane Market** (tube: Chancery Lane) offers a good variety of items for sale: fruit from carts, vegetables, books, men's shirts and sweaters, and women's clothing. There are no try-ons at this outdoor market.

New Caledonian Market is commonly known as the Bermondsey Market because of its location on the corner of Long Lane and Bermondsey Street (tube: London Bridge, then bus 78 or walk down Bermondsey Street); at the extreme east end, it begins at Tower Bridge Road. It is one of Europe's outstanding street markets in the number and quality of the antiques and other goods offered. The stalls are well known, and many dealers come into London from the country. Prices are generally lower here than at Portobello Road and the other street markets. This market gets under way on Friday at 7am and—with the bargains gone by 9am—closes at noon.

Petticoat Lane (tube: Liverpool Street) still functions only on Sunday from 9am to 2pm. There's furious bargaining for every conceivable kind of object, from old clothing to just plain junk, and the air vibrates with voices, canned and human. In spite of the market's famous reputation, many readers have found that a Sunday-morning trip here is no longer worth the effort.

A magnet for collectors of virtually anything, **Portobello Market** (tube: Ladbroke Grove or Notting Hill Gate) is mainly a Saturday happening from 6am (it's best to go early) to 5pm. Once known mainly for fruit and vegetables (still sold, incidentally, throughout the week), Portobello in the past four decades has become synonymous with antiques. But don't take the stallholder's word for it that the fiddle he's holding is a genuine Stradivarius left to him in the will of his Italian great-uncle. It might just as well have been "nicked" from an East End pawnshop.

The market is divided into three major sections. The most crowded is the antique section, running between Colville Road and Chepstow Villas to the south. (*Warning:* A great concentration of pickpockets is in this area.) The second section (and the oldest part) is the "fruit and veg" market, lying between Westway and Colville Road. In the third and final section, Londoners operate a flea market, selling bric-a-brac and lots of secondhand goods they didn't really want in the first place. But it still makes interesting fun for a look-around.

Shepherd Market (sometimes mistakenly called Shepherd's Market) was not named for sheep herders but for Edward Shepherd, who had earned his fortune developing Mayfair. In 1735, he obtained a grant from King George II to open a market here between what is now Queen Street and Curzon Street. The market developed on the site of the infamous May Fair, launched in 1686 by Lord St. Albans. Instead of a fair, one wag at the time called it "that most pestilent nursery of impiety and vice." Even as late as the 1990s, "this former field of debauchery" still has a reputation (now fading) as a "red light district," with prostitutes plying their trade in the narrow lanes branching off from the market. However, in recent days, many of these working women have retired or gone elsewhere.

Today's Shepherd Market is filled with grocers, boutiques, shops, pubs, restaurants, and some small private houses lived in by who knows. Although it's not a market today in the sense of the markets previously previewed, it provides for an interesting stroll at least. Tube: Green Park.

From many of the stores, the serious collector can pick up a copy of a helpful official guide, *Saturday Antique Market: Portobello Road & Westbourne Grove,* published by the Portobello Antique Dealers Association. It lists where to find what, ranging from music boxes to militaria, from lace to 19th-century photographs. The serious collector can visit any of some 90 antiques and art shops during the week when the temporary market is closed.

2 Shopping A to Z

ANTIQUES

Alfie's Antique Market

13–25 Church St., NW8. ☎ **0171/723-6066.** Tues–Sat from 10am–6pm. Tube: Marylebone or Edgware Road.

This is the biggest and one of the best-stocked conglomerates of antique dealers in London, all crammed into the premises of what was built before 1880 as a department store. Named after the father of the present owner—an antiques dealer in London's East End before the war—it contains more than 370 stalls, showrooms, and workshops scattered over 35,000 square feet of floor space.

Antiquarius Antiques Centre

131–141 King's Rd., SW3. ☎ **0171/351-5353.** Mon–Sat from 10am–6pm. Tube: Sloane Square.

Antiquarius echoes the artistic diversity of King's Road. More than 120 dealers offer specialized merchandise, usually of the small, domestic variety, such as antique and period jewelry, porcelain, silver, first-edition books, boxes, clocks, prints, and paintings, with an occasional piece of antique furniture. You'll also find a lot of items from the 1950s.

Bond Street Antiques Centre

124 New Bond St., W1. ☎ **0171/351-5353.** Mon–Fri from 10am–5:45pm, Sat from 10am–4pm. Tube: Bond Street or Green Park.

In the heart of London's finest shopping district, the stores grouped together in this center enjoy a reputation for being London's finest center for antique jewelry, silver, watches, porcelain, glass, and Asian antiques and paintings.

Chenil Galleries

181–183 King's Rd., SW3. ☎ **0171/351-5353.** Mon–Sat from 10am–6pm. Tube: Sloane Square or South Kensington.

Originally built in 1905 as studio and exhibition space for artists, this building has functioned since 1979 as the headquarters of about 30 different antique dealers. Each focuses on a different style of art object, and some carry limited but carefully chosen carpets, porcelain, dolls, furniture, and paintings. Although it operates under the same management as the above-mentioned Antiquarius Antiques Centre, its ambience is calmer, quieter, slow-paced, and deliberately genteel.

Grays and Grays in the Mews

58 Davies St., and 1–7 Davies Mews, W1. ☎ **0171/629-7034.** Mon–Fri from 10am–6pm. Tube: Bond Street.

These antiques markets are housed in two old buildings that have been converted into walk-in stands with independent dealers. The term antique here covers items from oil paintings to, say, the 1894 edition of the Encyclopaedia Britannica. Also sold here are exquisite antique jewelry; silver; gold; antiquarian books; maps and prints; drawings; bronzes and ivories; arms and armor; Victorian and Edwardian toys; furniture; art nouveau and art deco items; antique lace; scientific instruments; craft tools; and Asian, Persian, and Islamic pottery, porcelain, miniatures, and antiquities. There is a café in each building.

Mall at Camden Passage

Islington, N1. Tues, Thurs, and Fri from 10am–5pm; Wed from 7:30am–5pm; Sat from 9am–6pm. Tube: Angel.

This mall contains one of Britain's greatest concentrations of antiques businesses. Here, housed in individual shop units, you'll find some 35 dealers specializing in fine furniture, porcelain, and silver.

ART

Berkeley Square Gallery

23A Bruton St., W1. ☎ **0171/493-7939.** Mon–Fri from 10am–6pm, Sat from 10am–2pm. Tube: Green Park.

Established in 1987, this busy, friendly gallery sells graphics done by such masters as Francis Bacon, Matisse, Chagall, Picasso, Braque, and David Hockney, as well as sculpture by Lynn Chadwick. In the competitive art world of London, the Berkeley Square is considered innovative and creative.

BOOKS, MAPS & ENGRAVINGS

Hatchards

187 Piccadilly, W1. ☎ **0171/439-9921.** Mon–Fri from 9am–6pm, Sat from 9:30am–6pm, Sun from 11am–5pm. Tube: Piccadilly Circus or Green Park.

On the south side of Piccadilly, Hatchards offers a wide range of books in all subjects and is particularly renowned in the areas of fiction, biography, travel, cookery, gardening, and art, plus history and finance. In addition, Hatchards is second to none in its range of books on royalty.

Map House

54 Beauchamp Place, SW3. ☎ **0171/589-4325.** Mon–Fri 9:45am–5:45pm, Sat 10:30am–5pm. Tube: Knightsbridge.

An ideal place to find an offbeat souvenir, Map House was established in 1907 and sells antique maps and engravings and a vast selection of old prints of London and England, original and reproduction. An original engraving, guaranteed to be more than a century old, can cost as little as £5 ($7.90) although some rare or historic items sell for as much as £50,000 ($79,000).

Stanfords

12–14 Long Acre, WC2. ☎ **0171/836-1321.** Mon and Sat from 10am–6pm, Tues–Friday from 9am–7pm. Tube: Leicester Square or Covent Garden.

The world's largest map shop, Stanfords was established in 1852. Many of its maps, which include worldwide touring and survey maps, are unavailable elsewhere. It's also the best travel-book store in London (naturally, the staff has the good judgment to carry a complete selection of Frommer guides, in case you're going on to some other country after a tour of Britain).

W. & G. Foyle, Ltd.

113–119 Charing Cross Rd., WC2. ☎ **0171/439-8501.** Mon–Wed, Fri and Sat from 9am–6pm, Thurs from 9am–7pm. Tube: Tottenham Court Road.

Claiming to be the world's largest bookstore, W. & G. Foyle, Ltd., has an impressive array of hardcovers and paperbacks, as well as travel maps. The stock also includes records, videotapes, and sheet music.

BRASS RUBBING

London Brass Rubbing Centre

St. Martin-in-the-Fields Church, Trafalgar Sq., WC2. ☎ **0171/930-9306.** Mon–Sat from 10am–6pm, Sun from noon–6pm. Tube: Charing Cross.

In the big brick-vaulted 1720s crypt, London Brass Rubbing Centre stands alongside a brasserie restaurant, a bookshop, and a crafts market. In the crypt is a small art gallery. The center has 88 exact copies of bronze portraits of medieval knights, ladies, kings, and merchants waiting for visiting aficionados to use. Paper, rubbing materials, and instructions on how to begin are furnished, and classical music plays as visitors work away. The charges range from £1.50 ($2.35) for a small copy to £11.50 ($18.15) for the largest, a life-size Crusader knight. A gift area sells British products with a historical theme, including Celtic jewelry. The center has a selection of more than a thousand handmade brass rubbings for sale. Even beginners who have never made a rubbing take home impressive artworks for themselves. To make brass rubbings in countryside churches, you must obtain permission from the parish of your choice. Once you have received written permission, the center offers instructions and sells the necessary materials.

CHINA, SILVER & GLASS

Glasshouse

21 St. Albans Place, N1. ☎ **0171/359-8162.** Mon–Fri from 10am–6pm, Sat from 11am–5pm. Tube: Angel.

This glass workshop and gallery sells hand-blown studio glass by four of Britain's leading makers. It prides itself on creating specifically commissioned works of art based on customers' specifications. Visitors can watch the artists at work.

Lawleys

154 Regent St., W1. ☎ **0171/734-3184.** Mon, Wed, and Fri from 9:30am–6pm; Tues from 10am–6pm; Thurs from 9:30am–7pm. Tube: Piccadilly Circus or Oxford Circus.

Founded in the 1930s, this store contains one of the largest inventories of china in Britain. A wide range of English bone china, as well as crystal and giftware, is sold here. The firm specializes in Royal Doulton, Minton, Royal Crown Derby, Wedgwood, and Aynsley china; Lladró figures; David Winter Cottages, Border Fine Arts, and other famous giftware names. Lawleys also sells cutlery.

Reject China Shop

183 Brompton Rd., SW3. ☎ **0171/581-0739.** Mon, Tues, Thurs, and Sat from 9am–6pm; Wed from 9am–7pm. Tube: Knightsbridge.

This shop sells seconds along with first-quality pieces of china with such names as Royal Doulton, Spode, and Wedgwood. You also can find a variety of crystal, glassware, and flatware. There are several branches throughout London. If you would like to have your purchases shipped home for you, the shop can do it for a fee starting at £15.50 ($24.50) depending on the number of pieces you ship.

Thomas Goode

19 S. Audley St., Grosvenor Sq., W1. ☎ **0171/499-2823.** Mon–Sat from 10am–6pm. Tube: Bond Street or Green Park.

Though less visible outside of Britain than many other of the country's porcelain manufacturers, Thomas Goode enjoys an enviable reputation as some of the finest porcelain ever made. During its lifetime, it has acquired warrants from three different royal households (including those of Queen Victoria, George V, and Elizabeth II), and enjoyed the patronage of, among others, Edward VII. Established in 1827, the company flourished until the 1940s, when wartime bombings, timid management, and economic crises curtailed its expansion. Faced with crushing competition, it barely survived the 1980s, but in 1993, the company received massive infusions of capital from anonymous investors, new factories were acquired, and the company's landmark showrooms were renovated with their original Victorian accessories.

Visited for their nostalgic allure by architectural enthusiasts, the showrooms are today considered among the most famous merchandising emporiums in Britain. Originally built in 1876, they contain 14 different rooms loaded with porcelain, and the oldest automatic doors in the world. (Delicately calibrated with a complicated series of counterweights, they're considered an elegant relic of the Industrial Age.) On the premises is a minimuseum devoted to the company's archives, which include dinner services commissioned by Czar Nicholas II of Russia, Queen Victoria, and various Eastern potentates. Also on the premises, in an oak-paneled enclave of great charm, are a pair of rare, seven-foot-high Minton majolica elephants created for Paris's World Exhibition of 1889, and valued today at £2.5 million (about $3.95 million). Also on display is a 550-pound bomb that landed on the company's roof during the blitz of London in 1941 and failed to explode. About 80% of the inventory is by Thomas Goode. Inventories include everything from a small gift to unique dinner services with cresting, gilding, and monogram. Since 1990, the company has established a manufacture of contemporary pieces as well. Goodes, an in-store restaurant, serves lunch and dinner.

CLOCKS

Strike One Islington Limited

48 Balcombe St., NW1. ☎ **0171/224-9719.** Open by appointment only at any time. Tube: Baker Street.

Selling clocks, music boxes, and barometers, this store clearly dates and prices each old clock—from Victorian dial clocks to early English long-case timepieces—and every purchase is guaranteed worldwide for a year against faulty workmanship. Strike One specializes in Act of Parliament clocks. It also issues an illustrated catalog, which is mailed internationally to all serious clock collectors. The firm also undertakes to locate any clock a customer might request if no suitable example is in stock.

CRAFTS

Contemporary Applied Arts

43 Earlham St., WC2. ☎ **0171/836-6993.** Mon–Wed, Fri and Sat from 10am–6pm, Thurs from 10am–7pm. Tube: Covent Garden.

This association of craftspeople sells and displays contemporary artwork, both traditional and progressive. The galleries at the center contain a diverse retail display of members' work that includes ceramics, glass, textile, wood, furniture, jewelry, and metal—all selected from the country's most outstanding contemporary artisans. There is also a program of special exhibitions that focuses on innovations in the various crafts.

Crafts Council

44A Pentonville Rd., Islington, N1. ☎ **0171/278-7700.** Tues–Sat from 11am–6pm, Sun from 2–6pm. Tube: Angel.

This is the national body for promoting contemporary crafts. Here you can discover some of today's most creative work at the Crafts Council Gallery, Britain's largest crafts gallery. There is also a shop selling craft objects and publications, a picture library, a reference library, and a café.

Naturally British

13 New Row, WC2. ☎ **0171/240-0551.** Mon–Sat from 11am–7pm, Sun from noon–5pm. Tube: Leicester Square or Covent Garden.

This well-stocked gift shop has a traditional British ambience with old wooden floors and antique furniture. A wide range of English, Welsh, and Scottish goods are sold, including toys, cloths, ceramics, jewelry, and food. Many items can be made to order, including rocking horses, painted christening spoons, and furniture.

Neal Street East

5 Neal St., WC2. ☎ **0171/240-0135.** Mon–Wed from 11am–7pm, Thurs–Sat from 10am–7pm, Sun and bank holidays from noon–6pm. Tube: Covent Garden.

In this vast shop devoted to crafts and giftware from around the world, you can find dried and silk flowers, books, pottery, baskets, chinoiserie, and toys, as well as calligraphy, modern and antique clothing, textiles, and ethnic jewelry. The china and glass department is extensive.

DEPARTMENT STORES

Daks Simpson Piccadilly

203 Piccadilly, W1. ☎ **0171/734-2002.** Mon–Wed, Fri and Sat from 9am–6pm, Thurs from 9am–7pm. Tube: Piccadilly Circus.

Opened in 1936 as the home of DAKS clothing, Simpson's has been going strong ever since. It is known for menswear—its basement-level men's shoe department is a model of the way quality shoes should be fitted—as well as women's fashions, perfume, jewelry, and lingerie. Many of the clothes are lighthearted, carefully made, and well suited to casual elegance. More formal clothing is also sold by the always polite and thoughtful staff. A restaurant serves fine English food.

✪ Harrods

87–135 Brompton Rd., Knightsbridge, SW1. ☎ **0171/730-1234.** Mon, Tues, and Sat from 10am–6pm, Wed–Friday from 10am–7pm. Tube: Knightsbridge.

London's—indeed Europe's—top store, Harrods is an institution, and visitors have come to view it as a sightseeing attraction, like the Tower of London. Some of the goods displayed for sale are works of art, and so are the 300 departments displaying them. The sheer range, variety, and quality of merchandise is dazzling—from silver and pewter to clothing, from food to fabrics, from pianos to delicatessens. The store has been refurbished to restore it to the elegance and luxury of the 1920s and '30s.

The whole fifth floor is devoted to sports and leisure, with a wide range of equipment and attire. Toy Kingdom is on the fourth floor, along with children's wear. The Egyptian Hall, which opened in 1991 on the ground floor, sells crystal from Lalique and Baccarat, plus porcelain. There's also a men's grooming room, an enormous jewelry department, and the Way In department for younger customers. You have a choice of 11 restaurants and bars at Harrods. One of the highlights is the Food Halls, stocked with a huge variety of foods. In the basement you'll find a bank, a theater-booking service, a travel bureau, and Harrods Shop, offering a range of souvenirs, including its famous green-and-gold bag.

Liberty Public Limited Company

214–220 Regent St., W1. ☎ **0171/734-1234.** Open Mon, Tues, Fri and Sat from 9:30am–6pm, Wed from 10am–6pm, Thurs from 9:30am–7pm. Tube: Oxford Circus.

This major department store is renowned worldwide for selling high-quality, stylish merchandise in charming surroundings. Its flagship store on Regent Street houses six floors of fashion, china, and home furnishings. In addition to Liberty Print fashion fabrics, upholstery fabrics, scarves, ties, luggage, and gifts, the shop sells top-drawer goods from all over the world. Liberty offers a personal "corner shop" service, with helpful and informed assistants selling its often unique merchandise. It has branches around England, including one at Heathrow Airport Terminal 3.

Peter Jones

Sloane Sq., SW1. ☎ **0171/730-3434.** Mon, Tues and Thurs–Sat from 9:30am–6pm, Wed from 9:30am–7pm. Tube: Sloane Square. Bus 11, 19, 22, 137, 319, or C1.

Founded in 1877 and rebuilt in 1936, Peter Jones is known for fashion and household goods, including perfume, china, glass, soft furnishings, and linens. The store also displays a constantly changing selection of antiques. There's an abundance of gift items. Peter Jones also has a coffee shop and first-class licensed restaurant, both with extensive views.

Selfridges

400 Oxford St., W1. ☎ **0171/629-1234.** Mon–Wed, Fri and Sat from 9:30am–7pm, Thurs from 9:30am–8pm. Tube: Bond Street or Marble Arch.

One of the largest department stores in Europe, Selfridges has more than 500 divisions selling everything from artificial flowers to groceries. The specialty shops are particularly enticing, with good buys in Irish linens, Wedgwood china, leather goods, silver-plated goblets, cashmere items, and woolen scarves. There's also the Miss Selfridge Boutique.

To help you travel light, the Export Bureau will air-freight purchases anywhere in the world, tax free. In the basement Services Arcade, the London Tourist Board will help you find your way around London's sights with maps and advice.

FASHION

Aquascutum

100 Regent St., W1. ☎ **0171/734-6090.** Mon–Wed and Fri from 9:30am–6pm, Thurs from 9:30am–7pm, Sat from 9:30am–6:30pm. Tube: Piccadilly Circus.

The magazine *Time Out* said this about Aquascutum: "It is about as quintessentially British as you'll get this side of Savile Row, and it's a popular stop-off for American tourists wanting to look more British than the Brits." On four floors, this classic shop offers only high-quality British and imported clothing (including leisurewear) for men and women. The Season's Café is on three.

Austin Reed

103–113 Regent St., W1. ☎ **0171/734-6789.** Mon–Wed, Fri and Sat from 9:30am–6pm, Thurs from 9:30am–7pm. Tube: Piccadilly Circus.

Austin Reed has long stood for superior-quality clothing and excellent tailoring for both men and women. The suits of Chester Barrie, for example, are said to fit like bespoke (custom-made) clothing. The polite employees are unusually honest about telling you what looks good. The store always has a wide variety of top-notch jackets and suits, and men can outfit themselves from dressing gowns to overcoats. The first floor is devoted to women's clothing, with carefully selected suits, separates, coats, shirts, knitwear, and accessories.

Berk

46 Burlington Arcade, Piccadilly, W1. ☎ **0171/493-0028.** Mon–Fri from 9am–5:30pm, Sat from 9am–5pm. Tube: Piccadilly Circus.

Berk is one of those irresistible "fancy shops" for which London is famous. The store is believed to have one of the largest collections of cashmere sweaters in London—at least the top brands.

Burberry

18–22 Haymarket, SW1. ☎ **0171/930-3343.** Mon–Wed, Fri and Sat from 9:30am–6pm, Thurs from 9:30am–7pm. Tube: Piccadilly Circus.

The name Burberry has been synonymous with raincoats ever since Edward VII publicly ordered his valet to "bring my Burberry" when the skies threatened. An impeccably trained staff sells the famous raincoat, along with excellent men's shirts, sportswear, knitwear, and accessories. Raincoats are available in women's sizes and styles as well. Prices are high, but you get quality and prestige.

Hilditch & Key

37 and 73 Jermyn St., SW1. ☎ **0171/930-5336.** Mon–Sat from 9:30am–5:30pm. Tube: Piccadilly Circus or Green Park.

Perhaps the finest name in men's shirts, Hilditch & Key has been in business since 1899. The two shops on this street both offer men's clothing (including a bespoke shirt service) and women's ready-made shirts. Hilditch also has an outstanding tie collection.

Hyper-Hyper

26–40 Kensington High St., W8. ☎ **0171/938-4343.** Mon–Wed, Fri and Sat from 10am–6pm, Thurs from 10am–7pm. Tube: High Street Kensington.

Hyper-Hyper has been showcasing young designers since 1983, and the work of nearly 70 is on display at all times. The range is sportswear to evening wear, with plenty of accessories, including shoes. Menswear is also sold. Hyper-Hyper will thrill and intrigue.

Scotch House

84–86 Regent St., W1. ☎ **0171/734-5966.** Mon–Wed from 10am–6pm, Thurs from 10am–7pm, Fri from 10am–6:30pm, Sat from 9am–6:30pm. Tube: Piccadilly Circus.

For top-quality woolen fabrics and garments, go to Scotch House, renowned worldwide for its comprehensive selection of cashmere and wool knitwear for both men and women. Also available is a wide range of tartan garments and accessories, as well as Scottish tweed classics. The children's collection covers ages 2 to 13 and similarly offers excellent value and quality.

Thomas Pink

85 Jermyn St., SW1. ☎ **0171/930-6364.** Mon–Fri from 9:30am–6pm, Sat from 9:30am–5:30pm. Tube: Green Park.

This Jermyn Street shirtmaker, named after an 18th-century Mayfair tailor, gave the world the phrases "hunting pink" and "in the pink." It has a prestigious reputation for well-made cotton shirts, for both men and women. The shirts are created from the finest two-fold pure-cotton poplin, coming in a wide range of patterns, stripes, and checks, as well as in plain colors. Some patterns are classic, others new and unusual. All are generously cut, with extra-long tails, and finished with a choice of double cuffs or single-button cuffs.

Turnbull & Asser

71–72 Jermyn St., SW1. ☎ **0171/930-0502.** Mon–Fri from 9am–5:30pm, Sat from 9am–1pm. Tube: Piccadilly Circus.

Everyone from David Bowie to Ronald Reagan (a far stretch) has been seen in a custom-made shirt from Turnbull & Asser. Prince Charles was introduced to this shirt manufacturer by Lord Mountbatten. The manager of the store assured me that Charles has "a real sense of taste." Long before the prince showed up, Turnbull & Asser were putting up with the tastes of Winston Churchill and Liberace, who never ordered the same style shirt. Excellent craftspersonship and simple lines—even bold colors—distinguish these shirts. The outlet also sells shirts and blouses to women, a clientele that has ranged from Jacqueline Bisset to Candice Bergen. The sales department will inform you that it's made-to-measure service takes six weeks, and you must order at least half a dozen. Of course, the monograms are included. Ready-made shirts are also sold if you don't want to spend so much.

Westaway & Westaway

62–65 Great Russell St., WC1. ☎ **0171/405-4479.** Mon–Sat from 9am–5:30pm, Sun from 11am–6pm. Tube: Tottenham Court Road.

Opposite the British Museum, this is a substitute for a shopping trip to Scotland. Here you'll find a large range of kilts, scarves, waist coats, capes, dressing gowns, and rugs in authentic clan tartans. The salespeople are knowledgeable about intricate clan symbols. They also sell superb—and untartaned—cashmere, camel-hair, and Shetland knitwear, along with Harris tweed jackets, Burberry raincoats, and cashmere overcoats for men.

For Children

The best buys—in both quality and price—are generally found at leading department stores, notably:

Selfridges

400 Oxford St., W1. ☎ **0171/629-1234.** Mon–Wed, Fri and Sat from 9:30am–7pm, Thurs from 9:30am–8pm. Tube: Bond Street or Marble Arch.

Clothing for both babies and children can be found on the third floor. There's also a baby-changing area there.

For Men

Burtons West One

379 Oxford St., W1. ☎ **0171/495-6282.** Mon–Wed, Fri and Sat from 10am–7pm, Thurs from 10am–8pm, Sat from 9am–6:30pm. Tube: Bond Street.

At the Bond Street tube station, the new look in Burtons fashion is represented here at their flagship store. Incorporating "all lifestyles," its menswear ranges from casual to formal, with competitive prices.

Gieves & Hawkes

1 Savile Row, W1. ☎ **0171/434-2001.** Mon–Wed, Fri and Sat from 9am–6pm, Thurs from 9am–7pm. Tube: Piccadilly Circus or Green Park.

This place has a prestigious address and a list of clients that includes the Prince of Wales; yet its prices are not the lethal tariffs of other stores on this street. It's expensive, but you get good quality, as befits a supplier to the British Royal Navy since the days of Lord Nelson. Cotton shirts, silk ties, Shetland jumpers (sweaters), and exceptional ready-to-wear and tailor-made (bespoke) suits are sold.

For Women

Bradley's

85 Knightsbridge, SW1. ☎ **0171/235-2902.** Mon, Tues, Thurs and Fri from 9:30am–6pm; Wed from 9:30am–7pm; Sat from 10–6pm. Tube: Knightsbridge.

Bradley's is the best-known lingerie specialty store in London, selling items designed and made exclusively for them, as well as stocking quality wear from around the world. Some members of the royal family shop here. Established in the 1950s and very fashionable today, Bradley's fits "all sizes" in silk, cotton, lace, polycotton, whatever. You'll love the fluffy slippers, and the satin or silk nightgowns will make you feel like a well-accessorized movie star.

The Changing Room

10A Gees Court, St. Christopher's Place, W1. ☎ **0171/408-1596.** Mon–Wed, Fri and Sat from 10:30am–6:30pm, Thurs from 10:30am–7:30pm. Tube: Bond Street.

This small but well-staffed shop stocks the clothing and accessories of at least a dozen designers, including Betty Jackson, Issey Mikaye, Helen Story, and Ally Capellino. The establishment's expertise lies in its ability to coordinate items from different lines to create unique fashion statements for all types of women in all kinds of situations. It also sells scarves by Georgina von Etzdorf and clothing from a handful of other manufacturers you might or might not have heard about. The Changing Room maintains a second location near Covent Garden, in the Thomas Neal Development, Shorts Gardens, WC2. (☎ 0171/379-4158.)

Fenwick of Bond Street

63 New Bond St., W1. ☎ **0171/629-9161.** Mon–Wed, Fri and Sat from 9:30am–6pm, Thurs from 9:30am–7:30pm. Tube: Bond Street.

Fenwick is a stylish fashion store that offers an excellent collection of womenswear, ranging from moderately priced ready-to-wear items to designer fashions. A wide range of lingerie (in all price ranges) is also sold here. The store dates from 1891.

Laura Ashley

256–258 Regent St., W1. ☎ **0171/437-9760.** Mon and Tues from 10am–6:30pm, Wed and Fri from 10am–7pm, Thurs from 10am–8pm, Sat from 9:30am–7pm. Tube: Oxford Circus.

This is the flagship store of the company whose design ethos embodies the English country look. The store carries a wide choice of women's clothing and home furnishings, and is one of 180 United Kingdom branches of this vast emporium of the Anglophiliac aesthetic. On the clothing floor, you'll find beautiful knitwear, casual clothes in easy-to-wear jersey, formal outfits, and dresses for special occasions, along with belts, handbags, hats, and a range of clothing for children. Upstairs, the home furnishing floor carries everything from basics such as fabric (sold by the meter), wallpaper, borders for bedlinen, lighting, cushions, curtains, and furniture.

Secondhand Designer Clothing

Pandora

16–22 Cheval Place, SW7. ☎ **0171/589-5289.** Mon–Sat from 10am–6pm. Tube: Knightsbridge.

A London institution since the 1940s, Pandora stands in fashionable Knightsbridge, a stone's throw from Harrods. Several times a week, chauffeurs will drive up with bundles packed anonymously by the gentry of England. One woman voted best dressed at Ascot several years ago was wearing a secondhand dress acquired at Pandora. Identities of former owners are strictly guarded, but many buyers are titillated at the thought that they might be wearing a hand-me-down of a royal person, perhaps Princess Di. Prices are generally one-third to one-half the retail value. Chanel and Anne Klein are among the designers represented. Outfits are usually no more than two seasons old.

FOOD

Charbonnel et Walker PLC

One, The Royal Arcade, 28 Old Bond St., W1. ☎ **0171/491-0939.** Mon–Fri from 9am–6pm, Sat from 10am–5pm. Tube: Green Park.

What may be the finest chocolates in the world are made here. The firm will send messages of thanks or love spelled out on the chocolates themselves. The staff of this bow-fronted shop will help you choose from the variety of centers. Ready-made presentation boxes are also available.

Fortnum & Mason Ltd.

181 Piccadilly, W1. ☎ **0171/734-8040.** Store, Mon–Sat from 9:30am–6pm; Fountain Restaurant, Mon–Sat from 7:30am–11pm. Tube: Piccadilly Circus or Green Park.

The world's most elegant grocery store, down the street from the Ritz, Fortnum & Mason, with its swallow-tailed attendants, is a British tradition dating back to 1707. In fact, the establishment likes to think that Mr. Fortnum and Mr. Mason "created a union surpassed in its importance to the human race only by the meeting of Adam and Eve." The chocolate-and-confectionery department is on the ground floor, while other floors will tempt you with china and glass, leather goods and stationery, antiques of all kinds, and more.

In the Mezzanine Restaurant, you can mingle at lunch with caviar-and-champagne shoppers; the pastries are calorie-loaded but divine. The Fountain Restaurant has both store and street entrances (Jermyn Street), and is open late for the benefit of theatergoers. The St. James's Room Restaurant on the fourth floor is open during normal store hours.

Tea House

15A Neal St., Covent Garden, WC2. ☎ **0171/240-7539.** Mon–Sat from 10am–7pm, Sun and national holidays from noon–6pm. Tube: Covent Garden.

This shop sells everything associated with tea, tea drinking, and mugs, among other items.

IRISH WARES

Irish Shop

14 King St., WC2. ☎ **0171/379-3625.** Mon–Sat from 10am–7pm, Sun from noon–6pm. Tube: Covent Garden.

Since 1964, this small family business has been selling a wide variety of articles shipped directly from Ireland. The staff will be happy to welcome you and answer questions on the selection of out-of-the-ordinary tweeds, traditional linens, hand-knit Aran fisherman's sweaters, and Celtic jewelry. Merchandise includes Belleek and Royal Tara china, tapes of Irish music, souvenirs, and gift items. Waterford crystal in all styles and types is a specialty.

JEWELRY

Asprey & Company

165–169 New Bond St., W1. ☎ **0171/493-6767.** Mon–Fri from 9am–5:30pm, Sat from 10am–5pm. Tube: Green Park.

It's as well-entrenched a name in luxury gift items as anything you're likely to find within Britain, with a clientele that includes the likes of the sultan of Brunei and Queen Elizabeth. (Some of her jewelry comes from the place.) Don't come with the idea of going slumming: There are about 14 different departments scattered over four floors of a dignified Victorian building whose decor was originally installed in 1841. The emporium itself dates from 1781. You'll find antiques, porcelain, leather goods, crystal, clocks, and enough unusual objects of dignified elegance to stock an English country house. Some of the jewelry sells for up to $8 million; a worthy selection of engagement rings cost around $5,000 each, and some utilitarian objects go for around £10 ($15.80) each. Looking for something for someone who has everything? Try a gilded toothbrush, an engraved swizzle stick, or any of a wide assortment of whisky flasks.

Sanford Brothers Ltd.

3 Holborn Bars, Old Elizabeth Houses, EC1. ☎ **0171/405-2352.** Mon–Fri from 10am–4:30pm. Tube: Chancery Lane.

A family firm, Sanford Brothers Ltd. has been in business since 1923. It sells all manner of jewelry, both modern and Victorian; silver of all kinds; and a fine selection of clocks and watches. The Old Elizabethan buildings that house the shop are among the sights of old London.

MUSIC

Virgin Megastore

14–16 Oxford St., W1. ☎ **0171/631-1234.** Mon and Wed–Sat from 9:30am–8pm, Tues from 10am–8pm, Sun from noon–6pm. Tube: Tottenham Court Road.

If a recording has just been released—and if it's worth hearing in the first place—chances are this store carries it. It's like a giant "grocery store" of recordings, and you get to hear the release on a headphone before making a purchase. Even the rock stars themselves come here on occasion to pick up new releases. A large selection of classical and jazz recordings is also sold as are computer software, video games, and video movies. In between selecting your favorites, you can enjoy a coffee at the café or perhaps purchase an airplane ticket from the Virgin Atlantic office. Another Megastore is at 527 Oxford St., W1. (☎ 0171/491-8582).

Tower Records

1 Piccadilly Circus, W1. ☎ **0171/439-2500.** Mon–Sat from 9am–midnight, Sun from noon–9:30pm. Tube: Piccadilly Circus.

Attracting the throngs from a neighborhood whose pedestrian traffic is almost overwhelming, this store claims to be the largest tape, record, and CD store in Europe. Sprawling over four floors, it's practically a tourist attraction in its own right, an icon to the changes sweeping over the entertainment and information industries. In addition to copies of most of the musical expressions ever recorded, it inventories everything on the cutting edge of information technology, including interactive hardware and software for CD-ROM, computers, and laser discs. Its collection of books and periodicals includes most of Britain's magazines, including esoterica such as *Soil Monthly* and *How to Redesign the Hull of Your Boat.* There's also an impressive collection of travel guides and maps.

PHILATELY

The Museum Shop

National Postal Museum, King Edward Building, King Edward St. (without number), EC1. ☎ **0171/239-5420.** Mon–Fri from 9:30am–4:30pm. Tube: St. Paul's.

Previously described as a sightseeing attraction (see "Museums" in Chapter 6), this complex also houses The Museum Shop. On sale are postcards, NPM ties, a selection of model vehicles (including a circa 1950 clockwork toy van), and letterboxes, along with various publications, including *Postal Reform & The Penny Black: Appreciation.*

POSTERS

London Transport Museum Shop

Covent Garden (without number), WC2. ☎ **0171/379-6344.** Daily from 10am–6pm. Closed Dec 24–26. Tube: Covent Garden.

This museum carries a wide range of reasonably priced posters. The London Underground maps in their original size as seen at every tube station can be purchased here. This unique shop also carries books, cards, T-shirts, and other souvenirs.

SHOES

Charles Jourdan

39–43 Brompton Rd., SW3. ☎ **0171/581-3333.** Mon, Tues and Thurs–Sat from 10am–6:30pm, Wed from 10am–7pm. Tube: Knightsbridge.

Charles Jourdan, the France-based chain, offers a wide variety of men's and women's shoes in a store with more square footage than any other upscale shoe boutique in London. The inventory reflects sober good taste and style, and includes designs by Lagerfeld for Jourdan and Michelle Perry for Jourdan. Also available are bags, handbags, and a boutique-style collection of clothing for men and women.

Church's

143 Brompton Rd., SW3. ☎ **0171/589-9136.** Mon–Sat from 9am–7pm. Tube: Knightsbridge.

Well-made shoes, the status symbol of well-heeled executives in financial districts around the world, have been turned out by these famous shoemakers since 1873. Today, well-outfitted English gents often prefer to stamp around London in their Church's shoes. These are said to be recognizable to all the maîtres d'hôtel in London, who have always been suspected of appraising the wealth of their clients by their footwear. Always a bastion of English tradition, Church's has gradually changed with the tides of style and now offers a limited selection of more modern designs along with their traditional wingtips. There is also a fashionable selection of shoes for women. This branch, though not the largest in terms of floor space, has probably the most complete inventory of the company's products of any store in the world. Incidentally, it lies a few steps away from Harrods.

Lilley & Skinners

360 Oxford St., W1. ☎ **0171/629-6381.** Mon–Wed, Fri and Sat from 9:30am–6:30pm, Thurs from 10am–8pm. Tube: Bond Street.

Lilley & Skinners is the largest shoe store in Europe, displaying many different brands of shoes over three floors of showrooms staffed by an army of salespeople. It specializes in not particularly glamorous names, and offers good value and a wide selection of difficult-to-find sizes.

Natural Shoe Store

21 Neal St., WC2. ☎ **0171/836-5254.** Mon, Tues, and Sat from 10am–6:30pm; Wed–Fri from 10am–7pm; Sun from noon–5:30pm. Tube: Covent Garden.

This store sells all manner of comfort and quality footwear, from Birkenstock to the best of the British classics, for men, women, and children. It will also repair shoes.

SHOPPING MALLS

Whiteleys of Bayswater

Queensway, W2. ☎ **0171/229-8844.** Mon–Sat from 10am–8pm, Sun from noon–6pm. Tube: Bayswater or Queensway.

Once, this was a store that gave Harrod's some competition, but it eventually went belly-up. Occupying its former premises is an Edwardian mall, whose chief tenant is a branch of Marks & Spencer, but in addition to that, there are around 70 to 80 shops (the number varies from year to year), mostly specialty outlets. On the uppermost floor is an array of some 10 restaurants, cafés, and bars. There's also an eight-screen movie theater.

SPORTING GOODS

Lillywhites Ltd.

24–36 Lower Regent St., Piccadilly Circus, SW1. ☎ **0171/915-4000.** Mon and Wed–Fri from 9:30am–7pm, Sat from 9:30am–6pm. Tube: Piccadilly Circus.

Europe's biggest and most famous sports store, Lillywhites has floor after floor of sports clothing, equipment, and footwear. Established in 1863, it also offers collections of stylish and fashionable leisurewear for both men and women.

TOILETRIES

Floris

89 Jermyn St., SW1. ☎ **0171/930-2885.** Mon–Fri from 9:30am–5:30pm, Sat from 10am–5pm. Tube: Piccadilly Circus.

A variety of toilet articles and fragrances can be found in the floor-to-ceiling mahogany cabinets that line Floris's walls and are considered architectural curiosities in their own right. They were installed relatively late in the establishment's history (that is, 1851), long after the shop had received its Royal Warrants as suppliers of toilet articles to the king and queen. The business was established in 1730 by a Minorcan entrepreneur, Juan Floris, who brought from his Mediterranean home a technique for extracting fragrances from local flowers.

Fashionable residents of St. James's flocked to his shop, purchasing his soaps, perfumes, and grooming aids. Today, you can still buy essences of flowers grown in English gardens, like stephanotis, lily of the valley, and lavender. Other items include men's cologne, perfume bottles, and badger-hair shaving brushes.

Penhaligon's

41 Wellington St., WC2. ☎ **0171/836-2150.** Mon–Sat from 10am–6pm. Tube: Covent Garden.

This Victorian perfumery was established in 1870, holding Royal Warrants to HRH Duke of Edinburgh and HRH Prince of Wales. All items sold are exclusive to Penhaligon's. It offers a large selection of perfumes, after-shaves, soaps, and bath oils for women and men. Gifts include antique-silver scent bottles, grooming accessories, and leather traveling requisites. For mail order call 0181/880-2050.

TRAVEL CENTER

British Airways Travel Department Store

156 Regent St., W1. ☎ **0171/434-4700.** Mon–Fri from 9:30am–6pm, Sat from 10am–4:30pm. Tube: Piccadilly Circus or Oxford Circus.

The retail flagship of British Airways, housed on three floors, offers not only worldwide travel and ticketing, but also a wide range of services and shops, including a clinic for immunization, a pharmacy, a bureau de change, a passport and visa service, and a theater-booking desk. The ground floor offers luggage, guidebooks, maps, and other goods. There are various other services such as a Holiday Centre and a coffee shop. Passengers with hand baggage only can check in here for a BA flight. Travel insurance, hotel reservations, and car rentals can also be arranged.

TOYS

Hamleys

188–196 Regent St., W1. ☎ **0171/734-3161.** Mon–Wed from 10am–6:30pm, Thurs from 10am–8pm, Fri from 10am–7pm, Sun from noon–6pm. Tube: Oxford Circus.

The finest toy shop in the world is found here—more than 35,000 toys and games on seven floors of fun and magic. A huge choice is offered, including soft, cuddly animals, as well as dolls, radio-controlled cars, train sets, model kits, board games, outdoor toys, and computer games.

WOOLENS

British Designer Knitwear Group

2–6 Quadrant Arcade, 80 Regent St., W1. ☎ **0171/439-4659.** Mon, Wed, and Fri from 10am–6pm; Thurs and Sat from 10am–7pm. Tube: Piccadilly Circus.

For woolens from all over the British Islands, including the Shetlands in Scotland, this is one of the city's best-recommended outlets. It even offers Irish pullovers from the fog-shrouded Aran Islands. The woolens are handmade, and often, many of the designers are well known. Some of the woolens will make you look like the "tweedy" English, if that is your desire; others are more high fashion.

9

London After Dark

The London nightlife establishments cover the entire social spectrum of the city, from the sleekest haunts to the plainest proletarian strongholds, from overstuffed Victorian plush palaces to Edwardian–era rooms, often in formerly dilapidated buildings. The range of entertainment is equally wide: from classical theater productions to blasting rock bands, nude female performers, and even drag shows.

Geographically, about 90% of the bright lights burn in the area roughly defined as the West End. The core of this region is Piccadilly Circus, which, with Coventry Street running down to Leicester Square, resembles New York's Broadway. To the north lies Soho, chockablock with entertainment in various hues of scarlet. To the northeast is the theaterland of Covent Garden, to the east Trafalgar Square, and to the west the fashionable and expensive night world of Mayfair.

Weekly publications such as *Time Out* and *Where* give full entertainment listings. They are available at newsstands and contain information on restaurants and nightclubs, as well as theaters. Daily newspapers, notably *The Times* and *The Telegraph,* also provide listings.

Nightlife in London can be divided into pre- and post-midnight. This "midnight curtain" operates against simple nighttime pleasures. It prevents you, for instance, from just dropping into a place for a drink (you must have something to eat with a drink served after 11pm). It doesn't prevent you, after hours, from paying a cover charge (frequently disguised as a membership fee) and enjoying a stage show, taking a spin on a dance floor, trying your luck at a gambling table, eating a five-course meal, or drinking yourself into oblivion.

Many of the places I'll describe in this chapter have some kind of front-door policy that passes as membership enrollment. What it amounts to is a so-called temporary membership, which satisfies the letter (if not the spirit) of the law and enables you to get in without delay. In many cases the temporary membership fee is deducted from the cost of dinner. There is, however, no hard-and-fast rule.

At this point I'd better add a word for the benefit of male travelers. London's club world is full of "hostesses." Their purpose is to make you buy things—from drinks to dolls and cigarettes—and they can shoot up your tab to much more than you intended to spend. However, London's recognized meeting spots, especially for the younger set, are ballrooms and dance clubs, neither of which employs hostesses.

1 The Performing Arts

South Bank Centre

Royal Festival Hall, South Bank, SE1. ☎ **0171/928-8800.** Tickets £5–£35 ($7.90–$55.30); AE, DC, MC, V. Box office daily 10am–9pm. Tube: Waterloo and Embankment Station.

In the aftermath of World War II, London's musical focus shifted to a uniquely specialized complex of buildings that were erected between 1951 and 1964 on the site of a bombed-out 18th-century brewery. Rising from industrial wastelands on the rarely visited south side of the Thames, across Waterloo Bridge from more glamorous neighborhoods of London, rose three of the most comfortable and acoustically perfect concert halls in the world. They include Royal Festival Hall, Queen Elizabeth Hall, and the Purcell Room. Within their precincts, more than 1,200 performances a year are presented, including classical music, ballet, jazz, popular music, and contemporary dance. Also here is the internationally famous Hayward Gallery, showcasing both contemporary and historical art. Recent exhibitions have included work by Andy Warhol, Pierre-Auguste Renoir, Jasper Johns, Leonardo da Vinci, Le Corbusier, and Salvador Dalí.

Royal Festival Hall opens at 10am every day and offers an extensive range of things to see and do. There are free exhibitions in the foyers and free lunchtime music at 12:30pm. The Poetry Library is open from 11am to 8pm, as well as shops providing a wide selection of books, records, and crafts.

The Festival Buffet offers a wide variety of food at reasonable prices, and there are numerous bars throughout the foyers. The People's Palace offers lunch and dinner as well as a spectacular view of the River Thames.

✪ London Coliseum

St. Martin's Lane, WC2. ☎ **0171/632-8300.** Tickets £8–£12 ($12.65–$18.95) balcony, £10–£48 ($15.80–$75.85) upper dress circle or stalls. Performances usually Aug–June. Tube: Charing Cross or Leicester Square.

The home of the English National Opera, this is the city's largest and most splendid theater, built in 1904 as a variety theater and converted into an opera house in 1968. The ENO performs a wide range of works, from great classics to operetta to world premieres, and every performance is in English. With a repertory of 18 to 20 productions, it plays five or six nights a week.

✪ Barbican Centre

Silk St., the City, EC2. ☎ **0171/638-8891.** Tickets £6–£30 ($9.50–$47.40). Box office daily 9am–8pm. Tube: Barbican or Moorgate.

Barbican Centre is said to be Western Europe's largest arts complex. It was created to make a perfect setting in which to enjoy good music and theater from comfortable and roomy seating. In addition to the theater, which is the London home of the Royal Shakespeare Company, the concert hall is the permanent home of the London

Central London Theaters

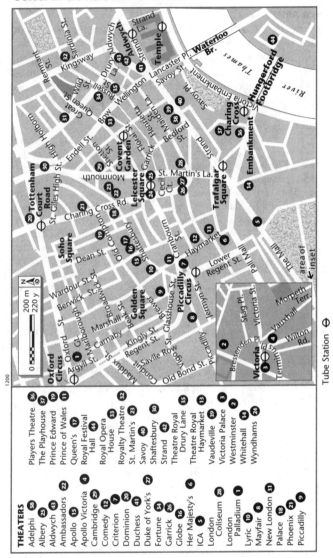

Symphony Orchestra and host to visiting musicians from all over the world. There are also a studio theater known as The Pit; the Barbican Art Gallery, a showcase for the visual arts; exhibition spaces; Cinemas One and Two, showing recent mainstream films; and The Barbican Library, a general lending library with strong emphasis on the arts. In addition, you'll find one of London's largest plant houses, The Conservatory, three restaurants, and a handful of bars.

Royal Albert Hall

Kensington Gore, SW7. ☎ **0171/589-8212.** Tickets £8–£120 ($12.65–$189.60), depending on the show. Box office daily 9am–9pm. Tube: South Kensington.

Opened in 1871 and dedicated to the memory of Victoria's consort, Prince Albert, the building encircles one of the world's most famous auditoriums, with a seating capacity of 5,200. It is also a popular venue for music by such stars as Eric Clapton and Shirley Bassey, or perhaps the latest in rock and pop. Sometimes, sporting events (especially boxing) figure strongly here, too.

Since 1941, the hall has been the setting for the BBC Henry Wood Promenade Concerts ("The Proms"), a concert series that lasts for eight weeks between mid-July and mid-September. (The Proms has been a British tradition since 1895.) Although most of the audience occupies reserved seats, true aficionados usually opt for standing room in the orchestra pit for close-up views of the musicians performing on stage. The programs are considered outstanding, and often present newly commissioned works for the first time. The last night of The Proms is the most traditional, as such rousing favorites as "Jerusalem" or "Land of Hope and Glory" echo through the hall. For tickets call Ticketmaster at 0171/379-4444 instead of Royal Albert Hall directly.

In addition to the musical venues, there are two restaurants on the premises, one of which is open daily at 5:30pm.

London Palladium

Argyll St. (corner of Oxford St.), W1. ☎ **0171/494-5100.** Tickets £10–£30 ($15.80–$47.40), depending on the show. Show times vary. Tube: Oxford Circus.

This theater is a show-business legend, having figured into the dreams of every up-and-coming star in the British repertoire. (Even Alfred Hitchcock used it as a setting for scenes in some of his thrillers.) In days of yore, the Palladium hosted such stars as Judy Garland, Tom Jones, Perry Como, and Sammy Davis, Jr., In recent years, it's been the setting for gangbuster musicals such as *Oliver!*, *Fiddler on the Roof*, and *Joseph and the Amazing Technicolor Dreamcoat*.

Royal Opera House

Bow St., Covent Garden, WC2. ☎ **0171/304-4000.** Tickets £2–£64 ($3.15–$101.10) ballet, £4–£133 ($6.30–$10.10) opera. Box office Mon–Sat 10am–8pm. Tube: Covent Garden.

The central shrine of London opera and ballet is the Royal Opera House, a classical building on Bow Street (actually the northeast corner of Covent Garden) and the home of the Royal Opera and the Royal Ballet, the capital's leading international opera and ballet companies. Newspapers give details on performances. The opera house's box office is at 51 Floral St., WC2 (☎ 0171/304-4000).

Sadler's Wells

Rosebery Ave., EC1. ☎ **0171/278-8916.** Tickets £5–£32.50 ($7.90–$51.35). Performances usually 7:30pm. Tube: Angel.

Sadler's Wells is in a theater that has stood here since 1683, on the site of a well that was once known for the healing powers of its waters. Today, the theater is a showcase for British and foreign ballet and modern dance companies and international opera. The box office sells tickets Monday through Saturday from 10am to 8pm.

Wigmore Hall

36 Wigmore St., W1. ☎ **0171/935-2141.** Tickets £4–£35 ($6.30–$55.30). Performances nightly, plus Sun Morning Coffee Concerts and Sun concerts at 4 or 7pm. Tube: Bond Street or Oxford Circus.

An intimate auditorium, Wigmore Hall is where you'll hear excellent recitals and concerts. After an expansion of its facilities, it reopened in 1992. There are regular series of song recitals, piano and chamber music, early and baroque music, and concerts featuring composers or themes. A free list of the month's programs is available from Wigmore. A café-restaurant is on the premises.

Kenwood Lakeside Concerts

Kenwood, Hampstead Heath. ☎ 081/348-1286. Reserved deck chairs £10–£15 ($15.80–$23.70) adults, £8–£12 ($12.65–$18.95) students and over 60. Lawn admission £8.50–£11 ($13.45–$17.40) adults, £5.50–£9 ($8.70–$14.20) students and over 60. Performances every summer Sat at 7:30pm mid-June to early Sept. Tube: Golders Green or Archway, then bus 210.

On the north side of Hampstead Heath, these top-class outdoor concerts have been a British tradition for some 50 years. Laser shows and firework displays enliven an otherwise dignified cultural scene. Music drifts across the lake from the performance bandshell.

2 The London Theater

London today is the theatrical capital of the world by any criterion you want to apply. It shows both more and better plays than any other city, enjoys a standard of acting unequaled anywhere, and holds a wide lead in both the traditional and the experimental forms of stagecraft.

This is partly, but only partly, because of a theatrical tradition going back well over 400 years. The city's first theater, in the Fields at Shoreditch, opened in 1576 under the patronage of Queen Elizabeth I. The following year saw the debut of the Curtain, and in 1598, the most famous of all—the Globe. This was Shakespeare's and Marlowe's stage, and as long as the shrewd, tough, and efficient Queen Bess ruled England, the legitimate theater held its own against such rival attractions as bullbaiting, cockfighting, and public executions.

From then on, however, the nation's dramatic glory suffered periodic declines that almost extinguished it, the first under Cromwell's official puritanism, which banned *all* stage performances (along with the celebration of Christmas) as "heathenish and un-Godly."

In more recent times, the causes lay in the social and moral rigidity Britain had acquired along with her Empire. At the turn of the century France became the country with the best theater. In the 1920s Germany took the lead. During the '30s the focus shifted to the United States, while England floundered in the most dismal theatrical shallows of her history, and turned out her worst movies to boot.

This doesn't mean that country at any time lacked great playwrights, actors, or directors. But the stage and film craft had become largely removed from real life. It tended to reflect little beyond the stilted formalism of a thin upper-middle crust who went to the theater to admire their own petrified reflection in a kind of polite distortion mirror.

Attempts in earthier directions were rigorously sat upon by an official called the Lord Chamberlain, who had unlimited powers of censorship and used them like the proverbial "Little Old Lady from Dubuque." This Mandarin figure was responsible for the creation of London's theater clubs, which—being private rather than public stages—were outside his jurisdiction. One such club was specially founded to present Arthur Miller's *A View from the Bridge* to English audiences, who would have been deprived of this masterpiece otherwise.

The Great Thaw occurred sometime during the mid-1950s, although it was more like a volcanic eruption. The pressures of talent, creativeness, and expressive urges had been building up ever since the second world war. Now they broke loose in a veritable lava stream of stage and film productions, which flooded the globe, swept away most of London's dusty theatrical mores, and swung open the gates of a second Elizabethan dramatic era. Britain hasn't looked back since. The tide is still running, originality still rampant. No one can say for how long. So my advice is to use your stay in London for a theater orgy: You may never get opportunities like this again.

London's live stage presents a unique combination of variety, accessibility, and economy. No other city anywhere can currently boast a similar trio of advantages.

Variety is assured by the sheer number of productions on view. London currently has more than 35 active theaters, and this figure does not include opera, ballet, amateur stages, or the semiprivate theater clubs mentioned earlier.

HOURS AND TICKETS

London theaters generally start and finish earlier than their American cousins. Evening performances start between 7:30 and 8:30pm, midweek matinees at 2:30 and 3pm, Saturday matinee at 5:45pm. Many theaters offer additional trimmings in the shape of licensed bars on the premises and hot coffee during intermissions, called "intervals."

Matinees are performed Tuesday through Saturday and they are cheaper, of course, than regular performances. Prices for London shows vary widely—usually from £15 to £52.50 ($23.70 to $82.95), depending on the seat.

Many theaters will accept telephone bookings at regular prices if you have a credit card. They will hold the tickets for you at the box office, where you present your credit card when you pick them up at show time.

Beware of unlicensed ticket agencies, which flourish in London. You may end up paying £25 ($39.50) for a ticket worth only £15 ($23.70). According to law, the face value of a ticket sold at a premium should be declared to the consumer at the time of sale. However, this code is not enforceable. The Society of West End Theatre reports that it receives complaints of overcharging on a frequent basis. The society advises that you try to book your ticket at the theater box office either by telephone or in person—credit cards can be used.

Visitors interested in ordering tickets days, weeks, or months in advance can contact **Edwards & Edwards** at the Palace Theatre, Shaftesbury Avenue, W1 (☎ 0171/734-4555), or at 12 Lower Regent St., SW1 (☎ 0171/839-3952). Tickets to almost anything in London can be arranged in advance by telephone. In most cases, a personal visit is not necessary. Tickets will be mailed or delivered to the box office of any particular theater, usually with a service charge of 10% to 20% added. Some North Americans opt to order tickets for London plays through Edwards & Edwards' New York office, 1 Times Square Plaza, New York, NY 10036 (☎ 212/944-0290 in New York City, or toll free 800/223-6108 from the rest of the U.S.).

If you want to see specific shows, particularly hits, you'll have to reserve in advance through one of the many London ticket agencies, including **Keith Prowse/First Call** (☎ 0171/836-9001). For various locations near you, look under "Keith" in the telephone book. This agency has an office in the United States, where you can reserve weeks or even months in advance for hit shows. Contact Keith Prowse, Suite 1000, 234 W. 44th St., New York, NY 10036 (☎ 212/398-1430, or toll free 800/669-8687). The fee for booking a ticket is 20% to 25% in London or 28% in New York.

One of the most sure-fire ticket agents is **British Airways,** which has some of the best seats available for London productions (including musicals), Stratford-upon-Avon, and the Edinburgh Festival. The service is available only to passengers flying transatlantic or long distances on BA. An up-to-date list of events is available, at prices that tend to be less than what you'd have paid a ticket agent or scalper in London. For information and reservations, call toll free 800/AIRWAYS in the U.S. or Canada.

Theatreline will provide details of London theater productions and ticket availability information at main theaters in the West End (and many venues beyond). The service provides theatergoers an alternative to making endless calls to theaters to find out if they can get a seat for later that day. Gathered by the theaters' trade association, The Society of London Theatre, information is updated by breakfast time each morning Monday through Saturday. Lines are open 24 hours a day, seven days a week. A brief description of the show is provided, as is information about the availability of tickets for that day, the theater box office's telephone number, and the address of the theater and how to get there. Numbers are as follows: musicals 0891/559-900; plays 0891/559-901; comedies 0891/559-902; thrillers 0891/559-903; opera, ballet, and dance 0891/559-904; and children's theater 0891/559-905. The cost of a call ranges from 39p to 49p (60¢ to 75¢).

Warning: Beware of "scalpers" who hang out in front of hit shows at London theaters. Even if their tickets are valid—and there are many reports of forged tickets—they charge very high prices.

THEATERS

Barbican Theatre

In the Barbican Centre, Silk St., Barbican, EC2. ☎ **0171/638-8891.** Barbican Theatre £7.50–£22 ($11.85–$34.75); The Pit £15 ($23.70) matinees and evening performances. Box office daily 9am–8pm. Tube: Barbican or Moorgate.

This is the London home of the Royal Shakespeare Company, one of the world's finest theater companies. The central core of its work remains, of course, the plays of William Shakespeare. It also presents a wide-ranging program of three different productions each week in the Barbican Theatre—the 2,000-seat main auditorium, with excellent sightlines throughout, thanks to a raked orchestra—and in The Pit, the small studio space where much of the company's new writing is presented.

Fortune

Russell St., Covent Garden, WC2. ☎ **0171/836-2238.** Tickets £8.50–£20 ($13.45–$31.60). Evening performances Mon–Sat 8pm; matinees Tues 3pm and Sat 4pm. Tube: Covent Garden.

A part of the ancient and odd theater concentration around Covent Garden, the Fortune is an intimate house of 440 seats. Bars open from one hour before performance.

Gielgud Theatre (The Globe),

33 Shaftsbury Ave., W1. ☎ **0171/494-5065.** Tickets £10–£20 ($15.80–$31.60). Check daily press or ticket agencies for shows and times of performances. Tube: Piccadilly Circus.

Originally named The Globe in honor of William Shakespeare's legendary playhouse (which actually stood rather far from here, beside the Thames of long ago), this theater was renamed Gieglud in honor of the actor, Sir John Gielgud. The Gielgud is one of a row of theaters on the same street, near Piccadilly Circus. Dramas, bedroom farces, Restoration comedies, and musicals are presented here, in a gilded-cage setting originally built in 1906.

Her Majesty's

Haymarket, SW1. ☎ **0171/494-5400.** Tickets £9–£30 ($14.20–$47.40). Evening performances Mon–Sat 7:45pm; matinees Wed and Sat 3pm. Tube: Piccadilly Circus or Charing Cross.

Big, plush, and ornate, this is one of London's traditional homes for top musicals—located on what used to be "the street for scarlet women." Recent extravaganzas have included *The Phantom of the Opera.*

Old Vic

Waterloo Rd., SE1. ☎ **0171/928-2651** or 0171/928-7616 (box office). Tickets £6–£22 ($9.50–$34.75) plays and musicals. Tube: Waterloo.

The facade and some of the interior of this 177-year-old theater has been restored to its original early 19th-century style. Also, the proscenium arch has been moved back, the stage has been trebled in size, and more seats and stage boxes have been added. It is air-conditioned and contains three bars. It presents short seasons of varied plays, and several subscription offerings have been introduced.

Open Air

Inner Circle, Regent's Park, NW1. ☎ **0171/486-2431.** Tickets £8–£20 ($12.65–$31.60). Performances May 27–Sept 10; Mon–Sat 8pm, matinees Wed–Thurs and Sat 2:30pm. Tube: Baker Street.

As the name indicates, this is an outdoor theater, right in Regent's Park. The setting is idyllic, and its theater bar, the longest in London, provides both drink and food. Presentations are mainly Shakespeare, usually in period costume. Both seating and acoustics are excellent. If it rains, you're given tickets for another performance.

Royal Court Theatre

Sloan Sq., Chelsea, SW1. ☎ **0171/730-1745.** Mon (all seats) £5 ($7.90) in both theaters; Tues–Sat £5–£18 ($7.90–$28.45) downstairs, £8 ($12.65) upstairs (unreserved). Sat matinees £5–£15 ($7.90–$23.70) downstairs, £5 ($7.90) upstairs (unreserved). Main theater, evening performances Mon–Sat 7:30pm, matinees Sat 3:30pm. Upstairs, Mon–Sat 7:30pm, matinees Sat 3pm. Tube: Sloane Square.

This is the place that caused a sensation at the turn of the century by presenting plays by George Bernard Shaw. In the 1950s it ushered in, with no less of a stir, the new wave of British plays by presenting John Osborne's *Look Back in Anger.* As home to the English Stage Company, it still presents "fringe productions" in its experimental theater upstairs; call the theater for programs and hours. The main theater downstairs features plays by better-known authors and new interpretations of the classics, among other offerings.

Royal National Theatre

South Bank, SE1. ☎ **0171/928-2252.** Tickets £8.50–£22 ($13.45–$34.75); midweek matinees, Sat matinees; previews cheaper. Tube: Waterloo, Embankment, or Charing Cross.

Home of one of the world's greatest stage companies, the Royal National Theatre is not one but three theaters—the Olivier, reminiscent of a Greek amphitheater with its open stage; the more traditional Lyttelton; and the Cottesloe, with its flexible stage and seating. The National presents the finest in world theater from classic drama to award-winning new plays, from comedy to musicals to shows for young people, offering the choice of at least six plays at any one time. The National is also a full-time theater center, featuring an unrivaled selection of bars, cafés, and restaurants, free foyer music and exhibitions, short early-evening performances, bookshops, backstage tours, riverside walks, and terraces. You can have a three-course meal in Mezzanine, the National's restaurant; enjoy a light meal in the brasserie-style Terrace Café; or have a snack in one of the coffee bars.

Theatre Royal Drury Lane

Catherine St., Covent Garden, WC2. ☎ **0171/494-5060.** Tickets £8.50–£30 ($13.45–$47.40). Box office Mon–Sat 10am–7:45pm. Evening performances Mon–Sat 7:45pm; matinees Wed and Sat 3pm. Tube: Covent Garden or Holborn.

Drury Lane is one of the oldest and most prestigious establishments in town, crammed with traditions, not all of them venerable. This is the fourth theater on this site, dating from 1812. The first was built in 1663, and Nell Gwynne, the rough-tongued cockney lass who became Charles II's mistress, used to sell oranges under the long colonnade in front. Nearly every star of the London stage has played here at some time. It has a wide-open repertoire but leans toward musicals, including long-running hits. Guided tours may be arranged by calling 0171/494-5091.

Young Vic

66 The Cut, Waterloo, SE1. ☎ **0171/928-6363.** Tickets £8–£18 ($12.65–$28.45) adults, £5–£6.50 ($7.90–$10.25) students and children. Performances usually Mon–Sat 7:30pm. Tube: Waterloo.

The Young Vic presents classical and modern plays in the round for theatergoers of all ages and backgrounds, but primarily for young people between 16 and 25. Recent productions have included Shakespeare, Ibsen, Arthur Miller, and specially commissioned plays for children.

DINNER THEATER

Gilbert and Sullivan Evenings

Grim's Dyke Hotel, Old Redding, Harrow Weald, Middlesex HA3 6SH. ☎ **0181/954-4227.** Tickets £36 ($56.90) per person. Dinner/performance on alternate Sundays at 8pm in winter; usually each Sun at 8pm the rest of the year. But program subject to change—always call to confirm.

The English Heritage Singers present Gilbert and Sullivan programs in the context of a dinner event. You arrive for cocktails in the Library Bar of the house where Gilbert once lived and worked on his charming operettas. Sullivan once visited the premises. A full Edwardian-style dinner is served, with costumed performances of the most beloved of Gilbert and Sullivan songs both during and after the meal. You can request your favorite melodies.

3   The Club & Music Scene

NIGHTCLUBS/CABARETS

Camden Palace

1A Camden High St., NW1. ☎ **0171/387-0428.** Cover £2–£4 ($3.15–$6.30) Tues–Wed, £8–£12 ($12.65–$18.95) Fri–Sat. Tues–Wed 9pm–2:30am, Fri 9pm–4am, Sat 9pm–6am. Tube: Camden Town.

Camden Palace is housed in what was originally a theater built around 1910. It draws an over-18 crowd who flock in various costumes and energy levels according to the night of the week. Since it offers a variety of music styles, it's best to phone in advance to see if that evening's musical genre appeals to your taste. Styles range from rhythm and blues to what young rock experts call "boilerhouse," "garage music," "acid funk," "hip-hop," and "twist and shout." A live band performs only on Tuesday. There's a restaurant if you get the munchies.

The Green Room at the Café Royal

68 Regent St., W1. ☎ **0171/437-9090.** Reservations recommended. Tues–Sat. Dinner at 7pm followed by 60- to 90-minute show. Tube: Piccadilly Circus.

Although it's a relative newcomer to London's nightlife scene, this cabaret has already become a much-talked-about force among world-class entertainers and their fans. Set one floor above street level, in a sober and modern function room poised amid the gilded and frescoed premises of the Café Royal, the establishment offers a changing cast of such singers and comics as Helen Shapiro, Barbara Dickson, Buddy Greco, and Blossom Deary. Many visitors opt for dinner before the show begins; others arrive just for the entertainment. A three-course dinner, without wine, followed by the show, costs £48 ($75.85) per person; the cover charge for the show without dinner is £20 ($31.60). Drinks cost from £4 ($6.30) each.

L'Hirondelle

99–101 Regent St., W1. ☎ **0171/734-6666.** £10 ($15.80) cover charge for nondiners, plus £5 ($7.90) cover charge added to first drink. Mon–Sat 8:30pm–3:30am. Shows at 10:45am–12:45am. Tube: Piccadilly Circus.

L'Hirondelle stands in the heart of the West End and puts on some of the most lavish floor shows in town. What's more, you can dine, drink, and dance without a "temporary membership" or an entrance fee. The shows are full-scale revues and go on at 11pm and 1am. Dancing to one of the few live bands in a London club begins at 10pm. Dancing-dining partners are available. The club offers a three-course dinner for £32.50 ($51.35) per person, including VAT and service charges, or you can choose from their very large à la carte menu; a bottle of wine costs from £24.50 ($38.70).

Tiddy Dols

55 Shepherd Market, Mayfair, W1. ☎ **0171/499-2357.** No cover. Daily 6pm–1am. Tube: Green Park.

Housed in nine small atmospheric Georgian houses that were built around 1741, Tiddy Dols is named after the famous gingerbread baker and eccentric. Guests come to Tiddy Dols to enjoy such dishes as rack of lamb, cock-a-leekie, plum pudding, and the original gingerbread of Tiddy Dol. While dining, they are entertained with madrigals, Noël Coward, Gilbert and Sullivan music, and music-hall songs. In summer, there is a large pavement café with parasols and a view of the "village" of Shepherd Market; in winter there are open fires. Set dinners cost £10.95 to £18.95 ($17.30 to $29.95), including the cover charge. Dancing is restricted to special evenings. All year there is a café and wine bar serving a full menu at lower prices, offering sandwiches and afternoon teas. A light fixed-price meal in the café goes for £15.95 ($25.20). Drinks are priced from £2.50 ($3.95).

COMEDY CLUB

The Comedy Store

Coventry St. and Oxendon, off Piccadilly Circus SW1. ☎ **0142/691-4433.** Cover £8 ($12.60) Mon–Fri, £10 ($15.80) Sat, £9 ($14.20) Sun. Daily from 8pm. Tube: Leicester Square or Piccadilly Circus.

Set in the heart of the city's nighttime district, this is London's most visible showcase for established and rising comic talent. A prerecorded telephone message announces the various performers scheduled during the upcoming week. Even if their names are unfamiliar (highly unlikely), you will enjoy the spontaneity of live comedy performed before a British audience. Visitors must be 18 and older; dress is casual. Reservations are accepted through Ticketmaster at 0171/344-4444, and the club opens $1^1/_2$ hours before each show.

ROCK

Marquee

105 Charing Cross Rd., WC2. ☎ **0171/437-6603.** Cover £5–£10 ($7.90–$15.80). Daily from 7pm. Tube: Leicester Square or Tottenham Court Road.

Marquee is considered one of the best-known centers for rock in the world. Its reputation goes back to the 1950s and another location, but it remains forever young. Groups like the Rolling Stones played at the Marquee long before they achieved world celebrity. Live bands perform daily from 7pm to midnight. Fortunately, you don't have to be a member—you just pay at the door. Those 18 or older can order hard drinks. Well-known musicians frequent the place on their nights off.

The Rock Garden

6–7 The Piazza, Covent Garden, WC2. ☎ **0171/836-4052.** Mon–Fri 8pm–3am, Sat 4–10pm, Sun 7:30–midnight. Tube: Covent Garden. Bus: Any of the night buses that depart from Trafalgar Square.

Long established as a site for the presentation of a wide array of electronic and rock-and-roll bands, this establishment maintains a bar and a stage in the cellar, and a restaurant on the street level. The cellar area, known as The Venue, has hosted such names as Dire Straits, Police, and U2 before they became more famous (and more expensive). Today, acts vary widely, incorporating the up-and-coming rock-related talents of Europe as well as, quite simply, some bands you might never hear from ever again. In the restaurant, meals include T-bone steaks, chili, salads, and hamburgers.

The restaurant is open Monday to Thursday and Sunday from noon to midnight, Friday and Saturday from noon to 1am. Main courses cost £6 to £13 ($9.50 to $20.55); full meals, from £12 ($18.95). In the Venue, admission is £5 ($7.90) for nondiners (diners enter free); lager costs £1.75 to £2.50 ($2.75 to $3.95), depending on the time of day.

JAZZ & BLUES

The Blue Note

1 Hoxton Sq., N1. ☎ **0171/729-2476.** Cover £4–£10 ($6.30–$15.80). Mon–Sat 10pm–3am, Sun noon–2am. Tube: Old Street.

Formerly operating under the name "The Bass Clef," this club is located in a brick-fronted building that functioned as an important hospital in the early 20th century. It presents performances that range from traditional jazz, such as the music of Jessica Williams, all the way to contemporary hip-hop and funk. There is a restaurant on the premises serving café-style fare with meals priced from £5 ($7.90) each. Restaurant daily from noon to 11pm. Call for show times. Drinks are priced from £3 ($4.75).

Bull's Head

373 Lonsdale Rd., Barnes, SW13. ☎ **0181/876-5241.** Cover £2–£8 ($3.15–$12.65). Mon–Sat 11am–11pm, Sun noon–10:30pm. Transportation: Tube to Hammersmith,

then bus 9A to Barnes Bridge, then retrace the path of the bus for some 200 yards on foot; or take Hounslow Look train from Waterloo Station and get off at Barnes Bridge Station, then walk five minutes to the club.

This club has presented live modern jazz every night of the week for more than 30 years. One of the oldest hostelries in the area, it was a mid-19th-century staging post where travelers on their way to Hampton Court and beyond could eat, drink, and rest while coach horses were changed. Today, the place is known for its jazz, performed by musicians from all over the world. Jazz concerts are presented on Sunday from 12:30 to 3pm and 8 to 11pm. Monday through Saturday, you can hear music from 8 to 11pm. You can order food at the Carvery in the Saloon Bar daily or dine in the 17th-century Stable Restaurant. Main dishes in the Carvery cost £3.50 ($5.55). In the restored stables, the cook specializes in steak, fish, and other traditional fare; meals cost £8 ($12.65) and up. The Carvery is open daily to lunch only from noon to 3pm; whereas the Stable serves daily from 7pm till around midnight. Wine by the glass is priced from £1.75 ($2.75).

Pizza Express

10 Dean St., W1. ☎ **0171/437-9595.** Cover £6–£9 ($9.50–$14.20). Mon–Sat 8:30pm–1am, Sun 8pm–midnight. Tube: Tottenham Court Road.

Although this seems an unlikely venue for a night club, it offers some of the best jazz in London. While enjoying a thin-crust Italian pizza (the ordering of food is compulsory), you can hear either the local band or a hot group that's visiting, often from the U.S. Darkly lit, the club has cool jazz and hot food from the pizza oven. Sometimes it's important to reserve, as this place fills up quickly.

100 Club

100 Oxford St., W1. ☎ **0171/636-0933.** Cover Fri £7 ($11.05) members and nonmembers; Sat £7 ($11.05) members, £8 ($12.65) nonmembers; Sun £5 ($7.90) members, £6 ($9.50) nonmembers. Mon–Fri 8:30pm–3am, Sat 7:30pm–1am, Sun 7:30–11:30pm. Tube: Tottenham Court Road or Oxford Circus.

Although less plush and cheaper, 100 Club is considered a serious rival to the above venue among many dedicated jazz fans. Its cavalcade of bands includes the best British jazz musicians, as well as many Americans. Drinks are priced from £1.80 ($2.85).

Ronnie Scott's

47 Frith St., W1. ☎ **0171/439-0747.** Cover Mon-Thurs £12 ($18.95); Fri–Sat £14 ($22.10); with student ID, £7 ($11.05) Mon–Thurs only. Main Room Mon–Sat; the Upstairs Room Mon–Sat from 8:30pm–3am. Tube: Tottenham Court Road or Leicester Square.

Mention the word jazz in London and people immediately think of Ronnie Scott's, long the European citadel of modern jazz, where the best English and American groups are booked. Featured on almost every bill is an American band, often with a top-notch singer. In the heart of Soho, the place is a 10-minute walk from Piccadilly Circus along Shaftesbury Avenue—and worth an entire evening. You don't have to be a member, although you can join if you wish. In the Main Room you can either stand at the bar to watch the show or sit at a table, where you can order dinner. The Downstairs Bar is more intimate, a quiet rendezvous where you can meet and talk with the regulars, often some of the world's most talented musicians. The separate Upstairs Room has a disco called Club Latino. Drinks are priced from £2.10 ($3.30); a half-pint of beer, £1.10 ($1.75).

DANCE CLUBS/DISCOS

Diva

43 Thurloe St., SW7. ☎ **0171/584-2000.** No cover. Mon–Sat 7:30pm–3am. Tube: South Kensington.

This place combines a first-class Italian restaurant with a carefully controlled disco. The electronic music and flashing lights of the disco are separated from the dining area by thick sheets of glass, so diners can converse in normal tones. Full meals, costing from £25 ($39.50), include an array of Neapolitan-inspired dishes. Only clients of the restaurant are allowed into the disco. Drinks are priced from £2.30 ($3.65); beer £1.80 ($2.85).

Equinox

Leicester Sq., WC2. ☎ **0171/437-1446.** Cover £5–£10 ($7.90–$15.80), depending on the night of the week. Mon–Sat 9pm–3:30am. Tube: Leicester Square.

Built in 1992 on the site of a dance emporium (the London Empire) that witnessed the changing styles of social dancing since the 1700s, the Equinox has established itself as a firm favorite among London nightlifers. It contains seven bars, the largest dance floor in London, and a restaurant modeled along the lines of an American diner from the 1950s. With the exception of "rave" music, virtually every kind of dance music is featured here, including dance hall, pop, rock and roll, garage, and Latin. The setting is lavishly illuminated with one of Europe's largest lighting rigs, and the crowd is as varied as London itself. Drinks begin at £2.30 ($3.65).

Hippodrome

Corner of Cranbourn St. and Charing Cross Rd., WC2. ☎ **0171/437-4311.** Cover £2–£10 ($3.15–$15.80). Mon–Sat 9pm–3am. Tube: Leicester Square.

Here you will find one of London's greatest discos, an enormous place where light and sound beam in on you from all directions. Revolving speakers even descend from the roof to deafen you in patches, and you can watch yourself on closed-circuit video. Golden Scan lights are a spectacular treat. Lasers and a hydraulically controlled stage highlight visiting international performers. There are six bars, together with an à la carte balcony restaurant. Drinks are priced from £3 ($4.75).

Smollensky's on the Strand

105 The Strand, WC2. ☎ **0171/497-2101.** No cover, except £3.50 ($5.55) charge Sun night for live jazz. Mon–Sat noon–midnight, Sun 6:30–10:30pm. Tube: Charing Cross or Embankment.

This American eatery and drinking bar is a cousin of Smollensky's Balloon at 1 Dover St. (see below). At the Strand location, there is dancing on Thursday, Friday, and Saturday nights. On Sunday nights there is a special live jazz session, in association with Jazz FM, a radio station devoted to jazz. Many visit just for drinks, ordering everything from house cocktails to classic cocktails to deluxe cocktails. Beer costs from £2.20 ($3.50), drinks from £2.95 ($4.65). Meals, ranging from barbecue loin of pork to corn-fed chicken, average £20 ($31.60).

Stringfellows

16–19 Upper St. Martin's Lane, WC2. ☎ **0171/240-5534.** Cover £3–£15 ($4.75–$23.70), depending on the night of the week. Mon–Sat 8pm–3:30am. Tube: Leicester Square.

This is considered one of the relatively elegant staples on London's nighttime landscape, with a widely varied clientele and lots of velvet and glossy accessories. In theory, it's a members-only club, but—and only at the discretion of management—nonmembers may be admitted. Its disco has a glass dance floor and a dazzling sound-and-light system. On the premises is a restaurant suitable for late-night suppers, and it has two different drinking areas, one slightly less formal than the other. Beer costs £2.50 to £3.25 ($3.95 to $5.15), drinks from £3.25 ($5.15).

Wag Club

35 Wardour St., W1. ☎ **0171/437-5534.** Cover £5–£10 ($7.90–$15.80). Tues–Thurs 10:30pm–3:30am, Fri–Sat 10:30pm–5:30am. Tube: Piccadilly Circus.

This popular dance club is set behind an innocuous-looking brick facade in one of the most congested neighborhoods of London's entertainment districts. Its two levels are decorated with unusual murals, some with themes from ancient Egypt, others with snakes. Clients all seem to love to dance, and hail from throughout Europe and the rest of the world. Live bands are sometimes presented on the street level, while the upstairs is reserved for highly danceable recorded music. Various evenings of the week are set aside for different musical genres, including rock and roll, jazz, or "dance house." Beer costs £2 ($3.15). The Wag Club maintains the Café de Paris, a late-night restaurant around the corner at 3–4 Coventry St., W1, for those with late-night munchies.

4 The Bar Scene

PUBS, WINE BARS & BARS

American Bar

In the Savoy Hotel, The Strand, WC2. ☎ **0171/836-4343.** Jacket and tie recommended for men. Mon–Sat 11am–3pm, 5:30–11pm; Sun noon–3pm, 7–10:30pm. Tube: Charing Cross or Embankment.

At the American Bar, still one of the most sophisticated gathering places in London, the bartender is known for making such special concoctions as the "Savoy Affair" and the "Prince of Wales," as well as the best martini in town. Monday through Saturday evenings, jazz piano music is featured. The location—near so many West End theaters—is ideal for a pre- or post-theater drink. Drinks cost £4.50 to £8.50 ($7.10 to $13.45).

Bracewells Bar

In the Park Lane Hotel, Piccadilly, W1. ☎ **0171/499-6321.** Mon–Sat 11am–3pm, 5:30–11pm; Sun noon–2:30pm, 7–10:30pm. Tube: Green Park or Hyde Park.

Chic, nostalgic, and elegant, it's the kind of bar where Edward VII and his stylish companion, Mrs. Langtry, might have felt very much at home. The plush, comfortable decor has touches of Chinese lacquer, upholstered sofas, soft lighting, and an ambience like that of an elegant private club. The bar adjoins Bracewells (see Chapter 5), one of the finest hotel restaurants in London. Drinks are priced from £5.90 ($9.30); a glass of champagne £5.75 ($9.10); beer from £2.70 ($4.25).

Cocktail Bar

In the Café Royal, 68 Regent St., W1. ☎ **0171/437-9090.** Mon–Sat noon–11:30pm, Sun noon–5pm. Tube: Piccadilly Circus.

In the business since 1865, this bar was once patronized by Oscar Wilde, James McNeill Whistler, and Aubrey Beardsley. Decorated in 19th-century rococo style, with one of the most beautiful frescoed ceilings in London, it is one of the more glamorous places to order a drink. Café Royal cocktails, including Golden Cadillac and Prince Williams, begin at £5.50 ($8.70). Nonalcoholic drinks are also served, and you can order wine by the glass from the superb wine cellars. A traditional English tea, served between 3 and 5pm, costs £11 ($17.40). Drinks are priced from £3 ($4.75).

The Dorchester Bar

In the Dorchester, Park Lane. ☎ **0171/629-8888.** No cover. Mon–Sat 11am–11pm; Sun noon–3pm, 6–10:30pm. Tube: Hyde Park Corner or Marble Arch.

This is a fun and sophisticated modern hideaway on the lobby level of one of the most lavishly decorated hotels in the world. Amid its champagne-colored premises, you'll find an internationally diverse clientele with commonly shared assumptions about the pleasure that only taste and lots of money can buy. You can order upscale bar snacks, lunches, and suppers throughout the day and evening, including selections from an Italian cuisine. Cold appetizers from the antipasti buffet—available only at lunch—cost £13 ($20.55). Otherwise, the bartender can make any drink ever conceived on the planet. A pianist performs every evening after 7pm. Drinks are priced from £5 ($7.90).

Lillie Langtry Bar

In the Cadogan Hotel, Sloane St., SW1. ☎ **0171/235-7141.** Mon–Sat 11:30am–11pm; Sun noon–2:30pm, 7–10:30pm. Tube: Sloane Square or Knightsbridge.

This bar, next to Langtry's Restaurant, exudes a 1920s aura and epitomizes the charm and elegance of the Edwardian era. Lillie Langtry, actress and society beauty at the turn of the century (notorious as the mistress of Edward VII), used to live here. Oscar Wilde, who was arrested in this bar, is honored on the drinks menu with Hock and Seltzer, his favorite libation here, according to Sir John Betjeman's poem "The Arrest of Oscar Wilde at the Cadogan Hotel." The most popular drink is a Cadogan Cooler. An international menu is also served in the adjoining restaurant. Choices change daily but are likely to include roast rack of lamb, Scottish salmon, Dover sole, and breast of duck. On Monday through Friday, a set luncheon is offered for £16.90 ($26.70), increasing to £17.90 ($28.30) on Sunday. Not available on Saturday, the lunch menu includes three courses and a half bottle of the house wine. The Cadogan set dinner costs £21.90 ($34.60). Open for lunch Monday to Friday and Sunday from noon to 2pm; dinner daily from 6 to 10pm. Drinks are priced from £4.75 ($7.50); a glass of wine, from £2.95 ($4.65).

Rumours

33 Wellington St., WC2. ☎ **0171/836-0038.** Mon–Sat 5–11pm. Tube: Covent Garden.

Inspired by the kind of modern cocktail-style bar that might cater to a young and hip crowd in New York or Newport, this is the kind of place where you might expect Tom Cruise to turn up as bartender. Set behind a purple and fluorescent-pink exterior, within what functioned a century ago as a wholesale flower market, Rumours contains Gothic candlesticks, soaring columns camouflaged as palm trees, and a decor that mingles elements of 18th-century England with Miami Beach. This place is a popular watering hole for the neighborhood's young and restless, who order such frothy concoctions as strawberry homicides, little devils, corpse revivers, and double zombies. Cocktails cost from £3 to £4 ($4.75 to $6.30).

Smollensky's Balloon

1 Dover St., W1. ☎ **0171/491-1199.** Mon–Sat noon–midnight; Sun noon–10:30pm. Tube: Green Park.

A basement restaurant, this American eatery and drinking bar is packed during happy hour (Monday to Friday from 5:30 to 7pm) with Mayfair office workers fortifying themselves before heading home. The place has a 1930s piano bar atmosphere, with polished wood and a mirrored ceiling. Steaks and french fries are favorite fare, though you can also order well-prepared vegetarian dishes. Meals start at £13 ($20.55); house cocktails (good measures), at £3.95 ($6.25); beer at £2.25 ($3.55). A pianist/singer entertains Monday through Saturday evenings.

BOUZOUKI

Elysée

13 Percy St., W1. ☎ **0171/636-4804.** Cover Mon–Thurs £3 ($4.75), Fri–Sat £4 ($6.30). Tube: Goodge Street or Tottenham Court Road.

Elsyée is for *Never on Sunday* devotees who like the reverberations of bouzouki and the smashing of plates. The domain of the Karegeorgis brothers—Michael, Ulysses, and the incomparable George—it offers hearty fun at moderate tabs. You can dance nightly to the music by Greek musicians. Two different cabaret shows are presented (last one at 1am), highlighted by brother George's altogether amusing art of balancing wineglasses (I'd hate to pay his breakage bill). You can book a table on either the ground floor or the second floor, but the Roof Garden is a magnet in summer. The food is good, too, including the house specialty, the classic moussaka, and kebabs from the charcoal grill. A complete meal with wine costs £25 ($39.50). Lunch Monday to Saturday from noon to 3pm, dinner Monday to Saturday from 7:30pm to 4am.

5 The Gay & Lesbian Scene

The most reliable source of information on gay clubs and activities is the Lesbian and Gay Switchboard (☎ 0171/837-7324). The staff runs a 24-hour service for information on places and activities catering to homosexual men and women.

CLUBS

Heaven

The Arches, Villiers and Craven sts., WC2. ☎ **0171/839-3852.** Cover £5–£9 ($7.90–$14.20). Tube: Charing Cross or Embankment.

A London landmark, established by the same investors who brought the world Virgin Atlantic Airways, this club is set within the vaulted cellars of Charing Cross Railway Station. Painted black inside, and reminiscent of a very large air-raid shelter, Heaven is one of the biggest and best-established gay venues in Great Britain. It's divided into at least four distinctly different areas, each of these connected by a labyrinth of catwalk stairs and hallways. Its design allows for different activities to occur simultaneously within the club. It features different "theme nights," where, depending on the night of the week, gay men, gay women, or for-the-most-part heterosexual people seem to predominate. Typical nights include Thursday, an extravaganza to virtually all forms of sexuality, including plain old heterosexuality. Festivities are pronounced "mad" regardless of the orientation. Friday is ultraviolet night, when everything appears purple, and Saturday is always gay, gay, gay. Specially scheduled Sundays when young Asians can meet their admirers are frequent. Even guest lectures are presented here, including one recent topic devoted to "Aliens from Other Planets."

Madam Jo Jo's

8 Brewer St., W1. ☎ **0171/734-2473.** Cover £9–£12 ($14.20–$18.95). Mon–Sat 10pm–3am. Tube: Piccadilly Circus.

Set side by side with some of Soho's most explicit girlie shows, Madame Jo Jo's also presents "girls," but they are in drag. This is London's most popular transvestite showplace, with revues staged nightly at 12:15am and 1:15am. There is also a popular piano bar. In fact, many patrons appreciate the place as much for its bar area as for its shows. Drinks from £3 ($4.75).

Roy's West End

11 Upper St. Martin's Lane, WC2. ☎ **0171/836-5121.** Mon–Sat 6–11:30pm. Tube: Leicester Square.

Roys, which was originally launched on Fulham Road and now sits in the midst of London's theaterland, is the leading gay restaurant in town. It enjoys a garden-inspired setting, with a color scheme of cream and terra-cotta. Menu items include deep-fried garlic mushrooms, pan-fried chicken livers cooked in Armagnac, smoked salmon with lemon and capers, a traditional English beefsteak with kidney pudding, or sliced breast of Aylesbury duckling with a red wine sauce. Most meals average from £15 to £20 ($23.70 to $31.60). It is open only for dinner.

Steph's

39 Dean St., W1. ☎ **0171/734-5976.** Mon–Thurs noon–3pm, 5:30–11:30pm; Fri noon–3pm, 5:30–midnight; Sat 5:30–midnight. Tube: Piccadilly Circus.

Looking like a stage set for Pink Flamingos, Steph's is one of the most charming restaurants of Soho, near the exclusive Groucho Club. Owner Stephanie Cooke, a much-traveled former British schoolteacher, is today the sophisticated hostess of this well-run little restaurant. Her partner is Richard Thiel. A theatrical crowd, among others, is attracted to the place. Overall, the clientele is mixed—straight, gay, lesbian, bi, or whatever.

You conceivably could go here just to have fun, but the food is worthy in its own right. Everything is cooked fresh, so sit back, relax, and enjoy such specialties as Snuffy's chicken, beef-and-oyster pie, or selections from the charcoal grill, including filet steak with barbecue sauce. Steph might even suggest her own "diet"—a plate of wild Scottish smoked salmon and a bottle of champagne. The ubiquitous burger also appears on the menu, as do salads and even a vegetarian club sandwich (how fashionable can you get?). Meals cost from £16 ($25.30).

Wild About Oscar

In the Philbeach Hotel, 30–31 Philbeach Gardens, SW5. ☎ **0171/373-1244.** Daily 7–10:30pm. Tube: Earl's Court.

Catering to a mostly gay clientele, this French restaurant lies on the garden level of an interconnected pair of Victorian row houses. Decorated in blues and greens, with portraits of Oscar Wilde (the restaurant's namesake), the establishment overlooks a view of the brownstone's garden. There's a small cocktail bar open only to restaurant patrons and residents of the gay hotel that contains it. Reservations are required. A two-course fixed-price menu goes for £15 ($23.70), with three courses priced at £20 ($31.60).

Brief Encounter

41 St. Martin's Lane, WC2. ☎ **0171/240-2221.** Mon–Sat 11am–11pm; Sun noon–3pm, 7–10:30pm. Tube: Leicester Square or Charing Cross.

This place stands across from the Duke of York's Theatre, in the very heart of West End theaterland. In fact, it's the most frequented West End gay pub. Bars are on two levels, but even so, it's hard to find room to stand up, much less drink. The crowd's costumes vary. Some men are in jeans, leather, whatever, whereas others are dressed in business suits. There's a disco every night from 8pm until closing. Lager from £1.88 ($2.95).

Coleherne

261 Old Brompton Rd., SW5. ☎ **0171/373-9859.** Mon–Sat 11am–11pm; Sun noon–3pm, 7–10:30pm. Tube: Earl's Court.

This leather-and-denim bar in Earl's Court must have been featured in every guide to the gay scene in Europe ever written. As a consequence, it's often jammed. Lunch and afternoon tea are served in an upstairs dining room. Lager is priced from £1.88 ($2.95).

The Duke of Wellington

110 Balls Pond Rd., N1. ☎ **0171/249-3729.** Mon–Sat from noon–midnight, Sun from noon–5pm and 7–10:30pm. Tube: Highbury.

Originally built in the late 19th century as a workingman's pub, this is now one of the most popular gay bars in North London, with a higher percentage of gay women than that attracted by many of London's other gay bars. Divided into two rooms, each with its own bar and its own devoted corps of aficionados, it hosts Saturday-night disco parties (free entrance) and live music at least one night a week. Its name as bandied about by patrons of this place? The Dyke of Wellington, in honor of its large number of lesbian fans. Pint of lager from £1.85 ($2.90).

The Fridge

Town Hall Parade, Brixton Hill, SW2. ☎ **0171/326-5100.** Cover £3–£9 ($4.75–$14.20), depending on the scheduled event. Tues 10pm–3am, Thurs–Sat 9pm–3am. Tube: Brixton.

Set within a 15-minute tube ride southwest from Piccadilly and Leicester Square, this club occupies what was originally built during the 1920s as a movie theater. Open only three (and sometimes four) nights a week, it caters each night to a specific group of clients, many of whom are young and deliberately trendy. The club features a well-engineered sound system with up-to-date music. On the premises are two bars (one on street level, another on a balcony upstairs), and a restaurant. Tuesdays and Saturdays are most heavily patronized by gays (mostly men), Thursdays and Fridays are favored by persons of unknown sexuality, who would probably respond, if asked, that they were straight. It's a good idea to phone before setting out for this place, as its venue might change even during the lifetime of this edition.

Halfway to Heaven

7 Duncannon St., WC2. ☎ **0171/930-8312.** Mon–Sat noon–11pm; Sun noon–3pm, 7–10:30pm. Tube: Charing Cross of Embankment.

Contained within a century-old structure whose beamed ceiling might remind you of a setting in a novel by Charles Dickens, this is perhaps the least frenetic gay bar in the Trafalgar Square neighborhood. Remarkable for crossing many generational lines, it welcomes a clientele aged 18 to 65, none of who seem particularly interested in the current fashion trends. Lager is priced from £1.86 ($2.95).

79CXR

79 Charing Cross Rd., W1. ☎ **0171/439-7250.** No cover. Lager costs £1.85 ($2.90) per pint. Mon–Sat noon–1am, Sun noon–3pm, 7–10:30pm. Tube: Leicester Square.

Named after an abbreviation of the street that contains it (Charing Cross Road, near Leicester Square), this is a long, high-ceilinged bar whose clientele is almost overwhelmingly Gay and mostly male. There's no disco, no food service, and no entertainment, but something about the place contributes to a sense of camaraderie and fun. A balcony runs along the edges of the high-ceilinged room, looking down over the hubbub below.

6 More Entertainment

CASINOS

London was a gambling metropolis long before anyone had ever heard of Monte Carlo or Las Vegas. Victoria's reign changed all that, as usual, by jumping to the other extreme. For more than a century, games of chance were so rigorously outlawed that no bartender dared to keep a dice cup on the counter. However, according to the 1960 Betting and Gaming Act, gambling was again permitted in "bona fide clubs" by members and their guests.

There are at least 25 such clubs in the West End alone, with many more scattered throughout the suburbs. But under a new law, casinos aren't allowed to advertise, which in this context would mean appearing in a guidebook. Nonetheless, most hall porters can tell you where you can gamble in London.

You will be required to become a member of your chosen club, and in addition you must wait 24 hours before you can play at the tables . . . then strictly for cash. The most common games are roulette, blackjack, punto banco, and baccarat.

MOVIES

MGM Cinema

11–18 Panton St., off Leicester Sq., SW1. ☎ **0171/930-0631.** Tickets £3–£6 ($4.75–$9.50), depending on the time of day and the film. Tube: Piccadilly Circus or Leicester Square.

This streamlined black-and-white block houses four superb theaters. They share one lobby, but each runs a separate program, including at least one continental film, along with the latest releases, often from the United States.

National Film Theatre

South Bank, Waterloo, SE1. ☎ **0171/928-3232.** Tickets 40p (65¢) membership, £4.35 ($6.85) screenings with membership. Tube: Waterloo or Embankment.

This cinema is in the South Bank complex. More than 2,000 films a year from all over the world are shown here, including features, shorts, animation, and documentaries.

Odeon Leicester Square and Odeon Mezzanine

Leicester Sq., WC2. ☎ **0142/691-5683.** Tickets £4–£9 ($6.30–$14.20). Tube: Leicester Square.

The Odeon is another major London film theater, with one main screen and a mezzanine complex comprising another five screens. All screens feature the latest international releases.

STRIP SHOWS

Soho has many strip clubs, located mainly along Frith Street, Greek Street, Old Compton Street, Brewer Street, Windmill Street, Dean and Wardour streets, and the little courts and alleys in between.

Raymond Revuebar

Walker's Court, Brewer St., W1. ☎ **0171/734-1593.** Admission £19.50 ($30.80). Shows at 8 & 10pm, Mon–Sat. Tube: Piccadilly Circus.

The Revuebar dates from 1958. Proprietor Paul Raymond is considered the doyen of strip society and his young, beautiful, hand-picked strippers are among the best in Europe. This strip theater occupies the much-restored premises of a Victorian dance hall, with a decor of red velvet. There are two bars, which allow clients to take their drinks to their seats. Whisky costs £2.50 ($3.95) for a large measure.

Stork Club

99 Regent St., W1. ☎ **0171/734-3686.** Three-course dinner £35 ($55.30), or £10 ($15.80) cover charge for show only. Mon–Sat 8:30pm–3:30am. Tube: Piccadilly Circus.

This first-class nightclub incorporates good food, a Las Vegas–style cabaret with a lineup of attractive dancers who don't believe in overdressing, and an ambience noted for its good taste and theatrical flair. Located near the corner of Swallow Street in the upscale heart of Mayfair, it welcomes diners and drinkers to a decor of royal blue and peach with an art deco inspiration. Two shows are staged nightly, at 11:45pm and 1am. Foreign visitors don't have to go through the tedium of obtaining membership. Drinks are priced from £4 ($6.30).

10

Easy Excursions from London

You could spend the best part of a year—or a lifetime—exploring London, without risking either boredom or repetition. But since your stay is probably limited, I advise you to tear yourself away from Big Ben for at least a day or two, for the Thames metropolis is surrounded by some of the most memorable spots on earth: entire clusters of scenic resorts, historic sites, cultural and religious shrines, and just-plain-fun places, all within comfortable commuting range.

The only trouble is that there are too many of them. There's Shakespeare's town of Stratford-upon-Avon, the pilgrimage city of Canterbury, Churchill's country home at Chartwell, the Tudor turrets of Hampton Court, dozens of "stately mansions"—and resident dukes—awaiting your inspection, Windsor Castle of Queen Victoria's memory, the flowers of Syon Park, the great universities of Oxford and Cambridge, the roaming wild animals of Woburn Abbey, Stonehenge on the Salisbury Plain, Runnymede of Magna Carta fame—the roll call goes on and on.

The small county of Hampshire alone contains the medieval cathedral city of Winchester, the great seaport of Southampton, and the New Forest nature preserve with deer and shaggy wild ponies.

1 Brighton

51 miles S of London

Brighton's Asian-style Royal Pavilion represented fashionable wickedness when the prince regent built it in 1787. But today, the town is very much a family resort, boasting warm summer sunshine.

Although the beaches are pebbly and the water is cold, the seafront promenade and amusement piers make Brighton a fun place to visit. It has waxworks, aquariums, three live theaters, every conceivable form of sport, and the annual London-Brighton Veteran Car Run.

Nonetheless, the town still exudes Regency elegance, and, at night, the floodlights play on the Royal Pavilion and the floral boulevard.

GETTING THERE

BY TRAIN   Fast trains leave often from Victoria Station or London Bridge Station, with the trip taking 55 minutes (☎ **0171/834-2345**).

BY BUS   Buses from Victoria Coach Station (☎ **0171/730-3466**) take around two hours.

BY CAR   M23 (signposted from Central London) leads to A23, which will take you into Brighton.

WHERE TO DINE
MODERATE

Langan's Bistro
1 Paston Place. ☎ **01273/606933.** Reservations required. Appetizers £3.95–£5.95 ($6.25–$9.40); main courses £13.95–£14.95 ($22.05–$23.60); three-course fixed-price lunch £14.50 ($22.90). AE, DC, MC, V. Lunch Tues–Fri and Sun 12:30–2:15pm; dinner Tues–Sat 7:30–10:15pm. Closed two weeks in Aug. FRENCH.

Located near the waterfront, off King's Cliff, this is the latest branch of a well-known minichain of restaurants that gained fame in London. The limited menu is based on the freshest of market ingredients. You might, for example, begin with a salad made from warm scallops, then follow with grilled turbot with langoustine coulis or roast lamb served with a tomato and garlic confit. Vegetarian dishes are also available. Desserts are often sumptuous, as reflected by a crème brûlée flavored with apple and cinnamon.

2 Cambridge

55 miles NE of London

The university of Cambridge, along with Oxford, is one of the most ancient seats of learning in Britain. The city on the banks of the Cam River is also the county town of Cambridgeshire. In many ways, the stories of Oxford and Cambridge are similar—particularly the age-old conflict between town and gown. But beyond the campus, Oxford has a thriving, high-tech core of industry.

Oxford University predates Cambridge, but by the early 13th century, scholars began coming here, too. Eventually, Cambridge won partial recognition from Henry III, rising or falling with the approval of subsequent English monarchs. Cambridge consists of 31 colleges for both men and women. Colleges are closed for exams from mid-April until the end of June.

A word of warning: Unfortunately, because of the disturbances caused by the influx of tourists to the university, Cambridge has regretfully had to limit visitors, and even exclude them from various parts of the university altogether. In some cases, a small entry fee will be charged. Small groups of up to six people are generally admitted with no problem, and you can inquire from the local tourist office about visiting hours here.

The **Cambridge Tourist Office** is on Wheeler St. (☎ **322-640**), a block south of the marketplace. From April through October, it is open Monday and Tuesday and Thursday and Friday from 9am to 6pm, Wednesday from 9:30am to 6pm, and Saturday from 9am to 5pm. In winter, the office closes at 5:30pm, and from Easter through

Cambridge

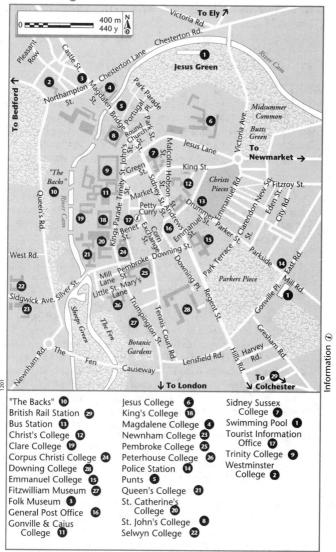

"The Backs" **10**	Jesus College **6**	Sidney Sussex College **7**
British Rail Station **29**	King's College **18**	Swimming Pool **1**
Bus Station **13**	Magdalene College **4**	Tourist Information Office **17**
Christ's College **12**	Newnham College **23**	
Clare College **19**	Pembroke College **25**	Trinity College **9**
Corpus Christi College **24**	Peterhouse College **26**	Westminster College **2**
Downing College **28**	Police Station **14**	
Emmanuel College **15**	Punts **5**	
Fitzwilliam Museum **27**	Queen's College **21**	
Folk Museum **3**	St. Catherine's College **20**	
General Post Office **16**	St. John's College **8**	
Gonville & Caius College **11**	Selwyn College **22**	

September, it is also open on Sunday from 10:30am to 3:30pm. Ask about two-hour walking tours of the city and some of the colleges.

GETTING THERE

BY TRAIN   Trains depart frequently from Liverpool Street Station(☎ **0171/928-5100**) and King's Cross Station (☎ **071/278-2477**), arriving an hour later. A same-day round-trip ticket is £11.80 ($18.65). A regular round-trip fare is £15.40 ($24.35)

BY BUS   National Express coaches (☎ 071/730-0202) run hourly between London's Victoria Coach Station and Drummer Street Station in Cambridge (trip time: 2 hr.) A one-way or same-day round-trip ticket costs £9.25 ($14.60).

BY CAR   Head north on M11 from London to Exit 11.

WHAT TO SEE & DO

The adolescent Henry VI founded ✪ **King's College** on King's Parade (☎ 331100) in 1441. Most of its buildings today are from the 19th century. The perpendicular **King's College Chapel,** dating from the Middle Ages, is its crowning glory and one of the architectural gems of England. The chapel, owing to the chaotic vicissitudes of the English kings, wasn't completed until the early years of the 16th century.

Among its most characteristic features are the magnificent fan vaulting—all of stone—and the great windows, most of which were fashioned by Flemish artisans between 1517 and 1531 (the west window, however, dates from the late Victorian period). The stained glass, in hues of red, blue, and amber, portrays biblical scenes. The rood screen dates from the early 16th century. Henry James called the King's College Chapel "the most beautiful in England." From June to October, the college is open Monday through Friday from 9:30am to 4:30pm, and on Sunday from 9am to 5pm. During term time, the chapel can be visited Monday through Saturday from 9:30am to 3:30pm, and on Sunday from 1:15 to 2:15pm.

There is an exhibition in the seven northern side alcoves showing why and how the chapel was built. A visit to the college and chapel, including the exhibition, costs £2 ($3.15) for adults, £1 ($1.60) for students and children 12 to 17. Those under 12 are admitted free.

After your visit to King's College, you can wander along the **"Backs,"** the name for the meadows and gardens running down to the banks of the River Cam. Some colleges open onto these "Backs." On Queen's Lane, adjoining the wide lawns that lead down from King's College to the Backs, stands **Queen's College** (☎ 335511), thought by some to be the loveliest of Cambridge's colleges. Dating back to 1448, it was founded by two English queens, one the wife of Henry VI, the other the wife of Edward IV. Its second cloister is the most interesting, flanked by the early 16th-century half-timbered President's Lodge. Admission is £1 ($1.60), and a short printed guide is issued. Normally, individual visitors are admitted daily from 1:45 to 4:30pm, but during July, August, and September, the college is also open to visitors daily from 10:15am to 12:45pm. Entry and exit is by the old porter's lodge in Queens' Lane only. The old hall and chapel are usually open to the public when not in use.

After a visit, continue south to Trumpington Street, site of **Peterhouse College** (☎ 338200), visited largely because it's the oldest college in Cambridge, founded in 1284. The founder was Hugh de Balsham, the bishop of Ely. Of the original buildings, only the hall remains, but this was restored in the 19th century and now boasts stained-glass windows by William Morris. Old Court, constructed in the 15th century, was renovated in 1754; the chapel dates from 1632. Ask permission to enter the porter's lodge.

The **Fitzwilliam Museum** stands on the same street (Trumpington Street, near Peterhouse). This museum (☎ 332900) was the gift of the Viscount Fitzwilliam, who in 1816 gave Cambridge University his paintings and rare books—along with £100,000, to build the house in which to display them. Other gifts have since been bequeathed to the museum, and now it's one of the finest in England. The collection has also been beefed up by loans and purchases. It's noted for its porcelain, old prints, antiquities, and oil paintings. These include examples dating from Italy of the 17th century (Titian, Veronese, and Tintoretto); other works by Rubens, Van Dyck, and the French impressionists; and a superb collection of 18th- and 19th-century British paintings. Up to 20 temporary exhibitions are staged every year. A gallery for Japanese prints opened in 1992.

The museum's ground floor is open Tuesday through Friday from 10am to 2pm, and its upper floor from 2 to 5pm on the same days. Both floors are open on Saturday from 10am to 5pm, and on Sunday from 2:15 to 5pm. Admission is free.

After the museum, you can head north again, going along the main streets of Cambridge, including King's Parade and Trinity Street, until you reach St. John's Street, site of **St. John's College.** The college (☎ 338600) was founded in 1511 by Lady Margaret Beaufort, mother of Henry VII. A few years earlier, she had founded Christ's College. Before her intervention, and old monk-run hospital had stood on the site of St. John's. The impressive gateway bears the Tudor coat-of-arms, and Second Court is a fine example of late Tudor brickwork. But its best-known feature is the Bridge of Sighs crossing the Cam, built in the 19th century, patterned after the bridge with the same name in Venice. It connects the older part of the college with New Court, a Gothic revival on the opposite bank, from which there is an outstanding view of the famous "Backs." The Bridge of Sighs is closed to visitors, but can be viewed from the neighboring Kitchen Bridge. Wordsworth was an alumnus of St. John's College. The college is open daily from 10:30am to 5:30pm except in May and June. Admission costs £1 ($1.60) for adults and 50p (80¢) for children, but it is charged only in April, July, August, and September. Visitors are welcome to attend choral services in the chapel.

WHERE TO DINE
MODERATE

Midsummer House

Midsummer Common (without number). ☎ **0122/369299.** Reservations required. Fixed-price lunch £17–£23 ($26.85–$36.35); fixed-price dinner £32.50–£55 ($51.35–$86.90). AE, DC, MC, V. Lunch Tues–Fri and Sun 12:30–2pm; dinner Tues–Sat 7–9:30pm. FRENCH.

Located near the River Cam, between Elizabeth Way and Victoria Avenue, Midsummer House is reached by towpath. The preferred dining area is in an elegant conservatory, but an upstairs dining room is also available. The menu is wisely limited. Chef John Bishop was schooled in French cuisine, and every dish bears his own special imprint.

Twenty Two

22 Chesterton Rd. ☎ **0223/351880.** Reservations required. Fixed-price dinner £19.95 ($31.50). AE, DC, MC, V. Open: Dinner only, Mon–Sat 7–9pm. ENGLISH/ CONTINENTAL.

Who would expect to find one of the best restaurants in Cambridge in this quiet residential and hotel district? In the vicinity of Jesus Green, it is jealously guarded by the locals. Decorated in pink and gray, Twenty Two offers an ever-changing fixed-price menu based on fresh produce. Owners David Carter and Louise Crompton use time-tested recipes along with their own inspiration. Typical dishes include green pea and ham soup; pan-fried filet of pork with prunes and grain mustard, served with a timbale of sweet potatoes; and for dessert, perhaps homemade iced raspberry parfait in a confectioner's basket made from a recipe for brandy snaps.

3 Canterbury

56 miles E of London

Canterbury Cathedral, 11 The Precincts (☎ **01227/762862**), is the seat of the archbishop of Canterbury, the first of whom was St. Augustine who arrived in Kent in the year A.D. 597. The present structures reflect a building campaign that began in 1070 and ended in 1498—the period of the Benedictine community at Canterbury. The most famous archbishop was Thomas Becket whose martyrdom in the cathedral in 1170 made Canterbury a great center of European pilgrimage in the Middle Ages. The tomb of Edward the Black Prince, who died in 1376, is near the site of the shrine of Thomas. The artistic treasures of the cathedral include its stained glass dating back to the 12th century, its Romanesque sculptures in the crypt, and its sequence of architectural development from the Romanesque of the crypt to the crowning glory of the Perpendicular of the nave, completed in 1405.

GETTING THERE

BY TRAIN   Frequent trains from Victoria, Charing Cross, Waterloo, or London Bridge stations take 1¹/₂ hours (☎ **0171/834-2345**).

BY BUS   Buses leave twice daily from Victoria Coach Station (☎ **0171/730-0202**), taking two to three hours.

BY CAR   From London take A2, then M2. Canterbury is signposted along the way.

WHERE TO DINE

Sullys

County Hotel, High St. ☎ **01227/766266.** Reservations required. Set lunch £13.50 ($21.35) for two courses, £16 ($25.30) for three courses; set dinner £17 ($26.85) for two courses, £19.50 ($30.80) for three courses. AE, DC, MC, V. Lunch daily 12:30–2:30pm; dinner daily 7–10pm. CONTINENTAL.

The most distinguished restaurant in Canterbury is centrally located in its most distinguished hotel. Considering the quality of the ingredients, the menu offers good value. You can always count on a selection of traditional French dishes, but you might try a more imaginative selection, such as the pan-fried filet of duck with mango- and vanilla-flavored sauce.

Tuo e Mio

16 The Borough, ☎ **01227/761471.** Reservations recommended, especially at lunch. Appetizers £3.50–£5 ($5.55–$7.90); main courses £6–£12.50 ($9.50–$19.75). AE, DC, MC, V. Open: Lunch Wed–Sun noon–2:30pm; dinner Tues–Sun 7–10:45pm. Closed last two weeks in Aug and last two weeks in Feb. ITALIAN.

This is a bastion of zesty Italian cookery, the finest in town in its category. Signor R. P. M. Greggio, known locally as Raphael, sets the style and plans the menu at his casual bistro. Some dishes are standard, including the pastas, beef, and veal found on most Italian menus, but the daily specials have a certain flair, based on the shopping for fresh and good quality ingredients on any given day. Try especially the fish dishes, including skate, which is regularly featured. A selection of reasonably priced Italian wines accompanies your food selection. The dining room is a respectable, conservative bastion of white walls, white napery, white-coated waiters, and time-blackened ceiling beams.

4 Chartwell

2 miles S of Westerham off B2026, 26 miles E of London

For many years, former prime minister Winston Churchill lived at his fairly modest home two miles south of Westerham in Kent. Maintained by the National Trust, Churchill's house (☎ **01732/866368**) is open to the public. From April to October, the house, gardens, and studio are open on Tuesday through Thursday from 11am to 5:30pm and on Saturday and Sunday from 11am to 5:30pm. Last admission is one hour before closing. In March and November, only the house is open, on Wednesday, Saturday, and Sunday from 11am to 4pm. Admission to the house only, between March and November is £2.50 ($3.95); to the house and gardens from April to October £4.50 ($7.10); to the gardens only, £2 ($3.15); and to Churchill's studio only 50p (80¢). Children pay half price. A restaurant on the grounds operates from 10:30am to 5pm on days the house is open.

GETTING THERE

BY TRAIN   From London's Victoria Station (☎ **0171/834-2345**), trains run daily to Westerham, where you can take a taxi to Chartwell.

BY CAR   From London, head east along M25, taking the exit to Westerham, where B2026 leads to Chartwell (road is signposted).

5 Hampton Court

13 miles W of London

On the north side of the Thames is Hampton Court (☎ **0181/ 781-9500**; or write to Superintendent, Hampton Court Palace, East Molesey, Surrey KT8 9AU). Set amid rolling green country by the riverside, this ranks as the grandest of all the great palaces built in England during the Tudor period. It was intended as the home of Cardinal Wolsey, chancellor (meaning prime minister) to Henry VIII. But the wily cardinal presented it as a gift to his royal master, who then added a few luxurious touches of his own.

GETTING THERE

BY TRAIN   Frequent trains from Waterloo Station (Network SouthEast) go to Hampton Court Station. Round-trip tickets cost £3.60 ($5.70).

BY BUS   London Regional Transport buses no. 111, 131, 216, 267, and 461 make the trip, as do Green Line coaches (ask at the nearest London Country Bus office) on routes 715, 716, 718 and 726.

BY BOAT   Waterbus service in summer is offered to and from Westminster Pier four times daily. Take the tube to Westminster. Round-trips take three to four hours, depending on water conditions. Call **0171/930-4721** for schedules.

BY CAR   From London, take A308 to the junction with A309 on the north side of Kingston Bridge over the Thames.

WHAT TO SEE & DO

Walk into the palace and see the fantastic and still-working Astronomical Clock, made by Nicholas Oursian in 1540; it was regarded as one of the mechanical miracles of its period. Wander through the royal kitchens (restored as in the 1530s), where an ox could be roasted whole, and lounge on the original lawn where Henry VIII once serenaded Anne Boleyn—whom he eventually married and subsequently beheaded.

Later, baroque additions were made by Sir Christopher Wren for William of Orange and Queen Mary. Wren built the formal Fountain Court and the East Front facing the gardens. Still standing is the Great Vine (mentioned in Ripley's *Believe It or Not*), which was planted in 1769 and has a main branch now more than 100 feet long. You can also lose yourself in the Maze.

The gardens are open daily year-round from 7am until dusk, but not later than 9pm, and can be visited free. The cloisters, maze, courtyards, state apartments, great kitchen, cellars, and Hampton Court exhibition are open mid-March to mid-October, daily from 9:30am to 6pm; and mid-October to mid-March, daily from 9:30am to 4:30pm. The Tudor tennis court and banqueting house are open the same hours as above, but only from April to mid-October. Admission to all these attractions is £7.50 ($11.90) for adults and £4.90 ($7.70) for children (children under 5 are free). Students and senior citizens pay £5.60 ($8.80). A garden café/restaurant is in Tiltyard Gardens.

6 Oxford

57 miles NW of London

The city predates the university—in fact, it was a Saxon town in the early part of the 10th century. By the 12th century, Oxford was growing in reputation as a seat of learning, at the expense of Paris, and the first colleges were founded in the 13th century. The story of Oxford is filled with conflicts too complex and detailed to elaborate here. Suffice it to say, the relationship between the business interests of the town and its academic core wasn't as peaceful as it is today. Riots often flared, and both sides were guilty of abuses. Nowadays, the young people of Oxford take out their aggressions in sporting competitions.

GETTING THERE

BY TRAIN   Hourly trains from Paddington Station (☎ **0171/ 262-6767**) reach Oxford in 1¼ hours. A same-day round-trip ticket costs £12.40 ($19.60).

BY BUS   The X90 London–Oxford Express departs daily from London's Victoria Coach Station (☎ **0171/730-0202**) for the Oxford Bus Station. Coaches usually depart about every 20 minutes during the day, taking 1¾ hours. A day return ticket costs £6.75 ($10.70).

BY CAR   Take M40 west from London and follow signs.

WHAT TO SEE & DO

Ultimately, the test of a great university lies in the caliber of the people it educates. Oxford can name-drop a mouthful: Roger Bacon, Sir Walter Raleigh, John Donne, Sir Christopher Wren, Samuel Johnson, Edward Gibbon, William Penn, John Wesley, William Pitt, Matthew Arnold, Lewis Carroll, Arnold Toynbee, Harold Macmillan, Graham Greene, A. E. Housman, T. E. Lawrence, and many others.

Many Americans arriving at Oxford ask: "Where's the campus?" If a local resident shows amusement during his or her response, it's because Oxford University is, in fact, made up of 35 colleges. To tour all of these would be a formidable task. Besides, a few are of such interest that they overshadow the others.

For a bird's-eye view of the city and colleges, climb **Carfax Tower** at Carfax. This is the one with the clock and figures that stroke the hours. Carfax is the tower that remains from St. Martin's Church, where William Shakespeare once stood as godfather for William Davenant, who also became a playwright. A church stood on this spot from 1032 until 1896. The tower used to be higher, but after 1340, it was lowered after complaints reached Edward III that townspeople threw stones and fired arrows from it during town-and-gown disputes. Admission is £1.20 ($1.90) for adults, 60p (95¢) for children. The tower is open from late March to late October, daily from 10am to 6pm. For information, call 792653.

Word of Warning: The main business of a university is, of course, to educate—and this function at Oxford has been severely interfered with by the number of visitors who disturb the academic work of the university. So, unfortunately, visiting is restricted to certain hours and small groups of six or fewer. In addition, there are areas where visitors are not allowed at all, but the **tourist office** at St. Aldates Chambers, St. Aldates St. (☎ **01865/726871**), will be happy to advise you when and where you may "take in" the sights of this great institution. It is open Monday through Saturday from 9am to 5pm, and on Sunday from 10am to 3:30pm.

You can begin your stroll around the colleges at **Magdalen College,** right on High Street (☎ **01865/276000**), the main street of town. Pronounced "MAWD-len," this college was founded in 1458 by William of Waynflete, bishop of Winchester and later chancellor of England. Its alumni range from Wolsey to Wilde. Opposite the **botanic garden,** the oldest in England, is the **bell tower,** where the choristers sing in Latin at dawn on May Day. The grounds of Magdalen are the most extensive of any Oxford college and even contain a deer park. A favorite pastime is to take **Addison's Walk** through the water meadows—a stroll named after alumnus Joseph Addison, the 18th-century essayist and playwright noted for his contributions to *The Spectator* and *The Tatler.*

The college is open from Easter to mid-June Monday through Friday from 2 to 6pm, Saturday and Sunday from noon to 6pm. From mid-June through September hours are daily from 11am to 6pm. From October to Easter, it is open daily, only from 2 to 6pm. Admission costs £1.50 ($2.35), but it's charged only from Easter through September.

To the northwest, you can visit **New College,** New College Lane, off Queen's Lane (☎ **279555**), which was founded in 1379 by William of Wykeham, bishop of Winchester and later lord chancellor of England. His college at Winchester supplied a constant stream of students. The first quadrangle, dating from before the end of the 14th century, was the first quadrangle to be built in Oxford, and formed the architectural precedent for the other colleges. In the antechapel is Sir Jacob Epstein's remarkable modern sculpture of *Lazarus* and a fine El Greco painting of St. James. One of the treasures of the college is a crosier (pastoral staff of a bishop) belonging to the founding father. In the garden, you can see the remains of the old city wall and the mound. The college (entered at New College Lane) can be visited Easter through September, daily from 11:30am to 5pm. In winter, hours are daily from 2 to 5pm. Admission costs £1 ($1.60) from Easter through September; free off-season.

The other three most interesting colleges lie immediately to the southwest of New College. The first on the tour (see map) is **University College,** High Street (☎ **01865/276602**). University College traces its history back to 1249, when money for its establishment was donated by an ecclesiastic, William of Durham. More fanciful is the old claim that the real founder was Alfred the Great. The original structures have all disappeared, and what remains today is essentially a Gothic-like structure from the 17th century, with subsequent additions in Victoria's day, as well as in more recent times. The Goodhart Quadrangle was added as late as 1962. Shelley was originally "sent down" for collaborating on a pamphlet on atheism, but the poet is

Oxford

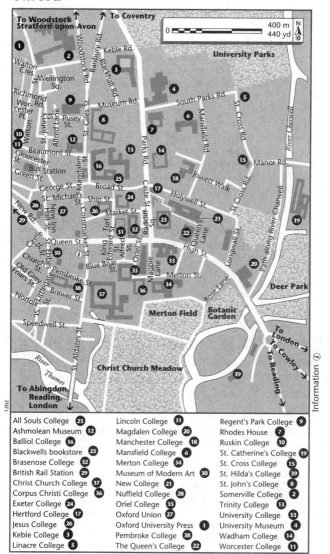

To Woodstock
Stratford-upon-Avon ↑   ↑ To Coventry

Walton Cres.
Keble Rd.
University Parks
Wellington Sq.
Richmond Wor-cester Pl.
Walton St.
Museum Rd.
South Parks Rd.
Pusey St.
Mansfield Rd.
St. Cross Rd.
Beaumont St.
Gloucester St.
Parks Rd.
Bus Station
Green St.
Manor Rd.
George St.
Jowett Walk
St. Michael's St.
Broad St.
Ship St.
New Rd.
New Inn Hall St.
St. Ebbes St.
Cornmarket St.
Market St.
Holywell St.
Radcliffe Sq.
Queen's Lane
Castle St.
Queen St.
King Edward St.
High St.
Church St.
Pembroke St.
Blue Boar St.
Oriel St.
Merton St.
Old Grey Friars St.
Littlegate St.
Brewer St.
Norfolk St.
Speedwell St.
St. Aldates St.

River Charwell
Path along River Charwell
Deer Park

Merton Field
Botanic Garden
Rose Lane

To London
To Cowley
To Reading

River Thames
Christ Church Meadow

To Abingdon, Reading, London

Information ⓘ

0   400 m
      440 yd

N

1202

All Souls College 23	Lincoln College 31	Regent's Park College 9
Ashmolean Museum 12	Magdalen College 20	Rhodes House 7
Balliol College 16	Manchester College 18	Ruskin College 10
Blackwells bookstore 25	Mansfield College 6	St. Catherine's College 19
Brasenose College 32	Merton College 34	St. Cross College 15
British Rail Station 29	Museum of Modern Art 30	St. Hilda's College 39
Christ Church College 37	New College 21	St. John's College 8
Corpus Christi College 36	Nuffield College 28	Somerville College 2
Exeter College 24	Oriel College 35	Trinity College 13
Hertford College 17	Oxford Union 27	University College 33
Jesus College 26	Oxford University Press 1	University Museum 4
Keble College 3	Pembroke College 38	Wadham College 14
Linacre College 5	The Queen's College 22	Worcester College 11

nonetheless honored by a memorial erected in 1894. It is open during college vacations daily from 2 to 4pm, charging adults £1.50 ($2.35) and children 60p (95¢).

Immediately to the south lies **Merton College,** Merton Street (☎ **01865/276310**). Founded in 1264, Merton is one of the three oldest at the university. It is noted for its library, which is said to be the oldest college library in England, built between 1371 and 1379. One of its treasures is an astrolabe (astronomical instrument used for measuring the altitude of the sun and stars), thought to have belonged to Chaucer. There is also a 13th-century chapel. It is open Monday through Friday from 2 to 4pm and on Saturday and Sunday from 10am to 5pm. It is closed one week at Easter, and one week at Christmas. Admission costs £1 ($1.60) for a visit of the ancient library and the Max Beerbohm Room (English caricaturist and parodist, 1872–1956).

By walking east for a few minutes (see map), you reach **Christ Church College,** St. Aldates (☎ **01865/276499**). Begun by Cardinal Wolsey as Cardinal College in 1525, Christ Church, familiarly known as The House, was founded by Henry VIII in 1546 and has the largest quadrangle of any college in Oxford. Tom Tower houses Great Tom, the 18,000-pound bell that rings at 9:05 nightly, signaling the closing of the college gates (it originally signified the number of students in residence). In the 16th-century Great Hall, with its hammer-beam ceiling, portraits by Gainsborough, Reynolds, and others depict prime ministers for whom Christ Church was training ground. There is also another picture gallery.

The cathedral, dating from the 12th century, is not only the college chapel but also the cathedral of the diocese of Oxford. The Norman pillars and the vaulting of the choir date from the 15th century.

The college and cathedral are open daily from 9:30am to 6pm in summer (until 4:30pm in winter). Admission is £2.50 ($3.95) for adults and £1 ($1.60) for children.

7 Stratford-upon-Avon

91 miles NW of London

As you probably know, Shakespeare was born here in 1564, and returned to live and die there after his successful and creative years in London had earned him enough money to settle down as the solid bourgeois he was at heart. You can trace his life story in Stratford, from his birthplace on Henley Street to his tomb in the Holy Trinity Church. There's still an aura of old Elizabethan England among Stratford's timbered inns and 16th-century houses with their oddly protruding upper stories. And the Avon is still the same gentle river in which young Will, the tanner's son, admired the reflection of his sprouting beard. The Bard was first honored at a "birthday celebration" in Stratford in 1769. Ever since, Will has drawn a steady stream of tourists to his hometown. By the way, in Stratford—especially to the prospering innkeepers and shop owners—don't put forth the theory that Francis Bacon really wrote those plays.

GETTING THERE

BY TRAIN Frequent trains from Paddington Station take 2¼ hours. Call **0171/262-6767** for schedules. Standard round-trip tickets cost £22.50 ($35.55).

BY BUS Eight National Express (☎ **0171/730-0202**) coaches a day leave from Victoria Station, with a trip time of 3¼ hours. A single-day round-trip ticket costs £13 ($20.55).

BY CAR   Take M40 toward Oxford and continue to Stratford-upon-Avon on A34.

INFORMATION

The Tourist Information Centre, Bridgefoot (without number; ☎ **01789/293127**), will provide any details you might wish about the Shakespeare properties. It's open March to October on Monday through Saturday from 9am to 6pm, on Sunday from 11am to 5pm. From November to February, it's open on Monday through Friday from 9am to 5pm.

WHAT TO SEE & DO

It's recommended that you go first to **Shakespeare's Birthplace,** on Henley Street. The Elizabeth dramatist was born there on April 23, 1564, the son of a "whittawer," or fine leather worker. Since 1847, when fans of the Bard raised money to purchase the property, the house has been operated as a national shrine. Built to honor the 400th anniversary of the writer's birth, the Shakespeare Centre next door was dedicated as a library and study center in 1964.

For many, the chief attraction here is **Anne Hathaway's Cottage,** in the small hamlet of Shottery outside of Stratford. Anne resided here as a child and while her husband went to London in 1587 to pursue his career as a playwright and actor at the Blackfriars and Globe theaters. Of the furnishings remaining, the "courting settle" evokes the most interest. If the weather is good, the best way to reach Shottery is from Evesham Place in town (the strolling path is marked), traversing a meadow. Otherwise, a bus leaves from Bridge Street in Stratford.

At the so-called **New Place,** on Chapel Street, Shakespeare retired in comfort in 1610. The house itself was later destroyed, but you can walk through the gardens (entered through the home of Thomas Nash, a man who married Shakespeare's granddaughter, Elizabeth Hall). The mulberry tree is said to have been rooted from a cutting of a tree that Shakespeare planted.

Although often ignored by the casual visitor, **Mary Arden's House** is a delight, built in the charming Tudor style. Shakespeare's mother, who like his wife was the daughter of a yeoman farmer, lived here in Wilmcote, a village about three miles outside Stratford. A farming museum is accommodated in the barns.

In the Old Town is the **Hall's Croft,** not far from the parish church. It was here that Shakespeare's daughter, Susanna, lived with her husband, Dr. John Hall. It is a Tudor house with a beautiful walled garden. Visitors are welcome to use the adjoining Hall's Croft Tearoom, which serves morning coffee, lunch, and afternoon tea. The house is only a short walk from the Royal Shakespeare Theatre, about a block from the river.

Although not administered by the Trust, the **Holy Trinity Church,** one of England's most beautiful parish churches, on the banks of the Avon, is also much visited. Shakespeare was buried here, his tombstone bearing the words "and curst be he who moves my bones." A contribution is requested from adults wishing to view Shakespeare's tomb.

From April to October, Shakespeare's Birthplace and Anne Hathaway's cottage are open from 9am to 6pm Monday to Saturday and Sunday from 9:30am to 6pm, and New Place, Mary Arden's House, and Hall's Croft are open from 9:30am to 6pm Monday to Saturday and Sunday from 10am to 5:30pm. In the off-season, Shakespeare's Birthplace and Anne Hathaway's Cottage are open from 9:30am to 4:30pm Monday to Saturday and Sunday from 10am to 4:30pm; and New Place, Mary Arden's House, and Hall's Croft are open Monday to Saturday from 10am to 4:30pm and Sunday from 10:30am to 4:30pm. Last admissions are 30 minutes before closing time.

You can purchase a comprehensive ticket admitting you to all five Shakespeare Birthplace Trust properties at any of the sights. The cost is £8 ($12.65) for adults and £3.60 ($5.70) for children. Seniors and students pay £7 ($11.05).

The Trust properties are in full operation from late March to mid-October. Generally, they are open at that time on Monday through Saturday from 9am to 6pm and Sunday from 9:30am to 6pm. In the off-season, Shakespeare's Birthplace and Anne Hathaway's Cottage keep the longest opening hours: 9:30am to 4:30pm Monday through Saturday and 10am to 4:30pm on Sunday. Other properties remain open but with reduced hours. Complete details are provided when you purchase your tickets.

Nearly every visitor to Stratford wants to attend at least one performance at the **Royal Shakespeare Theatre,** Waterside (☎ **01789/ 295623**), designed in 1932 to stand right on the Avon. The long season begins in April and lasts until January. Each season, five of the Bard's dramas and comedies are usually performed in repertory at the Royal Shakespeare Theatre; and five additional plays by Shakespeare, his great contemporaries, and later playwrights are staged at the small Swan Theatre Waterside. Ticket prices at the RST are £6 to £42 ($9.50 to $66.35) and at the Swan are £8 to £28.50 ($12.65 to $45.05). Reservations should be made in advance.

8   Windsor

21 miles W of London

Windsor means two things to an English person: a castle and a college. Windsor Castle, the largest inhabited castle in the world, has been the home of English sovereigns for just over 900 years. And nearby Eton College has been educating future sovereigns, along with lesser fry, for more than 500.

GETTING THERE

BY TRAIN   The train from Paddington Station (☎ **0171/262-6767**) takes 30 minutes. More than a dozen trains per day make the run, costing £5 ($7.90) for a same-day round-trip.

BY BUS   Green Line coaches (☎ **0181/668-7261**) no. 700, 701, 702, and 718 from Hyde Park Corner in London take about

1¹/₂ hours. A same-day round-trip costs from £4.35 to £5.50 ($6.85 to $8.70).

BY CAR   Take M4 west of London.

WHAT TO SEE & DO

✪ **Windsor Castle** (☎ 0753/868286 for public visiting hours) was built by William the Conqueror. Diarist Samuel Pepys called it "the most romantic castle in the world," and it is the longest continuously occupied royal castle in the world. The State Apartments are still used at certain times by the present monarch, Elizabeth II. The apartments can be visited unless the Royal Standard is up. In November 1992 a fire swept through part of Windsor Castle, severely damaging it. It has since been reopened, but until restoration is complete sometime in 1998, visitors can't see all the rooms they could before. For periods in April, June, and December, when the royal family is in residence, the castle is closed to the public. When it is open, hours are daily from 10am to 5pm March through November, and daily from 10am to 4pm November through February. One comprehensive admission ticket covers the castle precincts, the State Apartments, St. George's Chapel, the Gallery, and the Albert Memorial Chapel. The cost is £9 ($14.20) for adults, £6.50 ($10.25) for students and senior citizens, and £5 ($7.90) for children under 17.

Eton College, founded in 1440 by Henry VI, is still the most illustrious "public" (meaning private) school in Britain, and its pupils still wear Edwardian garb—top hat and collar—that makes them look like period fashion plates and carries massive snob appeal. You can visit the schoolyard and cloisters free daily from 2 to 5pm.

Two miles beyond Windsor lies the meadow of **Runnymede,** where King John, chewing his beard in fury, signed the Magna Carta. Runnymede is also the site of the John F. Kennedy Memorial, an acre of hallowed ground presented to the United States by the people of Great Britain.

9 Woburn Abbey

44 miles N of London, 8¹/₂ miles NW of Dunstable

The great 18th-century Georgian mansion of Woburn Abbey, Woburn, Bedfordshire (☎ 01525/290666), is the traditional seat of the dukes of Bedford and the most publicized of England's stately homes. A wondrous repository of art gems, it contains works by Rembrandt, Holbein, Van Dyck, and Gainsborough, plus antique furniture, silver, and tapestries. Guests have included Queen Victoria as well as Marilyn Monroe.

GETTING THERE

BY BUS   In summer, travel agents can book you on organized coach tours from London.

BY CAR   Take M1 north to the junction of 12 or 13, where Woburn Abbey directions are signposted.

WHAT TO SEE & DO

The Stately Antique Market consists of three streets of period shops selling objets d'art. Surrounding it is a 3,000-acre park containing the Safari Park, with herds of rare deer, American bison, and a pets corner, as well as amusement rides and a light railway. Light meals are available at the Flying Duchess Pavilion Coffee Shop.

From January 1 to March 25, the house and park are open only on Saturday and Sunday. Visiting times for the house and the park, 11am to 4pm (till 5pm on Sunday and bank holidays). From March 27 to October 30, the abbey is open daily, and the house can be visited on Monday through Saturday from 11am to 5pm. The park is open on Monday through Saturday from 10am to 4pm and on Sunday from 10am to 5pm. Admission is £6.50 ($10.25) for adults and £2.50 ($3.95) for children.

10 Stonehenge

100 miles SW of London

Two miles west of Amesbury, and about nine miles north of Salisbury, at the junction of A303 and A344/A360, is the renowned Stonehenge, Stone Circle (☎ **01980/623108**), believed to be anywhere from 3,500 to 5,000 years old. This huge circle of lintels and megalithic pillars is the most important prehistoric monument in Britain.

GETTING THERE

BY TRAIN A Network Express train departs hourly from Waterloo Station in London bound for Salisbury (trip time; 2 hr.), and Sprinter trains make a speedy journey from Portsmouth, Bristol, and South Wales, likewise departing hourly. There is also direct rail service from Exeter, Plymouth, Brighton, and Reading.

BY BUS Five National Express buses per day run from London Monday through Friday. On Saturday and Sunday, four buses depart Victoria Coach Station heading from Salisbury (trip time: 2¹/₂ hr.). Once at Salisbury, you can go the rest of the way to Stonehenge by taking a bus departing form the Salisbury rail station. The first bus—marked STONEHENGE—leaves Salisbury at 8:45am daily. The last bus back from Stonehenge departs at 4:20pm. Trip time is 40 minutes, and a round-trip ticket costs £3.75 ($5.95).

BY CAR From London, head west on M3 to the end of the run, continuing the rest of the way on A30. Some visitors are disappointed when they see that Stonehenge is nothing more than concentric circles of stones. Perhaps they do not understand that Stonehenge represents an amazing engineering feat since many of the boulders, the bluestones in particular, were moved many miles (perhaps from southern Wales) to this site.

WHAT TO SEE & DO

The boulders, many weighing several tons, are believed to have predated the arrival in Britain of the Celtic cult, the Druids.

Your ticket permits you to go inside the fence surrounding the site that protects the stones from vandals and souvenir hunters. You can go all the way up to a short rope barrier about 50 feet from the stones.

Admission is £2.85 ($4.50) for adults, £1.40 ($2.20) for children, £2.15 ($3.40) for students. Stonehenge is open April, May, and September daily 10am to 6pm; June through August daily 10am to 7pm; November through March, daily 10am to 4pm.

Appendix

1 Famous Londoners

Clement Richard Attlee (1st Earl Attlee) (1883–1967). A 20th-century socialist and a Labour member of Parliament (1922–55), he served in Churchill's war cabinet. During his six-year tenure as prime minister—beginning in 1945—much social legislation was enacted, major industries were nationalized, and India and Palestine were granted independence.

Robert Stephenson Smyth Baden-Powell (1st baron of Gilwell) (1857–1941). This aggressive soldier is known for establishing the Boy Scout and Girl Guide movements in 1908.

Aubrey Vincent Beardsley (1872–98). The most famous English illustrator of the Victorian era, he's considered a master of the art nouveau movement. His evocative illustrations, often erotic, accompany the texts of Alexander Pope's *Rape of the Lock* and Oscar Wilde's *Salome.*

Sir Cecil Beaton (1904–80). One of the most famous English designers and photographers of his era, he was designated "official photographer" by Wallis Simpson for her celebrated 1936 wedding in France. Americans knew him best for the sets he created for the New York City Ballet and for the costumes he designed for the stage and film productions of *My Fair Lady.*

Sir Thomas Beecham (1879–1961). A great conductor, he was instrumental in introducing London to Russian ballet and the music of Frederick Delius.

Annie Besant (1847–1933). Coeditor of the newspaper *National Reformer,* she was a well-known social reformer, believer in theosophy, and advocate of birth control and free speech. She was also active in politics in India.

William Blake (1757–1827). Artist and mystical poet, he received critical acclaim for his great poetry and his illustrations of *The Book of Job,* Dante's *Divine Comedy,* and Milton's *Paradise Lost.*

Anne Boleyn (1507–36). Mistress and then second wife of Henry VIII, she was accused of infidelity by the king, tried, declared guilty, and beheaded in the Tower of London. Her daughter eventually ruled as Elizabeth I.

William Booth (1829–1912). Minister and social worker, Booth founded the Salvation Army in 1878.

James Boswell (1740–95). His *Life of Samuel Johnson* and *London Journal* established him as an ardent and a colorful portrayer of 18th-century London, as well as a devoted biographer.

Benjamin Britten (Baron Britten of Aldeburgh) (1913–76). A celebrated composer, he is famous for operas like *Peter Grimes* and *Death in Venice*, for *A Ceremony of Carols*, and for his great *War Requiem*.

George Bryan Brummell (1778–1840). Considered the supreme arbiter of fashion in Regency England, Beau Brummell inherited a vast fortune in 1799 but was eventually ruined by gambling and his too many enemies; he died a pauper in a French asylum.

Thomas Chippendale (1718–79). The most famous furniture designer in English history, he set up a workshop in St. Martin's Lane and favored Louis XVI, Chinese, Gothic, and neoclassical styles.

John Constable (1776–1837). One of the finest painters of English landscape, his *View on the Stour* (1819) and *Hay Wain* (1820) won gold medals at the Paris Salon of 1824 and now hang in London's National Gallery.

Sir Noël Coward (1899–1973). A sophisticated wit and a captivating gossip, he wrote and produced plays that continue to delight, the most famous being *Private Lives*. He also wrote the screenplay for *Brief Encounter*, several novels, and many songs.

Benjamin Disraeli (1st earl of Beaconsfield) (1804–81). A Conservative politician and the author of five novels, Disraeli served as prime minister under Queen Victoria. He passed several important reform measures and significantly expanded the British empire.

Sir Arthur Conan Doyle (1859–1930). The creator of the detective Sherlock Holmes and his assistant, Dr. Watson, who were featured in a number of stories, including *The Hound of the Baskervilles* (1902), Doyle was born in Edinburgh and qualified as a physician. His eccentric Holmes solved more mysteries than anyone in Victorian London. Doyle also wrote historical romances such as *Micah and Clarke* (1889) and *The White Company* (1891), and a scientific romance, *The Lost World* (1912).

Edward Fitzgerald (1809–83). A poet in his own right, Fitzgerald is best remembered for his 1859 translation from the Persian of the 16th-century *Rubaiyat of Omar Khayyam*.

Ian Fleming (1908–64). A Reuters correspondent, he covered the trials of alleged British spies in Moscow during the height of the cold war. Fleming started an international industry when he wrote the first of the "007" books (*Casino Royale*) in two months. His suave fictional hero was named after the author (James Bond) of a standard British ornithological reference work.

David Garrick (1717–79). A great Shakespearean actor, theatrical producer, and playwright, he's honored with burial in Poets' Corner of Westminster Abbey.

Grinling Gibbons (1648–1721). This brilliant wood-carver was employed by Sir Christopher Wren during the reconstruction of London after the Great Fire. His bronze statue of James II is outside the National Gallery.

William Ewart Gladstone (1809–98). This Liberal prime minister and superb orator was noted for important reforms but strongly disliked by both Queen Victoria and rival politician Benjamin Disraeli.

William Hogarth (1697–1764). Painter and engraver, Hogarth created works that satirized the social customs, hierarchies, and foibles of his era. His most famous paintings are *The Rake's Progress* and *Marriage à la Mode.*

Edmond Hoyle (1672–1769). An expert on gaming, he wrote the authoritative *Hoyle's Games* (1746).

Jack the Ripper (1857?–88?). Capturing the imagination of amateur sleuths for more than a century, the real identity of this truly infamous Londoner has never been positively established. He murdered six London women, all found mutilated in the city's impoverished East End in 1888.

John Maynard Keynes (1883–1946). Considered one of the most brilliant economists of the 20th century, he advocated extensive government intervention in the economy, an idea now widely accepted.

Lillie Langtry (1852–1929). The greatest English beauty of her era, she achieved fame as the publicly acknowledged mistress of the son of Queen Victoria (later Edward VII). Born on the Isle of Jersey (and known variously as "The Lily of Jersey" or "Jersey Lillie"), she reigned as an arbiter of taste from her town house near London's Cadogan Square.

W. Somerset Maugham (1874–1965). The author of novels, short stories, plays, and essays on writing, his most famous works include *Of Human Bondage, The Circle,* and *The Constant Wife.*

John Milton (1608–74). After losing his sight, this poet and prose writer composed what ranks as the greatest epic poem in the English language, *Paradise Lost.*

John Osborne (1929–1994). "Damn you, England," he once wrote. "You're rotting now, and quite soon, you'll disappear." It was such anger that made Osborne famous with his 1956 drama, *Look Back in Anger,* which is said to have changed the course of British theater. One of the most forceful voices rising out of the new generation of postwar British dramatists, Osborne won an Oscar for best screenplay with his 1963 film, *Tom Jones.* He is also known for his play *The Entertainer* (1958) which was turned into a film in 1960, starring Sir Laurence Olivier.

Henry Purcell (1659–95). Organist at Westminster Abbey from 1679 until shortly before his death, he is considered the greatest English composer prior to the late 19th century.

Sir Joshua Reynolds (1723–92). The most famous portrait painter in the history of English painting, Reynolds created works that included *The Strawberry Girl* and *The Age of Innocence.*

Sir Arthur Seymour Sullivan (1842–1900). The musical half of the enormously popular Gilbert and Sullivan team—famous for such operettas as *The Mikado, The Pirates of Penzance,* and *H.M.S. Pinafore.* Sullivan also wrote one of the most famous hymns of the Anglican church, "Onward, Christian Soldiers."

Evelyn Arthur St. John Waugh (1903–66). This London-born author was a master of pessimistic and savage satire, often aimed at the pretensions of the English aristocracy and the institution of war. His most famous works include *Brideshead Revisited* and *The Loved One*.

John Wesley (1703–91). Founder of the Methodist branch of Protestantism, he wrote several works on grammar and history.

Virginia Woolf (1882–1941). Novelist (*To the Lighthouse, Orlando*, and *Jacob's Room*) and essayist (*The Common Reader*), she founded the Hogarth Press with her husband, social critic Leonard Woolf. She was a member of a brilliant circle of intellectuals, known as the Bloomsbury Group.

Sir Christopher Wren (1632–1723). The most famous architect and designer in English history, Wren studied mathematics and was a professor of astronomy in Oxford. After the Great Fire of London in 1666, Wren prepared a plan for rebuilding the city, but it was not adopted. Wren was commissioned, however, to rebuild 51 churches and St. Paul's Cathedral. He is buried in the crypt of what is generally believed to be his finest creation, St. Paul's.

2 Speaking British English

For many Americans it's a shock to discover that the British in fact speak British English, not American English. Believe it or not, there are enough differences to cause total communication breakdowns. For although the English use words and phrases you think you understand, they often have denotations quite different from their U.S. equivalents.

When the British call someone "mean," they mean stingy. And "homely," meaning ugly or plain in America, becomes pleasant in England. "Calling" denotes a personal visit, not a phone call; however, a person-to-person phone call is a "personal call." To "queue up" means to form a line, which they do at every bus stop. And whereas a "subway" is an underground pedestrian passage, the actual subway system is called "the Underground" or "the tube." The term "theatre" refers only to the live stage; movie theaters are "cinemas," and the films themselves are "the pictures." And a "bomb," which suggests a disaster in America, means a success in England.

In a grocery store, canned goods become "tins," rutabagas become "swedes," eggplants become "aubergines," and endive is "chicory" (while, conversely, chicory is "endive"). Both cookies and crackers become "biscuits," which can be either "dry" or "sweet"—that is, except for graham crackers, which are "digestives."

The going gets rougher when you're dealing with motor vehicles. When talking about the actual vehicle, very little means the same except for the word "car," unless you mean a truck, which is called a "lorry." In any case, gas is "petrol," the hood is the "bonnet," the windshield is the "windscreen," and bumpers are "fenders." The trunk is the "boot" and what you do on the horn is "hoot."

Luckily, most of us know that an English apartment is a "flat" and that an elevator is a "lift." And you don't rent a room or an apartment, you "let" it. Although the ground floor is the ground floor, the second floor is the "first floor." And once you set up housekeeping, you don't vacuum, you "hoover."

Going clothes shopping? Then you should know that undershirts are called "vests" and undershorts are "pants" to the English, while long pants are called "trousers" and their cuffs are called "turn-ups." Panties are "knickers" and panty hose are "tights." Pullover sweaters can be called "jumpers," with little girls' jumpers being "pinafores." If you're looking for diapers, ask for "nappies."

The education system offers such varied types of schools, identified by an equally wide variety of terms, that explain them all to the visitor would be too confusing. Briefly, however, the large English "public schools" (such as Eton) are similar to our large private prep schools (such as Andover). But the English also have other private, or "independent," schools on all levels. And all of the above charge tuition. In addition, there are "state schools," which we would call public schools. These include "primary schools" and secondary "comprehensive schools," "modern schools," and "grammar schools" that are equivalent to our junior and senior high schools.

In school and elsewhere, the letter Z is pronounced "zed," and zero is "nought." And if you want to buy an after-school treat, a Popsicle is called an "iced lolly."

Please note that none of the above terms—except the last—are slang. If you really want a challenge in that arena, you can always take on cockney. The cockneys are indigenous Londoners, although strictly speaking, the label refers only to people born within the sound of the bells of St. Mary-le-Bow in Cheapside.

The exact derivation of the word cockney is lost in the mist of antiquity, but it's supposed to have meant an "odd fellow." And the oddest feature about this fellow is undoubtedly the rhyming slang he has concocted over the centuries, based on the rhyme—or the rhyme of a rhyme—that goes with a particular word or phrase. So take my advice and don't try to delve further, unless you happen to be Professor Higgins—pardon me—'iggins.

And the British spell many words slightly differently than Americans do. Thus, British "colour" equals American "color," "cheque" equals "check," and "centre" equals "center."

3 Recommended Books

General & History Anthony Sampson's *The Changing Anatomy of Britain* (Random House, 1982) still gives great insight into the idiosyncrasies of English society. *London Perceived* (Hogarth, 1986), by novelist and literary critic V. S. Pritchett, is a witty portrait of the city—its history, art, literature, and life. Virginia Woolf's *The London Scene: Five Essays* (Random House, 1986), a literary gem, brilliantly depicts 1930s London. *In Search of London* (Methusen Publishers, 1988), by H. V. Morton, is filled with anecdotal history and well worth reading even though it was written in the 1950s.

In London: The Biography of a City (Penguin, 1980), popular historian Christopher Hibbert paints a very lively portrait. For 17th-century history, you can't beat the *Diary of Samuel Pepys* (1660–69), and for the flavor of the 18th century, try Daniel Defoe's *Tour Thro' London About the Year 1725.* Winston Churchill's *History of the English-Speaking Peoples* (Dodd Mead, 1956) is a four-volume tour de force, while his *The Gathering Storm* (Houghton-Mifflin, 1986) captures London and Europe on the brink of World War II.

Americans in London (William Morrow, 1986), by Brian N. Morton, is a street-by-street guide to the clubs, homes, and favorite pubs of more than 250 illustrious Americans—Mark Twain, Joseph Kennedy, Dwight Eisenhower, and Sylvia Plath—who made London a temporary home.

Another view emerges in *Rich Relations: The American Occupation of Britain 1942–1945,* by David Reynolds (Random, 1994). It tells what happens when three million "boisterous, materialistic, and decidedly horny" U.S. servicemen descend on Britain. Out-of-wedlock maternities, venereal disease, even the racial aspect of relations between British women and black GIs—it's all here.

Children of the Sun (Basic Books, 1976), by Martin Green, portrays the decadent post–World War I period in Britain and the lives of such people as Randolph Churchill, Rupert Brooke, the then Prince of Wales, and Christopher Isherwood.

George Williams's *Guide to Literary London* (Batsford, 1988) charts a series of literary tours through London from Chelsea to Bloomsbury. Peter Gibson's *The Capital Companion* (Webb & Bower, 1985), containing more than 1,200 alphabetical entries, is filled with facts and anecdotes about the streets of London and their inhabitants.

Unique among all guidebooks, Martin Fido's *Murder Guide to London* (Academy Chicago, 1993) is a step-by-step guide to the locations of some of the city's most notorious murders, including those by Jack the Ripper. *London,* by John Russell (Harry N. Abrams, 1994), is by the art critic who also wrote *Paris.* Russell surveys a great city, in the words of one reviewer, like a "kind uncle who knows whereof he speaks." It's not a guidebook, but a personal document filled with opinions and insights, but also firsthand reports of major events Russell has witnessed in London, such as Churchill's coffin traveling by water under Tower Bridge in 1965.

Architecture   *The Architect's Guide to London* (Reed International, 1990), by Renzo Salvadori, documents 100 landmark buildings with photographs and maps. *Nairn's London* (Penguin, 1988) is Ian Nairn's stimulating, opinionated discourse on London's buildings. Donald Olsen's *The City as a Work of Art: London, Paris, and Vienna* (Yale University Press, 1986) is a well-illustrated text tracing the evolution of these great cities. *London One: The Cities of London and Westminster* (Penguin, 1984) and *London Two: South* (Penguin, 1984) are works of love by well-known architectural writers Bridget Cherry and Nikolaus Pevsner. David Piper's *The Artist's London* (Oxford University Press, 1982) does what the title suggests—captures the city that artists have portrayed. In *Victorian and Edwardian London* (Batsford, 1969), John Betjeman expresses his great love of those eras and their great buildings.

Fiction and Biography   A good feel for English life, both urban and rural, has been created by some of the country's leading exponents of mystery and suspense fiction. Agatha Christie, P. D. James, Dorothy Sayers, and Ruth Rendell are just a few of the familiar names, but, of course, the great London character is Sir Arthur Conan Doyle's Sherlock Holmes. Any of these writers will give pleasure and insight into your London experience.

England's literary heritage is so vast that it's hard to select particular titles, but here are a few favorites. Master storyteller Charles Dickens re-creates Victorian London in such books as *Oliver Twist* (1838), *David Copperfield* (1850), *Great Expectations* (1860), and his earlier, satirical *Sketches by Boz* (1836).

Edwardian London and the 1920s and 1930s are wonderfully captured in any of Evelyn Waugh's social satires and comedies. Any work from the Bloomsbury Group will also prove enlightening—Virginia Woolf's *Mrs. Dalloway* (1925), for example, which peers behind the surface of the London scene. For a portrait of wartime London, there's Elizabeth Bowen's *The Heat of the Day* (1949).

For an American slant on England and London, Henry James's *The Awkward Age* (1899) portrays the age of Asquith. Colin MacInnes's novels—*City of Spades* (1957) and *Absolute Beginners* (1959)—focus on more recent social problems. Among contemporaries, Margaret Drabble and Iris Murdoch are both challenging, and there are many more.

The country has produced so many famous figures that it's virtually impossible to choose among biographies. *The Life of Samuel Johnson* (1791), by Johnson's friend James Boswell, is a superb examination of the life of this 18th-century writer.

The Wives of Henry VIII, by Antonia Fraser (Knopf, 1992), tells the sad story of the six women foolish enough to marry the Tudor monarch: Catherine of Aragón, Anne Boleyn, Jane Seymour, Anne of Cleves, Katherine Howard, and Catherine Parr. The great Elizabeth I emerges in a fully rounded portrait: *The Virgin Queen, Elizabeth I, Genius of the Golden Age* (Addison-Wesley, 1992) by historian Christopher Hibbert. Another historian, Anne Somerset, wrote *Elizabeth I* (St. Martin's, 1992), which was hailed by some critics as the most "readable and reliable" portrait of England's most revered monarch to have emerged since 1934.

No "man about town" in London became more famous than Shakespeare, and the Bard's life and the English Renaissance are illuminated in Dennis Kay's *Shakespeare: His Life, Work, and Era* (Morrow, 1992). Another interesting portrait emerges in *Shakespeare, the Latter Years,* by Russell Fraser (Columbia University Press, 1992).

An equally famous man about London was Sir Winston Churchill (1874–1965). Although no one told the story of his life more eloquently than did the prime minister, a Nobel Prize winner himself, the latest study emerges in *Churchill: A Life* by Martin Gilbert (Holt,

1991). This 1,000-page summary is a distillation of Gilbert's eight-volume official biography. *Churchill: The End of Glory—A Political Biography* (Harcourt Brace, 1993), was a controversial best-seller in England; its author, historian John Charmley, accused the former prime minister of "appeasement" in his political compromises with Stalin.

Richard Ellmann's *Oscar Wilde* (Knopf, 1988) is a masterpiece, revealing the Victorian era and such personalities as Lillie Langtry, Gilbert and Sullivan, and Henry James along the way. Quintessential English playwright Noël Coward and the London he inhabited, along with the likes of Nancy Mitford, Cecil Beaton, John Gielgud, Laurence Olivier, Vivien Leigh, Evelyn Waugh, and Rebecca West, are captured in Cole Lesley's *Remembered Laughter* (Knopf, 1977). More recently, *The Lives of John Lennon* by Albert Goldman (William Morrow, 1988) traces the life of this most famous of all 1960s musicians.

A more recent work, *Shakespeare—The Evidence: Unlocking the Mysteries of the Man and His Work,* by Ian Wilson (St. Martin's, 1994), is a richly illustrated, full-bodied biography, although it hardly unlocks the mystery of the Bard.

One of the most talked about biographies of 1992 was *Laurence Olivier: A Biography,* by Donald Spoto (HarperCollins). Spoto details the disappointments and triumphs of the great actor and provides anecdote and analysis for Olivier's most famous roles, including Macbeth.

No one had greater influence on London than did Queen Victoria during her long reign (1837–1901). The Duchess of York ("Fergie") and Benita Stoney, a professional researcher, capture the era in *Victoria and Albert: A Family Life at Osborne House* (Prentice Hall, 1991). Another point of view is projected in *Victoria: The Young Queen,* by Monica Charlot (Blackwell, 1991). Praised for its "fresh information," the book traces the life of Victoria until the 1861 death of her husband, Prince Albert.

In *Elizabeth II, Portrait of a Monarch* (St. Martin's, 1992), Douglas Keay draws on interviews with Prince Philip and Prince Charles to tell a lively story.

More recent works dealing with the royal family take a dimmer view, as exemplified by Anthony Holden's *The Tarnished Crown* (Random House, 1993) and A. N. Wilson's *The Rise and Fall of the House of Windsor* (W. W. Norton & Company, 1993). These authors take opposing points of view on the royal family; Wilson writes that the queen has performed her role "flawlessly," whereas Holden states the monarchy is a "ridiculously expensive exercise in folderol." But both authors agree that Prince Charles is a "twit."

Much of 1994 saw the publication of new works on the House of Windsor, a subject that has captured the imagination of the world. Books include *Queen Elizabeth: A Woman Who is Not Amused,* by Nicholas Davies (Birch Lane, 1994). Davies, a so-called royal expert, finds little to fault in the queen, except for her habit of feeding her corgis at table and reading the *Racing Times.* Philip, on the other hand, characterized as a "boorish philanderer," is accused of having a 20-year affair with his wife's cousin, Princess Alexandra of Yugoslavia, and of fathering two children with a French cabaret artist. *The Queen,* by Kenneth Harris (St. Martin's, 1994), presents a more even-handed profile. Harris even makes suggestions that could rescue the monarchy in the '90s from its current crisis. *The Windsors: A Dynasty Revealed,* by Piers Brendon and Phillip Whitehead (Hoddar & Stoughton, 1994), suggests that royal scandal isn't new, as he romps through pre-Fergie, pre-Charles, and pre-Di indiscretions. Invading the Windsor family closet, he recaps such events as Edward VIII's abdication, or Princess Margaret's ill-fated romance with Peter Townsend.

Index

Now Save Money on All Your Travels by Joining

Frommer's
TRAVEL BOOK CLUB

The Advantages of Membership:

1. Your choice of any **TWO FREE BOOKS.**

2. Your own subscription to the **TRIPS & TRAVEL** quarterly newsletter, where you'll discover the best buys in travel, the hottest vacation spots, the latest travel trends, world-class events and festivals, and much more.

3. A **30% DISCOUNT** on any additional books you order through the club.

4. **DOMESTIC TRIP-ROUTING KITS** (available for a small additional fee). We'll send you a detailed map highlighting the most direct or scenic route to your destination, anywhere in North America.

Here's all you have to do to join:

Send in your annual membership fee of $25.00 ($35.00 Canada/Foreign) with your name, address, and selections on the form below. Or call 815/734-1104 to use your credit card.

Send all orders to:

FROMMER'S TRAVEL BOOK CLUB
P.O. Box 473 • Mt. Morris, IL 61054-0473 • ☎ 815/734-1104

YES! I want to take advantage of this opportunity to join Frommer's Travel Book Club.

[ ] My check for $25.00 ($35.00 for Canadian or foreign orders) is enclosed.
   All orders must be prepaid in U.S. funds only. Please make checks payable to Frommer's Travel Book Club.

[ ] Please charge my credit card: [ ] Visa or [ ] Mastercard

   Credit card number: _____

   Expiration date: ___ / ___ / ___

   Signature: _____

   Or call 815/734-1104 to use your credit card by phone.

Name: _____

Address: _____

City: _____ State: _____ Zip code: _____

Phone number (in case we have a question regarding your order): _____

Please indicate your choices for TWO FREE books (*see following pages*):

   Book 1 - Code: _____ Title: _____

   Book 2 - Code: _____ Title: _____

For information on ordering additional titles, see your first issue of the *Trips & Travel* newsletter.

Allow 4–6 weeks for delivery for all items. Prices of books, membership fee, and publication dates are subject to change without notice. All orders are subject to acceptance and availability.   AC1

The following Frommer's guides are available from your favorite
bookstore, or you can use the order form on the preceding page
to request them as part of your membership in
Frommer's Travel Book Club.

FROMMER'S COMPLETE TRAVEL GUIDES

*(Comprehensive guides to sightseeing, dining and accommodations,
with selections in all price ranges—from deluxe to budget)*

FROMMER'S $-A-DAY GUIDES

(Dream Vacations at Down-to-Earth Prices)

FROMMER'S COMPLETE CITY GUIDES

(Comprehensive guides to sightseeing, dining, and accommodations in all price ranges)

Amsterdam, 8th Ed.	S176	Miami '95-'96	S149
Athens, 10th Ed.	S174	Minneapolis/St. Paul, 4th Ed.	S159
Atlanta & the Summer Olympic		Montréal/Québec City '95	S166
Games '96 (avail. 11/95)	S181	Nashville/Memphis, 1st Ed.	S141
Atlantic City/Cape May,		New Orleans '96 (avail. 10/95)	S182
5th Ed.	S130	New York City '96 (avail. 11/95)	S183
Bangkok, 2nd Ed.	S147	Paris '96 (avail. 9/95)	S180
Barcelona '93-'94	S115	Philadelphia, 8th Ed.	S167
Berlin, 3rd Ed.	S162	Prague, 1st Ed.	S143
Boston '95	S160	Rome, 10th Ed.	S168
Budapest, 1st Ed.	S139	St. Louis/Kansas City, 2nd Ed.	S127
Chicago '95	S169	San Antonio/Austin, 1st Ed.	S177
Denver/Boulder/		San Diego '95	S158
Colorado Springs, 3rd Ed.	S154	San Francisco '96 (avail. 10/95)	S184
Disney World/Orlando '96		Santa Fe/Taos/	
(avail. 9/95)	S178	Albuquerque '95	S172
Dublin, 2nd Ed.	S157	Seattle/Portland '94-'95	S137
Hong Kong '94-'95	S140	Sydney, 4th Ed.	S171
Las Vegas '95	S163	Tampa/St. Petersburg, 3rd Ed.	S146
London '96 (avail. 9/95)	S179	Tokyo '94-'95	S144
Los Angeles '95	S164	Toronto, 3rd Ed.	S173
Madrid/Costa del Sol, 2nd Ed.	S165	Vancouver/Victoria '94-'95	S142
Mexico City, 1st Ed.	S175	Washington, D.C. '95	S153

FROMMER'S FAMILY GUIDES

(Guides to family-friendly hotels, restaurants, activities, and attractions)

California with Kids	F105	San Francisco with Kids	F104
Los Angeles with Kids	F103	Washington, D.C. with Kids	F102
New York City with Kids	F101		

FROMMER'S WALKING TOURS

(Memorable strolls through colorful and historic neighborhoods, accompanied by detailed directions and maps)

Berlin	W100	San Francisco, 2nd Ed.	W115
Chicago	W107	Spain's Favorite Cities	
England's Favorite Cities	W108	(avail. 9/95)	W116
London, 2nd Ed.	W111	Tokyo	W109
Montréal/Québec City	W106	Venice	W110
New York, 2nd Ed.	W113	Washington, D.C., 2nd Ed.	W114
Paris, 2nd Ed.	W112		

FROMMER'S AMERICA ON WHEELS

(Guides for travelers who are exploring the U.S.A. by car, featuring a brand-new rating system for accommodations and full-color road maps)

Arizona/New Mexico	A100	Florida	A102
California/Nevada	A101	Mid-Atlantic	A103

FROMMER'S SPECIAL-INTEREST TITLES

Arthur Frommer's Branson!	P107	Frommer's Where to	
Arthur Frommer's New World		Stay U.S.A., 11th Ed.	P102
of Travel (avail. 11/95)	P112	National Park Guide, 29th Ed.	P106
Frommer's Caribbean		USA Today Golf	
Hideaways (avail. 9/95)	P110	Tournament Guide	P113
Frommer's America's 100		USA Today Minor League	
Best-Loved State Parks	P109	Baseball Book	P111

FROMMER'S BEST BEACH VACATIONS
(The top places to sun, stroll, shop, stay, play, party, and swim—with each beach rated for beauty, swimming, sand, and amenities)

California (avail. 10/95)	G100	Hawaii (avail. 10/95)	G102
Florida (avail. 10/95)	G101		

FROMMER'S BED & BREAKFAST GUIDES
(Selective guides with four-color photos and full descriptions of the best inns in each region)

California	B100	Hawaii	B105
Caribbean	B101	Pacific Northwest	B106
East Coast	B102	Rockies	B107
Eastern United States	B103	Southwest	B108
Great American Cities	B104		

FROMMER'S IRREVERENT GUIDES
(Wickedly honest guides for sophisticated travelers and those who want to be)

Chicago (avail. 11/95)	I100	New Orleans (avail. 11/95)	I103
London (avail. 11/95)	I101	San Francisco (avail. 11/95)	I104
Manhattan (avail. 11/95)	I102	Virgin Islands (avail. 11/95)	I105

FROMMER'S DRIVING TOURS
(Four-color photos and detailed maps outlining spectacular scenic driving routes)

Australia	Y100	Italy	Y108
Austria	Y101	Mexico	Y109
Britain	Y102	Scandinavia	Y110
Canada	Y103	Scotland	Y111
Florida	Y104	Spain	Y112
France	Y105	Switzerland	Y113
Germany	Y106	U.S.A.	Y114
Ireland	Y107		

FROMMER'S BORN TO SHOP
(The ultimate travel guides for discriminating shoppers—from cut-rate to couture)

Hong Kong (avail. 11/95)	Z100	London (avail. 11/95)	Z101